Baedeker

D0766678

Vietnam

www.baedeker.com

Verlag Karl Baedeker

SIGHSEEING HIGHLIGHTS ★★

Vietnam has more to offer to tourists than just the remnants of war: historical monuments and palaces testify to thousands of years of history and culture, and the country's unspoilt natural treasures captivate its visitors. So you don't miss out on any highlights, we have listed the most important destinations here.

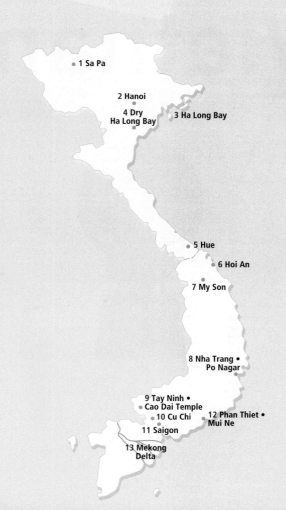

1 Sa Pa
2 Hanoi
4 Dry Ha Long Bay
3 Ha Long Bay
5 Hue
6 Hoi An
7 My Son
8 Nha Trang
Po Nagar
9 Tay Ninh
Cao Dai Temple
10 Cu Chi
12 Phan Thiet
Mui Ne
11 Saigon
13 Mekong Delta

1 ✶✶ Sa Pa
Far up in the north, Sa Pa enjoys an idyllic location in the midst of the mountains – and attracts hoards of tourists, who come to visit the hill tribes' colourful markets and set out from here on mountain hikes.   ► page 360

2 ✶✶ Hanoi
The heart of the country is today one of the most beautiful cities in Asia, whose French charm is accompanied by typical Vietnamese hustle and bustle.
► page 245

3 ✶✶ Ha Long Bay
This primeval landscape, rich in legend and peppered with grottoes and caves, is best explored on board a junk.   ► page 231

4 ✶✶ Dry Ha Long Bay
South of Ha Long Bay, a fairy-tale world with karst mountains and paddy fields awaits.   ► page 223

5 ✶✶ Hue
The old imperial city's palaces, temples, tombs, gardens and lakes appear on UNESCO's list of World Cultural Heritage Sites.   ► page 295

6 ✶✶ Hoi An
A whiff of China wafts across this old harbour town, with its beautiful trading houses and richly decorated assembly halls.   ► page 282

7 ✶✶ My Son
Even if only ruins of the temple complex remain, visitors to the spiritual and cultural centre of the Cham Empire can sense its former glory.   ► page 325

8 ✶✶ Nha Trang · Po Nagar
It is water sports, beaches and nightlife that attract great numbers of visitors to the harbour town. But the Buddhist place of worship is worth a look, too.   ► page 333

9 ✶✶ Tay Ninh · Cao Dai Temple
A unique religious community has its headquarters in Tay Ninh. Visitors to its temple can feast their eyes on the overwhelming abundance of colours and designs.   ► page 400

»Oncoming traffic« in a canal on the Mekong

10 ✶✶ Cu Chi
Memories of the resistance during the Vietnam War live on in Cu Chi's infamous tunnel system.   ► page 191

11 ✶✶ Saigon
Saigon captivates through its very own mix: the old French city centre, the colourful Chinese quarter of Cholon, and the charming colonial buildings alongside mirror-glass high-rises.   ► page 366

12 ✶✶ Phan Thiet · Mui Ne
This fantastic peninsula is the shooting star among Vietnam's bathing resorts. Every year surfers and kitesurfers breeze in for the »Fun Cup«.   ► page 345

13 ✶✶ Mekong delta
The delta is a genuine piece of Southeast Asia: small hamlets with houses on stilts, numerous tributaries and lush vegetation.   ► page 316

BAEDEKER'S BEST TIPS

We have put the most interesting Baedeker tips in this book together for you below. Experience and enjoy Vietnam at its very best!

🔳 Looking over the artist's shoulder
Witness the production of lacquerware up close in the state and family-run businesses in Hanoi and Saigon. ▶ page 81

Ship ahoy!
Conditions around Nha Trang are ideal for cruises

🔳 Da Nang Water Park
It is possible to ride the waves in the middle of town at the imaginatively designed Da Nang Water Park.
▶ page 210

🔳 A walk in the park
Hiking trails lead to the attractions in Cuc Phuong National Park. Excursions with a guide last from one to three days, with overnight accommodation in a Muong village. ▶ page 227

🔳 Sleeping on the water
A night away from the hoards of tourists on board a junk in the middle of Ha Long Bay is a very special holiday experience.
▶ page 238

🔳 Typical tube house
Tube houses are a special architectural feature of Hanoi. A typical example can be viewed on Ma May Street. ▶ page 257

🔳 Rice wine tasting
One of the specialities of the highlands is the honey-yellow ruou can: a mild (20% alcohol) wine made from rice, sticky rice or grain, which is traditionally sipped through long, bendable »straws« from a clay mug. ▶ page 176

🔳 *Easy Rider*, Vietnamese-style
A group of motorcyclists take guests on meandering tours of Da Lat and the highlands on old Russian and East German bikes. ▶ page 202

Beware: snake liquor cannot be taken home as a souvenir under the Convention on International Trade in Endangered Species

Sensibility...
is required when visiting the hill tribes near Sa Pa

🔢 Nuoc mam fish sauce
The fish sauce that is used as a dip without which no Vietnamese meal is complete is made in Mui Ne.   ► **page 345**

🔢 Rules of conduct amongst the hill tribes
Those visiting the villages of ethnic minorities should observe certain codes of behaviour.   ► **page 365**

🔢 Overview
That first overview of Saigon is best achieved from way up high.   ► **page 366**

🔢 Snake village Le Mat
Those who aren't afraid of snakes should take a side trip to Le Mat, where snakes are bred and snake liquor is produced.
► **page 279**

🔢 Cao lau
Visitors to Hoi An should give its culinary specialities a try. Cao lau, dumpling noodles with soybean sprouts and a few slices of pork in a light soup, is one of them.   ► **page 283**

🔢 Culinary specialities
Hue's delicacies include banh khoai – small, crispy pancakes with shrimps, pork and bean sprouts – and a special type of rice noodle soup.   ► **page 297**

🔢 A walk in the park II
Six walking trails lead through the rain-forest of the Bach Ma National Park, and there are places to spend the night along the way.   ► **page 313**

🔢 Cham Museum
Those interested in learning more about Cham culture should visit the small Cham Museum in Phan Rang.   ► **page 343**

Those wishing to see the magnificence of Cao Dai Temple in peace and quiet should come early

🔢 Ceremony without the crowds
It makes sense to plan an extra day to visit Cao Dai Temple and attend one of the less crowded services.   ► **page 402**

Paddy fields
A green mosaic covers the land – Vietnam is one of the world's largest rice exporters
▶ Seite 31

BACKGROUND

Dragon fruit
Rich in vitamins, these fruit taste mildly sour and grow predominantly in the south
▶ page 344

PRACTICALITIES

China's heritage
In Hoi An cages in which birds chirp and tweet are hung in the doorways
► **Seite 282**

TOURS

SIGHTS FROM A to Z

Price categories
► **Hotels**
Luxury: from 2 million VND / 90 GBP
Mid-range: from 500,000 VND / 22 GBP
Budget: up to 500,000 VND / 22 GBP
for one night in a double room

► **Restaurants**
Expensive: from 200,000 VND / 9 GBP
Moderate: up to 200.000 VND / 9 GBP
Inexpensive: up to 100,000 VND / 4.50 GBP
for one main meal

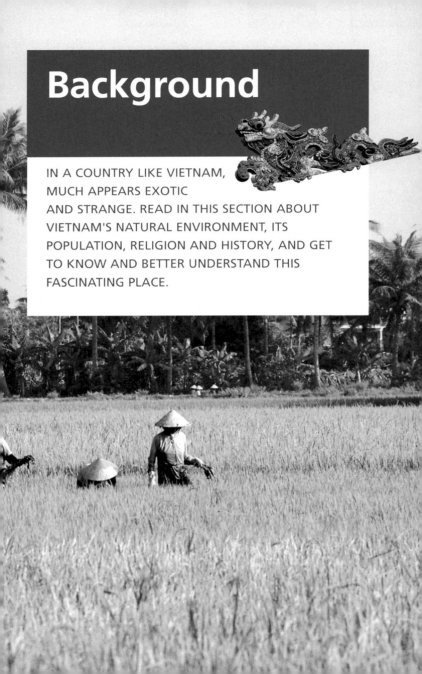

Background

IN A COUNTRY LIKE VIETNAM,
MUCH APPEARS EXOTIC
AND STRANGE. READ IN THIS SECTION ABOUT
VIETNAM'S NATURAL ENVIRONMENT, ITS
POPULATION, RELIGION AND HISTORY, AND GET
TO KNOW AND BETTER UNDERSTAND THIS
FASCINATING PLACE.

GOOD MORNING, VIETNAM!

First came the Chinese. A thousand years later Vietnam was colonized by the French, followed by the Japanese, who were in turn soon replaced by the Americans. Today, they all come at the same time, but on a peaceful mission – as tourists. Throughout its 4000-year history, Vietnam has suffered war and foreign rule like no other country in the world.

But this small country is now rising from the ashes like the proverbial phoenix, a David that has battled and defeated multiple Goliaths. It appears to be leaving the world's poorest countries behind – at first glance at least. The Vietnamese people are often referred to as the Germans of Asia. Although their country was bombed and burned with napalm, their industriousness has helped them work their way up to become one of the world's largest rice exporters within a few years, ahead of the United States, which now ranks only third. In the 1990s, Vietnam surprised the world with near double-digit growth rates.

Dragon
Symbol of wisdom and power

Necessity is the Mother of Invention

In the streets, everywhere you go, there is hammering and drilling, planing and filing, cooking and frying. Here, an improvised bicycle repair stand is made from a wooden stool, an air pump and a water bucket; there, a mobile cart offers a modest range of refreshments – perhaps ten cans of drink. Like other innovations inspired by difficult times, the Vietnamese people have turned their numerous war zones into lucrative tourist attractions, the most famous being the tunnels of Cu Chi and the legendary Ho Chi Minh Trail.

Vietnam appears to have succeeded in overcoming the division of North and South and the whole nation of »sons of gods and dragons« are unified in the pride in their historical ancestry. The monuments, palaces and temples, copiously covered in moss and patina, bear witness to a thousand-year-old culture. Vietnam enchants its visitors with its natural heritage, such as the prehistoric landscape of Ha Long Bay – seemingly inhabited by mythical creatures – and the many parts of the country that even napalm and explosives could

Temples and pagodas

Almost every world religion has left its traces in Vietnam. In contrast to Europe, religious belief plays an important role in everyday life here.

Sun and sea

The potential of the endless coast has also meanwhile been discovered. White sandy beaches, fringed by palms, attract more and more holidaymakers to the country.

People and markets

Experience the country and its people up close at the loud, colourful markets, where a whole variety of goods is on sale: mountains of exotic fruits, sacks of rice, living or freshly plucked poultry, seafood, wickerwork and cone hats.

Rulers and heroes

Great dynasties, emperors and statesmen have all come and gone in the long history of Vietnam. They left behind them magnificent palaces, splendid historical monuments and imposing tombs.

Bays and deltas

Water shapes the landscape: whether in the Red River delta in the far north, in the primeval Ha Long Bay with its fissured karst mountains or in the estuary of the Mekong in the south.

Highlands and mountains

Several mountain ranges run north to south through Vietnam. In the far north loom the fissured mountains of Tonkin, where Indochina's highest mountain, Fan Si Pan, towers upwards.

not rob of their beauty, such as the widely ramified Mekong delta in the south or the mountainous regions in the north.

The »Galápagos of Southeast Asia«

Although Vietnam is one of the most densely populated countries in the world, with a population of approximately 84 million, the World Wildlife Fund considers it to be one of the most biologically diverse countries in Asia. In remote areas and particularly in mountainous regions a variety of zoological oddities are to be found here. Animal researchers even refer to Vietnam as the »Galápagos of Southeast Asia«. During the 1980s and 1990s, researchers discovered some primate species long thought to be extinct, such as Delacour's langur and the grey-shanked douc langur (1997). Also found was the skull of a giant munjack, as well as a new deer species, and the antelope-type saola, also known as Vu Quang ox. These are two out of only six newly discovered mammalian species found worldwide in the 20th century!

Tradition Meets the Modern Age

The Vietnamese people have an unyielding desire for their country to emerge into the 21st century at the forefront. Moving further away from the tourist centres, however, there is less and less evidence of this attitude. While rural areas are still characterized by peasants wading through paddy fields, in Ho Chi Minh City (still commonly referred to as Saigon) and Hanoi the colonial backdrop is inevitably being eclipsed by skyscrapers, and mobile-carrying businesspeople are part of the scene. But in spite of the move to modernity, countless mythological figures have survived the millennia. The Vietnamese pantheon of gods is huge: temples and pagodas are overcrowded with gods and demons, Buddhas, guardian angels, princes of darkness, dragons, unicorns and other creatures, and all demand to be pacified with offerings. Ancestors play the most important role. To prevent the soul from mutating into a poltergeist, the bereaved families offer tea, rice and vegetables, and burn small presents made of cardboard on holidays and commemorative anniversaries for the deceased. Still today, the temples exude an atmosphere of timelessness – a world where drum beats ring out through the dim light and thick incense.

Cone hats *are ubiquitous on Vietnam's streets*

Facts

Find out here what animals in Vietnam are endangered, how a Communist country and a capitalist economy fit together, and where to find hand-crafted souvenirs. The facts and figures presented on the following pages will help you gain a better understanding of Vietnam.

Natural Environment

Vietnam is shaped by **natural borders**. The South China Sea to the east and vast highlands to the northwest and west offer protection from the neighbouring countries. Vietnam's two lowland regions, the Red River delta in the north and the Mekong delta in the south, are limited to a smaller area and make up the two »rice bowls« of Vietnam. Due to the positioning of these fertile lowlands and the shape of the country, Vietnam is sometimes referred to as the »bamboo pole with two bowls of rice«. The name is derived from the way in which loads are carried with the help of a bar and one basket on each side in Vietnam (and China).

»Bamboo pole with two bowls of rice«

The north is framed by the deeply fissured landscape of the Tonkin plateau, which continues into the Chinese province of Yunnan and into Laos and covers nearly three quarters of North Vietnam. Close to the border towers **Fan Si Pan**, the highest mountain in Indochina at 3143m/10,312ft. The mountain area (1000m/3300ft–1500m/5000ft) encloses the Red River delta and its tributaries that open into the Red River northeast of the capital Hanoi. Due to the difference in altitude, the Red River picks up a lot of debris and silt on its 1200km/746mi journey, which results in the creation of the country's most fertile soil. In the past, redirecting waterways and breaching the natural river dams regularly resulted in disastrous flooding, which could only be kept under control by means of artificial dykes. Bac Bo forms the heart of Vietnam with a population of approximately 40% of the 82 million inhabitants, who are scattered quite unevenly across the different regions. While the mountain areas are close to deserted, the Red River delta is occupied by nearly 2000 inhabitants per sq km (approx. 5000 per sq mi), making it one of the world's most densely populated regions.

North Vietnam (Bac Bo)

Central Vietnam, historically the region of Annam, constitutes the 900km/559mi-long »bamboo pole« of the country. In the north of the region, the mountains form a narrow cordillera that runs parallel to the South China Sea and in places stretches to the coast. The lowlands are therefore limited to small bays with big cities, for example Hue and Da Nang. The mountains in the southern part of Central Vietnam expand into highlands. The altitude drops continuously from north to south. Central Vietnam is quite sparsely populated as it has few mineral resources and agricultural cultivation is limited to the narrow coastal strip – 40% of the landmass is home to only 25% of the population. The more densely populated regions are the small lowland areas along the coast around Hue, Da Nang and Nha Trang, while the population of hill tribes is considerably smaller.

Central Vietnam (Trung Bo)

← *Bamboo comes in a variety of forms – it is used as a foodstuff, a building material, in the garden and much more*

Hill country near Da Lat

South Vietnam (Nam Bo) South Vietnam, also known as Cochinchina, constitutes approximately 35% of Vietnam and consists of broad, low hills in the north that gradually merge into the **Mekong delta** in the south. The Mekong River flows through Vietnam for the last 200km/124mi of its length and creates a delta on the coast that, at 45,000 sq km/27,900 sq mi, is three times bigger than the Red River delta in the north. It is the country's second biggest rice bowl. In contrast to the Red River, the Mekong has a storage basin in the form of the giant Tonlé Sap (Cambodia), which helps to regulate the course of the river and makes the Mekong delta less prone to flooding than in the north.

Islands and archipelagos Several archipelagos in the South China Sea and Gulf of Siam belong to Vietnam. One of the most scenic attractions in the north, close to the Chinese border, features thousands of bizarre-looking limestone islands jutting out from the sea in Ha Long Bay. South of Cambodia's coast lies Phu Quoc, the biggest island, and Vietnam's oil and gas resources, which have become the country's biggest source of foreign currency, are found just beyond the Mekong delta and the islands of Con Dao.

Flora

Rain forests Year-round humidity combined with high temperatures creates very fast-growing, lush vegetation in the tropical rain forest. There is no distinct time of blossoming, ripening or defoliation – everything appears to happen in parallel. Due to the tropical climate, the decomposition of organic material happens very rapidly and it is possible for a tree to regenerate itself with its own foliage.

In the flood-hazard zones of the river deltas and sea coasts there are lots of bog and mangrove forests. The movement of the tides means they are flooded twice a day, when only the upper trunks and tree tops remain above water. The trees have high stilt roots as well as respiratory roots that loom out of the water at low tide.

Mangrove forests

The tropical lowland forests feature the highest diversity of species, with 40 to 100 different types of trees. The dense canopy formed by the tree tops, over five to six levels, **filters out the sun** and in the forest interior a permanent half-light predominates. Ground vegetation is scarce, but epiphytes, creeping plants and many types of orchid strive to reach the sun. In addition, an abundance of parasitic plants use trees not only as a means to access more sunlight, but also as a source of nutrients, which will eventually lead to the death of the host plant.

Dry forests in the highlands and lowlands

Above 700m/2300ft–900m/2950ft lowland forest gives way to **tropical mountain forest**. The lower temperatures make it species-poor and growth is much slower. Tree ferns and low palm trees are characteristic of the moist and moderately warm climate of these elevations, and there are also deciduous trees such as oaks, as well as conifers.

The arms of the Mekong River are lined with palms

Deforestation

Deforestation started in the lowland regions of the Red River and the Mekong deltas, which are ideal for rice cultivation. These rice valleys are so closely connected to our image of Vietnam that they are hardly considered man-made. It was not until the overpopulation problems of the 20th century that deforestation had an impact on the mountain forests.

The method of slash-and-burn shifting cultivation is used to clear forested land units for agriculture. These lands are then cultivated until they are incapable of further yields and, while the soil is left to regenerate, the farmers move on to clear land in a different location. At the end of this period, and once the soil has recovered, they return to the point of origin to start a new rotation cycle. When the population grows, however, either the rotation cycle speed has to be increased – leading to the soil not being able to recover completely – or bigger land units need to be cleared, which results in increased deforestation. Consequently, forest stands were reduced from 80% to 50% between the beginning and the middle of the 20th century.

Consequences of war

Consequences of warA further cause for the enormous reduction of forest stands was the Vietnam War. The United States waged both a military and an **ecological war**. They bombed dams and dykes, caused artificial landslides and destroyed the vegetation by spraying a defoliant known as Agent Orange from the air as part of a herbicidal warfare programme. These measures were used primarily in the forests of the Mekong delta to uncover the natural hiding places of the Vietcong, who were operating from within the thick forests.

In the past, forests were cleared to develop new cropland. Recently however, the forest itself has become the focus of attention, as a supplier of tropical **precious woods**, such as teak or sandalwood. These are chiefly used as exports. The great variety of plants in the tropical rain forests make the cutting and transporting of every single tree an extremely complex operation, as large areas need to be cleared. Since the early 1990s, major efforts have been made to undertake reforestation, even though this does not entirely compensate for the annual deforestation. In addition, reforestation with fast-growing softwood trees, such as **eucalyptus**, does not offer the same ecological protection as a tropical rain forest rich in plant species.

Crops

Approximately 7000 different plant species have been counted in Vietnam. The exact number is estimated to be closer to 12,000 species, of which approximately 40% are native species. About 2300 herbal plants are used in everyday life as foodstuffs, pharmaceuticals and animal feed. The most important crops are rice (▶Baedeker Special p.320), tea, coffee, caoutchouc (natural rubber) and tobacco. Others include sweet corn, sweet potato, manioc, peanuts, cotton, sugarcane, and soy beans. The Mekong delta is rich in fruit and vegetable plantations in which mainly delicious fruits such as rose apples, pineapples, rambutan, jackfruit, pomelos, mangos, pawpaws and bananas are grown.

In addition there are approximately 1500 wood species, including palm, bamboo, teak, oak and spruce, as well as mangrove trees along the coast. Also to be seen are colourful and exotic flowers such as frangipani, hibiscus and hundreds of wild orchid species.

Frangipani: the scent of flowers creates well-being

Fauna

Vietnam is a veritable paradise for zoologists. In no other country have as many animal species been (re)-discovered in recent times: the grey-shanked douc langur in 1997 is an example. Approximately 280 **species of mammal** can be found in Vietnam, a lot of them endangered, such as the Javan rhino and the Asian elephant. 180 reptile species, 80 different amphibian species and 2600 fish species have also been recorded. Researchers have also listed between 773 and 850 types of bird, 11 of which are indigenous, and approximately 6000 different insect species further enrich Vietnam's fauna.

Rhinos

The rhino numbers among the world's most endangered animal species. In Asia, the species is on the brink of extinction. A small number of Javan rhinos are said to live in Cat Tien National Park. They are hunted in China, Taiwan and Korea for their precious horn, which is used to treat impotency, fever, nose bleeds, insomnia and epilepsy.

Elephants

Approximately 400 to 600 wild elephants can be found in various provinces such as Lai Chau, Da Lat, Kon Tum, Dac Lac and Tay Ninh. Cat Tien National Park is one of Vietnam's most important habitats for elephants. Like rhinos, elephants are critically endangered due to the demand for ivory. They have been domesticated in

Vietnam for centuries, particularly by hill tribes, who use them for heavy labour. Elephants are bred in the Central Highlands close to Buon Ma Thuo in the village of Ban Don. The village hosts a folk festival in spring that lasts several days and features costumes, dances and elephant races. These seemingly slow animals accelerate to almost 40kmh/25mph without any difficulty.

Tigers   The population of tigers in the wild in Vietnam has declined by 95% since the 19th century. Today, the maximum number of tigers is said to range from 100 to 150 in Vietnam's national parks and in areas bordering Laos and Cambodia. Due to the increasing loss of their natural habitat, their chances of survival are diminishing. Until a few centuries ago, these felines were **hunted on a large scale**. Tigers are hunted for their fur, bones and other body parts. Tiger bones are found in Vietnam in a well-known rheumatic balm, while Laos uses the skin of tigers in the treatment of dog bites and tiger teeth to reduce fever. In 1993 and 1994, the trade in tiger parts and derivatives was banned in the main countries of consumption, namely China, Taiwan and South Korea.

Monkeys   There are a large number of monkey species in Vietnam's forests, the most widespread being the macaque monkey. Among the gibbon

The first photo of a Vu Quang ox shows a four to five-month-old female calf in Hanoi's Botanical Gardens

species, the crested gibbon is native to Vietnam. During the early 1990s Delacour's langurs was rediscovered in Cuc Phuong National Park. One of the critically endangered species is the Tonkin snub-nosed monkey; only about 300 of these animals are said to exist in the northern limestone regions, and sightings of the monkeys are extremely rare since they often hide in the treetops.

The significance of the water buffalo as working animal used to till the fields is not to be underestimated

In 1992, the amazing discovery of a new **antelope species** in Vu Quang Nature Reserve in the northwest of Vietnam made world headlines. This elusive and nocturnal bovid (Pseudoryx nghetinhensis or the Vu Quang ox), with its long, sharp, furrowed horns, was identified during a joint survey by the WWF and the Ministry of Forestry of Vietnam, and is one of only **six newly discovered mammalian species** in the world during the 20th century. Experts estimate a population of 300 to 400 specimens.

Turtles

The Ho Guom turtle is the biggest freshwater turtle in the world and can weigh up to 130kg/285lbs. In Vietnam enjoys renown mainly for its role in the legend of King Le Loi (►Hanoi). Only a few specimens are said to live in the lakes of Hoan Kiem and Hoa Binh.

Domestic and working animals

One of the most important traditional domestic animals in Vietnam is the water buffalo, which was introduced from China about 2000 years ago. The water buffalo is the quintessential pack and draught animal of Vietnam, without which the country's agricultural landscape is unimaginable. Cattle, geese, chickens, goats, cats, dogs and pigs also find a place in the rural homestead. The pot-bellied pig is a typical Vietnam variety – for the most part, they run wild in villages and on farms. Inhabitants of rice-growing regions will keep domestic animals merely for their labour needs, but hill tribes and inhabitants of drier areas also rear livestock (cattle, sheep). In the Central Highlands near Buon Ma Thuot, elephants are trained to become working animals. The Hmong are well-known for **breeding horses and cattle**, and dairy farming is becoming increasingly important.

Bird life

Roughly 800 different bird species live in Vietnam, eleven of which, such as the Collared Laughingthrush, are native. Some bird species are critically endangered since their habitat, mainly marshland, is becoming more and more confined.

Only a few of our feathered friends can be seen in and around the paddy fields, and as a consequence ornithologists from abroad are showing an increased interest in **Vietnam's national parks**, whose lagoons and marshes attract rare birds such as cranes, cormorants, pheasants, peacocks, hornbills and short-toed eagles. Among the most important observation areas are Cat Tien National Park, the forests of the Tam Dao Plateau near Hanoi, Cuc Phuong National Park, the My Hoa Bird Reserve near Ben Tre, the Truong Son Mountains and the areas surrounding Da Lat.

Nature Conservation and Protection of Animals

Measures It was not until 1992–93 that the Vietnamese government passed a law for the protection of its flora and fauna. A ban on timber exports has been in force since 1992. Two years later, Vietnam joined the Convention on International Trade in Endangered Species of Wild Fauna and Flora (**CITES**), which officially prohibits trade in endangered species. However, the enforcement and control of this treaty leaves a lot to be desired.

International animal rights groups have been supporting the Vietnamese government since the mid-1980s in their attempt to protect their extensively rich fauna. All rare and endangered species have been listed in the »red book« since 1990. At present, the list consists of approximately 78 animal species, 83 birds and 54 reptiles and amphibians, making hunting for these animals strictly prohibited. Throughout Asia, however, superstition is still widespread and there is a strong belief in the healing power of animal-sourced substances and extracts.

Breeding programmes have been put in place to protect wildlife from being hunted to extinction. These programmes also create a source of income for local people. Since the 1970s, many farmers and hunters have been entrusted with the breeding of endangered species, such as snakes, crocodiles and elephants. The idea behind this initiative is that, thanks to their extensive knowledge of the animal's natural habits, former poachers and members of hill tribes will become valuable animal-rights campaigners. Other government projects include support and development of caoutchouc and cinnamon plantations, set up to bring alternative sources of income to certain areas and diversify the sources of income of the inhabitants, for example former tree fellers.

Population · Politics · Economy

Rapid population growth Vietnam's population of 82 million, over 20 million more than that of the UK, makes it one of the most populous countries in Southeast Asia. Between 1960 and 1993 the population doubled in size, though

it is unequally distributed. The contrast between the densely populated lowland regions and the all but deserted highlands is striking.
From 1963, North Vietnam has attempted to curtail population growth through education about **birth control** and **family planning**. The directive aims to limit the average family size to two children, to increase the marital age of women and to determine that the first child should not be born before a woman reaches the age of 22. In addition, the recommended age difference between the two children should be at least five years.

Befitting the high birth rate, Vietnam's population is overwhelmingly young. More than 50% of Vietnamese are younger than 20 and 71% are under the age of 30, meaning that more than two-thirds were born after the war or are too young to have consciously witnessed the war. This is also a reason for the rapid change in society which can be observed in Vietnam today, and the pragmatic stance towards the United States, once Vietnam's arch enemy.

Very young population

Vietnam enjoys a relatively well developed education system. Attendance up to 6th grade is free. Thus, since 1979, the **illiteracy rate** has decreased from 16% to less than 6%, although the standard of literacy is still relatively low. According to a 1997 World Bank study, various issues still need to be addressed, including oversized classes, an insufficient number of lessons, unskilled and underpaid teachers, and a high number of school drop-outs.

Education system

More than half of all Vietnamese are under 20 years of age

Women of the hill tribes in their traditional costume (from left to right):

Woman of the Nung people
Lao woman with hand-made jewellery
Meo girl with typical hairstyle
Woman from the Flower Hmong people
Black Hmong woman

A COLOURFUL MIX

About nine million inhabitants of Vietnam belong to one of the numerous ethnic minorities. While the lowland peoples often differ from one another only in terms of their traditions, religion or way of life, the hill tribes can be identified as separate groups by their appearance alone.

The **Chinese** (Hoa) are the largest minority group. Most of them live in the south of Vietnam and engage mainly in business and trading. When South Vietnam was taken over by the north, the Chinese gained control of 100% of wholesale trading, as well as almost all import and export business and 80% of heavy industry, as well as textile production and food processing. However, their situation deteriorated rapidly when businesses were nationalized in 1978. This took place at the same time as the increased tension between China and Vietnam, which resulted from the Vietnamese policy on Cambodia and even led to war between the two countries in 1979. The consequence was mass flight, reducing the Chinese population by over one million to half of its previous level. As boat people (▶ Baedeker Special p.62) the refugees

fled to their Chinese motherland or overseas. However, government economic reforms that began in the late 1980s allowed the Chinese to take up their traditional fields of activity once again.

The Cham

The Cham, who also live in the lowlands, are descendants of the people of Champa, a once-mighty kingdom that lay in today's Cambodia before it was conquered in conflicts with Vietnam and the Khmer kingdom. In the centuries after the occupation of their state, the Cham population was increasingly absorbed by the Vietnamese, so that today only about 100,000 people identify themselves with this ethnic group. Once Hindu, the Cham are **now Muslims**, and thus not only an ethnic but also a religious minority.

The Khmer

The Khmer populate the **Mekong delta**, which was occupied by Vietnam in the 18th century. Their numbers, now about 900,000, were swelled by refugees from Cambodia during the rule of the Khmer Rouge (1975–79). Like their kin across the border, they are adherents of Theravada Buddhism, and consequently differ considerably from the Vietnamese in their attitude to life. As they are entirely devoted to gaining a better reincarnation, they do not strive for material wealth. Their belief that each person must search for his or her own way to enlightenment means that they lack the marked communal feeling of the Vietnamese. This is evident even in their settlements, as Khmer villages consist of scattered wooden houses built on stilts.

Hill tribes

In their appearance and habits the hill tribes are so different from the Vietnamese that they are instantly recognizable as being separate ethnic groups. The French called them **Montagnards**, a term that has survived and is used by the hill tribes themselves. The Vietnamese, however, often refer to them as »moi«, i.e. wild people, which expresses their reservations towards a lifestyle that in some respects differs greatly from their own.

In contrast to the Vietnamese they do not live from cultivating rice in paddy fields, but keep livestock and practise **shifting cultivation**, clearing land by burning and moving on. They live not in compact villages like the Vietnamese but in loosely scattered settlements in houses built on stilts or, in some places in the south, in longhouses. The cultivation of coffee, tea and tobacco, which flourish only in tropical highlands, is being extended. The introduction of these new crops is intended not only to reduce the widespread growing of opium, but also to encourage the hill tribes to settle in one place.

In order to tie the mountain regions more closely to the heartlands of Vietnam, more and more ethnic Vietnamese are being settled there, which is increasingly making the hill tribes a minority in their own regions.

Children from the Red Dao hill tribe

The entire mineral resources of the country are situated in the mountain regions of the north.

Hill tribes of the south

The largest group among the minorities in the mountains of the south are the **Jarai**, of whom there are 250,000. They keep cattle and livestock, and originally planted dry rice, vegetables and sweet potatoes in shifting cultivation, but today increasingly grow tea, coffee and tobacco. Their origin in Southeast Asia is still evident from the fact that they dwell in longhouses of the type that are built on the island of Borneo.

Hill tribes of the north

The northern hill tribes wear **their own costumes** much more often than those of the south. This distinguishes them not only from the Vietnamese

but also from each other. For tourists it is a real experience to walk around a market and admire their colourful costumes. Many of the women wear silver jewellery, which is quite untypical for the Vietnamese. The largest group are the **Tay**, of whom 1.2 million live in the area bordering China. They are regarded as having been strongly »Vietnamized« in cultural and religious matters and are well represented in politics and government. Other minority groups include the **Nung**, who come from southern China and engage in shifting cultivation and livestock keeping, as do another group, the **Thai**, who are subdivided into the Red, White or Black Thai according to their clothing and are also to be found in Laos, China and Thailand. The **Muong** are thought to be descended from the original inhabitants of Vietnam, i.e. have been settled in the country for a long time, while the **Hmong** (Meo) did not come to Vietnam from China until the 19th century.

Approximately 88% of the country's population is Vietnamese. Thus, Vietnam – like Cambodia and Thailand – is one of the Southeast Asian countries with a relatively **uniform population structure**. The Vietnamese people originated from an ethnic mixture of Austro-Indonesian peoples who travelled overseas to the north and Mongolian tribes who travelled overland, crossing large rivers and interjacent mountain ranges. Their economy has always been based on the cultivation of wet rice, which is limited to lowland regions. Only very few Vietnamese people live above 100m/328ft.

The Vietnamese people

Vietnam *Ethnic Minorities*

While **settling** these lands and adapting to heavy seasonal fluctuations in water level and the frequently changing courses of rivers, they tamed the bodies of water by building dykes. With the exception of Hanoi (and later Saigon), no real cities emerged in Vietnam until the French colonial occupation. Even today, 80% of Vietnam's population live in villages, which are strictly hierarchically structured so that every individual serves the community.

Ethnic minorities
Baedeker Special
p.24 ▶

Ethnic minorities in Vietnam only account for 12% of the population, but this still amounts to around nine million people. In Vietnam, there is a marked contrast between the small, densely populated lowland regions inhabited predominantly by Vietnamese and the vast but scarcely populated highlands inhabited mainly by ethnic minorities. Minority groups are a colourful mix made up of very different population groups with a variety of origins. There are a total of **54 different ethnic groups**, their numbers ranging from a few thousand to several million.

The lowland minority groups often have features in common, and foreigners cannot distinguish between them since they are, in their appearance, very similar to the Vietnamese. The main differences lie in tradition, religion, lifestyle and habits. Ethnic minorities living in mountainous regions, however, can easily be identified as independent groups on the basis of their physical appearance.

! Baedeker TIP

Hanoi Museum of Ethnology
Visit the Museum of Ethnology in Hanoi to find a wide range of information on the different ethnic groups. The exhibits focus on the different tribes and their cultural idiosyncrasies.

Politics

State

The Socialist Republic of Vietnam emerged in 1976 as a result of the unification of the Democratic Republic of Vietnam – formerly North Vietnam – and the Republic of South Vietnam. The preamble of the constitution, based on a phrase attributed to the former US President Abraham Lincoln, reads: »The Socialist Republic of Vietnam is a state of the people, by the people, for the people«.

Communist Party

According to the constitution, the Communist Party of Vietnam (CPV) – with more than 2 million members – is the country's only political power. Not only does it determine the political guidelines, but its members also occupy all political and administrative high offices. The party is omnipresent in all levels of society. Every citizen is urged to join either the party or one of its sub-organizations.

The **Sixth National Party Congress**, held in 1986, made history with its reform programme, when the new economic policies of doi moi were introduced. At the Seventh National Party Congress in 1991 these policies were officially enacted, the acquisition of property certified and private property guaranteed. Since the National Party Congress only meets approximately every five years, its duties are assigned to the Central Committee in the interim. It consists of over 170 members and has bi-annual meetings known as plenum.

Facts and Figures *Vietnam*

Location and Area
► Southeasternmost country of the Indo-Chinese subcontinent
► Approx. 332,800 sq km/128,500 sq mi
► Length from north to south: 1650km/1025mi
► Width from east to west: between 40km/25mi and 550km/340mi
► Capital: Hanoi
► Neighbouring countries: Laos, Cambodia and China

Population
► Approx. 84 million inhabitants
► Ethnic groups: 88% Vietnamese, 1% Chinese, 2% Thai, 1% Khmer and other ethnic minorities, which are divided into 54 groups
► Population density: 256 people per sq km/663 per sq mi (80% in villages)
► Average age: 24 years
► Illiteracy rate: 6%

Religion
► 55% Buddhist
► 8% Christian
► 3% Caodaist
► 1% Muslim
► Approx. 17% other

State
► Socialist republic with one-party system (Communist Party of Vietnam, CPV)
► Head of state: President Nguyen Minh Triet
► Head of government: Prime Minister Nguyen Tan Dung
► Parliament: National Assembly with 498 seats elects the 17-person State Council
► Administrative structure: 59 provinces and 5 municipalities

Economy
► Per capita income: approx. 540 euros p.a. (2007)
► Unemployment rate: approx. 3%
► Employment structure: 67% agriculture and fishing, approx. 20% services and commerce, 13% industry and handicrafts
► Economic growth: 8%
► Tourists: approx. 3.5 million p.a. (2007)

National Assembly and State Council

The National Assembly – a unicameral parliament with approximately 500 ministers – is the highest legislative political body in Vietnam. It is elected, or rather validated, by the people every five years. Nevertheless, **compulsory voting** prevails in Vietnam. The National Assembly meets bi-annually for a fortnight to discuss bills that have often been previously mandated by the Politburo or the party itself. These meetings end, sometimes after controversial debates, in the eventual unanimous passing of these bills. The National Assembly decides on issues of war and peace and presides over the Supreme Court. Even the appointment and release from duty of high state officials, such as ministers, judges etc., is part of their responsibility.

The 17 members of the **State Council** are elected from the ranks of the National Assembly. The State Council is both the highest institution of the National Assembly and the highest representative of the state. With the amendment of the constitution in 1992, collective governance was replaced by a state president. In June 2006 this role was assigned to Nguyen Minh Triet, who took over from former president Tran Duc Luong.

Council of Ministers

The Council of Ministers appoints the government and consists of a prime minister and departmental ministers, whose responsibility it is to implement and enforce the bills passed by the National Assembly.

Recent politics

Since the end of the war, Vietnam has undergone many changes in all areas of political life. This is especially noteworthy as from the division of the country up until September 1997 the political leaders had changed very little. A change at the top was therefore inevitable, if only for reasons of age. President Tran Duc Luong and Prime Minister Phan Van Khai took office in 1997. During the Ninth National Party Congress in April 2001, the previous chairman Nong Duc Manh – rumoured to be the illegitimate son of the still very much admired state founder Ho Chi Minh – was able to establish himself as General Secretary of the Communist Party, succeeding the conventional Le Kha Phieu. Both the Vietnamese population and foreign businesspeople embraced Nong's election as a strengthening of reformist factions in Hanoi. President Nguyen Minh Triet and Prime Minister Nguyen Tan Dung were elected into office in June 2006. These appointments marked a major reshuffle in the Communist Party and a move to bring in younger leaders.

Economy

Structure of the economy

Since time immemorial, Vietnam's economy has been based on **wet rice cultivation** in the lowlands, the Red River delta in the north and the Mekong delta in the south. Commercial fishing also plays an important role: in part due to the country's long coastline, but also because of the fish farming that is practised in the numerous and extensive irrigation reservoirs in rice-growing areas. Even today, 66%

of Vietnam's population still work in agriculture. Surprisingly, the industrial sector is underdeveloped and employs only 13% of the population. The same applies to the service sector, which accounts for 20% of employment. As a consequence, Vietnam has the characteristics of an economically underdeveloped country. Statistically, it numbers among the poorest countries in the world, with an average yearly income of €520/US$660 in 2004.

The conditions for **agriculture** in Vietnam are not at all bad. Fertile lowlands allow for extensive rice cultivation, which not only covers national requirements but also makes Vietnam one of the **world leaders in rice exports**. The range of cultivated products is complemented by typical highland products, such as coffee, tea, sweet potato and caoutchouc.

? DID YOU KNOW …?

■ … that Vietnam is the world's largest producer of black pepper, the second largest producer of coffee (after Brazil), rice and cashew nuts, number four in rubber production and the seventh largest producer of tea?

Women workers plant the small rice plants

Industry ▶ Conditions are also good for the creation of a stronger industrial sector in Vietnam: the country is rich in mineral resources, such as hard coal and metals, e.g. iron ore, bauxite, manganese, chrome, zinc and silver, and possesses energy reserves in the form of charcoal and crude oil.

Natural constraints Vietnam is still among the world's poorest countries, which is to some extent due to natural constraints. Mineral resources, with the exception of crude oil, are found in the far north of the country. This leads to transportation problems due to the country's size and an uneven population distribution.

However, above all it was a cause-and-effect chain of **misguided development**, flawed decision-making and both political and economic catastrophes that prevented Vietnam from undergoing the development experienced by other big Southeast Asian countries such as Thailand, Malaysia and Indonesia. Other reasons include its exploitation by the French colonists, the division of the country after France's retreat, and the Vietnam War.

North Vietnam, following its invasion of the south, took over a country that – economically – had suffered greatly from the consequences of war. In addition, it faced the challenge of unifying two completely differently-structured parts of the country. In doing so, the

Brickworks in South Vietnam

northern economic system was applied to the south. Initially, this meant the **collectivization** of the agricultural sector. The farmers, hitherto used to their independence and private economic activity, were pushed into joining increasingly bigger cooperatives. From 1978, industry and trade sectors were also nationalized, which as a result took away the economic basis of Chinese residents based in South Vietnam.

Foreign trade The Vietnamese invasion of Cambodia and the ensuing war with China ruled out any further trade relations with its northern neighbour. In addition, the United States imposed a **trade embargo** on Vietnam, which was also joined by the ASEAN states. As a consequence of this, Vietnam turned to the states of the Warsaw Pact and became a member of the Council for Mutual Economic Assistance. Against this backdrop, Vietnam fell into a severe economic crisis at the end of the 1970s when even rice – Vietnam's main food resource – had to be imported.

Much like in the Soviet Union, the year 1986 was a turning point for Vietnam. With the death of the head of state, Le Duan, younger, less dogmatic politicians came into power. At the **Sixth National Party Congress** in December they decided on a new, progressive economic policy that came to be known as doi moi: the economic structure was to be changed from a closed to a free market economy, which meant that the state and party should withdraw from the economy and only uphold political offices.

New economic policy doi moi reforms

Families in the agricultural sector were assigned long-term tenancy agreements of the once collectivized soil. Production and sales was now their own responsibility, while ordering fertilizers and machinery or agricultural implements continued to be incumbent on the cooperatives. In the industry sector, too, planning requirements were not imposed as of 1987; the procurement of raw materials as well as production and financing were now managed by the businesses themselves.

◄ New ownership structure

The implementation of the economic reforms was planned in two stages. The first stage from 1991 to 1995 was intended to overcome the economic crisis. The second stage was to conclude the annexation to the neighbouring countries by the year 2000. Until then, the plan was to have increased the national income per capita from US$200 to US$400 per annum. In addition, 80% of the population were to get access to clean water, 95% were to be equipped with radio, and 80% with television. These allowances could not be entirely met; nevertheless, over the course of these years the average **economic growth** was between 6% and 8%.

◄ Two-stage plan

The United States lifted the economic embargo in 1994 and officially entered a diplomatic relationship with Vietnam in 1995. In 2000, the two countries signed an economic agreement. In 1995 Vietnam had joined the Association of Southeast Asian Nations (ASEAN states) – once founded as an association of anti-Communist countries.

Vietnam had to import food up until 1988, though in 1989 the country exported 1.4 million tons of rice and six years later 2 million tons. Today it is one of the world's main exporters of rice. Cultivated areas in the highlands were expanded and the range of cultivated produce was complemented by products primarily used for export, such as coffee, tea and caoutchouc. The agricultural share of Vietnam's **gross domestic product** was approximately 21% in 2004. Because of its long coastlines and its often artificially created inland lakes, Vietnam has always been an important exporter of fish produce. Here, too, export volumes have increased significantly.

Economic sectors
◄ Agriculture

The industrial sector in particular was badly hit by the new economic policy. Heavy industry, established with support from the Soviet Union and initially also from China, was particularly unprofitable. In contrast to agricultural holdings it was difficult for these businesses to adopt a privately-run economic tradition, since they had been state-run companies from the start. The **abolition of subsidies** led to

◄ Industry

a rapid decline in production and many workers faced unemployment. Conversely, light industry, such as the food and clothing industries, is only in its early stages, so production and export of industrial produce are still maintained at a low level. Nevertheless, the industry sector contributed approximately 40% of Vietnam's gross domestic product in 2004.

Mineral resources ▶ Vietnam is rich in mineral resources, which can mainly be found in the north of the country, including large stocks of high-quality anthracite coal near Hai Phong not far from the Chinese border. Available reserves are estimated at several billion tons. Near Lao Cai in the northwest there are enormous iron ore resources as well as phosphate deposits. Also to be found are smaller deposits of chrome, manganese, titanium, copper, zinc, tin, and bauxite, as well as the precious metals gold, silver and antimony. Large **oil and natural gas resources** were discovered in the South China Sea. Oil production accounted for approximately 17 million tons in 2002, which accounts for 20% of the exports.

Services ▶ The tertiary sector has also been evolving rapidly in recent years and generated 39% of the gross domestic product in 2004. In particular, small family-run businesses supplying any number of goods or services shape daily life in every Vietnamese city.

When the seawater has evaporated, the salt must only be swept up

One of the driving forces for this is the growth of the emergent tourist industry: Vietnam is becoming an increasingly popular holiday destination. In 2005, approximately 3.5 million people visited Vietnam. The number of **newly built hotels** grew accordingly, not only catering for travelling salespeople or groups of tourists but also for single travellers. As in many other areas, it is the south that is setting the pace for growth. Vietnam's proximity to Thailand becomes especially noticeable when it comes to tourism, as within just a few years an economic sector has developed that allows even single travellers to find everything they need, from small, private hotels and a versatile range of gastronomy to private transport systems with mini-buses.

◄ Tourism

Despite the positive progress of the recent years, the transition towards a free market economy entails plenty of challenges for Vietnam, the biggest obviously being the number of unemployed people. With the closing down of a number of unprofitable state-owned companies many employees have been laid off, while numerous workers are also returning to Vietnam from overseas, primarily from countries that had previously joined the Warsaw Pact. Simultaneously, because of the population increase additional jobs would have to be created for 1 million people every year.

Problems with the new economic policy
◄ Unemployment

Another issue is the increasing gap between poor and rich. Through economic reforms, a small number of people became well-off very quickly, yet the vast majority of the population lives barely above the poverty line. According to the CIA, in 2002 29% were even living below the poverty line, and in 1998 that figure was as much as 37%.

◄ Social distinctions

Religion

As a country situated both politically and culturally in an area of conflict between southern and eastern Asia, virtually all world religions have left their mark on Vietnam. Unlike its neighbouring countries Laos and Cambodia, where Buddhism is omnipresent, a far greater spiritual diversity prevails in Vietnam. The country itself brought about the worshipping of ancestors and animism. Several influences came from the outside, such as Buddhism, both from China in the form of Mahayana (Greater Vehicle) and from India in the form of Hinayana (Inferior Vehicle). Hinduism was the religion of the Cham in Central Vietnam, whose descendants are still followers of Islam. European mis-

Spiritual diversity

? DID YOU KNOW ...?

■ ... that white clothing is worn during a funeral or for obsequies? The exceptions to the rule are the grandchildren, who are dressed in red, and the great-grandchildren, who wear yellow.

The ancestors are commemorated at small altars in flats and pagodas

sionaries eventually brought Catholicism to the country. There are also several mostly regionally operating sects, which in the recent past had greater significance, also in the political arena. Unlike in Europe, philosophy is an important part of daily life, first and foremost Confucianism and Taoism.

Religious tolerance The different spiritual streams do not compete but rather complement each other. While it is nearly impossible for Europeans to be both Christian and Buddhist, or for an Indian to be both Hindu and Christian, for a Vietnamese it is no problem to embrace both religions. Hence, **double entries** when stating religious denomination are quite common.

Ancestor worship Ancestor worship can be considered prototypical for Vietnam as it was not introduced to the country from abroad. It never faced rejection from other religions, but was always practised alongside other sets of belief. Based on the notion that humankind consists of more dead than living beings, a worthy way of worshipping the deceased is given great importance. It is not death that is at the focus of attention here, but rather the deceased themselves who, according to Vietnamese belief, live on as spirits and require continuous care from the living. The spirit not only provides a connection between the living and the dead, but also a bond with future generations.

The burning of incense and offerings (e.g. food) at the ancestor altar on major holidays or birthdays and death anniversaries is a sign of respect toward the deceased. The ancestral spirits are summoned for important decisions, and informed about all new developments. Ancestor worship is the foundation of all religiousness of the Vietnamese, particularly of their belief in ghosts and demons.

Belief in ghosts and demons

Being primarily a rural people and therefore strongly dependent on favourable or unfavourable natural conditions, the Vietnamese developed a very distinct form of animism. It is founded on the idea that the universe is divided into **three realms**: heaven, earth and humankind. Ong troi, the honourable heaven, watches over their balance together with the gods of the earth, water and mountains. Within this hierarchy there are four sacred animals, which make an appearance on numerous monuments in Vietnam. The dragon symbolizes the king (as well as power and intelligence), and the phoenix represents the queen, beauty and peace. Long life is assigned to the tortoise, which also secures the protection of the empire. Finally, the mythical Kylin, a kind of unicorn, is associated to wisdom.

The belief is that nature is animated by ghosts and demons that can either be good or evil towards humans. Offerings are a way to appease them. These spirits can live everywhere, for example in stones, plants or animals. Every house and village has their own guardian spirits, which are worshipped at temples and community houses. Sometimes the spirit may be a legendary character such as the Bach Ma mountain, a Taoist deity or a historic figure.

Confucianism

Approximately 2500 years ago, the Chinese philosopher Confucius designed a strictly hierarchical social model which allocates each individual to his proper place within the community, with closely defined rights and duties. The stricter an individual adheres to the model, the better the society functions and the stronger is the empire. According to Confucius the state is much like a **big family** – both are structured following the same set of rules.

? DID YOU KNOW ...?

- ... that in temples the plates with fruit offerings are highly significant? A coconut, for example, symbolizes frugality, while a papaya means pleasure. The custard apple grants a wish, prunes promise old age, the pink dragon fruit provides power and strength, and »dragon eyes« (longans) are said to have relaxing properties.

Within his society model he distinguishes five different forms of shared existence: ruler – subject, master – servant, husband – wife, elder brother – younger brother and friend – friend. While the first four pairs describe a relation of dominance and subordination, the last is a relation of equals. A sense of duty is the basic requirement for all members of society. Subordinates also need to be loyal and obedient towards their master or ruler and to accept their place, while the latter function as role models and need to care for their subordinates.

Confucian idea of man

Confucius searches for nobleness in human beings; a noble person embodies all **virtues** such as education, tolerance, a sense of duty, public spiritedness, and justness. The more a person matches this ideal, the more he or she is entitled to become a leader in a state. However, these virtues are not innate, but need to be acquired through education and study. Therefore, irrespective of social class, education is of the utmost importance for Confucius. He therefore disapproves of a hereditary monarchy, instead making a case for the strict selection of rulers on the basis of tests.

Impact

The major impact of Confucianism in later years is mainly due to the fact that Confucius's teachings were also understood by the general public. To him, a philosophy that could not be practiced had no right to exist. By providing only a few clear rules, he allowed the people to practice them as well. However, his teachings were not spread until centuries after his death. They were to serve as a **state philosophy** for over 2000 years. In 1908, during the final stages of the Chinese Empire, Confucius was even canonized. Confucianism came to Vietnam in the 2nd century and became the predominant philosophy here. Up until 1915, aspiring civil servants had to pass exams in Confucian teachings in **Mandarin** before they could take up a position (▶p.264).

Respect for elders is a pillar of Confucianism

Though Confucianism remained the predominant philosophy for a long time, it slowly degenerated. For example, in Vietnam rulers were not elected; instead the system of dynasties was maintained, which often led to incompetent people governing the country. While the rulers were willing to claim Confucian rights, they did not live up to the corresponding duties. Alongside this there emerged a scholarly guild that considered it their duty to preserve the untainted teachings, but not to develop them any further. As a consequence, Confucianism froze in a backward-oriented movement that glorified the past and was less and less able to face new developments. Not least because of this trend, Europe's colonial powers easily gained ground in Vietnam in the 19th century.

Change

To this day, Confucianism plays an important role in daily life in Vietnam. Any changes that have occurred over the past 100 years have been unable to dissipate the hierarchical structures of state and family. This becomes especially noticeable in any conversation, where the first question is always about **age**. The rule of thumb is the older, the better. This helps establish a ranking between the two people, which allows assessment of one another. Furthermore, Vietnam has separate concepts for the elder and younger brother and for the elder and younger sister. This is also helps determine the hierarchical position of each family member.

Confucianism today

The effectiveness of Confucian ideas was confirmed through the victory of the north over the south: while the former were resolute in their organization both socially and politically, the latter were split into numerous groups and cliques who only had their own interests in mind.

Taoism

Unlike Confucianism, Taoism is a natural philosophy which can be traced back to the Chinese philosopher Lao Tse, who lived in Northern China in the 6th century BC. The central idea of his philosophy is the Tao (Dao), which can be literally translated as »the path«. Lao Tse's underlying idea is that all things have an innate force that cannot be perceived by our senses. It acts not through its strength, but through its apparent softness and subtlety. Water, for example, though the weakest medium, can still erode the strongest stone. Lao Tse does not weigh good against evil, as both are inherent in the Tao, and water can only work in interaction with the stone. This belief is emblematized through **Yin and Yang**, the ancient representation of male and female which creates harmony by mutual permeation and interaction.

Natural philosophy according to Lao Tse

The ideal of Taoism is the sovereign human (the sage). He has authority without being authoritarian. He guides humans solely through his presence and provides certainty that everything is in or-

The ruler of the north is said to have power over the winds

der. He acts much like a conductor who, with only few movements of his baton, makes an entire orchestra play together. Lao Tse rejects laws, orders or prohibitions as they demonstrate a lack of **sovereignty**. Although his teachings were written down in the ancient book of Tao Te Ching (Dao De Jing), Lao Tse is against written proclamations, as these would already be selective and therefore a restriction. Advice is not given as it would involve an assessment of good and evil. Instead, Lao Tse propagated his views in sometimes paradoxical aphorisms. For example, about the perfect leader he writes: »When the effective leader is finished with his work, the people say it happened naturally.«

Taoism and spirituality
Taoism finds its spirituality in the worshipping of gods, spirits and demons of nature. They are integrated into a hierarchical system led by the **Emperor of Jade** Ngoc Hoang. He is supported by Bac Dau (Star of the North) who watches over the dead, and Nam Tao (Star of the South) who keeps an account of the living. Their subjects are the four mothers representing the cardinal points of the compass, but also the four elements heaven, earth, water and wood. There are only a few purely Taoist temples in Vietnam. Taoist and Buddhist deities are often found side by side or worshipped in community centres or at family altars.

Buddhism

Buddhist teachings go back to Siddhartha Gautama, a prince who lived in northern India at the foot of the Himalaya during the 5th century BC. Raised in wealth and luxury, while out on a ride he came across an old man, a diseased person and a corpse, as well as a monk. To him, these encounters were crucial experiences: he decided to abjure courtly life to find the **meaning of life**. He followed various philosophical teachings without ever finding a satisfactory response to his questions. At about 30 years of age, however, he gained knowledge through his own meditation and became Buddha, which translates as »the enlightened one«. In the centuries to follow he travelled through India to propagate his teachings before, at about 80 years of age, he died, or rather entered nirvana.

Siddhartha Gautama – founder of Buddhism

Like all eastern religions, Buddhism also considers life as a cycle – an eternal succession of birth, death and rebirth. According to Buddha's teachings, life means suffering and the purpose of humanity is to break this cycle. In this context suffering means not physical pain but **futility and illusiveness**, because everything worldly perishes. The reason for human imprisonment within this eternal cycle of life is that they are attached to earthly concerns, above all to material objects. Only when they succeed in detaching themselves from perishable things in life will they achieve enlightenment and break this endless cycle. The enlightened will not be reborn but instead enter nirvana **nirvana**. Nirvana does not mean paradise in a Christian sense, but rather signifies leaving all earthly existence behind in a state of highest meditation.

Cycle of life

? DID YOU KNOW ...?

- ... that according to legend, Buddha needed more than 500 lives to reach enlightenment.

According to Buddha, the ability to reach enlightenment is inherent in all humans and only needs to be called forth. In order to reach enlightenment, Buddha came up with a set of rules called the Eightfold Path, which consist of: 1. the right view, 2. the right intention, 3. the right speech, 4. the right action, 5. the right livelihood, 6. the right effort, 7. the right mindfulness, 8. the right concentration.
Buddha did not assume that humans reach enlightenment during the course of one life, but that they need to work their way up from reincarnation to reincarnation until one day in a far existence they enter nirvana.

The Eightfold Path

Composure and confidence are Buddhist character traits. Believers know they do not miss out on anything, since whatever they are refused in this life can be made up for in the next. They are not ascetics, but do not strive for wealth as they believe anything earthly (material) is perishable. At the same time they are confident that

Buddhist concept of man

Guardian figure from Tay Phuong Pagoda near Hanoi

Strange and peculiar figures populate pagodas and temples

BUDDHA AND CO.

Visitors to the impressive shrines of Vietnam encounter a great number of strange-looking statues. These images all have special attributes by which they can be recognized, and after a while their appearance no longer seems so strange.

Buddha is worshipped in various forms. **Sakyamuni**, the historic Buddha Siddhartha Gautama, can usually be recognized by his plain appearance as an ascetic, often as a teacher with his favourite disciples. He generally sits on a lotus throne, and sometimes has elongated ear lobes, a third eye on his forehead and curly hair. **Amithaba**, the Buddha of the past, supports his adherents on the path to purification. In some representations he has a particularly long right arm, with which he can embrace the whole of humanity, or he is accompanied by merciful Bodhisattvas (see below). The Buddha of the future, **Maitreya** or Di Lac, is frequently to be seen. This Buddha laughs and has a fat stomach. He is said to return to earth every 5000 years for the salvation of humankind. **Bodhisattvas** are enlightened beings who do not enter nirvana but remain on earth in order to help others. The most popular of them is undoubtedly the goddess of mercy, **Quan Am**, a female Bodhisattva who is often depicted all in white. She can be seen in a great variety of forms:

holding a bottle with the water of purity, with 100 arms and eyes as a sign of her power, or standing on a lotus leaf with a child in her arms as a promise of fertility to childless women. The best-known male Bodhisattva is **Avalokiteshvara**. He is usually shown in the posture of meditation, holding a water vessel and lotus flower. Sometimes he also has four arms and carries a rosary and book.

Guardians and hell's judges

Figures regularly found in Buddhist pagodas include guardians, the Ten Judges of Hell and the 18 arhat. The benevolent white-faced **Ong Thien** and the malevolent red-faced **Ong Ac** are guardians of the Buddhist faith. The **Ten Judges of Hell**, usually arrayed in two rows of five, await people after death. Each of them is responsible for a different sin (murder, fraud etc), and when the deceased have been judged by one, they are passed to the next. After the final verdict of all judges, the poor soul is finally handed over to **Mother Meng**. She serves the soup of forgetting to the now-purified

sinners, so that they can be reborn entirely pure and without sin. Vietnamese pagodas, especially in the north, often house realistic depictions of the **arhat** (La Han), holy ascetics.

Other figures

The side altars are home to statues of the donors of the pagoda, particularly holy monks, the spirits of ancestors, heroes and other non-Buddhist protective deities. Taoist gods and demons have been admitted to Buddhist sanctuaries. The most important of them is the **Jade Emperor** with his assistants Bac Dau (star of the north) and Nam Tao (star of the south), who keep record of the dead and the living. In courtyards the grottoes of natural spirits can often be discovered.

Essential figures in Chinese pagodas and halls of assembly are **Thien Hau**, the patron of sailors, and **Quan Cong**, the Chinese General of the Three Kingdoms with his helpers and magic horse. Thien Hau, originally the daughter of a fisherman from the Chinese province of Fujian, is usually portrayed seated with a flat crown. The green-faced Thien Ly Nhan and the red-faced Thuan Phuong help this goddess to predict the weather.

Symbols of fortune

Temples are adorned with all sorts of symbols of fortune, for example many types of **dragons**, which are regarded as divine and beneficent in Asia, rather than dangerous and evil as in Western fairy tales. Some visitors may be surprised to see **swastikas** on temples, graves or sarcophaguses. Originally this was a sign of luck to the Buddhists, before the Nazis adopted it and falsified its true meaning. The swastika symbolizes Buddha's heart and stands for a long life. It is depicted rotating either to the left or to the right. The **yin-yang symbol**, finally, originated in Taoism. An S-shaped line divides a circle, separating a dark from a light area. This represents the dualism that is in the nature of all things.

Altar with various Buddha statues and an abundance of offerings

they can, one day, leave their earthly existence behind. They are **lenient** toward all fellow beings as they, just like the Buddhists themselves, are also travelling the tedious path to enlightenment.

Mahayana Buddhism Buddhism came to Vietnam in the 2nd century from two directions – from the north via China in the form of Mahayana (the Greater Vehicle), and from the south via India in the form of Hinayana (the Inferior Vehicle). Mahayana, which is widespread in East Asia, represents the **main school of Buddhism** in Vietnam. According to its interpretation there are not only Buddhas, but also Bodhisattvas. These people have already reached the state of enlightenment, but voluntarily do not enter nirvana in order to help others on their way. They help not only monks but also ordinary mortals to reach enlightenment.

Hinayana Buddhism Hinayana, which is common mainly in Burma, Thailand, Laos and Cambodia, teaches that every individual needs to find the path to enlightenment on their own. Furthermore, a person can only reach enlightenment as a **monk**. Therefore, the path to nirvana is only open to a few people, hence the name »the Inferior Vehicle«.

Impact of Buddhism Buddhism was most strongly promoted from the 10th to 12th century when it became a state religion in Vietnam. Many temples and monasteries were built during this time. However, from the 13th century onwards it was repressed by Confucianism which accused it of not being state-friendly and lacking commitment to social engagement. Buddhism became a religion of the individual, but it found fewer followers within the educated social classes than among the common people.

Since most people were not familiar with the theoretical framework of Buddhism, they found help and refuge in Bodhisattvas. At the very top of the hierarchy of Buddhist deities are Buddhas of three generations (the past, the present and the future). The Buddha of the past A Di Da (Amitabha) supports people during catharsis. The Buddha of the present Thich Ca Mau Ni, on the other hand, relates to the historical Buddha Siddharta Gautama and is considered a teacher, while Di Lac (Maitreya), the Buddha of the future, is always portrayed laughing and round-bellied. One of the most popular figures among the Bodhisattvas is the goddess of charity (Quan Am or Guan Yin). The Buddhist healers, however, were combined with other deities from various religions to form an entire pantheon of gods. Therefore a lot of Buddhist temples often also feature Taoist deities or elements of ancestor worship (►Baedeker Special p.42). *Buddhism and spirituality*

Christianity

European discoverers were generally followed directly by missionaries – both in Asia and America. Unlike in America, however, Christianity had to compete with religions that were already in existence. *Proselytization of Vietnam*
The first records of missionary activities date from the early 16th century: as early as 1533 the »teachings of Jesus« were forbidden. This was followed by proselytizations through Dominicans from Spain, Portugal and France and from the 17th century also by Jesuit priests, who had previously been expelled from Japan. Alexandre de Rhodes is especially worthy of mention at this point. He was first active in Annam (Central Vietnam) and later also in Tonkin (North Vietnam). Alongside his activities as a missionary he developed the first Vietnamese to Spanish/Portuguese dictionary bringing Latin writing to Vietnam, which is still in use today. At the end of his stay, the estimated Christian community in Vietnam numbered approximately 300,000 people.

Although persecution of Christians took place throughout the 18th century, the number of believers rose to 400,000 by the beginning of the Nguyen dynasty in the early 19th century. Due to a tendency to follow the teachings of Confucius, further persecution was recorded between 1825 and 1883, when approximately 100,000 Christians were killed. *Persecution of Christians*

When the Communists assumed power in 1975, Christians were forced to accept the same restrictions as other religious communities, *Christianity after the unification* such as limited mobility, working on Sundays, closing of seminaries, etc. However, despite the changing course of history, today about 4 million Vietnamese people are Christians, mainly Catholics. Thus, Vietnam has the second highest number of Christians in Asia – second only to the Philippines.

Islam

Islam »light« The number of Muslims in the Vietnamese population today amounts to approximately 0.5%. The Cham are the main followers of this religion. From the fourth to the 14th century the Cham formed a regional power in Central Vietnam with Hindu beliefs. After their subordination by the Vietnamese they converted to Islam. This new belief was also brought to Southeast Asia between the 7th and 10th century by Arab traders and seafarers, though it did not find many followers. Today, the Cham represent an **isolated island of faith**, unconnected to the central ideas of Islam. The religious commandments are therefore fostered less than in Arab countries. Vietnamese Muslims do not go on a pilgrimage to Mecca, and the prayers that are normally performed five times a day are performed only on Fridays; the month of Ramadan is shortened to three days. Furthermore, other common forms of religious faith are fostered in Vietnam alongside Islam, such as, for example, animism or the worship of ancestors.

Sects

Caodaism As previously mentioned, several different religions are practiced side by side in spiritually diverse Vietnam. The denomination of the Cao Dai goes one step further. With approximately two million believers today, it is limited to **South Vietnam** and aims to unite all of Vietnam's religions into one. The Cao Dai sect was founded in the 1920s by the spiritualist Ngo Van Chieu.

Cao Dai sees itself as the third and last revelation of religions that have already manifested themselves twice – first through Moses and the mythical creatures of Eastern religions, later through the historical figures Confucius, Lao Tse, Buddha, Jesus, and Muhammad. The third revelation comes in the shape of the Cao Dai, the Supreme Being, which will guide people to salvation. Their symbol shows an eye framed by rays of light watching over the earth. Its teachings take elements from all other religious doctrines, but to an outsider seem somewhat randomly selected. During spiritualistic sessions its members try to make contact with the Supreme Being. Historical figures can act as a medium, such as the French author Victor Hugo or the founder of the Chinese Republic, Sun Yat-Sen.

The Cao Dai are tightly structured and are oriented towards the Catholic Church, with one difference being that women can also become priests. The headquarters of the Cao Dai, the so-called high

tower, is located in the Tay Ninh province northwest of Saigon, close to the Cambodian border.

The **Hoa Hao sect** was founded in 1939 by the monk Huynh Phu So and named after his native village in the Mekong delta. He preached a **reformative Buddhism** that renounces pomp and prestige and propagates a simple life. Due to his bond with spiritualists, Huynh Phu So was pronounced insane by the French and sent to a mental home where he managed, however, to persuade the director of the institution of his religion. During the Second World War, with the help of the Japanese, he built a strong army, which controlled parts of the Mekong delta. After a falling-out with the Vietminh, Huynh Phu So was assassinated in 1947. Nine years later the sect's military branch was destroyed by the Diem government.

Symbol of Caodaism: the all-seeing eye

The number of followers of the Hoa Hao sect is estimated at approximately 1.5 million believers. It is difficult to determine the exact number, since it does not maintain any temples and its followers do not attract attention through any particular style of clothing.

History

The Chinese, the French, the Japanese and later even the mightiest power on earth, America – all staked claims of various kinds on the small nation in Southeast Asia. And all were defeated and forced to retreat empty-handed.

Early Empires and Civilizations

7th to 3rd century BC	Bronze Age (Dong Son culture) and the Van Lang Empire of the legendary Hung Kings
3rd century BC	Union of several princedoms to form the Au Lac kingdom
111 BC	Start of 1000 years of Chinese domination
931–938	Victory over China, independence instituted

Early-history legends

There are different theories about the ethnological origin of the Vietnamese. Today it is generally suggested that the Viet were a highly fragmented ethnic group of Melanesian-Indonesian origin that settled in the south of China. In the 4th century BC their families gradually moved to the southern **Red River delta**.

Much of the first millennia of the approximately 4000-year history of the Vietnamese is lost in legends in which dragon kings and mountain fairies as well as the Han and Viet peoples play a major role. In the third millennium BC, 100 Viet princedoms allegedly emerged from the Bach Viet kingdom of the dragon lord Lac Long Quan and the immortal fairy Au Co. Yet all Viet tribes were almost completely Sinicized (i.e. they underwent the process of becoming Chinese) in the 3rd and 2nd century BC under the influence of the Han Chinese. The Van Lang kingdom is thought to have been one of the last legendary dynasties, though this theory has not yet been scientifically proven.

Dong Son culture

The Dong Son culture was named after a village in North Vietnam (Thanh Hoa province), where in 1924 archaeologists found hatchets, daggers and belt buckles. Some of the most fascinating relics of the Dong Son era are **bronze drums** (►p.230, 386), of which more than 150 were discovered in Vietnam.

Kingdom of Au Lac

In the 3rd century BC Vietnam left the realm of myths and legends with the newly founded kingdom of Au Lac. Some princedoms in the Red River delta had presumably merged under An Duong Vuong (also Thuc Phan) around 257 BC in order to fend off Chinese invasions.

Independent kingdom of Nanyue

The Chinese commanding General Zhao Tuo defeated Au Lac after several unsuccessful attacks. He founded the Nanyue kingdom around 200 BC and laid the foundation for the Trieu dynasty. The capital of his kingdom, which was largely independent of China, was situated close to what is now Guangzhou (Canton).

← *King Tu Duc's life is described on his tomb stele*

Chinese Colony and Independence

Chinese protectorate of Giao Chi

In 111 BC Emperor Wu of Han captured Nanyue and turned it into the Chinese protectorate of Giao Chi. This marked the beginning of roughly 1000 years of Chinese domination of the »barbarians« in Vietnam. Their submission resulted in the exploitation of resources in Vietnam, regular tribute payments and the continuous immigration of the Chinese. Under the Chinese, everyday life changed so dramatically that the Viet nobility finally revolted and fought for its national identity. In AD 40 the **Trung sisters** and their followers made a stand against the Chinese. They appointed themselves queens and ruled for three years until they were defeated by the Chinese army; many Viet noblemen either emigrated or were banished. Although the Chinese called the Vietnamese region of Annam the »pacified south« from the 7th century onwards, there were still more uprisings and upheaval against the Chinese occupiers. During the 2nd century, Indian pilgrims started bringing the **teachings of Buddha** to Vietnam. Later, most Vietnamese adopted the Dhyana doctrine of the Indian monk Bodhidharma (6th century), the founder of Zen Buddhism.

These stakes are said to have pierced Chinese ships at the battle on the Bach Dang River (History Museum, Hanoi)

As the downfall of the Trang dynasty weakened the Chinese empire, the Vietnamese general Ngo Quyen, after years of battle, brought independence to Vietnam in 939 and founded the Ngo dynasty – the **first purely Vietnamese dynasty**. Co Loa, the old seat of the Au Lac kingdom, was to be its capital. After Ngo Quyen's death in 944, generals and princes competed for power until one of them, Dinh Tien Hoang, prevailed in 968 and established the Dai Co Viet kingdom.

Dai Co Viet kingdom

The Great Dynasties

1009–1225	Ly dynasty introduces the civil service system.
10th century	Confucianism becomes the state religion.
1288	Tran Hung Dao defeats the Mongols.
16th century	Trinh and Nguyen split the country in two.
1771–1802	Tay Son uprising
1802	Hue is made capital under Emperor Gia Long (Nguyen).

The Ly dynasty was the first major dynasty in Vietnam. In 1010, on the order of the first king, Ly Thai To, the capital was moved to Thang Long (now Hanoi). Many important and **far-reaching reforms** were implemented during his reign: he created a civil service system, financed through tributes and taxes and consisting not only of members of the royal family. In addition, general conscription was introduced, science and culture thrived, and the Chinese-Vietnamese script Chu Nom developed. Early dyke constructions successfully held off the yearly floodings of the Red River delta.

Ly dynasty

The rulers of the Ly dynasty were greatly devoted to Buddhism; when it came to the education of scholars, however, they promoted Confucian philosophy, which became a **state religion** in the 10th century. The common people mixed Buddhist, Confucian and Taoist beliefs with animist elements – this »People's Buddhism« is still largely practised today. The third king of the Ly dynasty, Ly Thanh Tong, defeated the Cham in the 11th century, occupied their provinces in the north and renamed the entire country Dai Viet.

The Tran clan, related to the Ly dynasty, established a new dynasty in Dai Viet. One Tran family member in particular became widely known through his glorious victories over the Mongols: in 1288, Tran Hung Dao drove out the outmanned army of the **Mongol ruler Kublai Khan** at the Bach Dang River. But the Tran dynasty also expanded its empire peacefully, for example by the marriage of one of the king's sisters to the Cham king in the south in the early 14th cen-

Tran dynasty

tury. The kingdom of Champa became a tribute-paying vassal state, until Cham troops invaded the capital, Thang Long, in 1371 and 1377, destroyed the imperial palace and annexed the southern provinces.

Diarchy of the Trinh and the Nguyen

In 1527 the ambitious provincial governor Mac Dang Dung had temporarily seized power over the gradually collapsing Le dynasty – though his dominance was only short-lived. The Le dynasty, reinstated in 1533, practically ruled in name only, for it was members of the feudal families Trinh and Nguyen that actually pulled the strings. Vietnam saw a time of thriving arts, and its **ceramics** in particular were greatly sought-after and mimicked throughout Asia.

The famous Dynastic Urns in Hue: a symbol for the emperors of the Nguyen dynasty

The initially more powerful Trinh took control over the marionette king from the Le dynasty by marrying into the imperial family and by taking over strategically important military posts in the north of the country. From the late 16th century the Nguyen also extended their influence as they built their palaces in Central Vietnam. For decades, the two families fought a civil war, until around 1673 they divided Vietnam in two. The Nguyen managed to continually expand their territory southward to the Gulf of Siam, receiving military support from the Portuguese, who meanwhile had arrived with their ships. At the end of the 17th century they had an enormous fleet of 133 vessels. In 1678, the Nguyen clan chose Phu Xuan (now Hue) as their seat of government. From here they invaded Cambodia in 1767 and evicted the Khmer from the Mekong delta, where they had earlier founded the city of Gia Dinh (Saigon) around 1694.

Tay Son uprising

The uprising against the Trinh and Nguyen dynasties began in 1771, headed by three brothers from Tay Son, who with the help of dissatisfied soldiers and peasants rebelled against the high taxes, disastrous corruption and **poor economic conditions** in the country. Eventually, in 1776–77, the Tay Son rebels were able to conquer the territories of the Nguyen dynasty. In turn, the Chinese of the Qing dynasty used these years of upheaval to stage another attack on the separated nation, worn down by peasant uprisings and internal power struggles. This attempt was in vain, however, and in 1789 the Chinese were expelled again by one of the Tay Son brothers (who now called himself Emperor Quang Trung).

The only surviving Nguyen prince, Nguyen Anh, defeated the Tay Son brothers after two decades of battle and thus ended his exile in Siam – albeit with French assistance. He reclaimed first Saigon, then Hue, and proceeded to march on Hanoi. In 1802, under the name Gia Long, he pronounced himself the first emperor of the last Vietnamese dynasty, the Nguyen dynasty. During military campaigns the neighbouring countries of Laos and Cambodia were turned into vassal states. Hue was made capital of the reunited empire of Viet Nam (from 1804). During this period, Vietnam faced claims to power from two foreign rivals: China and France. Under the rule of the Emperor's son, Minh Mang and his successor, Thieu Tri, French-Vietnamese relations deteriorated noticeably.

Nguyen dynasty

Under Foreign Rule

1862–63	French colonization begins.
1940–45	Japan occupies Vietnam.
1946–54	First Indochina War
1954	Geneva Conference: division of Vietnam

French Colonial Rule

French battleships landed in Da Nang (formerly Tourane) in 1858. By only one year later, the French had conquered Gia Dinh (Saigon); later, towards the end of the 19th century, they took the north, including Hanoi. The colonial army gradually occupied all of Indochina (Cambodia, Laos and Vietnam). In 1862–63, the country's governance was contractually taken from the Nguyen and given to France. Vietnam was split into the colony of Cochinchina in the south, the Annam protectorate in the centre and Tonkin in the north. In particular, it was the **rich mineral resources** (especially coal and tin) as well as agricultural products (such as caoutchouc, rice, tobacco, tea and coffee) that made the operation in the Far East worthwhile.

However, the country's infrastructure – the road network, railroads, docks, mines, and factories – was also developed with French assistance. These projects were financed by taxes and the state's monopoly on the opium trade.

During the 20th century, signs of an anti-colonial movement became increasingly noticeable. It stemmed particularly from the educated upper class, some of whose sons and daughters even went to French schools and universities. In 1930 the Communist Party of Vietnam

First resistance movements

French colonial master in a rickshaw with a coolie (early 20th century)

(later CP of Indochina) was founded in Hong Kong. In Central Vietnam the resistance against the French reached its most violent later that year with an uprising of the farmers and workers in **Nghe An**. The French colonial rulers put the nationalist movements and revolts down with utmost brutality and banished all opposing factions to the prison island of Con Dao, including nearly all leaders of the Vietnamese CP. Eleven years later the Communist League for the Independence of Vietnam, or Vietminh (Viet Minh) was founded, with Ho Chi Minh (►Famous People) as its leader. In the following years the United States provided weapons for the Vietminh to support its fight against Japanese occupation.

Second World War During the Second World War, Vietnam experienced yet another period of co-sovereignty: although the Japanese occupied the country from 1940, they still tolerated the French administration. Japan granted independence to Vietnam only in 1945, having disarmed and interned the French colonial army at the end of the war after all. Nguyen Emperor Bao Dai (►Famous People) was now allowed to temporarily rule the country under Japanese supervision, a situation that persisted until the Japanese capitulated in August of the same year.

Declaration of independence With the capitulation of Japan, Ho Chi Minh took the opportunity to call for an **armed revolt**. In Hanoi, on 2 September 1945, he proclaimed the nation's independence – the Democratic Republic of

Vietnam (DRV) was born. Bao Dai had to abdicate, and, for the first time in Vietnam, elections were held in January 1946, with a victory for the Vietminh.

First Indochina War

Even though the former French colonial rulers, in signing the French-Vietnamese Agreement of Hanoi, had recognized the independence of the DRV, they occupied Saigon and Hanoi again only shortly afterwards. The bombardment of the Hai Phong harbour in November 1946 was the official beginning of the First Indochina War between France and Vietnam, a guerrilla war that was to last several years. Ho Chi Minh's government was forced to go underground and hide in the north in the inaccessible mountains near Cao Bang. In 1948 the former emperor, Bao Dai, was reinstated by the French as regent of the formally independent state of Vietnam. In this way this once purely colonial conflict evolved into an international proxy war and split the entire world at the time of the Cold War: while China and the Soviet Union supported the north with

Painting of the declaration of independence in the History Museum, Hanoi

weapons and considered its government to be legitimate, the western states took sides with France and its marionette leader Bao Dai.

Battle of Dien Bien Phu ▶ The French army failed for years to make any real headway against the liberation movement. In 1954, the decisive battle of Dien Bien Phu took place in the far north, near Dien Bien Phu. Soldiers of the Vietnamese People's Army (VPA) besieged, bombarded, starved and eventually defeated the French troops in their own stronghold. During this 55-day siege, which ended on 7 May 1954, about 3000 French soldiers died. The Vietnamese commander-in-chief, General Vo Nguyen Giap, later also repeatedly challenged the US troops.

Division of Vietnam

Second division of Vietnam In April 1954 all war opponents involved, i.e. Vietnam's neighbouring countries Laos and Cambodia as well as the four world powers (the USA, the Soviet Union, China and Great Britain) met at the **Geneva Conference** in Paris to determine the future of the Southeast Asian nation. The provisional **demarcation line** at the 17th parallel at Dong Ha was only meant to divide the country up until the all-Vietnamese elections in July 1956. But Dong Ha became a permanent border for the next 21 years. The Geneva Conference was signed by neither South Vietnam nor the United States.

The North – Democratic Republic of Vietnam Under Ho Chi Minh the Communists ruled in the north of the newly separated country from the capital Hanoi. The socialistic Democratic Republic of Vietnam became a one-party state (the CP) where all urban and rural family businesses were put under state control. Those in power began to systematically cleanse the country north of the 17th parallel, which caused about one million North Vietnamese to **flee** to the south. Every day alleged traitors were denunciated or executed. A rigorously enforced land reform in 1955–56 increased the feeling of insecurity among the population and led to more uprisings in the north.

The South – Republic of South Vietnam The Republic of South Vietnam was proclaimed in the capital of the pro-West south, Saigon, in October of 1955. The anti-Communist and Catholic Ngo Dinh Diem became head of state. Fearing a likely victory for the Communists, he simply cancelled the all-Vietnamese elections of 1956 that had been agreed upon at the Geneva Convention. Instead Ngo Dinh Diem had himself appointed president after a manipulated referendum in the south. The French army only left South Vietnam in 1956. Starting in the mid-1950s, however, the United States sent military help and advisors to solve the conflict with the north. Meanwhile, the South Vietnamese head of government gradually transformed into a **dictator** who took action against Buddhists and political dissidents with relentless violence. In 1963, Buddhist monks publicly **self-immolated**, while South Vietnamese students demonstrated in the streets.

Vietnam War

1963	Overthrow of South Vietnam's dictator Diem
1964–75	Second Indochina War
1975	North Vietnamese invade (FNL) Saigon and seize power.

The Vietcong (Vietnamese Communists) was a guerrilla organization from South Vietnam and had been part of the resistance from 1956 onwards. The regular troops of South Vietnam were already considerably weakened due to widespread corruption and numerous cases of defection. Driven underground by political persecution, in 1960 the South Vietnamese opposition founded the NLF, the **National Liberation Front**, with Communist support from Hanoi. With the beginning of the 1960s, the US continuously sent more military advisors to South Vietnam: their number increased from 2000 (at the end of 1960) to 16,300 (at the end of 1963). The reason for this action was the so called domino theory: Western politicians (the Americans in particular) feared a Communist victory in Vietnam would cause a domino effect in the neighbouring countries. After several attempted coups that all failed, the military removed Ngo Dinh Diem from office and executed him in 1963. All of this was supported by the CIA and silently approved by President John F. Kennedy.

Preparations for war

The so-called **Gulf of Tonkin Incident** is considered to be the official cause for the Vietnam War (Second Indochina War). In August 1964 the US destroyer *Maddox* engaged in a gun battle with two torpedo boats off the North Vietnamese coast. Later American investigations revealed that the *Maddox* had been involved in a secret manoeuvre with the South Vietnamese navy. US President Lyndon B. Johnson used this incident as a pretext for sending reinforcement troops to South Vietnam and for ordering the bombing of North Vietnam, both with the consent of the US Congress. Oddly, the so called Tonkin Resolution had already been sitting in the President's drawer months before the alleged attacks – as the *New York Times* reported with extracts from the top secret »Pentagon Papers«.

Gulf of Tonkin Incident

The Americans never officially declared war on North Vietnam. The task force »**Operation Rolling Thunder**« was the starting point for the US entry into North Vietnam. In March 1965, 25,000 soldiers went ashore in the area of Da Nang. Within the following four years their number rose to a half a million.

With state-of-the-art weaponry, the US military was to drive the Communist soldiers out of South Vietnam and defeat the north. The Vietcong, however, employed **guerrilla tactics** against US troops and fought on familiar territory, partly supported by the rural popula-

»Tiger traps« against US tanks

tion. Due to their repressive governance in the years before, the rulers in Saigon had long lost the sympathy of many farmers in the hard-fought areas. A multitude of casualties within the civilian population did the rest – a lot of South Vietnamese refugees joined the Communists. In order to cut down the supplies to the Vietcong, a great part of the rural population was eventually relocated to the cities or to so called fortified villages. »Charlie«, as the US troops soon came to call the South Vietnamese underground fighters, inflicted huge losses on the Americans by means of land mines, tiger traps, surprise attacks and acts of sabotage. The **tunnels of Cu Chi** enabled the Vietcong to become virtually invisible. Using this underground complex the Communist fighters even managed to close in on Saigon. Today these tunnels are open to the public. During the day, US troops seemed to prevail, but at night the Vietcong fought back and was able to strike serious blows against the world power. An overall victory by the Communist guerrillas, however, was impossible due to the superiority of American, South Vietnamese and other allied forces (among them Australia and South Korea). More than 600,000 allied troops fought against 200,000 Communist soldiers from the north and south. To bring this **military stand-off** to an end, the US military even considered the use of nuclear weapons.

Vietnam War Map

©Baedeker

In order to win this jungle war, US Army Chief of Staff, General Westmoreland ordered the release of »**Agent Orange**«, a chemical pesticide containing dioxins. Vast areas were declared »free-fire zones«. The favourite target of these defoliation operations was the so-called **Ho Chi Minh Trail** (▶ DMZ). The US forces dropped napalm and conventional bombs on this 16,000km/ 10,000mi-long, heavily branching network of trails, part of which crossed over to Laos and Cambodia. North Vietnamese fighters ceaselessly travelled these trails bringing (military) supplies from the north to the south and immediately returning for new assignments.

Without doubt one of the most formative images of the 20th century:
Nick Ut pressed the shutter as a crying girl ran towards him from Trang Bang

The turning point of the war took place on 31 January 1968, the Vietnamese New Year's Day or »Tet«. Despite the ceasefire agreed for this holiday, the fighters of Ho Chi Minh and the Vietcong attacked positions of the American and the regular South Vietnamese forces. Though the attacks were not a military success and the Communists suffered huge losses (approximately 30,000–50,000 casualties), the consequences for the American government were severe. The news footage showed several Vietcong soldiers on the US embassy grounds, thus proving the American war propaganda about a near end of the war to be all but lies. These pictures came as a shock to the American public.

In 1968, United States public opinion finally shifted. More and more war veterans and injured GIs joined the **anti-war movement**, and millions of people in America and Western Europe gathered in the streets to protest against the Vietnam War. The same year, President Johnson announced official peace negotiations that finally began in May in Paris, even though the ceasefire, one of the conditions for negotiation, lasted only a short while – operations soon continued and were officially extended to the neighbouring countries of Laos and Cambodia. Vietnamization of the conflict was conducted under President Richard Nixon as of July 1969: the gradual withdrawal of the US Army was to be counterbalanced by the rearmament of the regular South Vietnamese troops.

In no other war did the uncensored media coverage have such a resounding impact – an entirely different impact, however, from what had been planned by American military strategists. Reports about the **My Lai Massacre** (16 March 1968) changed public opinion for good. During a 90-minute »search and destroy« operation US soldiers killed 504 villagers: elderly people, women, children and babies. The pictures of Trang Bang (1972) had an even more powerful and symbolic impact on the world's public, and continues to do so to this day. Amongst other things, they showed a naked girl, crying as she ran from the destruction of her village by napalm bombs and towards photographer Nick Ut.

In spite of peace talks and secret negotiations, the war continued for several more years, with heavy bombings of the city of Hanoi. It was not until 27 January 1973 that the opponents signed the **Paris Peace Accords** that were to end the war and guarantee the withdrawal of the US forces.

A national reconciliation, however, was yet to come. After the withdrawal of the US troops in 1973 the North Vietnamese government pushed for a victory over South Vietnam and launched a large-scale attack at the beginning of 1975. Thousands of South Vietnamese soldiers defected and fled when the North Vietnamese troops could not be stopped from closing in on **Saigon**. President Nguyen Van Thieu stepped down and fled as well – to Great Britain. On 30 April 1975 the North Vietnamese and Communist troops marched into Saigon and conquered the presidential palace with no resistance of note offered by the South Vietnamese army. The Republic of South Vietnam surrendered without conditions.

The outcome, however, can only be described as horrible: millions of casualties, and hundreds of thousands injured, crippled or missing. In addition, approximately 10 million homeless refugees and former soldiers roamed the devastated country. Roughly 1600 US soldiers remain unaccounted for to this day; they are the so called MIAs (»missing in action«).

Even today the millions of litres of **toxic gas** claims its victims who can be found both among the children of US veterans and in the babies with numerous deformities born in Vietnamese hospitals. Dioxins have a long-term effect on the food chain and, years after the end of the war, are cited as the cause of uterine cancer. The whole country was bombed to the ground. Endless factories, schools and hospitals, traffic infrastructure, villages and almost half of all cities lay in ruins. Much of the country's wildlife and the better part of the Vietnamese forest were destroyed as well.

Unity and the Socialist Period

1976	Socialist Republic of Vietnam is founded.
1978	Ban on private trade
1979–89	Occupation of Cambodia, overthrow of terror regime
1979	China attacks Vietnam, severe economic crisis
1986	Reforms decided at Sixth National Party Congress
1994	End of the US trade embargo
2001	The moderate Nong Duc Manh becomes the new head of the Communist Party.
2003	Tourism crippled by SARS and bird flu
2007	Vietnam becomes a member of the World Trade Organization (WTO).

Consequences of the reunification

As expected, the first ever Vietnamese elections in April 1976 were won by the Communists. On 2 July 1976 the Socialist Republic of Vietnam (SRV) was founded and the north and south were reunited. Ho Chi Minh did not live to see this triumph: the North Vietnamese president had died back in 1969. The reintegration of the capitalistic south after 20 years of separation was now rigidly executed by the Communist Party. In addition to the nationalization of the South Vietnamese economy, the new republic also set up so called re-education camps. The effects of this radical change in the south were catastrophic. Religious freedom was seriously restricted and political persecution did not spare artists, journalists and intellectuals. The number of expropriations led to a flood of refugees – in particular, the population of Chinese origin fled overland and across the South China Sea. About 2 million people left Vietnam between 1975 and 1990, mostly as boat people (►Baedeker Special p.62). In terms of foreign policy, Hanoi moved closer to the Soviet Union, much to the displeasure of the Chinese.

Occupation of Cambodia

Vietnam's old ambitions for expansion towards Laos and Cambodia were gradually beginning to show again. At the end of 1978 Vietnam launched an attack on the neighbouring country Cambodia. In January 1979 the Vietnamese army marched into the Cambodian capital Phnom Penh and overthrew Pol Pot's terror regime. The genocide was over and a 10-year period of occupation began. The Cambodian government was controlled by the Vietnamese until September 1989. The Chinese, who had supported the terrible regime of the Khmer Rouge, countered the Vietnamese advance into Cambodia with an invasion on Vietnam. This conflict, the Sino-Vietnamese War, took place on the North Vietnamese border in the spring of 1979.

A Vietnamese climbs on board the US Marine supply ship »White Plains«, which had apprehended a boat with 29 refugees

A refugee boat capsizes as it docks with the »C Anamur«. All refugees were saved however. »C Anamur« was a German aid ship that saved lives of about 9000 Vietnam refugees in the 197

FLIGHT BY SEA

After the end of the Vietnam War in 1975 about two million so-called boat people fled the country, which was now a Communist state. Those who left the Socialist Republic of Vietnam were mainly ethnic Chinese, well-to-do business people who were persecuted by the new regime.

Many had worked for the Americans or for multinational companies during the war. Now thousands of them were dispossessed and sent to »re-education camps«. Some lost their work permits for decades: former traders and business people were now expected to earn their living in the »New Economic Zones« as fishermen, on factory production lines or making deliveries by bicycle. Many more fled to avoid prison, as they or members of their family had fought »on the wrong side«.

Dangerous passage

Take the example of Huynh Hanh, who was just 17 years old when he precipitately fled Vietnam in 1977. After the Communist takeover in the south his brothers, who had served in the South Vietnamese army, were regarded as traitors. His father's pharmacy in Saigon was immediately confiscated. Hanh was forced to flee alone. The fishing boat in which he escaped to Thailand was tossed to and fro by waves that were metres high. There was only one day's supply of

drinking water on board for 24 refugees. Pirates, attracted by their scant possessions, attacked the boat. Via camps in Thailand and Italy Hanh eventually reached Germany, where his refugee status was recognized. He served an apprenticeship there, and before long his father joined him. Today the rest of the family is scattered around the world. Hanh returned to Vietnam when his grandmother was on her deathbed. Confucian ethics require children and grandchildren to honour and look after relatives until they die. In conversation Hanh, now a car mechanic in a German company in Saigon, appears more European than Vietnamese. He complains about the **arbitrary behaviour of the authorities** and the widespread poverty in his old and new homeland. It came as a shock to return there after 18 years living in a consumer society run with German efficiency and discipline. His first impression was that the ideology of Karl Marx had given way to ubiquitous corruption: at the airport he had to pay 100 dollars extra for a visa in a

clandestine transaction in order to be allowed to re-enter his home country without difficulties.

Quota refugees

Hanh was just one of hundreds of thousands of victims of what became an **international humanitarian crisis**. From the camps set up in Thailand, Malaysia, Indonesia and elsewhere there were reports that inmates were being mistreated, including rapes and beatings by guards. Hong Kong, already overcrowded, accepted over 100,000 refugees, which led to tensions with local residents and violent clashes with the security forces in the 1990s. Some harrowing cases of suffering on the high seas were well publicized in the media. The willingness of Western countries to accept Vietnamese varied, and was expressed in **quotas of permitted immigrants**. The United States took in over 800,000, France about 140,000, Canada and Australia over 100,000, Germany 38,000 and the United Kingdom 19,000. From the late 1980s the numbers wishing to make a getaway from Vietnam declined, and by the mid-1990s, as the economy in Vietnam revived and repatriation continued, the camps in Southeast Asia began to close.

Reluctant return

After a repatriation agreement of 1990, and with financial support from the EU, it was mainly so-called economic refugees who returned home, few of them willingly. Each of them received US$410 for **reintegration**, at the time more than the average annual income in Vietnam.

The presence of the United Nations High Commission for Refugees in Hanoi and Saigon was intended to prevent discrimination against those who returned. However, it was not possible for a handful of United Nations observers to monitor the situation of 100,000 repatriated Vietnamese scattered over the whole country. They were by no means welcomed with open arms. The return of the boat people at the same time as the repatriation of workers contracted abroad to other Communist countries led to a **huge rise in the numbers of unemployed**. Most of them had difficulties in finding work, in addition to their problems with a lethargic bureaucracy and corruption. This was why many of them did everything they could to avoid repatriation, even resorting to self-mutilation and threats of suicide, as happened when the last boat people were forcibly deported from Hong Kong.

Present-day Vietnam

**Reforms –
doi moi**

The collapse of the Vietnamese economy had already been looming since 1979, and for obvious reasons: the country's infrastructure was destroyed, and its industry crippled; there had been natural catastrophes; military expenses were huge, and economic aid from China had stopped in 1978; the embargo had been extended of to all of Vietnam by the USA and other Western states; the inflation rate was disastrous (about 1000%), capital had been lost and the educated parts of the population were moving to other countries; corruption had increased, ethnic resistance movements had sprung up and Vietnam suffered broad international isolation after the occupation of Cambodia. Even the rulers in Hanoi realized that profound **reforms** had become inevitable. During the 1980s a new political generation came into power which led to the »renovation of thinking« (doi moi). At the Sixth National Party Congress in 1986 the delegates agreed on economic reforms that should for example promote decentralization and the market economy, permit individual businesses and joint ventures and establish productivity bonuses for workers and companies. At the latest by the collapse of the Soviet Union and the Eastern Bloc in 1989, Vietnam had no choice but to put these reforms into action. At the beginning of 1988 there was yet another **famine** in the north. As a consequence the government abolished the agricultural cooperatives for good: now farmers were allowed to lease some land and sell their goods on their own. The new constitution from 1992 guaranteed the right to private property; on the other hand, the right to free education and health care was abolished.

**Phase of
opening and
normalization**

Since the 1990s, foreign observers have regarded Vietnam, with its double-figures growth rate, as another Asian »tiger« or »dragon« – just like Hong Kong, Taiwan, South Korea, Singapore and Thailand. The export industry in particular flourished when the country turned away from the strongly supported heavy industries and embraced once again the typical and still prevailing Vietnamese agricultural industries. Vietnam is now one of the **biggest exporters of rice** worldwide, despite the fact that the exporting of rice was only re-established in 1989. The horrendous rate of inflation has dropped down to a normal level. Vietnam attracts foreign capital with its enormous oil deposits, its liberal laws, its highly motivated workforce and its low wages.

**Towards the
21st Century**

In the meantime, economic growth has slowed, and moreover the downsides of the booming economy have become apparent, for example in the form of high unemployment and the inevitable collapse of many unprofitable state-controlled businesses. The living conditions of the people in the cities have, however, improved; it is they who profit the most from the (re-established) investments by their relatives abroad. In 1990 President Bush was the first US president to

Historical handshake

once again hold talks with government representatives from Vietnam. Four years later, the United States lifted their trade embargo from 1975 for good. With the **re-opening of the American embassy** in Hanoi in 1996, relations between the former enemies have largely returned to normal. In November 2000 Bill Clinton was the first US President to visit Vietnam after 25 years. During his speech, which was broadcasted live on television, he emphasized America's intention to further improve the relations between the two countries.

In April 2001 the moderate representative Nong Duc Manh was elected to be the new leader of the Communist Party – for the first time a member of an ethnic minority (Thai) was to be the head of the party.

In the congressional elections of April 2006 the Communist Party confirmed Nong Duc Manh's appointment as General Secretary for a second term. In June 2006, President Nguyen Minh Triet and Prime Minister Nguyen Tan Dung were elected into office.

Bird flu was first detected in Vietnam in 2003, and by 2005 the UN was warning of a possible pandemic that could kill 150 million people. By February 2006, 40 people had died of the disease in Vietnam. Although the risk to tourists was low, Vietnam's tourism industry was hit hard. Outbreaks occur to this day, prompting emergency measures to prevent the spread of the disease from poultry to humans.

Prospects

In recent years the last of the approximately 90,000 boat people who had fled after the end of the Vietnam War in 1975 and had not been confirmed as official refugees (►Baedeker Special p.62) had to return to Vietnam. International observers still worry about the country's enormous population growth of almost 1.3% (2002) annually. The political system is still ruled by the **one-party government** in Hanoi – neither an opposition party nor true democratic change towards a multi-party system in Vietnam is anywhere to be seen, and political opponents are still threatened with many years of imprisonment. In spite of all the economic liberalization, the comrades of the Vietnamese Communist Party, the sole political power in Vietnam, still have a firm grip on the country. The removal from office of Vice-President Ngo Xuan Loc at the end of 1999 was a huge success for the anti-corruption campaign. The fight against corruption has continued since then, most recently with Nguyen Minh Triet, who became president in 2006.

Art & Culture

Which was the golden age of Vietnamese arts and architecture? What are sapeke clappers? How are the pictures that can be seen everywhere during the Tet New Year's Festival produced? Find all the answers here.

Art History

Architecture and Sculpture

When travelling through Vietnam, a great variety of architecture can be observed: simple thatched houses made of bamboo, elegant colonial mansions, clinical socialist buildings made from prefabricated slabs and postmodern high-rise buildings with reflective glass fronts.

Vietnam's architecture in overview

The most impressive buildings are palaces and emperor's tombs, temples, pagodas and community houses. They were built from more »durable« wood, stone or bricks and often adorned with carvings and sculptures. Of the numerous fortresses built during the 18th and 19th centuries only ruins or watchtowers have remained – with the exception of **Hue**. The citadel of Hue, in particular, clearly exhibits the foreign influences of the time, taking Beijing's Forbidden City and French fortresses as models. Here,

 Geomancy

- According to Chinese teaching more than a thousand years old, every location has both good and bad characteristics. When constructing burial sites, palaces and temples, as well as residential buildings, the aim is to find a balance of the elemental forces »yin« and »yang«. The characteristics of each location can be ascertained with the help of a compass-like instrument featuring a magnetic needle.

and for nearby burial sites, it is not only aesthetics but also geomancy that play an important role. The aim was to achieve absolute harmony of art and nature in order to positively influence destiny.

During their period of colonial rule, the French built administrative and prestigious buildings as well as city mansions adorned with stucco and colonnades in both **Hanoi** and **Saigon**. As befitting the tropical climate, shutters and patios were added. The residential buildings outside the centre and at resorts, such as Da Lat and Sa Pa, were given a more rustic look with tiled roofs and timber constructions. To this day, a third of Hanoi's colonial buildings, such as the opera and the residence of the British ambassador, still show traces of Art Deco, combined with some Asian elements. During the 1930s Vietnamese architects developed the puristic design used for the building of Bao Dai's mansions in Da Lat, Vung Tau and So Son.

Vietnam's sculpture focused almost exclusively on **religious themes** and complemented the elaborately built pagodas and burial sites. Sacred buildings – often adorned with carved columns and gracefully curved roofs – often unites symbols of different persuasions. Besides Buddhas and Bodhisattvas, Taoist deities, spirits of ancestors and national guardians can be found (► Baedeker Special p.42). Their design is a display of formidable craftsmanship, be it artistically shaped

Sculpture

← *Calligrapher in Thien Hau Pagoda in Cholon*

lattice work, imaginative paintwork, remarkable wooden sculptures or overwhelming roof ornaments. The rock stelae in some pagodas are equally impressive. They tell of the laying of the foundation or another important historical event. The most interesting characters and reliefs emerged, without a doubt, during the culture of the Cham people.

History of the Cham

The old and fascinating towers found between Phan Thiet and Da Nang are relics of the Cham dynasty, which ruled over parts of Central and South Vietnam for more than 1400 years. According to Chinese records, a man named Khu Lien collaborated with local princes near Quang Triin in 192 BC to fend off the Han Chinese in the north and to establish an independent state. Soon **Champa** united the coastline from Phan Thiet to Dong Hoi, and at the end of the 4th century it extended across four provinces: Amaravati (surroundings of Hue and Da Nang), Vijaya (around Qui Nhon), Kauthara (around Nha Trang), and Panduranga (today ranging from Phan Thiet to Phan Rang). Simhapura (lion citadel) became the capital of the first united empire. Around the same time the building of the My Son temple site began. Due to its location between the Khmer in the south and Viet groups in the north (which were still under Chinese rule at the time), Champa had to incessantly ward off its neighbours. Between the 3rd and the 5th century there were repeated conflicts with the Chinese. The battles against the Khmer were most severe during the 12th and 13th centuries and culminated in the partial destruction of Angkor, in what is now Cambodia. Under Binasuor the kingdom expanded even further, though following his death in 1390 the Viet had already seized control over the region around Indrapura. The Viets finally took over Vijaya in 1471. The Cham were forced to move their capitals south and their power decreased immensely. Over the following centuries they ruled nominally in the area between Phan Rang and Phan Thiet. When the last inde-

Cham Shrines *Map*

Hanoi

100 mi
150 km
©Baedeker

Than Hoa

Vinh

Ron
Dong Hoi

Quang Tri

Hue

LAOS

Da Nang
← **Amaravati**

← **Vijaya**
Qui Nhon

CAMBODIA

← **Khautara**
Nha Trang

Phan Rang
← **Panduranga**
Tay Ninh
Phan Ri

Saigon
Phan Thiet

The temple group near Nha Trang is consecrated to the Mother Goddess Po Nagar

pendent Cham king died in 1697, this once powerful empire was hardly more than a Viet vassal state. The emperor Minh Mang also put an end to this around 1820. Approximately 100,000 descendants of the Cham still live in Vietnam today.

If there ever was a golden age of Vietnamese art and architecture, it would be that of the Cham empire. Sadly, due to weathering in the hot tropical climate, pillage, and bombings, only around 20 of the once 250 sites have been preserved. The most interesting Cham sites are Po Klong Garai, Po Re Me (both ►Phan Rang), Po Nagar (►Nha Trang), Thap Doi (►Qui Nhon) and My Son. The excellent collection in the Cham Museum in Da Nang gives a good overview.

Culture of the Cham

The earliest pieces are part of the **My Son temple** and date back to the 8th century. Although they resemble Indian arts of the time, they have a distinctive character, especially in its naturalistic portrayal of humans.

The religion of the Cham was Hinduism, riddled with Buddhist elements and popular beliefs. Islamic influences were added in the late 14th century. Monuments and sculptures were mainly used for religious purposes. Dead rulers were worshipped as god-kings and affiliated to Hindu deities, especially Shiva. Ganesha, Vishnu and Lakshmi were also borrowed from Hinduism. The universal mother, Uroja, seems to be based on local beliefs. Often she is portrayed as a bust or nipple (photo p.328). She can, however, also show traits of Shiva's

THE VIETNAMESE PAGODA

It was during the Ly and the Tran dynasties (11th–14th centuries) that pagoda architecture reached its high point, but only a few buildings have been preserved from this time. Wood was the main construction material, and because it quickly weathered in Vietnam's hot, damp climate, the shrines had to be renewed at regular intervals. This often meant not only rebuilding but also restructuring.

🕐 Visiting times:
The best time to visit is the 1st or the 15th day of the lunar month (half moon or full moon), as most believers come at these times.

Site
The structure of the Vietnamese pagoda is strongly modelled on Chinese examples. The ground plan is mostly in the shape of a reclining H or a T standing on its head. As a rule the pagoda area, set up around a north-south axis, is surrounded by a 2–3m/6–10ft-high wall.

① Gate (tam quan)
A three-element gate leads into the temple site. Some gates are magnificent constructions with a tiled roof and rows of columns; others consist of simple posts with crossbeams.

② Temple building (chua)
The function of the temple also demands its division into three parts. The increasing religious importance moving from the entrance to the main altar is underlined by means of ascending levels.

③ Main entrance
The main entrances to the pagoda are opened only on feast days. The best spatial impression of the site is gained from here.

④ Front hall (tien duong)
Items for temple festivals, along with statues of ancestral spirits or local deities and tutelary spirits, are kept in the front hall.

⑤ Central hall (thien huong)
In the centre of the incense offering room stands an altar, at which prayers are said and sacrifices laid. The Buddha child is enthroned on the altar, often accompanied by other statues. The room is decorated with carvings on the columns and entablature.

⑥ Main altar hall (thuong dien)
The statues in the main altar hall throng around a steeply towering altar rising up to the entablature: the three generations of Buddha, the Jade Emperor with his disciples, the Kings of Hell. There are also statues of the donors and of other deities here.

⑦ Living quarters
The monks live in the galleries around the chua or in a plain building behind the pagoda, and pilgrims also find accommodation here. The living quarters contain statues of the donors and builders as well as pictures of the abbots.

⑧ Bell tower
The bell tower stands in the courtyard. In simple pagodas it is only a wooden framework; often, however, elaborate pavilions testify to the wealth of the pagoda.

⑨ Stupas
In the courtyard of the pagoda the ashes of the monks and abbots are buried in tomb-like monuments, so-called stupas. The height of the stupa depends on the age and rank of the dead person.

Vietnamese Pagoda Plan

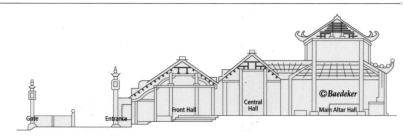

Gate   Entrance   Front Hall   Central Hall   Main Altar Hall   ©Baedeker

Along...
court...
in Sc...
of pa...
acter...
show...
facto...

The...
elem...
the f...
nize...
sitor...
thro...

spouse, Bhagavati – in the Po Nagar Towers near Nha Trang she is revered as a woman. Kala and Makara sculptures and the boat-like roof construction in some buildings also exhibit Javanese influences.

To honour their gods appropriately, Cham kings had impressive brick buildings built. At the centre of a typical complex stood the **kalan (tower)**, whose interior housed the sanctum with an image of a deity, mostly a lingam, the phallic symbol for Shiva. During cleansing rituals it was doused in holy water, which drained off through a gorge at the base, symbolizing the female counterpart (the yoni).

The Vietnamese pagoda

While originally the Vietnamese term »chua« only described a Buddhist pagoda, the concept is now also used for temples of other religious beliefs. Most Buddhist sanctuaries also display guardian spirits or Taoist and Confucian deities (▶ Baedeker Special p.42). Most buildings that can be visited today are from the 18th and 19th centuries. During restorations they were often not only reconstructed, but also remodelled. A three-part gate (tam quan) in the south leads to the temple buildings, which are situated in the middle of a park, sometimes even around a lake or with a bell tower. The chua is always tripartite and subdivided into a bigger hall and three altar chambers. From the outside it becomes obvious that despite their size and the abundance of ornamentation, the curved roofs appear relatively light – this effect is created by means of elevated roof endings and adorned ridges.

In the atrium, often simple in design, wardens and regional deities are found. The central hall, which is slightly elevated, is followed by the main sanctuary. An altar and tables with incense and food oblations are stored in the second chamber. Once again a variety of statues are found here, such as childlike portrayals of Buddha or the laughing Buddha of the Future. Their arrangement differs from one temple to another and can amount to up to 100 statues. Generally an uneven number must be placed on the individual steps, while the most significant figure stands in the middle. The Buddhas of the three generations reside at the very top.

! **Baedeker TIP**

Shoes off, please!

Before entering the main sanctuary of a Buddhist pagoda you will need to remove your shoes. Those who do not want to enter the site barefoot or find the slippers provided uncomfortable should always bring a pair of socks for sightseeing.

At the rear of the complex are the living and sleeping rooms of the monks or nuns. Sometimes inconspicuous altars in the halls commemorate the deceased members of the order; other pagoda gardens feature small stupas with burial sites of the former residents of the monastery.

Music, Theatre and Film

Music

At the time of the Vietnam Empire, music was one of the six liberal arts (along with ceremonies, shooting, horseback riding, law and arithmetic). Along with chess, poetry and painting, it was considered one of the four »joys in life«. According to Confucian belief that music has an ennobling effect on people, Vietnamese rulers always appreciated and promoted the art of music. When the last Vietnamese emperor abdicated in 1945, the royal court of musicians, mime artists, singers and dancers disappeared as well. Feudal and aristocratic culture was to have been finally overcome. In the meantime, however, numerous groups have committed themselves to the court art form. Such performances can be seen in Hue.

Court music

Buddhist priests proclaim their sutras and prayers in a mixed form of loud reading and singing, while the mostly evenly-spaced rhythm of the prayers is underlined by bells or a small gong. Very often, priests will also use tambourine-shaped wooden drums, ornately decorated with carvings. At some ceremonies they are also accompanied by fiddles, lutes, wooden rattles or a small one-skinned drum.

Religious ceremonial and cult music

Musicians with traditional instruments

At funeral services in southern Vietnam, five musicians provide ceremonial or funeral music to enhance the ambience for the various ritual acts. They usually play ceremonial drums, a buffalo horn beaten with a wooden stick, an oboe, gongs and cymbals, as well as the one-skinned goblet drum. Singing during these ceremonies is strictly restricted to the pallbearers: whilst carrying the coffin they chant songs to accompany the soul of the deceased.

Classical music At the beginning of the 18th century **»music from Hue«** was at the height of its popularity. It is performed either by a solo musician or by small ensembles consisting of three to six different instruments. Most commonly string instruments are used, but there are also flutes, drums and sapeke clappers (see below). Today this virtuoso music is being performed publicly again, at the former Imperial Palace in Hue for example. The **»music of lovers«** from southern Vietnam stems from the same tradition as the music from Hue. Singing is an essential part of both types of music; while the music from Hue is mainly sung by women, male vocalists are also to be found in the

Traditional folklore group in the Temple of Literature, Hanoi

south. Larger audiences will hear such music in »cai luong« theatre performances – so-called renewed or reformed theatre. One of the most popular and tear-jerking songs in southern Vietnamese music is called *Longing for the Past* (vong co).

Folk songs

The most essential element in folk music consists of tunes (hat) about the life of the ordinary people and the »Vietnamese soul«, which expresses itself through melodies, songs, poetry and lyricism and is often filled with sentimentality, profound melancholy and patriotism. Many folk songs are about unhappy love, the transience of life – and work. In Vietnam, all professions and crafts have their own tunes. Traditionally, those of farmers and peasant workers are represented the most.

Music of ethnic minorities

More than 6% of the population of Vietnam belong to ethnic minorities. Most of them live in isolation in the Central Highlands or in the mountainous regions of the north. All of them maintain their own traditions of music and dance, which are related to Indonesian, Thai or Burmese forms.

Sapeke clapper

An example of an authentic Vietnamese percussion instrument is the sapeke clapper (Sinh Tien). Made of wood, it combines the characteristics of clappers, rattles and ratchets. It is played by rubbing a wooden stick along its notches or beating it rhythmically. Sapeke clappers can be heard in both classical and folk music. If, in water-puppet theatre or in »hat cheo« theatre, musicians wish to create an evening atmosphere in the countryside, they will use a wooden instrument resembling sugar tongs. When the flexible tongs are pressed together and the small tines hit against each other and start to vibrate, it sounds like croaking frogs.

Monochord

One rather unique instrument is the monochord (dan bau), a narrow, stretched zither with only one string, which is attached to a peg at one end and to a wooden hemisphere at the other. This hemisphere is connected to a flexible, slightly bent bamboo rod. The player can change the pitch by bending the rod sideways with his left hand. With his right hand he plucks the string with a bamboo plectrum, while constantly changing the tension of the string. This instrument is most common in North Vietnam.

Theatre

Folk theatre (hat cheo)

Hat cheo is a popular boulevard theatre found in central and North Vietnam. Plays were mostly performed in the courtyard of the town hall. Both costumes and make-up are extremely simple – all props easily fit into one box. Actors usually embody common stereotypes, such as the poor and the rich man, the old woman, the clown, the monk or the hero. Lines are often filled with sarcasm directed at the

Performance in the municipal theatre in Saigon

wielders of power, which has led to conflicts and occupational bans more than once in the past. The performances protest against vices and praise (Buddhist) virtues by depicting fates of the common people and the lives of heroes, often spiced with the most current social criticism. They play scenes and sketches or dance and sing folk songs. Even ancient songs of the various professions are still preserved. To this day, improvisational art – in which audiences often enthusiastically participate – is an integral part of the performance. A musical ensemble is also an important element for the performance of this kind of musical play.

Classical theatre (hat tuong)

Classical theatre, or hat tuong, dates back to the 12th and 13th centuries and is influenced by Chinese opera. It later became an integral part of court entertainment. Even Emperor Tu Duc himself wrote texts for the hat tuong. Generally, tuong plays are meant to strengthen **patriotism** and loyalty to the rulers. Topics are mainly derived from the country's history, for example the story of the Trung sisters or the liberator Le Loi. In South Vietnam this type of theatre is called hat boi, which denotes songs that are performed in costumes and using gestures. The costumes of the courtly hat tuong are more sumptuous than those of the cheo plays, and there are more ceremonial elements involved. The gestures of the actors are highly stylized, their message being that of **Confucianism**. As soon as the actors enter the stage the audience immediately recognizes the identities of the characters by their costumes and make-up: a red-painted face is associated with courage, honesty and loyalty, a white-painted face implies brutality and deceitfulness.

Water puppetry from North Vietnam is an art form that is unique in the world. Though it incorporates influences from cheo plays and even classical theatre, its main themes stem from old legends and the everyday lives of Vietnamese peasants. The wooden puppets float, dance, plough and plant above and in the water and enact small, yet exquisitely satirical tales. This fascinating form of theatre is accompanied by musicians playing an array of percussion instruments made of metal and wood, string instruments and various types of bamboo flutes. They also sing and lend their voices to the puppets (► Baedeker Special p.358).

Water puppetry (mua roi nuoc)

The origins of water puppetry lie within the religious ceremonies and water rituals of the rural population. This unique technique most likely developed when the puppeteers of the **Red River delta** tried to perform their plays in spite of heavy rain and immense flooding during the monsoon season.

Baedeker TIP

Water puppetry

Today water puppetry can be experienced in Hue (on the Perfume River), in Hanoi (e.g. at the Temple of Literature, or in the Thang Long Theatre close to Lake Hoan Kiem) and in Saigon at the Museum of History.

The earliest records of water puppetry performances date back to the 11th century, but it is commonly believed that this folk art existed even earlier in the rural areas. In the 16th century the first permanent theatre venues were built, including Thay Pagoda (Quoc Oai, Son Tay Province ► Hanoi, surroundings) and the Dong Temple (Dong Anh, Hanoi). The latter still features the small temples for the water god from which the puppeteers controlled their puppets.

Vietnam in Films

Utterly exhausted, completely filthy and carrying heavy backpacks, a group of young US soldiers is fighting its way through the jungle. Heat, mosquitoes, fear and despair are omnipresent. The Vietcong is everywhere and nowhere. The tension becomes unbearable. Then suddenly, mortar bombs pierce the humid air and the sweat-drenched bodies of the soldiers. Screaming, blood; wounded and dead.

Hollywood and Vietnam

Hollywood goes Vietnam. We have all seen films like this. Countless directors from the 1970s and 1980s used America's war against Vietnam as a backdrop for brutal battle scenes set against an exotic landscape – though most of these films were shot in studios and images of landscapes from Thailand and the Philippines simply edited in later. Because, up until recently, the Socialist Republic of Vietnam was closed to filmmakers. Still, the **clichés** of most Vietnam films, which have little or nothing to do with the actual country, are often mistaken for reality. The image of the »slit-eyed«, unpredictable Vietcong has been more deeply engrained in the minds of audiences around the world than many will care to admit. The majority are tough action films and what are known as war veteran films, but there are a few worthy exceptions which really do portray the country and its culture more accurately.

War films Undoubtedly, the most well-known film about the war in Vietnam is **Apocalypse Now** by Francis Ford Coppola. Shot in 1979 for a record sum of US$ 30.5 million, *Apocalypse Now* was awarded the Palme d'Or of Cannes as well as an Academy Award for best cinematography. But again, the story makes use of common clichés: an American captain is ordered to assassinate an insane colonel who is acting up as ruler in the jungle. *Rambo: First Blood Part II (USA 1985) with Sylvester Stallone, Full Metal Jacket* (directed by Stanley Kubrick, USA 1987) and *Missing in Action* (USA 1984) are similar in plot. The latter is about a Vietnamese penal camp with American prisoners of war.

In *Platoon* (written and directed by Oliver Stone, USA 1986), the tough guys are also the top dogs: there are lengthy waits in the torrid sun, dangerous patrols, sudden battles. Historical facts are not only negated here but completely distorted, a phenomenon which neither filmmakers nor audiences seem to mind. *Platoon* is inhabited by brawny lone warriors and uniformed surrogate fathers. To give an example: the **My Lai Massacre**, which took place on 16 March 1968, is turned into an idyllic spectacle where laughing GIs leave the burning village of My Lai wandering across lush green rice fields, carrying little children on their arms and shoulders. In reality, US soldiers brutally massacred more than 500 mostly defenceless civilians, most of them women, children and elderly people. The countless raping and mutilation of Vietnamese women are merely hinted at through the buttoning-up of a soldier's pair of trousers. With historical fact profoundly lacking, these films hint at the suppression of these wartime events in American society.

Veteran films The veteran film genre demonstrates the inflictions of war even more explicitly. They not only deliberately portray physical and psychological injuries, but also pose the GIs' desperate question of why they ended up in the Vietnamese jungle in the first place. These films show crippled war veterans whose physical and mental health were destroyed by their experiences in Vietnam. One example, *Coming Home* (USA, 1978), recounts the love triangle of the wife of a Vietnam warrior (Jane Fonda) who, during her husband's absence, has an affair with a Vietnam War invalid. *Heroes* (USA, 1977) or *Welcome Home* (USA, 1989) with Kris Kristofferson also number among the genre of the broken returnee. Most widely known, however, is **Born on the 4th of July** (USA, 1989) by Oliver Stone, the story of a now paraplegic GI and his transformation to become a committed opponent of war. *Ashes and Embers* (USA, 1982), on the other hand, describes the major difficulties in readjusting experienced by black American soldiers, underdogs in both the army and society at large.

Scene from »Apocalypse Now«

Exceptions to the constantly used stereotypes include the collage film *Dear America – Letters from Vietnam* (USA, 1987), which is based on letters by American soldiers to their girlfriends, mothers and wives. The film contains original battle footage and American news programmes from that time. The original war footage prevents any false romanticizing about adventures in the trenches.

Recommended exceptions within the genre

Another very worthwhile film is called **Good Morning, Vietnam** (USA, 1987). It demonstrates that it is even possible to make a comedy about this topic, and what's more one with depth and substance. The new disc jockey, Adrian Cronauer (Robin Williams) at an army radio station quickly becomes a favourite with his listeners for his saucy comments, but his smart mouth gets him into trouble with his superiors. When Cronauer's Vietnamese friend is debunked as a member of the Vietcong, the DJ is relocated. This tragicomedy shows empathy for the victims on both sides of the war, and manages to be thought provoking in spite of the breathtaking speed of the film.

Romantic films

What Asian romantic films lack in authenticity, they make up in thrilling exoticism and popular cliché. *The Lover* (France/England, 1991), based on the autobiographical novel by the French writer Marguerite Duras, depicts the famous Chinese movie star Tony Leung as a rich man who initiates a young French woman into the secrets of love. Another romantic film set in 1930s Indochina is the French melodrama *Indochine* from 1991, starring Cathérine Deneuve. It was the first European film that was actually shot at the original sites of Ha Long Bay, Dry Ha Long Bay and the caoutchouc plantations near Saigon. Set in the time shortly before colonialism ended, the colonial plantation owner recounts the story of a love triangle between her adoptive Vietnamese daughter and their joint lover.

Vietnamese perspectives on the war

After making several conventional Vietnam War films (*Platoon* and *Born on the 4th of July*) director Oliver Stone also made one from a Vietnamese point of view. The extensively modified adaptation of the novel *Born in Vietnam* by Le Ly Hayslip bore the film title **Between Heaven and Hell** (USA 1993).

The novel is the autobiographical story of Hayslip's youth in a village which is increasingly penetrated by the war. She grows up amidst bombings and Vietcong training, and is suspected of collaborating with the South Vietnamese. As a maid she flees to the city where she is made pregnant by her employer and fired by his wife. She works on the black market to earn a living for herself and her son, until finally a great opportunity presents itself: a soldier, played by Tommy Lee Jones, falls in love with her and takes her back to the United States. Neither the novel nor the film end here, for the story goes on to examine her social difficulties in a foreign culture and the longing to return home, even while being aware that her relatives are exposed to starvation and great danger. In 1986, directly after the opening of Vietnam's doors to the outside world, Le Ly visits her family and is painfully struck again by the sharp contrast between Vietnam and the United States. In the end, this film does not skimp on American emotionalism either.

Films by Vietnamese Directors

Vu Le My

Regrettably, there are hardly any films made from a Vietnamese perspective. A total exception, however, is **Where War Has Passed** directed by Vu Le My. This film, which won an award in 1997 at the Ecomedia Festival, depicts the consequences of the destructiveness of the war machine. In this documentary, victims speak about their suffering, and reveal that malformed children are still being born. They describe the pains and diseases they still have to cope with today. Children, their bodies and souls scarred, vegetate without any limbs or eyes, or with massive heads, even though they were born long after the end of the war. There is no financial and medical support from external sources.

Tran Anh Hung

European arthouse cineastes may be more familiar with the films by the Vietnamese director Tran Anh Hung. His first film, **The Scent of Green Papaya** (France, 1993), aesthetically depicts the life of a female servant in Vietnam at the start of the 20th century. Although this film, like so many others, was shot not in Vietnam but at French studios, it conveys an impressive and near-authentic feel.

Tran Anh Hung's second film **Cyclo** (1995) deals with present-day Vietnam. Buzzing streets, slums and the bars of Saigon provide the settings for this fast-paced, sinister and brutal film. Youth gangs fight their battles and the city shakes as if running a fever. Cyclo and his sister find themselves witnesses to a murder. The fast pace and the atmosphere draws the audience into the bewildering speed of the city. It shows how Vietnamese society is changing dramatically, with families losing their once strong ties. This affectionate and poetic film, along with the documentary *Where War Has Passed* by Vu Le My, portrays the most realistic and intense pictures of modern Vietnam.

Arts and Crafts

Arts and crafts are very common in Vietnam and found in great variety throughout the country, particularly in the cities of Saigon, Hue and Hanoi. This is because almost all inhabitants of the nearby villages make a living from those individual skills in which they have specialized. Gift shops tend to offer lacquerware, pottery, embroidery, wood carvings and intarsia crafts, whereas the local markets are the point of sale for beautiful bamboo and wickerwork items. The hill tribes have specialized in weaving, dyeing and embroidered textiles.

> **!** *Baedeker* TIP
>
> **Looking over the artist's shoulder**
> Those interested in the specific production process of lacquerware should pay a visit to the state and family-run businesses in Hanoi and Saigon where such goods are produced. The Hanoi Art Museum has dedicated a small exhibition to this special technique.

Originally from China, **lacquerware** has been in use in Vietnam for at least 1500 years and is sold throughout the country. The black or brown lacquer is produced from the sap of the sumac tree. However, there are immense quality discrepancies in manufacturing and processing. Well-made items were once characterized by up to 200 coats that were air-dried and polished for hours – a process which may have taken months or even years. Today, pieces are should be coated at least a dozen times. Only then will the motif be applied or carved into the inlays (seashells or eggshells). In Song Be province, southwest of Saigon, craftsmen have been manufacturing these goods for centuries.

During the Vietnamese Tet Festival, the most important holiday of the year (►Baedeker Special p.112), coloured woodcarvings (tranh tet), printed on silk or paper, are displayed above entrances to houses and apartments. They are supposed to ward off evil and bring happiness and fortune. Originally a rural tradition, the pictures have become commonplace throughout Vietnam since the 15th century.

New Year's pictures

The most treasured works come from the **village of Dong Ho**, approximately 50km/31mi from Hanoi. Every year, more than 500,000 of these prints are manufactured in Dong Ho by small family-run businesses and one cooperative. The manufacturing of the wood-carvings can be observed and admired in Hanoi on Hang Trong Street, in the craftsmen's quarter of the old town.

First, the artists create a draft. They then copy it onto a block of wood and carve a printing plate. After printing, the outlines of the motifs appear in black and the surfaces are coloured with a paint-brush. Traditional materials for manufacturing the colours are blossoms, fruits, bark, leaves, ashes and ground minerals – such formulations, developed especially by the artists in Dong Ho, are well-kept secrets. Nowadays, more and more synthetic (and cheaper) paints are replacing the natural ones. Finally, the pictures are coated with a glossy surface, which was originally supposed to be made of finely ground pearl oysters.

These prints depict events in the nation's history, folk tales, scenes of ordinary life (for instance a peasant woman with a water buffalo), heroes, guardian sprits and blessed animals: the rooster protects the house from evil, the goose stands for gentleness, the frog for courage, the pig for wealth and fertility, the peacock announces beauty and peace, while flowers bring happiness. For the entire year these lucky

Classically designed lacquerware and furniture

charms decorate the houses until they are replaced by new ones at the next Tet celebration, when once again there will be »fireworks in the yard and the picture of the rooster on the wall...«.

Water puppetry figurines (► Baedeker Special p.358) are carved out of the soft and light wood of the common fig tree. The figurines are between 30cm/12in and 1m/3ft tall, and take the shape of boats, **Water puppetry figurines**

balls, buffalos, ducks, dragons, peasants, children, kings and fairies. In order to protect them from the water, the puppets are coated with a waterproof resin and lacquer. Additionally, this layer is supposed to protect against woodworm. On top of this lacquer, paint as well as gold and silver are applied. The bodies of the puppets are made of one piece of wood, and the head and arms are fitted with joints to make them flexible. When performing the show in ponds or pools, the majority of the heavy puppet (1kg/2lbs–5kg/11lbs) lies submerged in the water. The puppets are moved with 3m/10ft–4m/13ft-long wooden or bamboo rods. Quite often they are also attached to little rudders and strings. The rods allow the puppeteer to move the puppet forwards and backwards or from side to side. The head, arms and other extremities are controlled by using the strings. The exterior of the puppets may look stylized, but their movements and expressions are often very realistic.

Lucky charms like this are exchanged as gifts during the Tet Festival

Vietnam's forests contain many precious woods such as mahogany, teak, ironwood and rosewood. The work of Vietnamese woodcarvers can be seen in the adornments of old community houses and the ornamentation of Chinese pagodas. In the old town of Hanoi and in the workshops of Hoi An, visitors can observe how little masterpieces (roof ornaments, figurines and furniture) come to life, some even crafted with mother-of-pearl intarsia. **Other woodcarvings**

Smaller figurines (mostly water buffalos and elephants) made of buffalo horn, ivory or tortoiseshell are also sold, but beware: according to the Washington Convention on International Trade in Endangered Species of Wild Fauna and Flora (CITES), such items may not be imported to Europe or the United States.

The production of ceramics has a long tradition in Vietnam. Originally, plated shapes were coated with clay and burnt; however, over the years, the procedures and shapes have progressed and gradually been refined. What is striking is that each dynasty apparently preferred different techniques, colours and motifs: items are coloured jade or blue, are more or less transparent, and the type of glazing is variable. **Ceramics and porcelain**

The art of glazing stems from China. During the Tran dynasty (1225–1400), bricks, tiles and ceramics were mainly coloured green, ochre and shades of brown, whereas in the 15th century the fashion was for blue and white ceramics, which are still manufactured today. In Hue during the reign of the Nguyen princes, bright blue porcelain was developed which showed Chinese influence in shape and decoration. To this day, Hue and the artisanal villages of Bat Trang and Tho Ha outside Hanoi (▶ p.279) have remained the pottery centres of Vietnam.

Silk painting and silk embroidery
Typically Asian motifs such as landscapes, flowers and village life are predominant in silk paintings and embroidery. Silk painting most likely developed in the 13th century and was originally a type of calligraphy, which was gradually complemented by small nature scenes. Tablecloths, blouses and kimonos are often decorated with dragons, birds and Chinese characters. The silk shops in Ho Chi Minh City and in the old town of Hanoi (Hang Trong), as well as the tailor's shops in Hoi An, are famous for these kinds of silk paintings. More elaborate silk embroidery may be marvelled at or purchased at the gallery in the Bao Dai Villa (Da Lat).

All manner of colourful ceramics are to be found at markets and make good souvenirs

In all parts of Vietnam, men and women work in the streets and fields. To protect themselves from the sun they wear conical hats: regardless of the time of day, they efficiently keep the head in the shade. They are made of young palm leafs, attached and weaved into a frame. The more simple hats are sold throughout the country, though the nicest hats are those from Hue. Here, romantic silhouettes and verses are laid between the palm leafs and shine through when holding the hat against the sunlight. There are also hats featuring colourful embroidery. The bands with which the hat is held in place are available in cotton, velvet and silk.

Weaving of conical hats

The ethnic minorities in Vietnam possess a wide range of handicraft skills, for example in manufacturing textiles, jewellery and baskets, to name but a few. The **Muong** are definitely worthy of mention for their **fine art weaving**, as are the unique indigo-dyed and embroidered **dresses of the Bahnar**. Those with a special interest in this subject should pay a visit to the Vietnam Museum of Ethnology in Hanoi, where many of the techniques are explained. The Craft Link shop and Hoa Sen Gallery on Van Mieu Street (next to the Temple of Literature) are well worth a visit for anyone interested in the multitude of local artisanal products (textiles, wooden figurines, paintings, etc.). The profits from these shops are used to finance projects in the hill communities and support children living on the street.

Arts and crafts of the ethnic minorities

Always a friendly smile

Famous People

Surely everyone knows the photograph of the nine-year-old girl running naked from her village after the detonation of a napalm bomb. But what has happened to Phan Thi Kim Phuc since then? Find out here!

Bao Dai (1913–97)

Bao Dai (born Nguyen Vinh Thuy) was the last emperor of the Nguyen dynasty, which ruled in Vietnam from 1802 to 1945. However, when Annam, the heartland of the empire, became a French protectorate in 1883, the monarchs became rulers in name only.

Last emperor of Vietnam

Following the death of his father, Khai Dinh, in 1925, Bao Dai officially became king. At that time, however, the 13-year old was being educated in Europe. It was seven years before he returned to his home country in order to fulfil his ceremonial duties. During the Second World War, Vietnam came under Japanese rule and around the same time the **Viet Minh** or National Liberation Movement was formed. This was a movement of opposition against the imperialist powers of Japan and France. In line with the Japanese surrender, Bao Dai was forced to abdicate on 24 August 1945. Initially however, he was to remain as an »advisor« to the Viet Minh government, which proclaimed the independence of the country on 2 September 1945.

In March 1946, Bao Dai decided to travel to Hong Kong and then to Geneva, where two years later he was persuaded by the French to return to Annam to help them expand their influence. On 14 June 1949 they even made him »head of state« within their sphere of influence (central and southern Vietnam). Bao Dai then assigned the Catholic Ngo Dinh Diem to be his close advisor. During the following years, his position was very vague as he spent most of his time on the Côte d'Azur. France left Indochina for good after their defeat at the Battle of Dien Bien Phu in 1954, but whilst the destiny of the country was discussed at the Geneva Conference, Bao Dai preferred to remain at his villa in Cannes. The negotiations resulted in a shaky ceasefire and the separation of the country at the 17th parallel. Diem became president of South Vietnam with support from the United States. When Diem abolished the emperor's guards, Bao Dai lost his last remaining foothold in Vietnam.

The result of a referendum held on 23 October 1955 led to the former emperor being dispossessed in 1957. It seems that by then he had already accumulated sufficient funds abroad, as he then lived in exile on the French Riviera, his preferred domicile. Bao Dai died on 31 July 1997 in Paris at the ripe old age of 83.

← *The Ho Chi Minh Monument outside the town hall in Saigon is one of the most popular subjects for a photograph amongst the Vietnamese*

Marie-Charles David de Mayréna (1842–90)

Adventurer
The story of the Frenchman Marie-Charles David de Mayréna is one of the most curious episodes in Vietnam's colonial history, and it shares some similarities with *Heart of Darkness* by Joseph Conrad. The novel is about a European who appoints himself ruler of a remote part of the Belgian Congo, a storyline that was later also used by Francis Ford Coppola in his film *Apocalypse Now*.

The life of the rather dubious de Mayréna was rather diverse. He attempted a professional career in the French Army and was also a banker and a planter in South Vietnam. In 1888, the governor sent de Mayréna on an expedition into the mountains accompanied by hundreds of carriers and soldiers. What exactly happened next is unknown, but in the end the only person with him (in Kon Tum) was Alphonse Mercurol. With the help of French missionaries, he met with the tribal chiefs of the Sedang, who were soon fascinated by him, possibly because of his blue eyes and imperious presence. De Mayréna took advantage of the situation and appointed himself Marie I, King of Sedang, while Mercurol became the Marquis of Hanoi. His residence was a straw hut; he designed his own flag, created laws, formed an army and declared war on the neighbouring Jarai tribe. But in spite of it all, he became bored of his majestic lifestyle after only a few months, as he was interested more in money than power. He packed up and set off to make money out of his title. Surrounded by courtiers, he lived in expensive hotels in Saigon. In Europe, too, he tried to convert his very presence into hard cash by selling fake titles and concessions. Over time, he could not prevent cracks appearing in his stories, and he became less and less credible. Eventually he returned to Asia in 1890 where he lived a moderate life on the Malaysian island of Pulau Tioman up until his death. De Mayréna is said to have died of a snake bite.

Ho Chi Minh

►Baedeker Special p.265

Phan Thi Kim Phuc (born 1963)

UNESCO ambassador
One of the most memorable press photographs of the last century shows a young unclothed girl fleeing her burning village together with other children. She screams whilst appearing to run towards the observer. The picture came to symbolize the Vietnam War and the horrors of war in general (►photo p.59).

The Vietnamese **photographer Nick Ut** arrived in Trang Bang on 8 June 1972, shortly after a Napalm bomb attack. Surrounded by gruesome scenes such as these, he pressed the shutter release button. Nine-year old Phan Thi Kim had suffered third-degree burns during the attack, which still affect her today. After lengthy hospital stays and studies in Cuba, the mother of two now lives in Canada. In 1997 Phan Thi Kim Phuc was appointed a UNESCO ambassador. The previous year she had forgiven the American responsible for the attack on her village during a personal encounter.

> **! Baedeker TIP**
>
> **The Girl In The Picture**
> More about the life of Phan Thi Kim Phuc can be read in her biography by Denise Chong (Penguin, 2001).

Alexandre de Rhodes (1591–1660)

Missionary

Vietnam is the only Asian country to have a writing system based on Latin letters. This came about when Alexandre de Rhodes, a French Jesuit missionary, came to Vietnam in 1627 as part of the proselytization of Southeast Asia. Apart from various European languages, he could also speak Chinese and was able to preach in Vietnamese after only six months of being there. In order to make the Gospel available to a greater audience he developed the »quoc ngu« script, a phonetic alphabet based on Latin letters which is still in use in Vietnam today. He then published a catechism and transliterated Vietnamese into Latin characters, hereby creating a complete Latin-Portuguese-Vietnamese dictionary, written in Latin and Chinese characters. Not only did the missionaries aid alphabetization and teach Christian beliefs, they also taught the Vietnamese basic skills such as shipbuilding and the manufacturing of clocks and firearms.
Constantly travelling between Hanoi, Macao, Paris and Rome in order to raise money and support for his work, Rhodes also became famous in Europe. His activities were the reason that the Vatican sent more French priests to Indochina to carry out missionary work – a fact that would later help the French tremendously when trying to gain ground and expand their power as colonial rulers. Rhodes had been a welcome guest at the court of Hanoi since 1627, though this was slowly starting to change. The monk's uncompromising views on Vietnamese traditions such as Buddhism, ancestor worship and polygamy, as well as increasing audiences during his sermons, were particularly disturbing for Confucian scholars. In 1630, Rhodes went to Macao after eventually being forced to leave the country. During the following years, he illegally returned to South Vietnam on various occasions until he was finally expelled in 1645. Alexandre de Rhodes died in Isfahan (Persia) in 1660 at the age of 69.

Thich Quang Duc (1897–1963)

Monk

During the early hours of 11 June 1963, several Buddhist monks from Xa Loi Pagoda in Saigon headed to the corner of Cach Mang Thank Tam/Nguyen Dinh Chieu Street. Having arrived from Hue, 66-year old Thich Quang Duc sat down on the street in a position of meditation. As a protest against the **discrimination of Buddhists** by the government of the Catholic President Diem, his companions doused him in petrol and set him on fire. As the flames started to slowly consume the body of Thich Quang Duc and passers-by threw themselves on their knees, Western journalists and photographers also joined the crowd. The day after this gruesome event, the story featured on the front pages of newspapers throughout the world.

However, the violation of monasteries, the demolitions and the slaying of many hundreds of nuns and monks continued, and Diem imposed martial law. Xa Loi Pagoda became the centre of protest and mass demonstrations. More than 30 monks and nuns followed in the footsteps of Thich Quang Duc as a protest against Diem's politics and the interference of the United States in South Vietnam. Two young US citizens also burned themselves publicly in November 1968, one of them in front of the Pentagon and the other near the Headquarters of the United Nations. The entire world was shocked about these **suicides**, and even more appalled by the cynical reaction of the president's sister-in-law, the legendary Madam Nu who commented: »Let them burn, we will applaud them.« Nevertheless, Thich Quang Duc's **self-immolation** initiated the beginning of the fall of President Diem. The world public turned away from him, and shortly afterwards he and his brother were killed during a military coup.

The Trung Sisters (died 43 AD)

Freedom fighters   The Trung sisters are the most famous and most admired heroines in Vietnamese history. Their rebellion against the Chinese in Vietnam, whose rule lasted for almost 1200 years, is still the most renowned and the most celebrated.

Vietnam was seized by the Chinese in 111 BC and was declared a protectorate of Giao Chi. Trung Tac was married to Lord Thi Sach, who was executed by the Chinese in AD 40. Together with her sister Trung Nhi she colluded with other sovereigns and successfully assembled and commanded an army that caused the Chinese governor to flee. The Trung sisters soon declared themselves **queens** of the now independent Vietnamese territory. Their leadership, however,

was short-lived: three years later the Chinese troops returned, this time putting a bloody end to the rebellion. Trung Tac and Trung Nhi were allegedly captured and beheaded, though another version of the story suggests that the sisters drowned themselves in the Hat Giang River to escape captivity. Vietnam still honours the sisters as symbols of this war of independence. Almost every city has a street named after them, many temples are dedicated to them and various monuments have been built in their memory. During the annual commemoration service on the second day of the fifth lunar month, the statues of both queens are carried into the river for a ritual ablution.

Alexandre Yersin (1863–1943)

Alexandre Jean Emile Yersin was born to French parents on 22 September 1863 in Rougemont in the Swiss Canton of Voud. After finishing his degree in medicine, he went to France where he met and for some time worked with Louis Pasteur. As a surgeon, he travelled to the Far East where he ended up in Nha Trang in 1891. Two years later, during one of his expeditions, he discovered the mountain village of Da Lat. Due to the beauty and moderate climate there, he recommended Da Lat as an eligible holiday location, turning it into a popular destination for the French. The following year, in 1894, he went to Hong Kong to help fight the cholera epidemic. Soon after returning to Nha Trang he built a laboratory, which in 1902 became the first Pasteur Institute outside France. At the institute, independently of the co-discoverer S. Kitasato, he managed to isolate the **pathogen that causes the plague** and developed an antiserum that was named after him. In addition, he set up a cattle farm to produce serums and vaccines. During the 50 years that he lived in Nha Trang until his death, Yersin made important reforms to the Vietnamese health system, often against the will of his employers. Apart from his medical successes, he also excelled in other areas: he has been credited with the importation of the coffee and rubber plants to Vietnam and was a driving force in promoting the industrial manufacture of rubber. Once he had retired from his active working life, he primarily concerned himself with astrology, photography and the characteristic water conditions of the Nha Trang Bay. On 1 March 1943, Alexandre Yersin died at the age of 79. He was buried in Suoi Dua, a village south of Nha Trang.

Tropical doctor

Practicalities

IS BIRD FLU DANGEROUS
FOR TOURISTS IN VIETNAM?
HOW DO YOU ADDRESS THE VIETNAMESE?
WHAT WILL TURN UP IF YOU ORDER »THIT HEO«
IN A RESTAURANT? PRACTICAL TIPS FOR A
SUCCESSFUL HOLIDAY.

Accomodation

Accommodations range from simple guesthouses and mini hotels to former colonial houses and mid-range hotels and on to luxury hotels and hostels, which are still largely limited to Saigon, Hanoi and the beach towns of Da Nang, Nha Trang and Phant Thiet/Mui Ne.

Guesthouses/ mini hotels

Guesthouses and mini hotels offer simple, small and mostly clean rooms without air conditioning, usually with sheets and sometimes also with towels, but without daily room service. They are particularly suitable for **backpackers**. Often these accommodations only offer shared shower and toilet facilities, but there are also true bargains to be found including an en-suite shower and bath with hot water. Those staying in one place for longer should not give up searching too quickly. While some rooms do not even have windows, others come with a balcony.

Middle-class hotels

Lower-range middle-class hotels do not always meet European demands in terms of service, cleanliness and fixtures. Sometimes the tap drips incessantly,and the air-conditioning sounds like a motorway next to the hotel. In this price range, rooms are equipped with shower, balcony and cupboard as well as TV, telephone, fridge and radio. Sometimes the room only has one window looking onto a courtyard or the hallway. Most hotels have their own restaurant, an elevator and sometimes even a pool. Often hotel staff do not speak English well.

Those searching for accommodation meeting certain international standards should choose a category higher than middle class.

First class

In this price range, rooms are equipped with a shower and/or bath, air conditioning, satellite TV and hotel videos, telephone, minibar, and room safe. The hotels also offer swimming pools, karaoke bars, discos, 24-hour coffee shops, fitness facilities and business centres, i.e. every form of entertainment and service imaginable. Reservations are often handled as **flat-rate bookings** by foreign travel agents, which usually means better prices. A lot of foreign business people stay for longer periods and can therefore expect better rates.

i ## Price categories

- Luxury: from 2 million VND / £75
- Mid-range: from 500,000 VND / £19
- Budget: up to 500,000 VND / £19
  (price for a double room without breakfast)

- Hotels and guesthouses ►Sights from A to Z

Luxury hotels

The top-class of accommodation meets the best international standards (5 stars) with all amenities and excellently trained staff. The rooms are luxuriously decorated and hotels come complete with a swimming pool and several speciality restaurants.

Arrival · Before the Journey

International airports are situated in Saigon (7km/4mi from the city centre) and in Hanoi (30km/19mi from the city centre). Tan Son Nhat International Airport in Saigon, however, is serviced more often by European airlines than Noi Bai International Airport in Hanoi, which tends to receive domestic flights and flights from Asian airports. A number of international flights also touch down at Da Nang Airport.

By air

British Airways does not currently fly to Hanoi. It does offer flights from London Heathrow to Saigon, with a change of planes necessary in Hong Kong or Singapore. Indeed, many airlines fly from Heathrow to Saigon, but there are **no direct flights**: Thai Airways fly via Bangkok, Air China via Beijing, Cathay Pacific via Hong Kong, and so on. Vietnam Airlines offers services from Heathrow to Saigon and Hanoi via Paris Charles de Gaulle, and to Hanoi via Frankfurt. A direct flight from Frankfurt to Saigon is also operated by Lufthansa Vietnam Airlines flies from Sydney direct to Saigon, and continues on to Hanoi without changing planes. Qantas flights to both Hanoi and Saigon involve changing in Hong Kong, Bangkok or Tokyo, for example. There are numerous flights from US and Canadian airports to Vietnam, but they always involve changing planes at an Asian airport (or Paris or Frankfurt). American Airlines, for example, flies from both J F Kennedy International Airport in New York and San Francisco International Airport to Saigon by way of Tokyo. Stopovers are of course possible in places such as Dubai, Bangkok, Singapore, Kuala Lumpur or Hong Kong.

From most Asian capital cities and all neighbouring countries there is at least one direct flight to Saigon and Hanoi every day. The flight time from Europe is 11 to 13 hours, depending on the route and possible stopovers. **Early booking** is recommended when travelling in October or later. Tickets get scarce around January/February as many Vietnamese ex-pats fly home for the Tet Festival (►Baedeker Special p.112).

Vietnam Airlines fly modern Airbus planes (ATR and Fokker machines are only used for flights to Cambodia, Laos and Canton). The connections and flight times to all larger cities and province capitals are listed in the tourist brochures (including *What's On in Saigon* and *Time Out*). With enough time before departure it is possible to reserve or purchase tickets in all major cities or travel agencies. Flights are usually on time, except during monsoon season when departures and landings are sometimes delayed due to bad weather conditions. There is a minibus service to the airports in Hanoi and Saigon, which is organized by Vietnam Airlines.

◄ Domestic flights

When leaving Vietnam, an airport tax is charged (currently US$12–14, also payable in VND). An extra counter is set up for payment of the charge. Flights must be confirmed by telephone two to three days prior to departure at the office of the airline in question.

◄ Leaving the country

● USEFUL ADDRESSES

VIETNAM AIRLINES

▶ **in the UK**
7 Lower Grosvenor Place
London   SW1W 0EN
Tel. 020 3263 2062
Fax 020 3263 2064
www.vietnamairlines.com
info@vietnam-airlines.co.uk

▶ **in the USA**
88 Kearny Street, Suite 1400
San Francisco, CA 94108
Tel. 415 677 8909 and 677 9788
Fax 415 677 9798

▶ **in Australia**
Level 13, 31 Market Street
Sydney NSW 2000
Tel. 2 9283 9658
Fax 2 9283 6355
vnaustralia@vietnamair.com.au

▶ **in Saigon**
Tel. 08/8 32 03 02 (international)
Tel. 08/8 25 83 77 (national)

▶ **in Hanoi**
Tel. 04/8 32 03 20
www.vietnamairlines.com

PACIFIC AIRLINES

▶ **in Hanoi**
Tel. 04/9 55 05 50
www.pacificairlines.com.vn

OTHER AIRLINES

▶ **British Airways**
Tel. 0844 493 0 787
www.britishairways.com
Saigon:
114A Nguyen Hue Boulevard
District 1
Tel: 829 2262
Fax 825 6578

▶ **American Airlines**
Tel. 1 800 222 2377
www.aa.com

▶ **Lufthansa**
Tel. (in the UK) 0871 945 9747
www.lufthansa.com

▶ **Qantas**
Tel. 13 13 13
www.qantas.com

AIRPORTS

▶ **Saigon**
(Ho Chi Minh City)
Tan Son Nhat International
Airport
Visitor Information and Service
Centre
Tel. 08/8 48 67 11 and 8 48 53 83
Fax 08/8 48 67 12
www.saigonairport.com
sasco@hcmc.vnn.vn
(daily 9am–11pm;
shuttle bus; taxi to the city centre:
£2/50,000 VND)

▶ **Hanoi**
Noi Bai International Airport
Tel. 04/8 86 65 27
(taxi to the city centre: £7/US$10;
shuttle bus to old town)

▶ **Da Nang**
International Airport
Tel. 05 11/81 18 11 and 83 03 39

TRAVEL AGENTS

▶ **Global Adrenaline**
25 East Washington Street
Suite 1458, Chicago, Illinois 60602
Tel. +1-866-884-5622
(toll free in USA)
Tel. +1-312-863-6300
(outside USA)
Fax +1-312-873-4440

Email: info@Global
Adrenaline.com
www.globaladrenaline.com
Vacations for the more adventurous traveller.

► **Mekong Travel**
Tel. (+44) (0)1494 674456
Fax: (+44) (0)1494 681631
www.mekong-travel.com
Tours to the Mekong delta and
beyond. From adventure tours and
cruises to beach and golfing
holidays.

► **Symbiosis**
in the UK:
2 Brambles Enterprise Centre
Waterberry Drive
Waterlooville PO7 7TH
www.symbiosis-travel.com
Tel. +44 (0) 845 123 2844

Fax +44 (0) 845 123 2845
in the USA:
Boston Center, P.O. Box 1585
Duxbury, MA 02332-1353
Toll free (US Only):
1-866-723-7903
Fax 1 617 848 4208
Complete holiday and expedition
planning service. Committed to
environmentally sensitive and
fair-trade tourism.

► **Travel Indochina**
2nd floor Chester House
21–27 George Street
Oxford OX1 2AY
Tel. 01865 268 940
www.travelindochina.co.uk
Specialists in small group holidays
to Asia. A host of tours to Vietnam
on offer, lasting from seven days to
four weeks.

Recently it has become possible to travel by train from Europe to   Overland
Vietnam, though it is not necessarily cheaper than flying. Specialized
agents can organize the entire trip, including the necessary connections (►Travel Agents p.96).
Visas are required to enter the country. They must be applied for in
advance and are valid for all international border crossings. Embassies and consulates can be found in all countries neighbouring Vietnam.
The opening of **border crossings** in this region, however, largely depends on the political situation in the area in question. In recent
years the region has stabilized, though short-term changes may occur
due to ongoing border conflicts and centuries-old animosities, so
check on the current political situation prior to departure and specifically whether it is possible to cross borders.

Since the spring of 1996, a train has again been running twice a week   By rail
from Hanoi to Kunming (Yunnan province) and Beijing in China.
The journey time is approximately 32 hours or longer (couchettes;
route is via the border crossing of Lao Cai–Heiku). Despite separate
handling, formalities may take a long time for foreign nationals;
quite often, and regardless of a valid visa, »special fees« are charged
as a small private extra income for customs officers. Be absolutely
sure that the **border crossing at Lao Cai** is entered on the visa applica-

tion, which is made through the immigration authority, the home embassy or consulate, or the travel agency. The train has 2nd and 3rd-class compartments, which should be reserved several days in advance.

By bus or shared taxi
Coming from China, the border crossing of Lang Son (Dong Dang) in Guangxi province is also open to Europeans. It is another 160km/99mi from here to Hanoi. There is another crossing at Hai Ninh (Mong Cai) in the northeast (Road 18) and at Lao Cai (Heiku) in the northwest, on the way to Yunnan. Travelling cross-country the now tarmacked Route 9 from the neighbouring country of Laos (Savannakhet) leads, via the border crossing in Lao Bao, to Central Vietnam (Dong Ha), and further north across the Keo Nua Pass near Cau Treo (near Vinh). From Phnom Penh in Cambodia it takes approximately 5 hours to reach Vietnam on the N 22 in Tay Ninh province (border crossing in Moc Bai).

By ship
Vietnam has a coastline of more than 3200km/2000mi, and there is a port in every large coastal town, making it an ideal destination for freighters and cruise ships. Though it is fairly expensive, travelling by cruise ship is increasingly popular. Cruises start in various countries in Asia, e.g. Thailand, or they travel from Vietnam to Thailand, Hong Kong and Singapore. The ports of destination in Vietnam are Hai Phong, Ha Long City, Da Nang, Nha Trang, Saigon and Vung Tau. Tours can be booked at Vietnam Tourism and Saigon Tourist (Star Cruises Company and Kien Giang Tourist Company).
For a number of years now, it has been possible to travel from South Vietnam to **Cambodia** (apply for a visa in advance) along the Mekong River from Chau Doc via the border town of Vinh Xuong (boat transfer) or Tinh Bien (road). Tickets for one of the daily express boats can be booked at the Victoria Hotel in Chau Doc or Kim Travel in Saigon. A visa for Cambodia is available within one day from the Cambodian Embassy in Vietnam.

Travel Documents

Passport and visa
To enter Vietnam a valid passport and visa are required. Visas for individual travellers or groups can be applied for at British or Vietnamese travel agencies (usually less expensive) or directly at the Vietnamese Embassy. Apply as early as possible – processing the application takes between 7 to 10 days. Visas can also be issued by embassies or travel agencies in the countries neighbouring Vietnam (embassies: ► Information). Visas are valid for two or four weeks (US$70/£47 or US$85/£57); they should be extended as necessary at immigration

> ! **Baedeker TIP**
>
> **Visa check**
> Immediately check the visa and entry date, as incorrect stamps from authorities have led to problems in the past (especially when it comes to »multiple entry« visas).

offices or local travel agents in Vietnam. If you do not do this, a charge of US$5 for every additional day is payable on leaving the country. Longer stays may be granted to those with official invitations.

Another possibility is to apply for a so-called **multi-visa**. Available in Hanoi, this costs US$117–133/£78–89 (including the authority fee)and is valid for longer stays. As multiple entries are rarely granted by the Vietnamese Embassy at home, visit a travel agency in Saigon or Hanoi before making a likely detour to Vietnam's neighbouring countries. It may even be possible to obtain a **re-entry visa** for Vietnam. Neighbouring countries also issue visas for Vietnam within 24 hours, e.g. at travel agents in Bangkok or Hong Kong.

Multiple (re-)entry from neighbouring countries

Travellers in Vietnam are not health-insured by the authorities at home. It is essential to arrange international travel insurance. Make sure the policy allows for transportation home in emergency cases.

Travel insurance

Customs Regulations

Entry cards and **customs declaration forms** are handed out on the plane.Present both documents along with your passport and completed visa application to the customs official. In addition, fill out the **white and yellow customs declaration form** before entering the country, keeping the yellow copy. The green copy of the migration card must also be kept until leaving the country, as it is required for hotel check-ins. It is prohibited to import weapons, ammunition and explosives, highly flammable materials, drugs (for such offences the death penalty can apply), anti-government literature and pornography. The importing and exporting of the national currency, the Viet-

Importing and exporting of goods in Vietnam

! *Baedeker* TIP

Foreign Office warning

Even the possession of small amounts of drugs is punishable by long prison sentences; in Vietnam the possession of 20kg/44lbs of opium or 600g/1lb 5oz of heroin may be punishable by death. This also applies to the sexual abuse of children. The death penalty has recently been applied in Vietnam, also to foreign nationals.

namese dong (VND), is also prohibited. The following quantities may be imported into Vietnam customs-free: 1.5 litres of spirits, 2 litres of wine, 200 cigarettes, 50 cigars, 250g of tobacco, gifts to a value of up to US$300 and up to US$3000 in cash.

Special attention should be paid to CITES (Convention on International Trade in Endangered Species of Wild Fauna and Flora) restrictions with regard to the protection of endangered species. Due to the growth of long-distance travel, customs officers at European airports are detecting ever increasing amounts of prohibited goods in travellers' suitcases. Vietnam is a hotspot for trading in products made

Trade in endangered species

from **endangered animal species,**which numerous shops sell openly. Never trust a vendor's claim that ivory comes from tame or dead elephants.

Any violation detected at European customs is punishable by fines of up to US$73,000/£49,000 or up to 5 years in prison. Consequently the following souvenirs are to be absolutely avoided: any product made from animal skin (e.g. snake leather, crocodile skin), fur (leopard, bear), shell (also tortoise shell), horn (rhinoceros, deer), claws (tiger), teeth (also ivory) and feathers, as well as »traditional far-eastern medicine« containing animal body parts (e.g. bear paw, tiger penis, snake liquor). Naturally, it is also prohibited to transport live animals such as tropical fish, birds, insects and reptiles, as well as souvenir boxes with pressed butterflies. Exporting orchids and cacti may also cause trouble if you fail to present proof of purchase from a respectable grower.

Beach Holidays

Beach towns in Vietnam

A coastline 3200km/2000mi long, with white sandy beaches fringed with palms and casuarina trees, is attracting an increasing number of beach holiday tourists to Vietnam. The infrastructure at many beach resorts, however, is not yet up to scratch. Many still lack nearby airports and many Western guests find comfortable access to the paradisiacal beaches lacking – there is no bungalow under palm trees directly on the beach like in Thailand or on the Philippines.

Vung Tau, Da Nang, Nha Trang and Phan Thiet (Mui Ne) are the most well-known beach resorts with the best infrastructure, though standards here still leave much to be desired. So far, only a few hotels meet the demands of an international clientele and offer, for example, bungalows and chalets directly on the beach. However, several **islands** are currently transforming into beach resorts, such as Lang Co, Con Dao, Tuan Chau (Ha Long Bay), Qui Nhon, Van Dou (Bai Tu Long Bay) and Phu Quoc. Unfortunately, when it comes to the expansion of tourist infrastructure, Asia often favours high-rise hotels complete with golf course, karaoke disco and Disneyland-type leisure facilities. Broad coastal strips in the south and the along the entire Mekong delta are covered by mangroves and are unsuitable for swimming due to the muddy waters.

Searching for an empty beach paradise in Vietnam is a rather futile endeavour, for it is a **densely populated country**, a fact that becomes very apparent all along the coast. If the odd small wonderland is found, it is likely that it is not even connected to the electricity grid, as is the case on the idyllic Lao islands off the coast of Da Nang. Tourists in Vietnam can expect to hear roaring fishing boats at dawn, when entire town communities come together to pull the nets out to shore and trade the freshly-caught fish and sea food, often directly next to people's deck chairs (e.g. in Phan Thiet/Mui Ne). At popular beaches countless travelling hawkers offer a variety of goods and services (from coconuts and pineapples to T-shirts and massages). Deck chairs and sunshades are almost always extra.

Beach Towns

The mountainous island of Con Dao (►Sights from A to Z, p.413) is a designated protected area and owes its popularity to a prison facility built by the French in the 19th century. Today the former prison is open to the public as a museum and memorial site. Here the wooded island mountains dramatically drop into the ocean and there are wide and deserted sandy beaches. Several flights per week connect the island with Saigon. A renovated middle-class hotel has already opened here. Best time to go: between March and July.

Con Dao

The beautiful long sandy beach of Cua Dai (approx. 5km/3mi west of Hoi An) along with the nearby islands of Cham and Cam Kim offer some fabulously comfortable beach resorts between the Song Do River and the dunes, including the luxurious Victoria Resort. Snacks and drinks are sold at food stands under casuarina trees. (Book early during the high seasons from August to October and December to February.)

Cua Dai

Even on the more remote beaches traders arrive with drinks and fruit

Da Nang /
China Beach

Da Nang is about to become an international beach town with numerous bars and karaoke clubs. The softly curved and seemingly endless beach south of Da Nang, China Beach (►Sights from A to Z, p.213), has become world famous. It is where the first US ground troops landed with their tanks in March of 1965, and where, ten years later, refugee boats set sail to unknown destinations. Now top-class hotels are opening their doors to foreign visitors. There may soon be as many hotels and B&Bs here as there are palm trees. Between August and October **typhoons** may rage in the area. Dangerous currents occur during wintertime in particular. Best time to swim: from April/May to July.

Around
Ha Long Bay
Tuan Chau ►

The Tuan Chau peninsula was literally built from scratch in 2002 (approx. 10km/6mi south of Ha Long City). The beach resort island gives an artificial impression. There is a connecting dam to the mainland and views to the cliffs of Ha Long Bay and the skyline of Ha Long City. There are some modern first-class hotels on the small strip of beach, with more inexpensive accommodation to be found on the second row up the slope. Travel agents here mainly seem to target Asian families. Events such as dolphin shows take place at the apparent smaller imitation of the Sydney Opera House located on the beach. An 18-hole golf course is in planning.

Cat Ba ►

On the biggest, largely rocky, national park island of Cat Ba, which has been a **biosphere reserve** under UNESCO protection since 2005, there are several idyllic, tiny beaches (Lan Ha, Cat Co and Cat Vang) though they become crowded during summer weekends. Most hotels are situated along the promenade of Cat Ba City. The only truly stunning luxury hotel so far is located on the small beach Cat Co 3, though more are currently being built on the bay nearby.

On the islands dotted around Ha Long Bay there are some attractive beaches, equipped with sunshades to a greater or lesser extent. The silted beaches of Bai Chay in Ha Long City are unsuitable for swimming, as is the crowded beach of Do Son near Hai Phong (which has a casino).

Van Don ►

More deserted beaches can be found in the nearby (to the east) and less crowded **Bai Tu Long Bay**, e.g. on the still rural peninsula of Van Don (simple to mid-range accommodation and a lower mid-range eco hotel with a small private beach set before imposing cliffs) and

Quan Lan ►

the two sandy beaches on the island of Quan Lan, which so far are only equipped with stilted huts and simple stone bungalows. More construction is in progress.

Best time for swimming in the entire Ha Long/Bai Tu Long Bay: May to September/October (rainy season in July and August, the odd typhoon between August and October), during winter (December/January to March/April) it is too cold and rainy to swim.

Lang Co

The best view of the small peninsula (50km/31mi south of Hue, ►Sights from A to Z, p.215) with its long sandy beach, can be en-

The Evason Hideaway enjoys an idyllic location on a bay near Nha Trang

joyed when crossing the Hai Van Pass – provided the cloud cover allows a look down on this phenomenal coastal stretch, where the blue ocean rolls into the golden shore, fishing boats rest under palm trees and a deep-blue lagoon extends into the hinterland. The small fishing town lies next to an upper mid-range beach resort. Take care when swimming: there are sometimes **dangerous currents** here.

A magnificent half-moon shaped beach stretches along the coast near the famous Cham ruins at Phan Rang (approx. 100km/60mi south of the beach town of Nha Trang). At Ninh Chu, a rather simple hotel with bungalows and a food stand are located on the mostly deserted beach. Ca Na, a little further south (approx. 25km/16mi.), is equally attractive with its beautiful and deserted beach – though it is directly behind the highly frequented N 1 motorway. There are some simple small houses and a diving resort at Ca Na.

Phan Rang, Ninh Chu and Ca Na

Vietnam's most famous beach resort was developed in the harbour town of Nha Trang (►Sights from A to Z, p.333) during the French colonial occupation. A 5km/3mi-long sandy beach stretches along the quayside, dotted with shady palm and flamboyant trees. At night it gets very busy in the many beach restaurants, cafés, food stands and bars. Water skiing, windsurfing, scooting, diving, snorkelling, sailing and parasailing are just some of the aquatic sports on offer.

Nha Trang

There are one-day boat trips to the off-shore islands and their beautiful beaches, e.g. the very popular **Bamboo Island** (Hon Tre) and the **coral reefs** of Hon Mun.

Doc Let ▶ Beyond Nha Trang there are a few more isolated sandy beaches, e.g. Doc Let on the Hon Khoi peninsula some 50km/31mi north, which has two fairly simple beach resorts. The Hon Gom peninsula (approx. 60km/37mi north of Nha Trang) has recently been made accessible by the opening of a new road. On its eastern side are sandy beaches with dunes and casuarinas. Only a five-minute speedboat ride away from the island village of Dam Mon is Whale Island (Hon Ong), with small, wonderful coves set amidst striking rocks (like those in the Seychelles) and hidden bays with crystal-clear water. So far, there is only one lovely bungalow resort here (with electricity). The resort is under French-Vietnamese management, and meals at the (seafood) restaurant are included. Visitors can follow in the flippered footsteps of Jacques-Yves Cousteau, who used to dive here back in the 1930s. With luck, **whales or whale sharks** can be spotted between April and July. Guests can also go snorkelling, windsurfing, sailing, or simply relax (best time to swim: June to October, diving from February to mid-October).

Hon Gom ▶

Hon Ong ▶

Dai Lanh ▶ On the mainland a little further north is another broad, deserted beach with casuarina trees, situated within a cove near the fishing village of Dai Lanh (approx. 70km/43mi north of Nha Trang). Behind the dunes stand a few hotels and camp sites, so far mainly frequented by Vietnamese tourists.

Phan Thiet/ The beach with the most hotels and bungalow resorts in all price
Mui Ne ranges is located some 10km/6mi from Phan Thiet (▶ Sights from A to Z, p.345). People coming here are looking for some peace and quiet on the miles of broad, sandy beaches interspersed with small fishing villages. Recreation is offered in the form of a multitude of water sports (especially windsurfing), a golf course, and trips to the famous Mui Ne sand dunes or the remains of a Cham sanctuary.

Phu Quoc This remote island close to the Cambodian coast – at 625 sq km/241 sq mi, the biggest island in Vietnam – was long considered an insider's tip (▶ Sights from A to Z, p.350). With several building projects in the pipeline, however, this is no longer a secret destination. Phu Quoc is situated in the Gulf of Thailand. During the holiday season, planes land several times a day from Saigon (flight time 1 hour) and there are at least three flights per week (30 minutes) from the small town of Rach Gia. Also from Rach Gia (in approx. 2 hours) as well as Hat Tien, both coastal towns in the Mekong delta, (night) ferries and modern speedboats ply to the island on a daily basis. Phu Quoc itself is covered by dense **protected rainforest** on hilly or mountainous terrain, and features countless uninhabited beach coves primarily in the south and west – with 40km/24mi of sandy beaches fringed with shady palm trees. In recent years, several cosy resorts with pools have opened directly on the beach, as well as simpler bungalow accommodation. Day-trip destinations include waterfalls, caves, pepper plantations and more than 100 off-shore islands – fishing boats take tourists here to snorkel above coral reefs. The area is one of the best diving grounds in all of Vietnam, with visibility of up to 50m/164ft.

In the south of the harbour town of Qui Nhon there are numerous attractive sandy beaches and coves hidden between dunes and rocks, and a newly developed international beach resort with great potential for tourism. The presence of the former Quy Nhon US Army base, including an airport and a lengthy runway, raises hopes that international tourism will thrive. So far, there is one luxury hotel in a small beach cove, as well as hotels in town and smaller places offering accommodation for backpackers.

Qui Nhon

The beach town of Vung Tau is still mainly frequented by Saigon locals, (▶Sights from A to Z, p.406) as it only takes two hours by car or one hour by speedboat to get there. At weekends and on holidays the many hotels and beaches are crowded with Vietnamese families, couples and people on company outings. The four beaches, however, do not quite meet Western requirements concerning swimming, hygiene and the beauty of the setting. Attractions include numerous souvenir stands, a few temples and a large statue of Christ rising into the sky from the hill above the sea. Somewhat less touristy and more peaceful is the small town of Long Hai in the north, which offers equally long, but fairly quiet beaches.

Vung Tau

Children in Vietnam

Sadly, the exotic world of Vietnam is also associated with a certain lack in hygiene. Though most children don't mind this, parents should take steps, even before the trip, and have their children vaccinated (e.g. against typhus and tetanus, besides vaccinations for all common children's diseases). Those travelling in malaria regions (outside cities, ▶ Health) should gather information in advance at tropical institutes on medication and preventive measures (mosquito nets, repellent, light clothes covering the entire body) at least 6 weeks prior to departure. See www.fco.gov.uk/en/travelling-and-living-overseas for the latest information. Also important: avoid non-peeled fruit, salads, raw vegetables, non-boiled water and milk, ice-cream and ice cubes, as well as spicy food. The basic rules for children are: no food from street vendors and especially no grilled meat. Even adults need to gradually become accustomed to »Vietnamese« bacteria, and children are more susceptible.

Preventive health measures

► TIPS FOR CHILDREN IN VIETNAM

► **Da Nang Water Park**
2–9 St. Hoa Cuong Ward, Da Nang, tel. 05 11/64 05 06
Surfing, whirlpools, waterfalls and mega slide
2km/1.2mi south of the city centre, down the extended Trung Nu Vuong towards My Khe Beach

► **Dolphin show**
Recreation centre on the Tuan Chau Peninsula (approx. 5km/3mi west of Ha Long City)
Trained dolphins, sea lions and seals perform tricks three times a day.

► **Water puppet theatre**
Thay pagoda on Dragon Lake
40km/24mi southwest of Hanoi, in the village of Sai Son

► **Phu Dong Waterpark**
Tran Phu Street, Nha Trang Beach
Tel. 0 58/52 18 44
North of the Ana Mandara Resort
Water slides, fountains, directly adjacent to a large fair with carousels

► **Zoo and Botanical Gardens, Saigon**
2 Nguyen Binh Khiem Street, Saigon
The Komodo dragons are an absolute highlight at Saigon Zoo

► **Dam Sen Water Park**
3 Hoa Binh, Saigon, District 11
www.damsenpark.com.vn
Rowing boats, super slides, mini train and much more

Travelling with children
Those taking their children to Vietnam must first survive the lengthy flight time (from Europe, 11 to 13 hours or longer), which often involves changing several times. Once in Vietnam, cross-country travel can be extremely strenuous: long rides in crammed (mini) buses; loud, hectic and dangerous traffic; and accommodation that is not always well equipped and clean.

Toddlers
Parents of babies should definitely bring a few specific items: passport and vaccination record, baby food, disposable nappies and sun lotion for children. All this hassle might be rewarded by the devotion and attention that the Vietnamese give to most toddlers – the rule would appear to be the blonder, the more excessive.

Electricity

The mains supply voltage in cities is 220V (50Hz) AC, in rural areas it may still be 110V. Sockets are either for Russian round two-pin plugs (in the north) or American flat two-pin plugs (in the south). European plugs will work in most hotels, but bring an adapter just to be sure.

Emergency

GENERAL EMERGENCY

► **Police**
Tel. 113

► **Fire department**
Tel. 114

► **Rescue service**
Tel. 115

AUTOMOBILE CLUBS

► **AA**
Tel. +44 (0)161 495 8945
(international enquiries)

► **RAC**
Tel. +44 (0)1922 727313
(general enquiries)

INTERNATIONAL AIR AMBULANCE SERVICES

► **Cega Air Ambulance (worldwide service)**
Tel. +44 (0)1243 621097
Fax +44 (0)1243 773169
www.cega-aviation.co.uk

► **US Air Ambulance**
Tel. 800/948-1214
(US; toll-free)
Tel. 001-941-926-2490
(international; collect)
www.usairambulance.net

Etiquette and Customs

The Vietnamese judge other people by their age and by the way they are dressed (shorts for both men and women are unsuitable in rural areas and are forbidden in all churches). Don't be surprised if asked for your **year of birth** first. This is rooted in Confucian belief: older people are always considered wiser and are more respected. But what if a traveller is younger than the travel guide, interpreter, street vendor or sales person? No problem, if you obey certain rules as a foreigner.

General rules

> ## *i* Addressing the Vietnamese
>
> ■ The Vietnamese always have three-part names that are read back to front: the family name comes first, the given name last. The middle name often hints at the person's gender: Thi is female, Van is male.

In Vietnam, keep any feelings of anger to yourself. Loud protests or displays of annoyance will only lead to everyone involved losing face. It is not uncommon for a question to be left unanswered: either the answer would have been negative or the person doesn't know the answer. And when it comes to making a date, it is also important to keep in mind that Asians have a rather different understanding of time and punctuality.

Behaviour in Public

Tipping

In Vietnam, it is uncommon to tip. In hotels (and often in bars and restaurants) up to 15% tax and service charge is already included, but considering the average monthly salary is only £38/US$57, it is polite to give a small tip. When invited to **pray** at a temple by monks or nuns, it goes without saying that visitors should drop a donation into the wooden boxes provided as a sign of gratitude. Usually one or three incense sticks are lit (the latter is common for deaths or problems), five means they are dedicated to the Mother of the Forest and seven to the wandering souls.

War veterans and begging children

Quite often, travellers in Vietnam will still encounter war veterans. As there is no longer free public healthcare in Vietnam, travellers may wish to make a donation (small dong notes). Beware that large numbers of gangs now deliberately inflict injuries and mutilations, or even »stage« injuries fit for Hollywood films with extra dramatic effect.

Beware of begging women with half-unconscious babies in their arms – apparently the children are not theirs and have been sedated with tranquilizers. It is up to the traveller whether to give sweets or money to begging children; just keep in mind that at some point children will earn more money begging than their working parents, so they may end up not going to school anymore. Child labour is widespread and is supported by buying postcards or cigarettes from them. Often children are exploited by gangs who will take away all their earnings at the end of the day. Of course, visitors can invite children to a meal, which most will happily accept.

> **! Baedeker TIP**
>
> **The smallest room**
>
> Toilets in restaurants are often still Asian (originally French) squat toilets, where flushing is done by hand with a scoop. Never forget to bring toilet paper (always to be dropped in the bin) on day trips or city tours.

Bargaining

▶Prices · Discounts

On the beach and by the pool

Do not under any circumstances bathe naked or without a bikini top. Also the beach (generally public) is an unsuitable place for acts of love, as romantic as the ocean sunset may be. This would clearly conflict with proper conduct in Vietnam.

Taking photographs

Before taking a photograph, locals should always be politely asked in advance; a »no« or disapproving nod should be accepted, even if it is accompanied by a hearty laugh. Women might be embarrassed when photographed in their street or work clothes. Also street vendors with black market products and certain hill tribes dislike being photographed. A nice gesture: buy something, ask them for their address and send them a copy from Europe.

A friendly request is all it takes… Most Vietnamese are happy to be photographed

Invitations

Nowadays the common way to greet in Vietnam is with a Western-style handshake (seniors first) – those who wish to greet the traditional way should cross their arms in front of their chest and bow slightly. When visiting a Vietnamese family at home the **shoes** of all residents are usually kept out on the doorstep. Taking one's shoes off is never wrong, even if the host waves it off with a smile. The only real discourtesy toward Buddhists is to face the soles of one's feet towards others.

Forms of greeting

When invited to dinner, it is customary to bring a small, nicely wrapped gift and present it with both hands (such as flowers, drawing pens for the children, fruit or cigarettes). Never forget to exchange business cards if the dinner is business-related – this is considered an obligatory ritual.

Presents

Outside Saigon and Hanoi don't be surprised if dinner is served on a mat on the ground if there are not enough chairs or space at the table (first the host and guests, then the rest of the family). It would be deemed impolite to refuse being served first as a guest. »Xin moi« means please start! Eating with the Vietnamese is usually a loud and leisurely

> ## ! *Baedeker* TIP
>
> ### Salutations
>
> The Vietnamese have a whole range of salutations, depending on age and social or Confucian rank, and to make it even more complicated some even vary from the north to the south, resulting in absolute confusion for tourists. Foreigners cannot go wrong, however, with this general greeting: xin chao (pronounced: sin chao).

affair, even at public restaurants: slurping, belching and the clicking of the tongue is just as common as talking on a mobile phone and smoking. Non-edible leftovers such as meat or fish bones and napkins are often just whisked off the table at the end. Never stick chopsticks into leftover rice – this will conjure up someone's death.

Festivals · Holidays · Events

For thousands of years the dates for traditional festivals have been calculated according to the position of the moon. The lunar year has twelve months and starts in the middle of January. Each year is marked by another animal of the Zodiac (tiger 2010, rabbit 2011, dragon 2012, snake 2013). Using this 4600-year-old calendar, astrologers still calculate the lucky and unlucky days.

▶ FESTIVAL CALENDAR

HOLIDAYS

▶ **Public holidays**

1 January: New Year's Day (adopted from the West)
3 February: Foundation Day of the Communist Party (1930)
30 April: Reunification Day and Fall of Saigon (1975)
1 May: International Labour Day
19 May: Birthday of Ho Chi Minh (1890)
2 September: Independence Day (1945)
3 September: Anniversary of Ho Chi Minh's death (1969)

▶ **Other holidays**

24–25 December: Christmas with midnight Mass (for Christians, mainly in the south)

JANUARY–FEBRUARY

▶ **Nationwide**

Tet Festival. The most important festival in Vietnam is the Vietnamese New Year (tet nguyen dan), which is celebrated for at least three days between mid-January and mid-February (sometimes early March): with offerings and gifts, family visits, festively decorated streets and houses and the consumption of tasty sticky rice cakes.

▶ **Sinh**

Wrestling festival. In the village on the southern bank of the Huong or Perfume River (Thua Thien, Hue province), thousands of proud young men gather from the neighbouring provinces, ready to fight. They measure their skill and strength in traditional wrestling matches. Afterwards they drink rice wine and »bia«.

MARCH–APRIL

▶ **Tay Nguyen/Buon Don**

Elephant race festival. Held on the Serebok River in Buon Don (Dak Lak province), where the M'Nong tribe, used to competing, demonstrates its skill around the 3rd month of the lunar calendar – or rather, the locally bred elephants do. During the races the portly looking animals can reach speeds of up to 40kmh/25mph.

APRIL–MAY

▶ **Nationwide**

Phat Dan – Buddha's birthday. Buddhists in Vietnam celebrate Buddha's birthday on the 8th day of the 4th lunar month – temples are filled with incense smoke, offerings and people praying.

MAY

► Thap Ba

Po Nagar Festival. A festival of the Cham people with boat races and traditional »boi« chanting.

► Mekong delta

Khmer New Year. The Khmer celebrate their new year at Khmer pagodas in the Mekong delta from the 13th to the15th day of the 4th lunar month.

APRIL–JUNE

► Nui Sam (Chau Doc)

Ba Chua Xu – Pilgrimage to the Nui Sam. The pilgrimage to Nui Sam Mountain takes place from the 22nd to the 26th day of the 4th lunar month.

JULY–AUGUST

► Nationwide

Trang Nguyen (Vu Lan) – Festival of Forgiveness. Another holiday commemorating ancestors and their wandering souls: on the day of the »Festival of Forgiveness« (15th day of the 7th lunar month) the Jade Emperor and the Princes of Hell deliberate over the sins of their earthly children, while the souls of the wandering dead return home for the day.

AUGUST

► Hue

Hon Chen Temple Festival. This temple festival takes place twice every year, during the 3rd and 7th lunar month: 10km/16mi west of Hue, at the Perfume River, the faithful gather to attend plays and processions and to worship the Holy Mother Thien Y A Na – the river is lit up by small illuminated boats.

SEPTEMBER

► Do Son

Festival of buffalo fighting. This famous festival on the 9th day of the 8th lunar month is for worshipping the tutelary deity of the Hai Phong fishermen, Dieu Tuoc Ton Than. Various rituals are followed by a (normally bloodless) buffalo fight. Sadly the winner does not benefit from its victory – both buffalos are slaughtered and eaten in honour of the tutelary god.

► Vung Tau

Nghinh Ong Festival.
At the Whale Temple in Vung Tau, a colourful festival, Lang Ca Ong (16th day of the 8th lunar month), commemorates the death of three whales that beached here on the shore. The fishermen, who still believe in the miraculous powers of this impressive mammal, celebrate this highly worshipped animal with a procession of flower-bedecked boats, a tuong opera, much chanting, kung fu displays and various offerings.

OCTOBER–NOVEMBER

► Soc Trang (Mekong delta)

Ghe-Ngo Festival (Ok Om Bok). On the 14th–15th day of the 10th lunar month the Khmer in the Mekong delta celebrate the full moon festival, Ok Om Bok, by making offerings to the Moon Goddess, who bestows luck and wealth on the people. Lanterns and flying lampions light the sky while offerings are presented to the Mekong River or one of its many tributaries on small banana leaf floats. The Ghe Ngo boat race takes place on the Soc Trang River at the same time.

The sale of calendars for the new year

HAPPY NEW YEAR!

The celebrations begin a full week before the first day of the New Year: on the 23rd day of the twelfth lunar month, in a ceremony held in the home, offerings such as fruit, flowers, food and paper gifts are laid on the domestic altar.

This puts the Hearth God Tao Quan in a good humour when he leaves the house and ascends to heaven, where he makes his annual report to the celestial ruler, the Jade Emperor, about the state of affairs on earth. He does not return until the evening of the New Year, which means that for one week the Vietnamese themselves have to protect their house against evil spirits. To this end they hang lights around the house and red banners on the streets, and adorn their living rooms with red and gold decorations, flowers and orange trees. In the villages bamboo poles draped with old clothing are often placed in the garden in order to drive away evil spirits. Tet, the New Year's festival, is the highlight of the year. As the lunar calendar is used in Vietnam, Tet is celebrated from the first to the seventh day of the first month, i.e. in late January or early February. Officially three days around New Year are public holidays, but most Vietnamese take a whole week.

Time for the family

Tet means not just the changing of the years, but an occasion for big family gatherings and feasting. It is the time to pay debts, make up disagreements, buy new clothes and send greetings cards. The Chinese characters painted on red silk paper that are hung up inside the house or on the front door are also wishes for good luck. All year round the inhabitants of the village of Dong Ho near Hanoi make traditional New Year's pictures (►p.83) showing scenes from legends and myths or symbols of fortune such as round, ripe fruit, fish or well-nourished children. Until 1995 fireworks and rip-raps were an indispensable part of

the Tet celebrations, but since then the government has banned this centuries-old tradition, as serious accidents involving a number of fatalities had taken place.

A New Year's celebration without a great banquet is unthinkable. Banh chung and banh day are an insepa-rable part of the feasting: these round cakes of sticky rice, filled with pork and soy beans and wrapped in banana leaves, symbolize earth and heaven. Even if the family cannot really afford it, everything that the food market has to offer will find its way onto the table, because the first day of the year is meant to set the pattern for the whole twelve months to come.

Honour your ancestors

The temples buzz with activity, espe-cially at midnight when the new lunar year begins. Many people gather at this hour to honour their ancestors and welcome the good spirits back to earth with choice dishes and a host of joss sticks. Presents are then ex-changed in the family circle.

Symbols

This is a time for superstition, too. Everything that happens around Tet is symbolic. Not only the first visit, but also the first sound that is heard in the New Year (apart from fireworks!) is thought to foretell what will happen in the coming year: a cock's crow, for example, means a lot of work and a bad harvest, while the barking of dogs signifies trust and optimism. A very bad year is in store for anyone who hears the cry of an owl, which is a harbinger of epidemics and ill fortune for the whole community. It is also unlucky at this time of the year to break glass, wash clothes, curse or engage in dirty talk – these are things that attract the evil spirits!

Food and Drink

Food as a philosophy

Food plays an important role in Vietnam. It means a lot more than just eating – it is part of an entire life philosophy. The Vietnamese never eat on the go, but have three wholesome meals a day at precisely the same time (good to know when planning a rental car trip with a guide and driver!). A French ethnologist even concluded when observing food rituals: »The Vietnamese are concerned about a filled rice bowl not only in their present life, but also for their next one.« This also explains the many **food donations** during ancestral worship at home.

The meaning of food is deeply rooted in Vietnamese history, which for millennia was marked by wars, droughts, floods, plagues and other catastrophes. Necessity is the mother of invention, and this is the reason that all kinds of animals still end up in the cooking pot.

Dishes are generally decorated with great love for detail

Just as the country is split into three main regions – the north, the central region, and the south – there are also three culinary traditions. The northern style is strongly influenced by **Chinese cuisine**. Stir-fries, stews, rice pudding and soups are especially popular in this region, where the climate is cooler and drier. The lack of herbs and spices here also make meals less aromatic. During winter, people often gather around a charcoal stove to boil meat and vegetables in a broth, just like in China. Well-known North Vietnamese meals are Hanoi soup (pho bac), asparagus soup with crab (mang tay nau cua) and spicy filled tofu slices (dau hu nhoi).

Regional preferences

In the area around Hue in the central region, the art of cooking came to play a significant part in a refined way of life. Special attention was paid to decoration and **displaying food**, said to please the royal palate. The cooks from Hue are known for their pork sausage, their sweet-and-sour rice cake and their soup ingredients with a mix of fried tomato puree, chilli and prawn sauce. Around Hue, many European types of vegetables are used as well: artichokes, cauliflower, asparagus and potatoes.

Southern cuisine is less complex but spicier than up north. Exotic fruit and top-quality vegetables grow well on this fertile land, and are served uncooked with meals. In this region quick stir-fries and sautés are preferred to fried or slowly stewed dishes; spicy curries are very common. The **French influence** is most evident in the use of asparagus, tomatoes and potatoes, which are prepared Vietnamese-style. Grilled dishes are equally popular here. A specifically southern tradition is to wrap fried or grilled meals with raw vegetables and herbs into a salad leaf. This little package is then dipped into a hot sauce.

> ## *i* Between Asia and Europe
>
> ■ Vietnamese cuisine is a culinary highlight within Asia, as the fusion of Asian and European styles results in light, delicious food. Compared to the spiciness of Thai or Indian food, Vietnamese dishes are fairly mild. The dominating flavour is determined by the addition of many fresh herbs, especially coriander.

Most Vietnamese start their day with a noodle soup. Even in the morning they are spiced with freshly cut chilli peppers. A wholesome breakfast is usually served bright and early. Boiled rice is served at lunch and dinner along with a mixture of spicy and mild dishes of meat, fish and vegetables. A characteristic of Vietnamese cooking is the use of additional ingredients of different consistencies to create flavours for the individual palate and taste. Colour contrast and the mixing of different aromas also play a major role. Many dishes combine cooked food with raw vegetables, and even stir-fries are prepared with only a little fat. In general, the Vietnamese use as little fat as possible and prefer vegetable oil.

Three big meals

The furniture in restaurants is often fairly simple and tourists should not be put off by wooden benches, plastic chairs and cutlery, or dirty

Restaurants

Hot food stalls are found everywhere – as well as soup, rice dishes, fried seafood and many other tasty treats are served here

table cloths. Foreigners are often given spoons and forks instead of chopsticks. In larger towns there are English and/or French menus, but waiters in Vietnamese restaurants rarely speak English. Sometimes menus do not list any **prices**, so make sure to ask the waiter when ordering. Often prices are stated for different portion sizes – the smallest portion is usually enough for one person. Green tea comes free of charge everywhere, while snacks such as salted almonds or dried fish in chilli sauce are normally extra, as is the damp towel.

Restaurants fill up relatively early with local customers (lunchtime is around noon, dinner time between 6pm and 8pm). Vietnamese like to eat in big groups with business partners or the entire family. The bigger the party, the more opulent the meal: all ordered dishes are served at the same time, and every guest can try each dish by putting some into a rice bowl using chopsticks (never take too much!). Eating out with the Vietnamese can be quite **lively** at times and is often accompanied by loud (live) music. Particularly at traditional, but also at finer restaurants, be prepared to hear the typical atmospheric noise of slurping, spitting and burping. People often smoke or talk loudly on their mobile phones.

Most restaurants serve poultry, marinated pork, beef, grilled pork ribs, thinly sliced beef and minced meat as well as fish in all shapes and sizes. Bun cha are noodle dishes with stuffed meat, usually served with raw vegetables on the side. The key ingredient is the **sauce**: it is said to be best in Hanoi and includes peppermint leaves. Fish, e.g. crab, shrimp, crayfish, lobster, mussels, snails, prawns, squid, mackerel, carp, tuna and shark, is a high-protein food that is affordable to many Vietnamese; in Vietnam, fish and shellfish are fairly inexpensive, delicious and always served fresh in coastal towns. Fruit is recommended for **dessert**: pineapple, water melon, banana, lychees, longan, mango, papaya and pomelo are just some of the delicious types of fruit grown in Vietnam. Better restaurants also offer fried bananas, pineapple flambéed with rice wine or traditional coconut desserts. Another common dessert is the rainbow drink, a cold sweet beverage made of ground mung beans, agar agar and coconut milk. Naturally, Western desserts such as crème caramel, ice cream or fruit sorbets can be ordered as well. In cities, many restaurants also offer good, though sometimes very sugary, cakes made of dough or sticky rice.

Restaurant food

Baedeker TIP

Beware of the fried dog?

Tourists need not worry about being served fried dog without their knowledge, and the same goes for such dishes as raw monkey brain or sliced python. These expensive delicacies are only offered at certain restaurants.

Individual Dishes

Rice

The Vietnamese have been growing rice for thousands of years (►Baedeker Special p.316); in fact, Vietnamese life is unimaginable without it. »Moi ong xoi com« (»Enjoy your rice«) is an old saying further illustrating its importance. Today people are more likely to say »Chuc an ngon!« or »Xin moi!« for »Enjoy your meal«. Unfortunately, most tourists in all Asian countries order fried rice, which is offered everywhere – blissfully unaware of what they're missing. These rice and vegetable fry ups, however, are considered to occupy the lower rungs of the Vietnamese culinary ladder. The Vietnamese mostly eat boiled rice and the ingredients are either mixed on the plate or served on the side.

Fish sauce (nuoc mam)

The Vietnamese simply love fish sauce, and it is far more than a substitute for salt. Nuoc mam is produced in factories in the Mekong delta and on the island of Phu Quoc (►pp.350). The recipe is very simple: salted sardines are stored and fermented in barrels for one year. At home, the bottled brew is refined with lemon juice, vinegar, fresh chilli, sugar, pepper, garlic and coriander.

Soups

In Vietnam there is a soup kitchen on every corner, and the streets are lined with travelling cooks who carry their kitchen over their shoulder or in a little cart. Soup kitchens serve traditional and very cheap soups for breakfast at low benches and stools. Soup is also an integral part of lunch and dinner.

The northern spicy soup **pho**, which has become a national dish, consists of rice or wheat noodles, thinly sliced beef, chicken or prawns and a few soybean sprouts as topping. The boiled (for hours!) meat broth is poured on top – a steamy and very spicy affair. On request, a raw egg is cracked on top. The soup is spiced with pepper, mint, coriander, ground chilli and lemon juice, but those who wish to can add a bit of fish or soy sauce, as well as the herbs provided on the table.

There are also sweet-and-sour (Chinese) soups, as well as purely sour soups with shrimp or fish, tomatoes and onions (**canh chua**). Noodle soups are eaten with spoons and chopsticks; tables are usually set with chopsticks. Mien is a Chinese glass noodle soup with meatballs, chao is a fairly thick rice soup, and the sweetish che soup is prepared with coconut milk. The steamboat, a kind of Vietnamese fondue, is definitely worth a try: the ingredients (fish, seafood, beef, vegetables, glass noodles) are simmered in stock in a large metal samovar or clay pot and cooked at the table.

Starters, side dishes and snacks

Small and zesty **spring rolls** (cha gio), either fried or steamed, can be stuffed with vegetables, minced meat, prawns, shrimp, glass noodles, chopped onion or soybean sprouts and are usually wrapped at the table in salad leafs or thin rice paper. This small package is then dipped in a sauce made from chilli, fish sauce, pepper and lemon juice (nuoc cham). A bowl with salad and herbs, such as coriander, lemon balm, mint, lemongrass and basil, is also provided on the table. Western travellers who are in Asia only for a short time should try and avoid raw vegetables, salads and herbs. **Vietnamese omelettes** are filled with various types of vegetables and meats. Samosas stuffed with shrimp or meat are another speciality along the coast. Crispy flatcakes made of sesame and rice flour are baked over charcoal, while spicy sa giang chips made of shrimp paste and flour (banh phong tom) are offered as a small starter in some restaurants and exported all over the world.

Food stands offer meat-stuffed pancakes (banh bao) and **baguette sandwiches** (com tay cam or banh mi pate), with often extremely spicy toppings with cheese, chicken, fish or pork, vegetables and onions. Meat grilled over charcoal is another popular roadside snack, as are scalloped bananas from the street vendors' baskets.

Noodles

The Vietnamese eat different types of noodles – either yellow (mi, made of wheat flour and eggs) or white (banh, made of rice). The thin, transparent glass noodles are mainly used for soups.

Mooncakes

During the full moon festival shops and food stands stock up on golden-brown banh nuong and banh deo – small, round »moon-

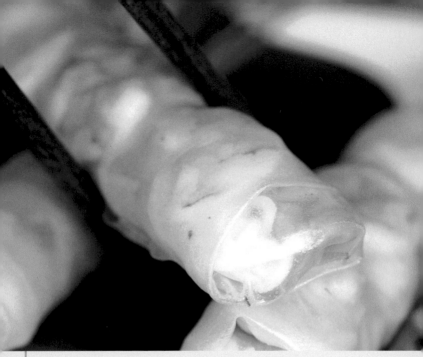

In contrast to China, Vietnamese spring rolls are wrapped in lettuce leaves or rice paper and eaten with a dip

cakes«. This typical Vietnamese treat is made of fried sticky rice, rice flour and sugared water. Bakeries create variations with a variety of flavours: coconut, sesame seed, pork fat, cashew and peanut, almond and egg, as well as chicken.

Beverages

Tea is usually brewed early in the morning to last the entire day, and is kept warm under a quilted tea cosy. It is offered to guests along with nuts, dried fruit and cake. The tea is poured in a bowl and diluted with hot water from a thermos. Although there are many types of tea, **green and black tea** are the most common. The difference lies in the way they are processed: green tea consists of unfermented tea leaves, roasted directly after picking. Black tea is first dried, fermented and then roasted. There are also many other kinds of tea that are flavoured with dried flowers. Particularly popular are chrysanthemum, jasmine, lotus, hibiscus and rose petal flavours. The dried petals remain in the teapot so they can spread their scent and their flavour.

The ever-present accompaniment: tea

It is also usual to find mineral water, **soft drinks** such as Coke and Sprite, sweet soybean milk (sua dau nanh), which is probably not enjoyed by many Westerners, **freshly squeezed fruit juice** and coconut milk. Many street stands (and restaurants) have a choice of coconuts that will be cracked open with a machete. Freshly squeezed sugar is also sold by street vendors. Needless to say, never drink tap water (▶Health).

French **coffee** (ca phe sua), which is coffee filtered in a glass at the table, is ordered afterdinner. The small metal filter is kept on the glass while the coffee seeps through. Often the glass comes in a bowl of hot water to prevent the coffee from getting cold. It is served with condensed milk and lots of sugar.

Alcohol
The Vietnamese word for **wine**, ruou, is used for various alcoholic beverages. One well-known national drink is called ruou de or choum. It is a strong, clear, alcoholic spirit made from sticky rice and is quite similar to Japanese sake. People drink it warm and normally only on special occasions when raising a toast.
In Vietnam, there are signs on every street corner advertising Tiger beer, from Singapore: the company brews a relatively strong **beer** in Vietnam. A French beer, BGI, is also brewed in Vietnam. However, Vietnamese bottled beers are tasty too: Ba-Ba-Ba (333) was the follow-up to Saigon Export and is mostly available in tins.

Menu   ▶Language

Health

Preventive measures
Particularly during your first days in Vietnam, beware of dishes that include raw vegetables, salads and non-peelable fruit. After that, consider every meal individually rather than categorically avoiding eating regional specialities. At a private dinner, it may be perceived as impolite to refuse dishes – especially when you are a guest or are being served first.

In Vietnam, your body will perspire a lot more than at home, so it is vital to drink at least 2 litres/day. Usually **ice cubes** do not bear any health risk as they are made from boiled water. Those who do not want any ice in their drink should tell the waiter: »khong co da« means »no ice, please«.

Soups are harmless even for sensitive stomachs, as they are served boiling hot and the accompanying uncooked vegetables can be avoided. **Meat** should always be well done and never eaten raw or lukewarm. In inland regions, it is best to avoid fish at simple restaurants because it may not have been properly cooled during transportation.

If, despite all preventive measures, digestive problems do occur, charcoal tablets, sufficient liquid and electrolytes often help.

To avoid sunburn and heatstroke, gradual **exposure to the sun** is advised. Use proper sun block with sufficient UV protection!

! **Baedeker TIP**

Bird flu

In Vietnam, avian influenza has been transmitted to humans, and there have been fatalities. Direct contact with our feathered friends at poultry markets and farms should therefore be avoided, though it is absolutely fine to eat chicken.

Vaccinations

There are no mandatory vaccinations required for entry to Vietnam, unless you are entering from a country affected with yellow fever. It

In the tropics you should drink as much as possible…

is recommended that travellers get booster vaccinations for polio, tetanus and hepatitis A, if it has been more than ten years since receiving one, and an oral vaccination for typhus. Catching cholera can be avoided by just drinking boiled water. In Vietnam there has been the odd case of dengue fever (also known as breakbone fever) and Japanese encephalitis.

Malaria prophylaxis

Malaria is prevalent in Vietnam, and while the risk in urban areas is considered low, there is a greater risk in rural anddensely wooded regions (e.g. Cat Tien National Park, Central Highlands, Mekong delta, etc.), on rivers or in coastal areas. Mosquitoes are widespread during and shortly after the **monsoon season**. It is advised, therefore, to take prophylaxis (prescription) or at least bring standby medication in case of emergencies. Consult a doctor approximately 6 weeks prior to departure. There have also been some cases of dengue fever, with similar symptoms to those of malaria.

To lower the risk of contracting malaria, bring a **mosquito net** (especially for hotels without air conditioning) and use mosquito repellent at dusk and at dawn. Thick, long socks as well as long-sleeved, light shirts offer some protection against mosquito bites. Mosquito coils also help.

In the case of flu-like symptoms such as fever, shivering, dizziness and headache go to the doctor immediately, even if they occur months after returning from Vietnam.

HIV/AIDS rate

Vietnam is among the countries with a rapidly rising HIV/AIDS rate. To avoid any risk of infection through foreign blood, bring disposable syringes and plastic gloves to any doctor's appointment. In Vietnam, there is extensive awareness of HIV and AIDS: almost every village has information centres.

Medical care

Though medical care in Saigon and Hanoi is comparable to European standards, this is not the case in the more rural areas. Pharmacies should have any common medication from Western pharmaceutical companies, but pay attention to the expiry date. A blood test to identify malaria can be carried out at all doctor's practices.

▶ USEFUL ADDRESSES

▶ **AEA International SOS**
24-hour emergency number, also for dental clinics
65 Nguyen Du Street, Saigon
Tel. 08/8 29 85 20 and
8 29 84 24

▶ **AEA International SOS**
31 Hai Ba Trung, Hanoi
Tel. 04/9 34 05 55 and 9 34 06 66

▶ **Bach Mai International Hospital**
Giai Phong Street, Hanoi
Tel. 04/8 69 37 31

Information

The Vietnam National Administration of Tourism (VNAT) has no offices in the UK or USA, but it does run an International Cooperation Department in Hanoi. Embassies and consulates can provide information regarding visas. Specialized travel agents are also a good source of reliable information (▶Arrival, pp.95–96).   Note

USEFUL ADDRESSES

IN THE UK, EUROPE AND THE USA

▶ **Indochina Services Travel Group**
Europe Sales Office
Enzianstrasse 4a
82319 Starnberg, Germany
Tel. 0 8151/77 02 22
Fax 0 8151/77 02 29
www.indochina-services.com

Americas Sales Office
870 Market Street, Suite 923
San Francisco, CA 94102
Tel. +1 (415) 434 4015
Fax +1 (415) 434 4145

in *Saigon*:
27 F, Tran Nhat Duat, District 1
in *Hanoi*:
Xay Dung Hotel (3rd floor), 20 The Giao Street, Hai Ba Trung District

▶ **Asia Society**
725 Park Avenue at 70th Street
New York, NY 10021
Tel. 212-288-6400
Fax 212-517-8315
E-mail: info@asiasociety.org
www.asiasociety.org

IN VIETNAM

▶ **Vietnam National Administration of Tourism (VNAT)**
80 Quan Su Street

Hoan Kiem District, Hanoi
Tel. +84 (0)4 3942 2070 / 3942 1061
Fax +84 (0)4 3942 4115
International Cooperation Department:
Tel. +84 (0)4 3942 2070 / 3942 1061
Email: icdvnat@hn.vnn.vn
www.vietnamtourism.com

▶ **Saigon Tourist**
23 Le Loi, District 1, Saigon
Tel. 08/8 29 22 91 and
8 22 58 74, 8 22 58 87, 8 29 50 00
Fax 08/8 24 32 39 and 8 29 10 26
www.saigon-tourist.com
saigontourist@sgtourist.com.vn

VIETNAMESE EMBASSIES AND CONSULATES

▶ **Embassy of Vietnam in the UK**
12–14 Victoria Road
London W8 5RD
Tel. 020 7937 1912
Fax 020 79376108
www.vietnamembassy.org.uk/consular.html
The London-based embassy is also responsible for diplomatic representation in the Republic of Ireland.

▶ **Vietnamese Consulate in Canada**
470 Wilbrod Street
Ottawa, Ontario K1N 6M8
Tel. 1 613 236 0772

Fax 1 613 236 2704
www.vietnamembassy-canada.ca

▶ **Embassy of Vietnam
in the USA**
1233, 20th Street, N.W. Suite 400
Washington DC 20036
Tel. 1 202 8610737
Fax 1 202 8610917
www.vietnamembassy-usa.org

▶ **Embassy of Vietnam
in Australia**
6 Timbarra Crescent
O'Malley, Canberra ACT 2606
Tel. 02 6290 1549
Fax 02 6286 4534
www.au.vnembassy.org

▶ **Embassy of Vietnam
in New Zealand**
Level 21, Grand Plimmer Tower
2-6 Glimer Terrace
PO Box 8042, Wellington
Tel. 04 473 5912
Fax 04 473 5913
embassyvn@paradise.net.nz

**DIPLOMATIC REPRESEN-
TATION IN VIETNAM**

▶ **British Embassy in Hanoi**
31 Hai Ba Trung St.
4–7th Fl. Central Bldg
Tel. 04 936 0500
Fax 04 936 0561/2
www.uk-vietnam.org

▶ **British Consulate in Hanoi**
40 Cat Linh St.
Tel. 04 843 6780
Fax 04 843 4962
behanoi@britishcouncil.org.vn

▶ **British Consulate in Saigon**
25 Le Duan St.
Tel. 08 829 8433
Fax 08 822 1971
bcghcmc@hcm.vnn.vn

▶ **Embassy of Ireland**
Ireland House, The Amp Walk 218
Jalan Ampang
50450 Kuala Lumpur, Malaysia
Tel. (60-3) 2161 2963
Fax (60-3) 2161 3427
ireland@po.jaring.my

▶ **Embassy of Canada in Hanoi**
31 Hung Vuong Street
Tel. 04 734 5000
Fax 04 734 5049
www.vietnam.gc.ca

▶ **Canadian Consulate in Saigon**
The Metropolitan Building, 235
Dong Khoi Street
Suite 1002, District 1
Tel. 08 827 9899
Fax 08 827 9937
hochi@dfait-maeci.gc.ca

▶ **United States Embassy
in Hanoi**
7 Lang Ha Street, Ba Dinh District
Tel. 04 772 1500
Fax 04 772 1510
www.hanoi.usembassy.gov

▶ **United States Consulate
in Saigon**
4 Le Duan Blvd, District 1
Tel. 08 822 9433
Fax 08 824 5571
www.hochiminh.usconsulate.gov

▶ **Australian Embassy in Hanoi**
8 Dao Tan Street
Ba Dinh District
Tel. 04 831 7755
Fax 04 831 7711
www.ausinvn.com

▶ **Australian Consulate in Saigon**
5th Floor, The Landmark Building
5B Ton Duc Thang, District 1
Tel. 08 829 6035
Fax 08 829 6031

► **New Zealand Embassy in Hanoi**
Level 5, 63 Ly Thai To St.
Tel. 04 824 1481
Fax 04 824 1480
nzembhan@fpt.vn

► **New Zealand Consulate in Saigon**
Level 5, Yoco Bldg
41 Nguyen Thi Minh Khai St.,
District 1
Tel. 08 822 6907
Fax 08 822 6905

ONLINE

► **www.fco.gov.uk/en/travelling-and-living-overseas**
The latest information on the country, getting there, safety, health, special travel warnings etc.

► **www.howtotravelvietnam.net**
Good source of information for travellers

► **www.discover-vietnam.com**
Round trips and tailor-made tours, travel tips, forum and information

► **www.vietnamtravelforum.net**
Tips from travellers

► **www.vietnamnews.vnagency.com.vn**
Homepage of the daily newspaper *Vietnam News*

► **www.savethechildren.org.uk**
Aid and education projects aimed at improving the lives of Vietnamese children

Language

Vietnam is the only Asian country to utilize a script with Latin letters. Most consonants follow their English pronunciation, though there are exceptions, which are listed in the table. The English letters f, j, w and z do not appear in Vietnamese. There are many vowel sounds, examples of which are listed in the table.

Latin script

Symbol	Pronunciation	Symbol	Pronunciation
a	as in father	ie	as in yes
ã	as a but longer	o	as in door
â	as in black	oa	as in French moi
ai	as in buy	oã	as in lack
ao	as in now	oai	as in why
au	as in Australia	oay	as in Uruguay
âu	as in go	oe	as in where
ay	as in day	oi	as in choice
ây	as in David	ô	as in Bordeaux
e	as in Claire	ôi	as in toy
ê	as in café	u	as in zoo
i	as in see	ua	as in Ecuador
ia	as in Asia	uê	as in question

Symbol	Pronunciation	Symbol	Pronunciation
ui	pronounced oo-ee	nh-	as the French gn in champagne
uôi	pronounced way-ee		
uy	as ü in German	ng-	as -nga- in long ago
uya	as in culture in French	ph-	as f in fur
uyen	as in when	r	as z in zero (N); as r in red (S)
uyu	as in new		
y	as in see	tr-	as ch in cheek (N); as tr in try (S)
ye	as in yen		
yeu	as in yeoman	th-	as a strongly aspirated t
d	as z in zero (N); as y in yes (S)	v	sometimes as y in you
		x	like an s
ð	as d in do	-ch	like a k
gh-	as g in go	-ng	as the ng in long but with closed lips
gi-	as z in zero (N); as y in yes (S)		
		-nh	as the ng in singing
kh-	as the German ch in ich		

Tones There are six tones in the Vietnamese language: level, high rising, low falling, dipping rising, high rising glottalized, and low glottalized. Vowels are spoken with a tone according to the diacritical mark they carry (none, acute, grave, hook, tilde, or dot below). These diacritical marks are in addition to the four accents attached to special consonants and vowels.

Tone	Example	Tone	Example
level	ma (ghost)	dipping rising	mả (tomb)
high rising	má (cheek)	high rising glottalized	mã (horse)
low falling	mà (but)	low glottalized	m (rice seedling)

VIETNAMESE LANGUAGE GUIDE

At a glance

Yes	Co; U, Da
No	Khong
Maybe	Co le
Please	Xin/Lam on
Thank you	Cam on
You're welcome.	Khong sao.
Excuse me!	Xin loi!
Pardon?	Lap lai/Lam on.
I (don't) understand.	Toi (khong) hieu.
What is this?	Cai nay la cai gi?
Could you (Sir/Madam)	Ong/Ba co the giup toi duoc

help me, please?	khong?
I (don't) want to ...	toi (khong) muon/can ...
I (don't) like it.	Toi rat (khong) thich.
Do you (Sir/Madam) have...?	Ong/Ba co ...?
How much is it?	Gia (tien) bao nhieu?
What's the time?	May gio roi?

Numbers

0	khong/linh]	17	muoi bay
1	mot	18	muoi tam
2	hai	19	muoi chin
3	ba	20	hai muoi
4	bon	21	hai muoi mot
5	nam	30	ba muoi
6	sau	40	bon muoi
7	bay	50	nam muoi
8	tam	60	sau muoi
9	chin	70	bay muoi
10	muoi	80	tam muoi
11	muoi mot	90	chin muoi
12	muoi hai	100	mot tram
13	muoi ba	1000	mot ngan
14	muoi bon	10 000	muoi ngan
15	muoi nam	1/2	mot phan hai
16	muoi sau	1/4	mot phan tu

Meeting people

Good morning! Good evening!	Loi chao.
Hello!/Hi!/Bye!	Chao!
... to an older/younger male	... Ong./Anh.
... to an older/younger female	... Ba./Chi./Co.
How are you?	Ong co khoe khong?
My name is ...	Ten toi la ...
Goodbye!	Tam biet!

Information

left/ right/ straight	Trai/Phai/Thang
close/far	Gan/Xa
Please, where is ...?	Lam on /o dau ...?
... the station?	... Nha ga
... the airport?	... Phi cong
... the hotel?	... Khach san

I'd like to rent a ... . Toi muon thue ...
... bicycle. .... xedap
... car/taxi. .... xe hoi/tac-xi
How far? .... May khoang cach?

Petrol station

Where is the next petrol station, please? .. O dau co tram xang gan nhat?
I would like ... litres. .... Toi muon ... Lit
Regular petrol/four-star (super)/Diesel. ... Xang binh thuong/Xang Supe/
        Dau.
Leaded/unleaded petrol. .... Dau niem chi/khong chi.
A full tank, please. .... Day Binh, lam on.

Accident

Help! .... Giup Do!
Watch out! .... Chu Y!
Quick, call... .... Ong lam on goi nhanh ...
... a doctor. .... Bac Si.
... an ambulance. .... Xe cuu thuong.
... the police. .... Cong an.
It was my/your fault. .... Toi co/Ong ta loi.
Please give me your name .... Ong lam on cho toi biet ten Ong
and address. .... va dia chi.

Shopping

Where can I find...? .... Toi tim o dau ...?
... pharmacy .... Nha thuoc tay
... photo service .... Tiem ban do chup hinh
... bakery/Brotladen .... Tiem banh mi
... department store/Geschäft .... Cua hang
... food store .... Hang thuc pham kho
... market .... Cho
When does the department store open /   Cua hang bach hoa tong hop mo
close? .... cua/dong cua/vao luc may gio?
What does this... cost? .... Quyen ... nay gia bao nhieu?

Bank

Where is the... .... O dau co ...
... bank? .... ngan hang?
... bureau de change? .... doi tien?

I would like to change... euros (US dollars) into dong.	Toi muon doi ... tien Euro (tien (tien Dola) ra dong.

Post office

How much is ...	Bao nhieu tien ...
... a letter?	... mot bi thu?
... a postcard?	... mot thiep goi?
... to Germany?	... toi nuoc Duc?

Accommodation

Could you please recommend	Ong co the tim cho toi ...?
... a hotel	... Khach san.
... a B&B	... Phong tro.
Do you still have...	Ong co con can ...
... a single?	... Phong rieng?
... a double?	... Phong doi?
... with shower/bath?	... voi Phong tam?
... for one night?	... cho mot dem?
... for one week?	... cho mot tuan?
How much is one room with...	Gia tien bao nhieu mot phong voi ...
... breakfast?	... an sang?
... half-board?	... an sang va an chieu?

Doctor

Can you recommend a doctor?	Omg co the tim, cho toi mot Ong bac si?
I have...	Toi co ...
... pains here.	... dau o' day.
... fever.	... sot.
... diarrhoea.	... tieu chay.
... headache.	... dau dau/nhu't dau.
... toothache.	... dau rang/nhu't rang.

Eating out

Where can I find ...	O dau co ...
... a good restaurant?	... nha hang ngon?
... a cosy bar?	... tiem bia lich su?
Please reserve us a table for tonight for four.	Ong/lam on, cho chung toi mot ban bon nguoi toi nay.
Cheers!	Chuc mung Ong!
Nice to meet you!	Han hanh duoc gap ong!

The food was delicious.	Thuc an rat ngon.
The bill, please.	Tinh tien, lam on!

Food and drink

Breakfast — **Bua an diem tam/bua an sang**

caphe den	black coffee
ca phe sua/da	coffee with milk /icecream
tra denh/xanh	black tea /green tea
bahn mi	bread/toast
bo	butter
pho mat	cheese
mut nhu	jam
doi	sausage
trung/luoc/chien	soft-boiled egg/hard-boiled egg/fried egg
trung op la	omelette
yoghurt	yoghurt

Soups and starters — xup

nuoc leo	chicken broth
bun thang	stew
chao	rice soup with added chicken, pork, mushrooms, spices, etc.)
canh chua ca	fish soup (sweet-and-sour)
lau	fish and vegetable soup
pho (bo/ga)	rice noodle soup (with beef/chicken)
mien luon/ga	glass noodle soup with eel/chicken
an chay	vegetarian dish (with tofu)
cha gio	spring roll

Fish and seafood — ca/do bien

ca	fish
ca luoi	sole
ca thu	tuna
ca ngu	pikeperch
ca map	shark
cua	prawns
tom nho	shrimp
tom lon/to	king prawns
muc	squid
so	oysters

Meat and poultry — cac mon thit

thit bo	beef

thit be	veal
thit cuu non	lamb
thit heo	pork
thit bam	minced meat
thit ga	chicken
thit vit	duck
thit chim	bird

Rice dishes ..... **com**

com trang/com chien	boiled/fried rice
banh cuon	steamed rice cake with mince meat
com tay cam voi ga/heo ...	rice, mushrooms, spices and chicken/pork
com xuon nuong	rice with roasted ribs
com chien nhan chau	fried rice with mixed ingredients (shrimp, pork, chicken)

Noodle dishes ..... **mi**

mi (chien)	(fried) noodles
bun xao	rice noodles
mien	glass noodles

Vegetables ..... **rau cai**

rau xao	boiled vegetables
mang	bamboo shoots
ca	aubergine
xa-lach	salad
bap cai/sup-lo	cabbage/cauliflower
ca rot	carrots
dua leo	cucumber
ca chua	tomato
hanh	onion
toi	garlic
gung	ginger
dua chua	sour beanseed salad
khoai tay (chien)	potatoes/fried potatoes
nuoc mam	fish sauce
mam tom	shrimp sauce
xa	lemongrass

Vietnamese specialities ..... **dat biet**

bo bay mon	beef prepared in seven different ways

cha	grilled pork
bun cha	grilled pork skewer
gio	minced pork cooked in leaves
cha ca	grilled meat skewer
mam chung	fermented fish with stuffed meat/vegetables
heo rung	wild boar
cho	dog (only in winter)
ech tam bot ran	frogs legs in batter
oc noi	snails (with pork)
ba ba	turtle
men	deer
ran ho/tran	cobra/python
doi	bat

Desserts   **trang mieng**

chao tom	grilled sugar cane
banh bao	small cakes stuffed with meat or vegetables
banh chung	sticky rice cake
banh xeo chay	sticky rice cake stuffed with fruit (and sesame)
banh xeo man	sticky rice stuffed with meat (and prawns, egg, salad)
banh dau xanh	bean cake
mut	candied fruit

Fruit   **trai cay/hoa qua**

bom/tao	apple
dao	peach
man	plum
le	apricot
quit]	mandarin
dau	strawberry
chanh	lime
chuoi	banana
cam	orange
nho	grapes
thom	pineapple
buoi	grapefruit
dua hau	water melon
mang cau	sugar-apple
roi	water apple
xoai	mango
bo	avocado
nhan	longan

khe	carambola (starfruit)
dua	coconut
sau rieng	durian
oi	guava
mit	jackfruit
vai	lychee
mang cut	mangosteen
dudu	papaya
trung ca]	passion fruit
tao ta	jujube (Chinese date)
hong xiem	sapodilla
hong	persimmon
sung/va	fig

Alcoholic drinks .... **ruou**

bia	beer
ruou trang/ruou do	white wine/red wine
mot ly/mot chai	a glass/a bottle
ruou de	rice wine
ruou nep thang	spirit made from sticky rice

Non-alcoholic drinks .... **nuoc ngot**

nuoc soi	hot water
nuoc suoi	mineral water
nuoc chanh	lemon juice/lemonade
nuoc dua	coconut milk
nuoc soda	soda/Seven-up
xa xi	cola mix
nuoc xoai	mango juice
nuoc cam	orange juice
nuoc bom	apple juice
nuoc da	ice cubes

Literature and Film

Burrows, Larry: *Vietnam* (Knopf Publishing Group 2002)   Non-fiction
Larry Burrows' definitive photographs of a war he did not himself
survive. Harrowing, technically brilliant images.

Chong, Denise: *The Girl In The Picture. The Remarkable Story of Vietnam's Most Famous Casualty* (Scribner, 2001)

A meticulously written, gripping reconstruction of the life of Kim Phuc, the Vietnam War and its aftermath. It emphasizes the incredible obscenity of war reporting – and its absolute necessity.

Ellis, Claire: *Culture Shock! Vietnam: A Guide to Customs and Etiquette* (Kuperard 2002)
A look at the customs, etiquette, culture and traditions of Vietnam aimed at helping visitors better understand the land and its people.

Fall, Bernhard B.: *A Street without Joy: The French Debacle in Indochina* (Stackpole Books 1994)
This description of France's staggering defeat in the Indochina War at the hands of Communist-led Vietnamese nationalists was published before the United States escalated its involvement in South Vietnam, but could have served as a warning. Now considered a classic.

McNamara, Robert S.: *In Retrospect: The Tragedy and Lessons of Vietnam* (Times Books, 1995)
The best political book on Vietnam. McNamara, US Secretary of Defence from 1961 to 1968, expounds his personal view on how the United States was dragged into the Vietnam War and why it could not be won.

Page, Tim: *Another Vietnam – Pictures From the Other Side* (National Geographic, 2002)
The Vietnam War from a different, North Vietnamese angle, with private photographs of Ho Chi Minh and Vietcong generals. US photo journalists and their Vietnamese colleagues recall events in the accompanying texts.

Plaster, John L.: *SOG: The Secret Wars of America's Commandos in Vietnam* (Dutton/Signet; illustrated edition 1998)
The war from an American perspective – a gripping account of the missions, sometimes heroic, sometimes suicidal, of the Studies & Observations Group, covert operatives sent to gather intelligence in enemy territory.

Routhier, Nicole: *The Foods of Vietnam* (Stewart, Tabori & Chang Inc., 1999)
With Vietnamese restaurants flourishing across the United States, Vietnamese cuisine has gained a large US following. Containing 150 traditional recipes, this book discusses the culinary history of Vietnam.

Taus-Bolstad, Stacy: *Vietnam in Pictures* (Lerner Publishing Group 2003)
A collection of colour photographs presenting Vietnam's geography, people, culture and more.

Wintle, Justin: *RomancingVietnam: Inside the Boat Country* (Signal Books Ltd 2006)
Justin Wintle was the first writer from the West to be allowed to journey around the whole of post-war Vietnam. This is his classic account of what he found.

Duras, Marguerite: *The Lover* (HarperPerennial, 2006)
Duras, herself born in Indochina, tells a delicate story of love and prostitution; the affair between a young French woman and an older Chinese man. An erotic novel without shame or coquetry.

Fiction

Greene, Graham: *The Quiet American* (Vintage, 2005)
A classic among literature focussing on Vietnam, this is a love story and a political thriller at the same time. The young Vietnamese girl Phuong leaves her lover during the colonial war with France and turns to an American, unaware of his secret assignment.

O'Brian, Tim: *The Things They Carried* (Broadway Books, 1999)
22 chapters of war memories of a US soldier give insight into the »fatal boredom« of war, into killing and dying in the battlefield and into the quirks of US soldiers and what they carried: the girlfriend's nylons, chocolate beans, the New Testament and first-class dope.

Duong Thu Huong: *No Man's Land* (Hyperion Books, 2006)
Possibly the most successful novel by any Vietnamese writer; it was also adapted into a screenplay.

Vietnamese writers

Duong Thu Huong: *Lovestory Told before Dawn* (1981)
Luu, a simple village woman, takes fierce revenge on her ex-husband. With the help of the Communist Party she has him spied upon. The private matters of a family become a public affair, and Luu's desire for power destroys all feelings of love.

Hayslip, Le Ly: *When Heaven And Earth Changed Places* (Doubleday, 1989)
On a trip into her own past Le Ly looks back on her youth as a farm girl and collaborationist during the Vietnam War. Possibly one of the best novels about Vietnam, this novel was turned into a film by Oliver Stone (*Heaven And Earth*).

Pham, Andrew X.: *Catfish and Mandala: A Two-Wheeled Voyage Across the Landscape and Memory of Vietnam* (Picador, 2000)
A young American depicts how in his childhood he and his family fled Vietnam as »boat people«, and his experiences on his return more than 20 years later, travelling the country on a bicycle – funny, thrilling and touching.

Pham Thi Hoai: *Sunday Menu* (Pandanus Books, 2006)
Eleven short stories of everyday life in Hanoi – ironic, witty and vaguely erotic. The writer paints a picture of a cold world, in which relationships are a lie, businesses shady, poets mainstream and officers corrupt.

Vietnam in films

Good Morning Vietnam (USA, 1987)
Robin Williams plays a DJ for a US Army radio station in Saigon. Thoughtful comedy.

Dear America – Letters from Vietnam (USA, 1987)
Original footage from the Vietnam War and a collage of letters from US soldiers.

Heaven And Earth (USA, 1993, directed by Oliver Stone)
The Vietnam War from a Vietnamese angle.

Cyclo (Vietnam, 1995, directed by Tran Anh Hung)
A film that depicts changes in Vietnamese society and the effects on the young generation.

The Quiet American (USA/Australia, 2002, directed by Phillip Noyce)
The most recent adaptation of Graham Greene's classic featuring Michael Caine as the British correspondent Thomas Fowler. During the Indochina War of the early 1950s he competes with the younger yet mysterious American, Pyle, for his beautiful mistress, Phuong.

Media

Newspapers

Vietnam offers several local daily and weekly newspapers in English, such as *Saigon Times Daily*, *Vietnam News*, *Vietnam Weekly*, *Vietnam Business* and *Vietnam Economic News*, though they are hard to find outside the bigger cities. The papers also contain listings and recommendations on restaurants and entertainment. International newspapers and magazines are available at the big hotels, at news stands and from street vendors in Saigon and Hanoi, e.g. *Bangkok Post*, *International Herald Tribune* or *Newsweek*.

Magazines

In most hotels, monthly or weekly magazines are provided especially for tourists. **What's On in Saigon?** and **Time Out** also include flight times and addresses of restaurants.

Television

Satellite TV receives stations including CNN, ABC, and STAR Plus, as well as French, Australian, Indonesian and Japanese stations. The English-language news is broadcast every night on state television.

Money

The dong is the currency in Vietnam. There are notes (100, 200, 500, 1000, 2000, 5000, 10,000, 20,000, 50,000, 100,000 and 500,000), some of which look very much alike, and coins (200, 500, 1000, 2000, 5000). The State Bank of Vietnam has pledged to apply all measures to keep the dong's foreign exchange rates stable in order to maintain economic stability and create market confidence.

Currency

Exchange rates

- 10,000 VND (dong) = € 0.42
- 10,000 VND = US$0.56
- 10,000 VND = £0.38
- €1 = 23,690 VND
- US$1 = 17,000 VND
- £1 = 26,640 VND

Hotels, restaurants, travel agencies, car rental agencies, stations, airports and even doctors still ask for **US dollars**, but it is of course also possible to pay with dong, the national currency. For visits to the market or post office, rides in a cyclo or travel in rural areas, make sure to always bring small-denomination dong or dollar notes. Although the euro

CONTACT DETAILS FOR CREDIT CARDS

In the event of lost bank or credit cards you can contact the following numbers in UK and USA (phone numbers when dialling from Vietnam):

► **Eurocard/MasterCard**
Tel. 001 / 636 7227 111

► **Visa**
Tel. 001 / 410 581 336

► **American Express UK**
Tel. 0044 / 1273 696 933

► **American Express USA**
Tel. 001 / 800 528 4800

► **Diners Club UK**
Tel. 0044 / 1252 513 500

► **Diners Club USA**
Tel. 001 / 303 799 9000

Have the bank sort code, account number and card number as well as the expiry date ready.

The following numbers of UK banks (dialling from Vietnam) can be used to report and stop lost or stolen bank and credit cards issued by those banks:

► **HSBC**
Tel. 0044 / 1442 422 929

► **Barclaycard**
Tel. 0044 / 1604 230 230

► **NatWest**
Tel. 0044 / 142 370 0545

► **Lloyds TSB**
Tel. 0044 / 1702 278 270

is meanwhile also accepted almost everywhere, it is advisable to carry US dollars in cash or travellers cheques if visits to remote areas are on the itinerary.

Credit cards Many hotels, restaurants, shops, supermarkets and travel agencies accept common credit cards (Visa, MasterCard, Diners Club or American Express), however sometimes high fees of 3 to 4% are payable – ask in advance. Cash withdrawals of up to US$130 are possible at an increasing number of ATM machines (especially in Hanoi, Saigon, Nha Trang) found at banks, shopping malls, airports and hotels. It is possible to get a cash advance using MasterCard or Visa in most cities, though a 3% commission will generally apply. **Traveller's cheques** are also highly recommended: they are cashable in banks and most hotels, post offices and airports on production of a passport (usually a 2% fee is charged). Banks are open from Monday to Friday (mostly closed for one hour at lunchtime).

Loss of cards ▶ If a bank or credit card is lost or stolen, notify the issuing bank immediately.

Opening Hours

Shops Most shops open daily at around 8am and close between 7pm and 10pm; sometimes they close for lunch. Department stores and supermarkets are open from 8am to 6pm, some until 9pm. Markets start as early as 6am and last until around 6pm; street markets are usually open for longer. Post offices with telephone exchanges are open daily between 7.30am and 7pm or 8pm. Most offices are open from Monday to Friday from around 7.30am to 4.30pm; information desks are not occupied around lunchtime (this varies between 11.30am and 2pm).
Restaurants are roughly open from 10am to 10pm or 11pm. **Bank** opening hours vary but are usually from Monday to Friday from around 7.30am to 11.30am and 1.30pm to 3.30pm or 4pm.

Museums ▶ Museums are generally open daily from 8am to 11.30am and 1.30pm to 4pm (some until 5pm or 5.30pm), but some are closed on Mondays and holidays.

? DID YOU KNOW …?

■ In Vietnam there is no guarantee that the opening hours of sights and museums will apply, so those printed in brochures are often not binding. Even if you call in advance to make sure, it can happen that the place is closed when you get there.

Banks, offices and some museums are closed on **public holidays**, but most shops stay open. During the festivities of the traditional Tet Festival in January/February many Vietnamese restaurants remain closed. Even the busy Vietnamese rest on Sunday, i.e. all offices and agencies are closed.

Personal Safety

It is safest to leave any valuable jewellery at home. Hotel safes are good for storing cash, while money belts and neck pouches are ideal for on the road.

Cash and jewellery

This sad chapter in Vietnam's tourism industry has until now been restricted mainly to Saigon: unfortunately, the number of crooks, both on a larger and a smaller scale, has increased greatly since the opening of the borders. Tourists walking along Dong Khoi Street may be attacked by whole gangs of children and distracted with noise while one of the youngest tries to pickpocket or steal a money belt. There are some highly skilled pickpockets among the newspaper and postcard vendors. Also beware of those who approach you with a friendly »hello my friend«, particularly if they don't speak another word of English. Always pay attention at crowded markets, airports and train stations – **pickpocketing** is very common here. Also watch out during leisurely cyclo rides: cyclo tourists are the most common targets of city gangs. Cyclo trips or walks at night are particularly risky. If you are the victim of a theft, call the police hotline: tel. 8 33 00 28, 8 39 92 50.

Confidence tricksters

At restaurants, always check the bill and complain if necessary: adding unordered fruit and other dishes to the bill is a very common way to trick tourists in Vietnam.

Undetonated mines and war scrap still pose a risk, particularly in the once highly bombed areas such as the former **Demilitarized Zone** at the 17th parallel (Dong Ha, My Son), the former Ho Chi Minh Trail and all regions bordering Laos and Cambodia. Even around Cu Chi it is still possible to spot people with a helmet and detector searching for mines. Never leave the marked paths during hikes or temple visits!

Mines and war scrap

Post · Telecommunications

International post should be sent directly from a post office. Many hotel receptions sell stamps and will accept letters for guests. Letters (postage: 12,000 VND) and postcards (8000 VND) to Europe take at least seven to ten days, sometimes longer. Sending a fax is always expensive (1 page costs approx. US$8).

Post

International calls are cheapest from the **internet and phone shops** (especially in Saigon and Hanoi). It is also possible to make international calls from post offices and hotels (for approx. US$1.30 per minute), or call direct with a telephone card from some public pay

Telephone calls

⏵ USEFUL NUMBERS

▶ **Country codes**
Australia: 00 61
New Zealand: 00 64
Republic of Ireland: 00 353
UK: 00 44
USA and Canada: 00 1
Vietnam: 00 84

▶ **Cheaper telephone calls**
By using one of the prefixes 171,

177 or 178 it is cheaper to phone home or within Vietnam: dial 171 + 00 + country code ... or 171 + 1 (wait for connecting tone) + country code ...

▶ **Directory enquiries**
116 (for telephone numbers)
1080 (information in English on schedules, hotel bookings, etc.)

phones (approx. US$0.65 per minute; cards available for 30,000 VND, 150,000 VND and 300,000 VND for international calls).

Mobile phones ▶ Before travelling to Vietnam it is wise to ask your mobile phone operator about current tariffs and roaming charges, but it is also possible to use a **Vietnamese SIM card** (pre-paid), which reduces the cost of calls to Europe by about half (approx. US$2 per minute; cards from 400,000 VND; no text message service). Rental mobile phones in Hanoi available at tel. 04/8 21 84 65, in Saigon at tel. 08/8 24 23 82. (For more information see Vietnamese operators: www.vnpt.com.vn, www.gpc.vnn.vn and www.gsmworld.com.)

Prices · Discounts

⏵ WHAT DOES IT COST?

Simple meal (countryside)
from 20,000 VND

Simple meal (city)
from 100,000 VND

Overnight stay in double room
from 300,000 VND

Noodle soup
from 5000 VND

Bottle of water
from 3000 VND

Train ticket Saigon–Hanoi
from 400,000 VND

In Vietnam babies (up to 2 years old) fly for free, and children up to ten years of age generally only pay half for transportation (flights and buses) or excursions. Sometimes foreigners will pay more than the Vietnamese, e.g. admission fees.

Those who don't bargain in Asia are fools to themselves, although haggling is not common everywhere: of course, supermarkets, restaurants, doctors, rail and air tickets have fixed prices. If an item only costs a few pennies, haggling would only be embarrassing. However, when looking for accommodation, making purchases at markets or fruit stands, hunting in souvenir shops or doing deals with rickshaw drivers, bargaining is a must – and is often rewarded with a one to two thirds reduction in price. Patience and a friendly smile are the keys to success. When bargaining with a rickshaw driver or a market trader it is always important to say whether you are paying in US dollars or dong – after all your efforts, you want to be certain that your negotiating partner doesn't expect a payment of five dollars instead of 5000 dong (25 cents).

Bargaining

Shopping

Besides classic souvenirs such as wickerwork, weaved items, ceramics and pretty conical straw hats, more extravagant decorative items for the home have dominated the souvenir market in recent years. Pillow cases and lamp shades made of paper and silk, or colonial-style furniture made of rosewood are examples – or how about trendy flip-flops with bamboo inner soles and cinnamon straps (an Ayurvedic method to combat sweating) ...?

In Vietnam the art of decorative woodcarving has been practised for more than 1000 years. The colourful or black-and-white woodcarvings are even popular among the Vietnamese, especially for the Vietnamese New Year celebrations, and mostly depict motifs with lucky charms, such as pigs or cockerels. These craftwork products are excluded from the wood export ban. The traditional **wood-carving village of Dong Ho** is near Hanoi (▶Sights from A to Z, p.279).

Vietnamese woodblock prints

> ! **Baedeker** TIP
>
> **Animal products prohibited**
> When buying souvenirs make sure you avoid any kind of animal product, such as snake skin, crocodile skin, reptilian claws, brandied snakes, tortoise shell, tiger fur, corals, mother-of-pearl or live tropical fish.

Pottery has also been around in Vietnam for nearly 1000 years. The roofs of many houses and temples were tiled withceramic tiles. Each

Ceramics

Figures from water-puppet theatre are a popular souvenir

dynasty had its own distinct style of pottery, such as the blue ceramics of the 17th-century Nguyen dynasty from Hue. The history museums in Hanoi and Saigon provide a good overview. In **Binh Hoa**, north of Saigon, there is a handicrafts centre with factories and family businesses manufacturing ceramic goods. Among the most popular souvenirs are the handmade elephants. Beware of so-called »antique« goods from centuries-old dynasties. If they really are genuine antiques, customs officials will certainly not turn a blind eye to them.

Silk   Sericulture and silk weaving has also been practiced in Vietnam for a millennium. Silk fabrics and tailored clothing are particularly inexpensive in Saigon. Within one or two days tailors can sew an item of clothing based on a model. Compare prices and ask for discounts for more than one item of clothing. Those travelling via **Hoi An** should definitely visit the tailor's shops on Le Loi Street. They make suits, kimonos and dresses cheaply overnight.

Lacquer ware   This handicraft, which originated in China, is now offered everywhere in Vietnam and has been practised for at least 1500 years. The black or brown lacquer is acquired from the resin of the sumac tree. Mother-of-pearl goods are particularly common and some are even quite cheap: jewellery boxes, writing utensils, betel nut bowls, ashtrays, china, chopsticks, musical instruments, altars, murals, cupboards and entire sitting room suites. Regular sightseeing tours stop at the **Lam Son lacquer ware factory** near the Omni Hotel in Saigon. Besides the traditional motifs and colours there are also more minimalist designs on offer, which seem more modern and less unconventional: pots, bowls and trays.

A lot of souvenir items and everyday utensils are made of **rattan and bamboo**, e.g. classical instruments. Hand-woven rugs and blankets also make good souvenirs. At markets there is a whole range of different green teas and spices on offer. Gold, silver and gemstones (ruby and jade) should only be bought by those who really know what they are buying, and in licensed shops only. Souvenir opium pipes may cause problems when leaving the country as selling them is technically not allowed.

Sport and Outdoors

Golf is now hugely popular in Vietnam. The establishment of several golfing facilities in the country in recent years was encouraged in particular by Asian and US tourists. In the highlands, however, golf was already played in imperial times – Bao Dai himself was known to swing a driver at the golf course in Da Lat.

Golf

Vietnam's 3200km/2000mi of coastline is an invitation to take part in water sports. Most first-class beach resorts in coastal towns offer a whole range of fun in the water: paddle and sail boats, catamarans, surfboards and parasailing, sometimes even jet skis. Several Western-run diving schools (with PADI certificate) have opened up on the coasts of Vietnam. The best time to dive is from May to June, but diving along Vietnam's coasts is possible even in winter (in Central Vietnam typhoons may occur from August to December; rainfall increases between October and November/December when the water visibility in Nha Trang is not as good). The best and deepest water visibility can be found around **Phu Quoc** (up to 50m/165ft), where there is at least one dive centre. Day tours including two dives cost around US$40–70 (£27–47).

Water sports

◄ Diving

The best regions for kitesurfing and windsurfing are around **Da Nang** (where the only Vietnamese surfing club is based) and **Mui Ne** near Phan Thiet.

◄ Windsurfing

The best kayaking region is to be found in the paradisiacal setting of Ha Long Bay and around the island of Cat Ba with its thousands of small islands jutting out of the emerald-green water like stone dino-

◄ Kayaking, rafting, canyoning

⏵ USEFUL ADDRESSES

GOLF

► **Vietnam Golf Club**
Long Thanh My Ward,
District 9, Saigon
Tel. 08/2 80 00-15/-16/-17
Fax 08/2 80 01 27
www.vietnamgolfcc.com

► **Vietnam Royal Country Club**
Tel. 08/8 99 74 84
Fax 08/8 99 13 52

► **Further information:**
www.vietnamgolfresorts.com
www.vietnamgolftours.com

DIVING

► **Jeremy Stein's Rainbow Divers**
52 Tran Phu, Nha Trang
Tel. 0 58/82 99 46 or 09 13/40 81 46
www.divevietnam.com

► **Blue Diving Club**
Hotel Vina, 66 Tran Phu, Nha Trang
Tel. 0 58/52 70 34
Fax 0 58/52 70 43
www.vietnam-diving.com
bluedivingclub@hotmail.com

KAYAKING, RAFTING, CANYONING

► **Asiatica Travel**
1203 (buildings M3-M4)
Nguyen Chi Thanh
Dong Da District, Hanoi
Tel. 04/2 66 28 16
Fax 04/2 66 28 18
info@asiaticatravel.com

► **Buffalo Tours in Hanoi**
11 Hang Muoi, Hanoi
Tel. 04/8 28 07 02
Fax 04/8 26 93 70
www.buffalotours.com
info@buffalotours.com

► **Buffalo Tours in Saigon**
Tel. 08/8 279179
saigon@buffalotours.com

► **Phat Tire Ventures**
73 Truong Cong Dinh, Da Lat
Tel. 0 63/82 94 22
Fax 0 63/82 03 31
www.phattireventures.com
info@phattireventures.com

TREKKING

► **Footprint Vietnam Travel**
6 Le Thanh Tong, Hanoi
Tel. 04/9 33 28 44
Fax 04/9 33 28 55
www.footprintsvietnam.com

► **Asiatica Travel**
►Rafting

► **Saigon Tourist**
►Information, p.123

CAVING

► **Footprint Vietnam Travel**
►Trekking

VETERAN TOURS

► **Vietnam Tourism**
►Information, p.123

► **Ho Guom Inserimex Tourist Company**
in Hanoi:
10 Hang Bot, Ton Duc Thang
Tel. 04/7 34 07 44
Fax 04/8 23 54 85
www.inserimex.com
inserhan@fpt.vn

in Saigon:
411 Dien Bien Phu, 3rd district
Tel. 08/9 29 01 99
Fax 08/9 29 02 00
insersaigon@hcm.vnn.vn

MOTORCYCLE TOURS

► **Saigon Tourist, Vietnam Tourism**
Both ►Information, pp.123

► **Viet Travel**
190 Pasteur Street, District 3, Saigon
Tel. 08/8 22 88 98
Fax 08/8 29 91 42
www.vietravel-vn.com
info@vietravel-vn.com

► **Further information**
www.minskclubvietnam.com
www.freewheelin-tours.com

CYCLING TOURS

► **Symbiosis**
►Arrival, p.97

► **Footprint Vietnam Travel**
►Trekking
Some tour organizers offering cycling tours will have the busy highways (e.g. N 1 and steep mountain roads) covered by bus, while cycling is reserved to quieter minor streets.

► **Further information**
www.cyclingvietnam.net
www.biking-asia.com

LANGUAGE HOLIDAYS

► **Hanoi Language Tours**
www.hanoilanguagetours.com

► **Department for Vietnamese Language for Foreigners at Saigon University**
www.vietnamese-language.com.vn

The golf course near Phan Thiet

After the fun in the water there are ball games on the beach

saurs. A canoe ride leads through mangroves and caves directly to the beaches. Usually people sleep on the boats or in tents on isolated beaches (a two-day tour starts at US$65/£44). Rafting or kayaking tours are also on offer (around Da Lat and into the national parks Cat Tien and Yok Don), as are canyoning and abseiling at waterfalls around Da Lat.

Trekking and hiking tours

Trekking and hiking tours are not allowed without official permission and a Vietnamese trekking guide. It is not a good idea to roam Vietnam's forests alone, if only because of the (as yet) unexploded bombs dating back to the war. There are often police checkpoints in hiking areas or national parks, and frequently summits may turn out to be in a military area. Actual trekking tours last up to a week with eight-hour hikes every day. The group sleeps in very simple wooden huts provided by members of hill tribes, e.g. the Hmong, Muong or Thai. Canoe trips, dinghy excursions or elephant rides are sometimes included in the programme. Those booking a one-day hiking tour with bus transportation are sure to end up in an ethnic minority village marketed specifically at tourists. During the **rainy season**, the high number of leeches and muddy paths make trekking tours a ra-

A group of hikers in the mountains is accompanied by members of the Red Dao tribe

ther unpleasant experience. Precautions against malaria and extensive mosquito protection are an absolute must in rural areas, particularly in the rainy season.

The following areas have been the first to become trekking regions: the provinces near Da Lat and Dac Lac, Cuc Phuong National Park in the north, the plateau at Tam Dao, and Hoa Binh/Mai Chau. Between November and April, Saigon Tourist offers trekking tours to Vietnam's highest peak, Fan Si Pan (3143m/10,312ft; sleeping in tents, porters on request). Around Fan Si Pan temperatures can plunge to freezing (best times are October/November and after winter from March to May).

Caving is a new adventure sport. At 19km/12mi the most famous and longest cave is the Phong Nha Cave (► Sights from A to Z, p.222), which has been protected by UNESCO since 2003. Now cave climbers can discover the legendary grotto on the heels of the old explorers. In addition, the karst region around Bac Bo is considered one of the best places for caving tours, particularly in the province of Lai Chau near Tam Duong, the area around Son La, Hai Giang and Cao Bang.

Caving tours

Other activities   Those into table tennis, badminton or volley ball can join Vietnamese sports enthusiasts in some early-morning exercise in the parks and squares of Saigon and Hanoi. Fans of Tai Chi can study the movements of (mostly older) Vietnamese.

Here, badminton and peteca are also played using one's feet. Ice skating is possible in Saigon (Ky Hoa Ice Skating, 16A Le Hong Phong, District 10). Those interested in horse races should consider mingling with the crowds at the race course in Phu Tho on the weekend – no extravagant hats, but pure fun with plenty of betting-crazed Vietnamese. Saigon and Hanoi offer bowling centres, cinemas and many other types of entertainment.

Special tours

Veteran tours   Vietnam markets its war history to tourists like no other country in the world. An example of this comes in the form of veteran tours. Veteran soldiers from (Western) allied countries visit the old battlegrounds and army bases, museums, markets of war items, the Demilitarized Zone and the rest of the Ho Chi Minh Trail. Old ruins and fortresses such as Khe Sanh in the north and tunnels such as those at Cu Chi are also part of the programme. Participants even get to meet the enemy of the past, members of the Vietcong.

Motorcycle tours   To some, it is a dream come true: riding on a motorcycle through Vietnam, from top to bottom or vice versa on National Highway 1. Often travellers will encounter whole fleets of motorcycles. As these tours may not yet officially be done alone – either on motorcycles or by car – many travel agents specialize in tours on two-wheels. Organizers take care of all the **necessary paperwork**, as a British or even an international drivers licence is often not accepted. Participants of these two to three-week-long motorcycle tours can choose between a Harley Davidson, BMW, Honda or Kawasaki, or various vintage bikes. Road conditions require decent driving skills and a fast reaction time.

Bicycle tours   Those doing the north-south route by bicycle can manage the approximately 1700km/2754mi-long stretch between Saigon and Hanoi within three to four weeks, depending on the number of stops. Either bring a bike by plane or simply buy a new one in Saigon.

Single travellers wishing to join a group tour should enquire at travel agents.

Helicopter tours   Those with little time but plenty of money to spare can experience a great way to see Vietnam – by air in a chartered helicopter. Destinations include Saigon, Cu Chi, Tay Ninh (landing on the Black Lady Mountain), Da Lat, Vung Tau (flying over the oil platforms in the South China Sea), Con Dau, and Hanoi, but also less accessible mountain regions such as Dien Bien Phu and Ha Long Bay in the north. Flying from Hanoi past the **limestone giants in the Ha Long Bay** is a spectacular experience. Prices for a one-day trip start at US$1000. Tours can be booked via Vietnam Tourism (▶ Information).

Time

Vietnam is seven hours ahead of Greenwich Mean Time. During British Summer Time the time difference is six hours.

Transport

In the City

In Vietnam there are traffic lights and zebra crossings. Nevertheless, pedestrians require a certain amount of assertiveness and courage to cross the road. Here are some rules: never wait too long for a gap in the seemingly endless stream of traffic! Just start walking and pay constant attention to cars and mopeds; use hand signals if necessary. Watch out when walking down country roads, even though the Vietnamese themselves often sit chatting on the tarmac.

Pedestrian behaviour

In cities the white and yellow taxis are practical if you have a lot of luggage. There are taxi stands in the cities of Saigon and Hanoi, Vung Tau and Da Lat; in other places it is possible to order a car and driver at the hotel reception. Fares are quite cheap and based on the turned-on taximeter (6000 VND/km); prices for longer tours (e.g. a day trip) are open to negotiation.

By taxi

On the three-wheeled pedal rickshaws, passengers sit in a more or less comfortable chair in front of the cyclo driver. Drivers either ride around the blocks or wait at markets, stations, hotels, restaurants and sights for potential customers. Ask someone at the hotel to write the desired destination on a paper to show the driver. Drivers waiting at hotel entrances are often used to better-paying customers than their cruising colleagues. Those who have not mastered the art of bargaining just yet, though are unwilling to pay often overpriced fares, should walk a few metres away from the hotel and wave down another driver. Cyclo drivers will often speak a few words of English (particularly in Saigon), though others don't even know the main streets. Some numbers in Vietnamese and sign language may be quite helpful when negotiating fares. For a dollar the cyclo driver will

By cyclo

take a passenger anywhere in the city centre. **At night**, due to repeated muggings and money disputes, it is best to take a taxi.

More and more roads in central Saigon and Hanoi are now being closed for pedal rickshaws (e.g. Dong Khoi, Nguyen Hue and Le Loi). Don't worry if the driver takes a seemingly wrong route. Once the destination is reached, drivers will often offer to wait until the customer returns. Clearly object if that is not your wish.

By moped taxi In Saigon, Hanoi or even in smaller cities such as Vung Tau and Nha Trang, moped drivers also offer a kind of taxi service. The fare must be negotiated in advance and it is a good idea to check the condition of the moped and the driver's driving skills. At night, this means of transportation is not recommended.

By bike Your own pedal power is another option, and a rented bike is a very pleasant way to explore smaller towns such as Hue, Da Lat, Nha

Amazing what will fit on a cyclo…

Trang or Vung Tau. Cycling in large cities like Saigon and Hanoi can be a very nerve-wracking and sweaty means of transportation – stuck in the endless stream of mopeds. Bicycles usually have neither bells, gears nor lights; brakes should definitely be tested in advance. Many places have **monitored parking lots for bikes**, which can be used for a small fee.

In Saigon and Hanoi there is a surprisingly large number of modern city buses, although the bus system may be a little confusing for foreigners. Those without a fixed sightseeing schedule can roam the city by bus and will definitely see some of the sights (e.g. the blue line runs between Me Linh Square to Cholon via Le Loi). The new buses are quite comfortable as they are rarely overly crowded.

By bus

Trains

The railway system in Vietnam covers approximately 3000km/ 4800mi and was established during the French colonial period. The still single-lane tracks are in dire condition, and some bridges destroyed during the war have only recently been rebuilt. The most important routes are the north-south connection from Saigon to Hanoi and Hai Phong, and to the border at Lao Cai. Particularly popular among tourists is the **reunification train** on the north-south route between Saigon and Hanoi, which runs several times a day and now also has air-conditioned compartments (32 to 41 hours).

By rail

Tickets should be reserved approximately three days in advance at the station or through a travel agency. There are four different classes; **booking is essential** for 1st and 2nd-class couchettes: passengers can choose between hard (straw mats) and soft beds (in a four-bed compartment) and between a hard and soft seat. Included in the fare are three meals. The interior of the train cannot be compared to European standards, but the ride is fairly comfortable, if a little cramped. **Couchettes** (soft berth) are the most comfortable option, but they are comparatively expensive – it would be much faster to fly for just about the same price. Foreign nationals always pay more than the Vietnamese. For a trip from north to south taking the train is still a better choice than a fairly tiresome journey on National Highway 1 (the only north-south connection) – there are fewer sights north of Da Nang than in the southern part of the country.

The **Victoria Express Train**, run by the Victoria Hotel, travels four times a week between Sa Pa, Hanoi and Lao Cai on the Chinese border (tel. 08/8 37 30 31; www.victoriahotels-asia.com, reservation@victoriahotels-asia.com).

Buses

Taking a cross-country bus is unsuitable for travellers with limited time. It is supposedly planned to replace the shabby fleet of regional

By express bus and mini bus

In the north the figures on the traffic signs sometimes still wear cone hats

buses with new ones. Broken-down buses or entire wrecks are often spotted by the side of the road. The seats of these rattling vehicles are designed for Asian figures, which can pose a special problem for Europeans and Americans.

Some major routes are also serviced by express buses, which do seem more comfortable and leave on schedule (mostly early in the morning) but are a little overpriced. To cater to the growing number of tourists, the main tourist towns are serviced several times a day by air-conditioned (mini) buses.

Inexpensive »**open-tour tickets**« (only for use on tourist buses) are a convenient way to travel cross-country, with fixed routes and departure times. It is possible to stop the bus at several places and there is a pick-up service from the hotel (example of prices: Saigon to Hanoi: US$22–28, prices are not subject to season; information: www.opentourvn.com). The driver's motto seems to be »just go for it«, as he bombs down the bumpy roads, often half-asleep at night. Day and night, the bus stops for breaks at the food carts and restaurants along the road.

Trips like these can be **booked** at the well-known and alternative Sinh Café travel agency (248 De Tham Street, District 1, Saigon, tel. 8 36 73 38, fax 8 36 93 22, www.sinhcafevn.com). A similarly inexpensive travel agent is Kim Travel, particularly for boat travel to the Cambodian border (270 De Tham Rd, Saigon, tel. 08/8 36 98 59). Mini and express buses should be reserved one day in advance at the station or travel agency; otherwise head to the bus terminal bright and early for a last-minute ticket. This may take a while so don't be on a tight schedule.

Boats, Ships and Ferries

By ship/ferry — Since 1990 cruise ships have been serving the 3200km/2000mi coast of Vietnam. They stop at the ports of Saigon, Vung Tau, Da Nang, Nha Trang, Hai Phong and Ha Long Bay/Hong Gai. The state-run shipping company Vinaship runs within Vietnam from Hai Phong to Saigon.

Boat tours are offered everywhere in the Mekong delta and Ha Long Bay, off the coasts and on the rivers. The **barque** *Cai Be Princess*, for instance, departs from Saigon and passes through the canals and ri-

The N 1 winds in tight bends over the Hai Van Pass

vers of the Mekong delta. It is also possible to cruise down the Perfume River (Huong) on a **house boat** in Hue. Old-style **junks** (sampans) are another popular way to explore the areas around Nha Trang, Hue and Ha Long Bay. From Saigon it is also possible to take a one-hour trip by **speedboat** to Vung Tau (run by Vinaexpress). There are ferry and hydrofoil services (by Greenlines) from Saigon to Vung Tau, daily express boats and private boats, as well as the Hotel Victoria ship to Cambodia. The new Tu Trang speedboat connects Saigon and Phnom Penh via stations in Can Tho (Cai Rang) and Chau Doc.

Rental Cars

By rental car The most comfortable way to explore Vietnam is by renting a car – however they can only be booked **with a driver** (who only rarely speaks English). Different models can be rented at car rental agencies, travel agencies and hotels in all major cities. The price is based on a mileage charge and sometimes there are additional costs for the driver (for accommodation and one meal). There are also package deals, however. As a general rule, it is wise to compare prices.

Driving A British or even international driving licence is not accepted in Vietnam. It is becoming increasingly popular among foreign tourists to explore the cities on a moped, which officially is not allowed. Those who take the chance must leave their passport with the rental company and be prepared to pay a fine if stopped by the police. It should also be taken into consideration that there is no insurance, and in the event of an accident the tourist, who is assumed to be rich, is usually the one at fault. In Vietnam they **drive on the right**. Street signs are quite rare in the countryside, though always written in Latin script.

Travellers with Disabilities

Disabled travellers may encounter extreme difficulties in Vietnam. At museums and hotels (except for luxury hotels) there are no lifts for people with walking disabilities, no pavement ramps and no adequately equipped means of transportation. It is therefore recommended to stick to large international hotel chains (most of which provide rooms suitable for the disabled) and to travel by rental car with a driver. Exploring the cities on foot can even be quite stressful and challenging for those without disabilities. The traffic is relentless. **Using toilets** is equally difficult: especially in rural areas, Asian (originally French) squat toilets are still very common.

Many Vietnamese, however, are very helpful and are used to assisting disabled people, as a large number of war veterans have disabilities. It is highly recommended that disabled travellers gather information regarding adequately equipped hotels and possibly enquire at specialized travel agents prior to the journey.

► **RADAR**
12 City Forum, 250 City Road,
London EC1V 8AF
Tel. (020) 72 50 32 22
www.radar.org.uk

► **SATH (Society for the Advancement of Travel for the Handicapped)**
347 5th Ave., no. 610
New York, NY 10016:
Tel. (21) 4 47 72 84, www.sath.org

When to Go

Due to its geographical length, Vietnam is split into two or three large climate zones, which, apart from the cooler highlands, are influenced by the monsoon winds. The Hai Van Pass between Hue and Da Nang is considered to be a meteorological divide. In the north the climate is subtropical with hot summers and mild winters, while the climate in the south is warm and tropical.

Two climate zones

A monsoon is a seasonal prevailing wind, carrying moist, rainy winds (from the southwest) or dry winds (from the northwest). From May to November it can get very wet, Vietnam numbering among the **most rain-laden regions** in the world. However, it hardly ever rains for long (except around Hue, Hanoi and Da Lat). In August and September/October typhoons and tropical cyclones with wind speeds of up to 160kmh/100mph rage along the coasts of central and northern Vietnam, crashing against palm trees and pushing a thick and grey veil of rain in front of them – resulting in entire regions getting flooded and banks, bridges and houses being damaged. High-risk regions should be avoided during monsoon periods. Generally the best time to travel in Vietnam is in December and January when there is little rain and it is not yet extremely hot.

Monsoon

ℹ Monsoon

- The word monsoon stems from the Arabic word »mausim« and describes a type of wind that changes its direction twice over the course of one year: during summer it blows from a southwesterly direction, during winter from the northeast. Arab people used these winds to sail their trading ships to India in summer and return in winter.

In the south it is hotter and more humid than in the north (especially in April and May). The average temperature is around 30°C/86°F. South Vietnam is hit by the southwest monsoon with strong but short rain showers – mostly from April/May to October – and high humidity of over 90%. The dry season is between November and April. The coolest, driest and most pleasant time to travel to the south is from November/December to January.

The south

Vietnam Climate Stations

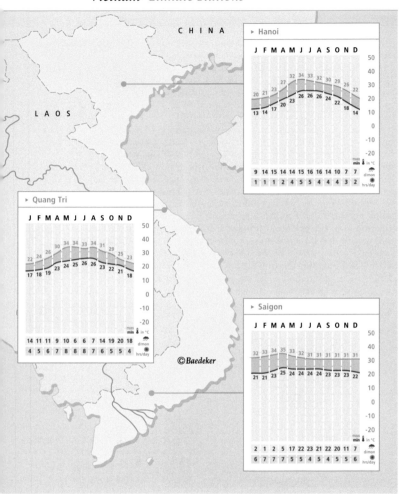

©Baedeker

Central Vietnam From August to December, when the **strong typhoons** of the north-east monsoon hit the coasts of central Vietnam, floods are very common: coastal roads and train connections may be closed off due to flooding, and some flights may even be cancelled. Of the tourist destinations, Hue is usually the most afflicted, with sometimes entire districts being flooded. Driving northwards from Hue can be very tedious during this time, as many rivers burst their banks. The best time to travel is the drier period between June and July/August. The southern central coast experiences less rain and in Nha Trang it rains mostly in October and November.

In the highlands around Da Lat, temperatures are cooler at around 20°C/50°F–25°C/59°F, and drop down even lower at night. Sometimes it rains here for several days non-stop; the driest period is between December and March.

The Central Highlands

There are two seasons in the subtropical north of Vietnam: summer and winter. The summer and rainy season is between May and October. With average temperatures of 25°C/59°F the climate is more pleasant than in the tropical south (Hanoi in January: average 17°C/45°F, in July: 29°C/66°F). The winters and nights are cooler, with lots of drizzle and temperatures dropping down to 10°C/50°F. Most rainfall occurs in July and August, though in the north there can be drizzle and fog even outside the monsoon season. Best time to travel: November to May.

The north

Intensive **exposure to the sun** can be avoided by wearing sun block with a high SPF, sunglasses and a sun hat, as well as long-sleeved shirts or a shawl (to avoid sunburn). A light cardigan or a jumper is recommended, as the air conditioning turns hotel rooms, restaurants, rental cars and taxis into ice coolers – the risk of catching a cold should not be underestimated. Otherwise bring loose clothes made of cotton or linen, stockings for dusk and long-sleeved light clothes for protection against mosquitoes. A waterproof can be advantageous in rainy periods.

Suitable clothing

Tours

VIETNAM LOOKS BACK ON 4000 YEARS OF HISTORY AND OFFERS A WEALTH OF HISTORICAL AND CULTURAL SITES, AS WELL AS UNSPOILT NATURE IN THE MOUNTAINS AND NEARLY 2000 MILES OF COASTLINE. THE TOURS SUGGESTED HERE LEAD TO THE MOST APPEALING DESTINATIONS.

TOURS THROUGH VIETNAM

Fancy a drive from the south to the north? Or perhaps you'd prefer a hike in the mountains? Visit the Mekong Delta, Ha Long Bay, or both? The following four suggested tours should make it easier to decide.

TOUR 1 **Through the Whole Country from South to North**
Start off in Saigon in the south and, heading northwards, visit famous colonial and imperial cities, historic ruins, palm-fringed beaches and the most beautiful landscapes in the far north of the country. ▶ **page 163**

TOUR 2 **From Saigon into the Highlands**
This short but varied tour leads into the mountains with a stop at one of Vietnam's most fauna-rich national parks (Cat Tien), home to the last Javan rhinos in mainland Asia. The trip concludes with a relaxing visit to the beach at Phan Thiet. ▶ **page 166**

TOUR 3 **Into the Mekong Delta**
Water as far as the eye can see: the Mekong delta boasts floating markets and fruit orchards, fish farmers and rice-paper producers, temples and pagodas. ▶ **page 168**

TOUR 4 **Mountains and Sea**
From the capital of Hanoi, tour 4 heads first for the mountains, either for some hiking or just to buy souvenirs from the hill tribes, who still today dress in traditional costume. From there, the UNESCO-listed Ha Long Bay beckons. One of the most magnificent settings in the country, it boasts dripstone caves and craggy limestone mountains in the middle of the sea – a place that could almost be home to mystical dragons. ▶ **page 170**

The islands of Ha Long Bay loom mysteriously in the morning mist

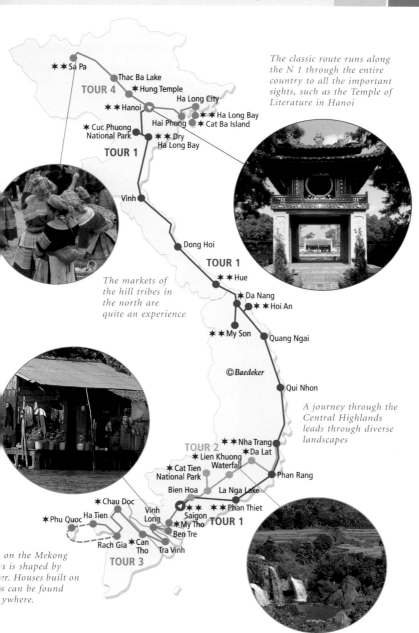

The classic route runs along the N 1 through the entire country to all the important sights, such as the Temple of Literature in Hanoi

★ ★ Sa Pa

TOUR 4

★ Thac Ba Lake
★ Hung Temple

★ ★ Hanoi

Ha Long City

★ ★ Ha Long Bay
★ Cat Ba Island

Hai Phong

★ Cuc Phuong National Park

★ ★ Dry Ha Long Bay

TOUR 1

Vinh

Dong Hoi

TOUR 1

★ ★ Hue

★ Da Nang
★ ★ Hoi An

★ ★ My Son Quang Ngai

©Baedeker

Qui Nhon

The markets of the hill tribes in the north are quite an experience

A journey through the Central Highlands leads through diverse landscapes

★ ★ Nha Trang
★ Da Lat

★ Lien Khuong Waterfall

TOUR 2

★ Cat Tien National Park

Bien Hoa La Nga Lake

Phan Rang

★ Chau Doc

Vinh Long

★ ★ ★ Saigon
★ My Tho

★ ★ Phan Thiet

TOUR 1

★ Phu Quoc Ha Tien

Ben Tre

Rach Gia ★ Can Tho Tra Vinh

TOUR 3

on the Mekong a is shaped by er. Houses built on s can be found ywhere.

Travelling in Vietnam

Variety   Vietnam offers a wealth of contrasts. From the port city of Da Nang in central Vietnam, for example, it is possible to visit three different **UNESCO World Cultural Heritage Sites**: the temple city of My Son, the imperial city of Hue and the ancient city of Hoi An. Hot on the trail of the colonial rulers, fans of famous authors such as Graham Greene or Marguerite Duras make pilgrimages through colonial buildings and weather beaten villas, where the floorboards creak and the bathtubs are perched upon lions' feet.

Signs of the war, which obviously did not spare the historical sites, are ever present. During the 1990s, Vietnam turned many remnants of the war into lucrative tourist attractions: dollar admissions to crawl through the Vietcong tunnels in Cu Chi, veterans' reunions at the former line of demarcation, motor rallies along the Ho Chi Minh Trail, and boat tours through the mangroves of the Mekong delta, once completely torched by napalm. Today, much of the havoc wreaked by the war is no longer visible. Yet, as harmless as the rice-paddy scenery appears, a third of all the bombs dropped during the war remain unexploded.

A little boy tending cattle in Cat Cat, in the mountains near Sa Pa

The »third face« of Vietnam is made up of the many **beaches and coastal areas**. The more than 3000km/1860mi-long coast holds unbelievable potential. The beaches of Vietnam have only been a destination for foreign tourists for the last decade or so – making the rapid increase in the number of luxurious and inventive beach resorts in recent years all the more amazing.

A fourth kind of vacation can be enjoyed in Vietnam, too: **a hiking holiday in the mountains**. »Ecotourism«, however, can sometimes come in strange forms. Don't be surprised if, during a several-day backpacking trek through the mountain villages around Sa Pa, neon lights compete with the starry night sky and your hosts serve Nescafé instead of Vietnamese coffee. The mountainous region around Sa Pa with Vietnam's highest peak (Fan Si Pan, 3143m/10,312ft), the high plateau of Tam Dao as well as the area around Mai Chau in the north are the most popular hiking areas in Vietnam. Others include the highlands near Da Lat and Dak Lak, and the national parks of Yok Don, Cuc Phuong and Bach Ma.

A hired car with a chauffeur is the best way to get to know the country on your own, and of course also the most expensive option. However, almost the entire country can be travelled relatively comfortably on **organized minibus tours**, departing from tourist hubs: all the bathing areas, cultural highlights, cities and national parks can be reached in this way (the special, very inexpensive Open Tour Tickets allow passengers to break the journey at various points). Contact with the local residents is more likely when using public bus services (or when travelling with private minibus firms not aimed at tourists); however, this requires somewhat more time.

By car or by bus

Travelling through a country by bike can often be a rewarding and intensive way of experiencing the land and its people. However, Vietnam does not offer any designated cycle paths like those in Europe, which means cyclists are always on the same roads as cars, herds of oxen and so on. This can sometimes be a rather hair-raising experience, bearing in mind the often adventurous **Asian driving style**. On quieter side roads, cycling in Vietnam can be recommended, but there are precious few of them. Those who dare to brave the big cities like Hanoi and Saigon on a bike should have especially strong nerves, be experienced and fit. A good alternative to cycling alone is to join the guided tour groups. Cyclists ride without a pack, supported by a bus. Numerous UK and American firms offer such tours, which run mostly through the Mekong delta or Ha Long Bay.

By bike

Tour 1 Through the Whole Country from South to North

Distance: approx. 1750km/1090mi   **Duration:** approx. 14–21 days

Natural attractions and historically significant sites lie along this route from the lively metropolis of Saigon in the humid south to Hanoi, the capital and administrative centrein the cooler north. Stops are possible at a number of bathing areas, as is a trip into the mountains.

The first part of the tour leads from ❶ ✳ ✳ **Saigon** on a four or five-hour drive past rice paddies, sugarcane fields, fruit stands and herds of cattle to Vietnam's expansive coast – an opportunity to go for a swim. About 20km/12mi away from the fishing harbour town of ❷ ✳ ✳ **Phan Thiet** are a number of very good hotel and bungalow complexes built along the beaches of the Mui Ne peninsula.

On the way north, it is worth stopping near ❸ **Phan Rang** to visit the remarkable Cham towers (Po Ro Me, Po Klong Garai). Further

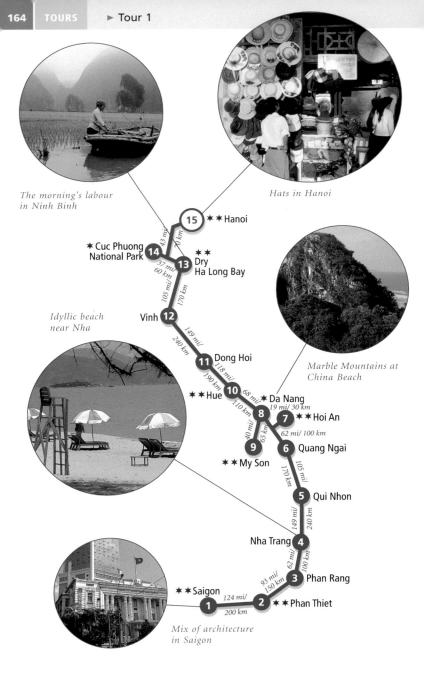

The morning's labour in Ninh Binh

Hats in Hanoi

15 ✹✹ Hanoi

43 mi/
70 km

✹ Cuc Phuong
National Park

14

37 mi/
60 km

13 ✹✹
Dry
Ha Long Bay

105 mi/
170 km

Idyllic beach near Nha

Vinh **12**

149 mi/
240 km

11 Dong Hoi

118 mi/
190 km

10 68 mi/
110 km

✹✹ Hue

Da Nang

19 mi/ 30 km

8

7 ✹✹ Hoi An

40 mi/
65 km

62 mi/ 100 km

9

6 Quang Ngai

✹✹ My Son

105 mi/
170 km

5 Qui Nhon

149 mi/
240 km

Nha Trang **4**

62 mi/
100 km

3 Phan Rang

93 mi/
150 km

Marble Mountains at China Beach

✹✹ Saigon **1**

124 mi/
200 km

2 ✹✹ Phan Thiet

Mix of architecture in Saigon

along, the route runs past the harbour of Cam Ranh, which was used as a base by the US Marines during the Vietnam War. Close to the resort of ❹ ✶✶ **Nha Trang** there are more Cham buildings (Po Nagar) to visit. For those staying for a number of days, the Oceanic Institute, which has an aquarium, a fish farming facility and offers diving expeditions to the outlying islands, should be an obligatory part of the itinerary.

Along the coast runs the spectacular beach and pass route: around 80km/50mi north of Nha Trang the bumpy surface of the Dai Lanh Pass runs above the coast, offering a marvellous view of the mountainous peninsula of Hon Gom. For the next 100km/60mi the mountains run closer to the coastline – a beautiful section of the route. The journey continues to ❺ **Qui Nhon**, a

DON'T MISS

- Mui Ne: stop for a swim at this golden beach.
- Nha Trang: boat tours, diving and snorkelling are on offer at this bustling resort.
- Da Nang: climb the Marble Mountains and visit the Cham Museum.
- Hoi An: the little city impresses with Chinese temples and trading houses.
- Hue: soak up the imperial atmosphere in palaces and tombs.
- Ninh Binh: jagged limestone mountains rise from rice fields in Dry Ha Long Bay.

coastal town with a number of the Cham towers influenced by the Khmer building style (Thap Doi; around 3km/2mi from the town centre).

Fishing harbours and palm-fringed beaches border National Highway 1 for 170km/106mi until ❻ **Quang Ngai** is reached. From here, after taking the bridge across the river, turn into a country road leading toward the sea and travel the 14km/9mi to Son My in order to see the memorial to the victims of the massacre at **My Lai**.

On National Highway 1 near Thanh Phuoc An a road branches to the right towards ❼ ✶✶ **Hoi An**. The small town on the Thu Bon River has played an important role as an Asian trading port for around 1000 years. It is worth a visit to see the pretty trading houses, the Chinese temples and the Japanese Covered Bridge. 30km/19mi further on is ❽ ✶ **Da Nang**, today Vietnam's fourth largest city, which looks back upon a millennium of history. China Beach, several miles in length, and the Marble Mountains are worth a visit.

Rough roads lead from Da Nang to the ruined temple city of the Cham, ❾ ✶✶ **My Son**. Do not under any circumstances leave the marked paths – My Son was heavily bombed during the Vietnam War.

A section full of magnificent panoramic views comes next: the coastal road runs between Da Nang and the old imperial city of ❿ ✶✶ **Hue** over the Hai Van Pass at an altitude of 496m/1627ft – in good weather, the Cloud Pass offers a breathtaking view of the peninsula and Lang Co lagoon.

The former Demilitarized Zone (DMZ) lies further north, at the 17th parallel in the area of the Ben Hai River. At Ho Xa the road branches off to Vinh Moc and the authentically preserved Vietcong tunnels there. Further along the N 1 is a chance to stop at ⑪**Dong Hoi** and visit the famous Phong Nha Caves. From there it is another 197km/122mi to ⑫**Vinh**. 15km/9mi west in Kim Lien stands the restored house in which Ho Chi Minh grew up.

Continuing toward ⑮✱✱ **Hanoi**, the National Highway reaches the Red River delta, a fertile and densely populated plain that has been visited by floods for thousands of years. Before that however, the road crosses the ⑬✱✱ **Dry Ha Long Bay**, a fantastic landscape with steeply rising, wildly overgrown giant limestone formations lying between the rice fields in the area around the city of Ninh Binh (93km/58mi south of Hanoi). Nearby it is possible to take a rowing boat through the canals, e.g. to the caves of Tam Coc.

Around 10km/6mi past Ninh Binh, the bumpy country road 12 A leads to ⑭✱ **Cuc Phuong National Park** the oldest and most visited national park in Vietnam. It is also possible to spend the night in the nature reserve, which is known for its giant trees and its caves.

Tour 2 From Saigon into the Highlands

Distance: approx. 600km/370mi   **Duration:** approx. 7 days

This route is among the most varied in Vietnam. It runs from the southern Vietnamese metropolis to one of the most diversely inhabited national parks in the Central Highlands at Da Lat, and continues over a breathtaking mountain pass back toward the coast to Nha Trang or Phan Thiet.

Along National Highway 1, around 30km/19mi northeast of ❶✱✱ **Saigon**, a first stop can be made at ❷**Bien Hoa**, a centre for handicrafts. Some miles further on, take National Highway 20 into the mountains. It runs past caoutchouc plantations and expansive fields with fruit trees. ❸**La Nga Lake** (also the Tri An reservoir) is home to houseboats and floating villages, where fishermen live. Those wishing to visit ❹✱ **Cat Tien National Park** (approx. 150km/93mi north of Saigon) should take the dirt road leading off to the left in Ma Da Gui.

From the national park, the dirt road leads back toward National Highway 20. This winds slowly upward to an elevation of 1500m/5000ft in the province of Lam Dong, where the pass runs through thick jungle. Along the side of the road are a number of picturesque temple shrines and waterfalls. The high plateau is reached at the town of Bao Loc, where nearby tea factories and silkworm farms can be visited. The ❺✱ **Lien Khuong Waterfall** is a nice place to take a

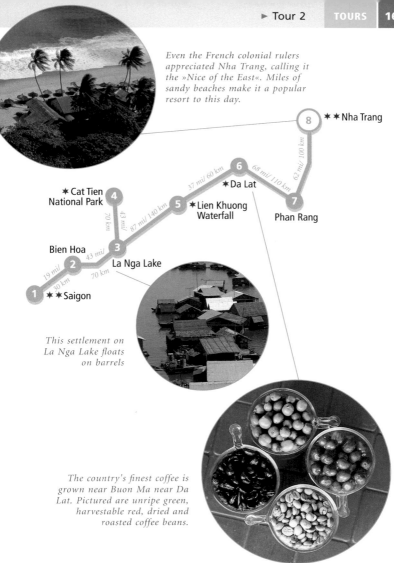

Even the French colonial rulers appreciated Nha Trang, calling it the »Nice of the East«. Miles of sandy beaches make it a popular resort to this day.

8 ✳✳ Nha Trang

62 mi/ 100 km

6 ✳ Da Lat

68 mi/ 110 km

37 mi/ 60 km

5 ✳ Lien Khuong Waterfall

4 ✳ Cat Tien National Park

7 Phan Rang

43 mi/ 140 km

87 mi/ 140 km

70 km

3

Bien Hoa

43 mi/

2

La Nga Lake

19 mi/

70 km

30 km

1 ✳✳ Saigon

This settlement on La Nga Lake floats on barrels

The country's finest coffee is grown near Buon Ma near Da Lat. Pictured are unripe green, harvestable red, dried and roasted coffee beans.

short break. Billboards as high as buildings eventually signify the beginning of the quiet mountain town of **6** ✳ **Da Lat** – its surroundings are ideal for hiking.

A side trip lasting several days can be made from here, for example westward from Da Lat along the inconsistently surfaced N 27 to the provincial capital of Buon Ma Thuot. The best coffee in Vietnam is said to come from this region. Visitors can find simple accommodation here, or stay with the Stieng, Ede or Mnong hill tribes. It is also possible to visit the village of Ban Don (Buon Don, approx. 45km/ 28mi northwest), where elephants are bred. The same road leads back to Da Lat.

Leave Da Lat from the south on the N 20 heading east to ❼**Phan Rang**. The journey leads past the Don Duong reservoir (also Da Nhim) and the huge hydroelectric power station. The Ngoan Muc Pass offers fantastic scenery – in good weather the coast 60km/37mi away is even visible. The pass road gradually winds from an elevation of around 1000m/3300ft down to the coast, where palms and cacti once again define the landscape. About 6km/4mi outside the coastal town of Phan Rang are the Cham sanctuaries of Po Klong Garai and Po Ro Me from the 13th and 14th centuries. Now follow National Highway 1 north to the fishing and resort town of ❽ ✱ ✱ **Nha Trang**. On the way are two more Cham towers (Hoa Lai) and, further north, the harbour Cam Ranh, which was used by the Americans as a Marine base between 1964 and 1973. Along this stretch, take a break at one of the restaurants built on stilts at the sea front.

Alternatively, it is possible to head back from Phan Rang on the N 1 along the coast south toward Saigon, stopping off for a swim after 150km/95mi close to Phan Thiet. Sand dunes, salt mines and fishing villages define the coastal scenery here.

Tour 3 Into the Mekong Delta

Distance: approx. 200km/125mi   **Duration:** approx. 2 days

It is just a quick hop from the hustle and bustle of Saigon to the amphibian world of the Mekong delta – the »rice bowl of the nation«. Pay a visit to the towns of Ben Tre and Can Tho – or take a couple of days to float along the nine arms and canals of the Mekong.

National Highway 1 runs south to the Mekong delta, but there is also a boat running from ❶ ✱ ✱ **Saigon** to My Tho. The branching arms of the river and canals criss-cross the landscape, which is characterized by rice fields, bamboo thickets, fruit plantations, orchid gardens and farms for fish and shrimp. The first stop is the provincial capital of ❷ ✱ **My Tho**, where it is possible to visit Vinh Trang Pagoda and a snake farm. Take the ferry further to ❸**Ben Tre**, where the famous fish sauce is produced and coconuts are processed. Day trippers can head back after a boat trip through the canals, which are lined with mangroves. Those with more time can spend the night in

④ Vinh Long in the heart of the Mekong delta – the little town lies between the two arms of the Mekong, the Tien and Hau rivers.
East of Vinh Long is **⑤ Tra Vinh**, where a number of Khmer pagodas can be marvelled at: Ba Om is said to be over 1000 years old. Cai Be is home to a floating market – a colourful attraction that can also be reached by boat. From here, take the ferry to **⑥ ✱ Can Tho**. Also worth a visit is the floating market near Phung Hiep, which can be reached by boat or by bus.

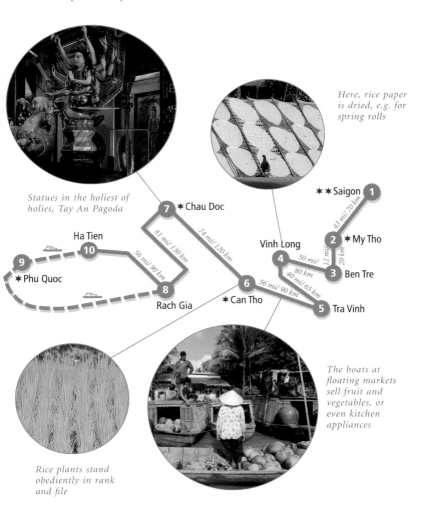

Here, rice paper is dried, e.g. for spring rolls

Statues in the holiest of holies, Tay An Pagoda

✱✱ Saigon ①

Ha Tien
⑩
81 mi/ 130 km
74 mi/ 120 km
Vinh Long
43 mi/ 70 km
② ✱ My Tho
⑨
56 mi/ 90 km
⑦ ✱ Chau Doc
④
50 mi/ 80 km
12 mi/ 20 km
✱ Phu Quoc
⑧
⑥
40 mi/ 65 km
③ Ben Tre
Rach Gia
✱ Can Tho
56 mi/ 90 km
⑤ Tra Vinh

The boats at floating markets sell fruit and vegetables, or even kitchen appliances

Rice plants stand obediently in rank and file

Another possibility is to travel further west (by boat of along Highway 91) to **⑦✶ Chau Doc**, near the Cambodian border, where the Sam mountain, a popular destination for pilgrims, towers upward. The route back takes the same road to Long Xuyen. From **⑧ Rach Gia** a modern speedboat brings visitors to Vietnam's largest island, **⑨✶ Phu Quoc**, in 2½ hours – the island constitutes the westernmost region of southern Vietnam and lies in the Gulf of Thailand. Those who wish to can take the relatively bad N 80 road a further 90km/56mi to the far southwest and the harbour of **⑩ Ha Tien**. The area is known for its tortoise farms and the bizarre rock formations in the sea. From here it is also possible to take a very long and uncomfortable ferry journey to Phu Quoc.

Tour 4 Mountains and Sea

Distance: approx. 1100km/680mi   **Duration:** 6–10 days

Mountains and sea – both can be combined on this magnificent tour. It starts by taking the train to the area around the picturesque little mountain town of Sa Pa, where it is possible to walk along the rice terraces and haggle over the price of souvenirs with the hill tribesmen. Over three or four days, the route then runs back along the coast via Hanoi – always in the direction of the sea – to Ha Long City, where the excursion boats and junks await to take visitors on a (sailing) voyage into the world of dragons.

Take the (night) train (7–10 hours) to reach a little mountain village, Lao Cai, near the Chinese border, and then board a bus or hire a taxi for the additional 38km/24mi to Sa Pa. Alternatively, make the somewhat tedious trip by bus from **①✶✶ Hanoi** (a total of 380km/236mi, approx. 8–10 hours including breakdowns), which offers even more views of the marvellous landscape. It is possible to take a side trip along the way to **②✶ Hung Temple** northwest of Hanoi (along the N 2 towards the industrial city of Viet Tri, where after a further 12km/7mi a sign points to the sanctuary of the legendary kings).
The journey continues back on the N 2 to Doan Hung, then turns left onto road no. 70 and passes **③ Thac Ba Lake**. It slowly becomes noticeable how the landscape is changing: suddenly there are terraced fields, palms with almost circular fronds and imposing houses on stilts. The last leg before Lao Cai (38km/24mi north of Sa Pa) runs along the Red River, with China lying on the opposite bank.

Heading southwest, the route leads to the highest mountain in Vietnam, Fan Si Pan (3143m/10,312ft), the immediate neighbour of

The islands of Ha Long Bay are riddled with dripstone grottoes

4 ✶✶ Sa Pa

99 mi/ 160 km

3 Thac Ba Lake

68 mi/ 110 km

2 ✶ Hung Temple

62 mi/ 100 km

1 62 mi/ 100 km

✶✶ Hanoi

Ha Long City

6

37 mi/ 60 km

5

Hai Phong

7 ✶✶ Ha Long Bay

8 ✶ Cat Ba Island

Tea is grown on large plantations in the hilly landscape north of Hung Temple

The residents of Cat Ba live increasingly from tourism. The national park covers around half of the island.

4 ✶✶ **Sa Pa**. Here it is possible to take mountain hikes or walks, or simply to visit the market, where the Hmong and Red Dao offer their goods.

Head back to Hanoi along the same route or by train, then take a car or a bus along the N 5 a further 100km/60mi east to **5** **Hai Phong**. From here it is another 60km/37mi on the new highway to **6** **Ha Long City** (the double city of Bai Chay and Hong Gai); it is also possible to get there by ferry from Hai Phong. From Ha Long City the boats and junks travel past the approximately 2000 bizarrely fissured rocky islands of **7** ✶✶ **Ha Long Bay** in the Gulf of Tonkin, docking at caves and floating villages, or visit **8** ✶ **Cat Ba Island**, the largest island in Ha Long Bay, and its national park.

Those with more time who are interested in less touristy places in the north of Vietnam can plan to make a trip by ferry to the island of Quan Lan and the Van Don peninsula in the neighbouring Bai Tu Long Bay.

Sights from A to Z

MANY TREASURES AWAIT IN VIETNAM: PATINA-COVERED PALACES, PAGODAS AND TEMPLES, THE PRIMORDIAL LANDSCAPES OF HA LONG BAY AND THE MEKONG DELTA. AND AFTER THE HUSTLE AND BUSTLE OF HANOI OR SAIGON, VISITORS CAN UNWIND BY ENJOYING WATER SPORTS AT FANTASTIC BEACHES.

Buon Ma Thuot

E 6

Province: Dak Lak (capital)
Population: 160,000

Region: Central Highlands

Waterfalls, magnificent rolling hills and elephants – these are the main attractions of the remote Dak Lak highlands around the provincial capital of Buon Ma Thuot. The nearby Yok Don National Park also lures the adventurous with its wilderness and wildlife, hiking trails and elephant safaris.

Delightful highland region
Coffee, tea and rubber plantations characterize the largest province in the country, but there are also rice and maize fields as well as herds of cattle. Despite the migration of many Vietnamese to this region, the hill tribes still play an important role, especially the Ede and the Mnong. The area is also known for its elephants. As late as the 1930s, the area around Buon Ma Thuots was considered a **hunting paradise**; to this day there is still a large game population in the forests. The lakes, above all Dak Lak in the south, are known for their high fish count. However, in certain parts of the forest, the effects of the deployment of Agent Orange and deforestation can hardly be overlooked.

What to See in Buon Ma Thuot

Victory Monument
Buon Ma Thuot's central square is dominated by an enormous monument commemorating the events of 10 March 1975, when Vietcong and North Vietnamese troops »liberated« the city, leading inevitably to the defeat of South Vietnam.

Such pile dwellings are found in the mountain regions in particular

► VISITING BUON MA THOUT

INFORMATION

Dak Lak Tourist
3 Phan Chu Trinh
Tel. 0 50/85 21 08 and 85 23 22
www.daklaktourist.com
Also in Hotel Dam San
(see below, daily 7am–5pm)

TRANSPORT

Buon Ma Thuot Airport
(10km/6mi outside the city)
Tel. 0 50/95 50 55

EVENTS

Elephant Festival
In March of each year, these heavy creatures compete in a race along the Serepok River. There is also a canoe race and numerous folklore displays with music and food. Further elephant spectacles are held in Ban Don, where the thick-skinned giants even play football.

MARKET

Those who enjoy watching the everyday life at the market should not miss the large food market on Quang Trung Street, open daily.

WHERE TO EAT

► Inexpensive

Quan Ngon
72–74 Ba Trieu, tel. 0 50/85 19 09
Large restaurant serving Vietnamese food in a stilt house or in the garden. Alongside the usual dishes, regional specialities such as smoked game and poultry are served.

WHERE TO STAY

► Mid-range

Cao Nguyen Hotel
65 Phan Chu Trinh
Tel. 0 50/85 59 60, fax 85 19 12
State-run hotel with upmarket standards. All of the rooms offer satellite television.

► Inexpensive

Dam San Hotel
212–214 Nguyen Cong Tru
Tel. 0 50/85 12 34, fax 85 23 09
damsantour@dng.vnn.vn
The best hotel in town, slightly east of the centre: attractive rooms with parquet floors, satellite TV and bathtub; pool, tennis courts, good restaurant.

The Dak Lak Museum (folklore and ethnology, on Nguyen Du Street, at the corner of Le Duan Street), where much can be learned about the province, its flora, fauna and culture, is worth visiting. The **exhibition about the region's ethnic minorities** – there are said to be 31 groups – is outstanding. Primarily on display are items of clothing and musical instruments, but equipment used for taming elephants as well as a model of an Ede stilt house are also on show.

Dak Lak Museum
⊙
Opening hours: daily
7.30am–11.30am, 1.30pm–4.30pm

Around Buon Ma Thuot

Around 20km/12mi southwest of Buon Ma Thuot (N 14), on the Serepok River, lies the »virgin waterfall«. Here, the adventurous can practice rock climbing and abseiling (bookings at the tourist office),

Trinh Nu Waterfall

survey the idyllic scenery either on foot or on the back of a horse or an elephant, explore caves, take a boat trip, or go fishing. Simple **accommodation** is offered in bungalows or a traditional long house; a local bar provides sustenance and refreshment.

Buon Tur The beautifully situated, mist-spraying Dray Sap Falls can be reached by travelling southwest from Buon Ma Thuot via Doc Lap. A worthwhile stop can be made after 14km/9mi, turning left to the village of Buon Tur, the inhabitants of which are from the Ede ethnic minority, and subsist from cattle breeding and growing vegetables. Although the village has been heavily influenced by Vietnamese culture, traces of the **Ede cultural identity** can still be found. The matriarchal system is still intact, and women occupy the prominent position as the head of the household and centre of family life. Living together with their extended families in 30m/98ft-long pile dwellings, each couple and their children have their own small living area. Cows, pigs and fowl scurry about below.

Dray Sap Falls A few miles away, in the midst of the rain forest, lie the arch-shaped Dray Sap Falls (accessible from 6am–7pm). With a height of almost 15m/49ft and a width of over 100m/328ft, the view of the falls is somewhat obstructed by the clouds of spray, which explains the name – Dray Sap means »**waterfall of mist**«. The spray is especially refreshing at the left side of the pool, which can be reached by walking through bamboo thickets and climbing over rocks.

! **Baedeker TIP**

Rice wine tasting

One of the specialities of the highlands is the honey-yellow Ruou can: a mild (20% alcohol) wine made from rice, sticky rice or grain, which is traditionally enjoyed in groups, sipped through long, bendable »straws« (can) from a clay mug (che). It is commonly consumed in combination with smoked game, roast veal, fried chicken or tasty Com lam (sticky rice cooked in bamboo).

With a total area of 115,000ha/444 sq mi, Yok Don National Park is the largest in Vietnam. It lies near the border with Cambodia, just 37km/23mi west of Buon Ma Thuot. Many types of pharmaceutically useable plants grow in the mixed forests, as do orchids and a number of varieties of bamboo. Elephants particularly enjoy the leaves of the bamboo trees – 80 to 100 of the thick-skinned creatures are said to live in the grassy forests of the national park. Game wardens claim to have counted a number of tigers and even **leopards** in an area which is closed to visitors. More commonly found are gibbons, Sambar deer, wolves, wild buffalo and crocodiles, as well as hornbills, peafowl and pheasants. Nearly 500 plant species, around 50 mammal species – about half of which are endangered – and 245 registered bird species can be encountered in the area.

✳ **Yok Don National Park**

It is especially popular to undertake an expedition on an elephant, which can be booked for a few hours or even for an entire day.

Alongside the pretty landscape and the particularly diverse wildlife of the area, remnants of the Ho Chi Minh Trail and a number of battlefields can be seen. It is best to plan a trip to Yok Don National Park as far as possible from the rainy season (April to October). Overnight accommodation can be found in the nearby villages and in a camp with huts.

The elephant village of Ban Don, just 2km/1.2mi from Yok Don National Park and approximately 45km/28mi northwest of Buon Ma Thuot, is known throughout the land. Settled in the vicinity are Khmer, Thai, Lao and Jarai. Ban Don itself is primarily inhabited by the Mnong and Ede minority groups, both of which are organized according to a matriarchal system. Wild elephants are hunted by the Mnong and domesticated with the help of tamed animals. Later they are mostly used for the **transportation of precious woods**. Around 50 of the animals live permanently in Ban Don. On the edge of the village, which is often overrun with tourists,

Elephant handlers in the village of Ban Don

lies the grave of the legendary Khonsonuk (1850–1924), who in his day was the most famous elephant hunter far and wide. Among the 244 elephants he tamed, there was said to be a white one which was a present to the King of Siam. Elephant tamers (Mahouts) still come here, bringing offerings and asking for success in taming their animals. A number of graves display peacocks upon tusks, which are seen as distinguished offerings for the next life.

★
**Elephant Village
Ban Don**

Also worth a trip is the 500ha/1.9 sq mi Lak Lake (Ho Dak Lak), which lies 50km/31mi south of Buon Ma Thuot. Its location at the foot of the Annamite range is very pretty, and it is worth a short climb to enjoy the view of the lake and its surroundings. The lake is well known for its high fish count and wide variety of bird life (including cranes and storks). On the banks of the lake are the remains of the small palace of the former emperor Bao Dai (►Famous People). Many Vietnamese come here, particularly in spring, to watch **boat and elephant races**. Also of interest is a visit to the neighbouring village of the Mnong. Visitors can make trips onto the shallow lake in rowing boats or even on the back of an elephant.

Lak Lake

✶ Can Tho

C 7

Province: Can Tho (capital)
Population: 500,000

Region: Mekong Delta

Can Tho, the largest city in the Mekong delta, is a good base for excursions into the amphibious everyday life of the region. From here it is possible – early in the morning is best – to visit the delta's floating markets, take a trip into the mangrove swamps in the far south of the country, and in the evening go for a stroll down the promenade of the Can Tho River.

What to See in Can Tho

✶
Munirang-syaram Pagoda

Munirangsyaram Pagoda (36 Hoa Binh Street) was built in 1946. It serves as a temple for the Khmer community of Can Tho (approximately 2000 members). Because the Khmer practice Theravada Buddhism, there are no depictions of Bodhisattvas, gods or patron saints, only likenesses of the historical Buddha Sakyamuni. The main court of the pagoda is reached through a mighty, richly decorated portal. On the upper floor is a 1.5m/5ft-high Buddha statue beneath a holy Bodhi tree. The resident monks are usually happy to welcome visitors, but the doors tend to be closed during lunchtime.

Can Tho Map

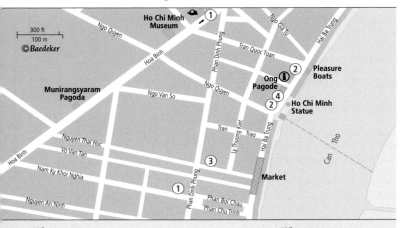

Where to stay
① Victoria Can Tho Hotel
② Quoc Te International Hotel
③ Saigon Can Tho Hotel
④ Tay Ho

Where to eat
① Quan Com Vietnam
② Nam Bo

Visitors to Munirangsyaram Pagoda are greeted by friendly Khmer monks

An impressive silver statue of Ho Chi Minh (► Famous People) marks the beginning of the pretty **esplanade**, which is decorated with flowers and trees and offers a number of nice cafés.

Nearby is Quang Thanh De Pagoda, which was built by the city's once-populous Chinese community. On the main alter is Quan Cong with his sentinels, to the left is Thien Hau (the sea goddess) and on the right is the god of luck, Ong Bon. At the table where incense sticks are sold there is usually a **calligrapher** writing Chinese characters into red prayer scrolls (opening times: daily 5am–8pm).

Quang Thanh De pagoda

⊙

Around Can Tho

Many travellers visit Can Tho for the various boat tours that are offered from here. It is possible to rent a small rowing boat, take trips through orange and mango plantations, or navigate the Mekong in large motorboats. A visit to one of the so-called **floating markets** is definitely worthwhile; all kinds of fruit and vegetables as well as drinks and kitchen appliances are sold here, and it is even possible to get a haircut. The little barges are often so heavily loaded that it seems they are just about to sink; many houseboats have crooked frames, scantly covered in an attempt to conceal the family's »living quarters«. Men and women strain at the overlapping oars of some of the sampans.

★
Boat tours on the Mekong

⊙ VISITING CAN THO AND SURROUNDINGS

INFORMATION

Can Tho Tourist
20 Hai Ba Trung, Ninh Kieu, Can Tho
Tel. 0 71/82 18 54 and 82 42 21
Mon–Sat 7am–11am,
1pm–5pm
www.canthotourist.com.vn
canthotour@hcm.vnn.vn

EVENTS

Each year, from the 13th to the 15th day of the fourth lunar month (April/May) the **Khmer new year's celebration** is held in the Mekong delta. Also, in the middle of the tenth lunar month (October/November) in Soc Trang, the Khmer holds the famous **Ghe Ngo Festival**, a race with traditional boats.

SHOPPING

The lively, colourful and clamorous market of Can Tho takes up the entire middle part of Hai Ba Trung Street, the section that is closed to traffic. From poultry to fish and seafood, fruit and vegetables to rice and noodles, everything the heart desires can be found here.

ENTERTAINMENT

Don't miss the chance to take a cruise down the river on one of the fairy-light-festooned **pleasure boats**, for example the Ninh Kieu ship: here, men and women present a programme of Vietnamese opera, words of wisdom and heart-rendering love songs (the ships depart from the esplanade in Can Tho from 7pm to 10pm for a round trip on the Bassac River).

DAY TRIP

A cruise on the Cai Be Princess: The elegant, traditional wooden ship departs from Cai Be Floating Market (maximum of 35 passengers), chugs along to Vinh Long to visit the fruit orchard and stops for lunch in Sa Dec, return to Saigon by road (information: tel. 08/51 09 25, CaiBe-PrincessCruise@yahoo.com).

WHERE TO EAT

► Inexpensive

① **Quan Com Vietnam**
16 Nam Ky Khoi Nghia, Can Tho
Tel. 0 71/82 31 65
A pleasant spot on Can Tho's »food street«, frequented by locals. Very good rice and noodle dishes.

② **Nam Bo**
50 Hai Ba Trung, Can Tho
Tel. 0 71/82 39 08
daily 8am–11pm
Eatery with a panoramic view: from the balcony overlooking the boardwalk you can keep and eye on the evening action of Can Tho, and the Western-Vietnamese dishes are good value.

Phuong Thuy Restaurant
Vinh Long, Vinh Long Province
(approx. 35km/22mi northwest of
Can Tho)
With a pleasant view over the Mekong, this restaurant, located directly
on the river, is a good place to break
the day trip for Vietnamese or
international cuisine.

WHERE TO STAY
► Mid-range
② *Quoc Te International Hotel*
12 Hai Ba Trung, Can Tho
Tel. 0 71/82 20 80
Fax 82 10 39
E-mail: ksquo-ct@hcm.vnn.vn
Small, modern hotel on the esplanade
with a good restaurant serving Vietnamese and international dishes.

③ *Saigon Can Tho Hotel*
55 Phan Dinh Phung, Can Tho
Tel. 0 71/82 58 31, fax 82 32 88
E-mail: sgcthotel@hcm.vnn.vn
Modern hotel on the main street with
slightly overpriced rooms (some
without windows). Karaoke and sauna.

► Budget
④ *Tay Ho*
36 Hai Ba Trung, Can Tho
Tel. 0 71/82 33 92
An inexpensive alternative to the top
hotels in Can Tho (mini hotel).

Baedeker recommendation

► Luxury
① *Victoria Can Tho Hotel*
283 Tran Van Khoe Cai Khe Ward, Can Tho
Tel. 0 71/081 01 11, fax 82 92 59
www.victoriahotels-asia.com
victoriact@hcm.vnn.vn
Accommodation on the riverbank with
colonial flair: splendid rooms with parquet
floors and every luxury. Two pools. Good
patio bar.

Truong An Tourist Villas
Vinh Long, Vinh Long Province
(approximately 35km/22mi northwest
of Can Tho)
Tel. 0 70/82 31 61, fax 80 02 40
The small bungalows of this complex
are found on the road to the ferry,
around 4km/2.5mi outside Vinh
Long. The park-like surroundings are
most inviting (mini hotel).

Phuong Nam Hotel
92 Phan Dinh Phung,
Ca Mau, Minh-Hai-Province
(approx. 150km/93mi south of Can
Tho)
Tel. 07 80/83 17 52 and 87 70 39,
fax 83 44 02
The best hotel in Ca Mau, rooms with
fan or air-conditioning, some with
TV. Breakfast included (guesthouse).

Two of the three larger floating markets in the area lie to the west of
Can Tho: the smaller one only 7km/4mi away in Cai Rang, the larger, very hectic one a further 10km/6mi away in Phong Dien.
The locality of Phung Hiep, 25km/15mi southeast of Can Tho, is a
transport hub where several canals meet, the longest of which leads
to the remote province of Minh Hai. Upon one of these waterways,
the Yang Canal, a small floating market is also held early each morning. It is very popular with tourists due to the fact that, from a
bridge, the activity of the market can be well observed – and photo-

★
Floating markets

◄ Phung Hiep

View of the floating market of Phung Hiep

graphed of course. Because Phung Hiep lies directly on the N 1, it is easily reached using public transport.

By boat, it is also possible to reach the island of My Phuoc in the Hau River, a branch of the Mekong. When travelling through the narrow canals, it is sometimes necessary to duck to avoid the mighty fronds of the coconut palms, which grow far beyond the banks. The route drifts past gardens and pretty houses. It is like a visit to the **Garden of Eden**, with stops at the many orchards where jackfruit, bananas, pineapples, mangos, papayas etc. can be sampled.

Soc Trang

Soc Trang, the main locality in the province of the same name, is located 30km/19mi southeast of Phung Hiep. The main attraction is the nearby Khmer Matoc Pagoda (also: Chua Doi, »bat temple«), ornately decorated with depictions of dancers and animals. The large **bats**, which live in the treesaround the sanctuary, are a peculiarity of the place. In the late afternoons they can be observed gradually awakening as the temperature drops, preparing themselves before flitting away on the evening's hunting trip. Some of them have a wingspan of 1.5m/5ft! The interior walls of the pagoda list the names of other Khmer congregations and depict scenes from the life of Buddha. The life-like portrayal of a monk, who even wears glasses, is quite astonishing.

Minh Hai Province

Ca Mau

As the economic centre of Minh Hai province, the most sparsely populated province of the Mekong delta, the town of Ca Mau – like all the other Mekong towns – has experienced rapid development in recent years.

Because Minh Hai is the only province in the Mekong delta without any of the major estuary creeks flowing through it, it is the site of much standing water, with swamps and moors. The countryside is covered with dense **mangrove and bog forests**. There are hoards of mosquitoes buzzing about. The place itself doesn't offer much worth seeing, but botanists and ornithologists are sure to have a field day in the area's wetlands.

Alongside a Catholic and a Protestant church, Ca Mau is also home to a large Cao Dai temple, which was built in the 1960s.

At Ca Mau's market, fish, tortoises and snakes are sold. The latter are still alive – connoisseurs agree that snake meat is best enjoyed freshly slaughtered. A large portion of the reptiles from the market in Ca Mau are brought to Saigon to be prepared in the finest restaurants.

U Minh Forest lies directly north of Ca Mau. This approximately 1000 sq km/386 sq mi primeval forest numbers among the largest self-contained mangrove forests on Earth. It is a habitat for birds and reptiles, which find ideal living conditions in this marshland. Because the area provided a very good hideout for the Vietcong, it long served as a retreating ground and field of operations against the Americans, who sprayed defoliants to deprive their invisible enemy of their natural cover. The trees are gradually recovering from this destruction, yet today the forest faces the new **danger of deforestation**, firstly to exploit the lumber, secondly to reclaim expanses of water for fish and shrimp harvesting. Measures taken by the government to limit deforestation have so far had little effect. The area can be reached by boat from Ca Mau.

✱ U Minh Forest

> **? DID YOU KNOW …?**
>
> ■ … that, according to the WWF (2005), the mangrove forests of the Mekong delta in the south of Vietnam are the third largest in the world? Larger forests are only to be found in Cuba and Bangladesh.

Around 50km/31mi south of Ca Mau are two bird sanctuaries: Hiep Hung and Than Khanh. It is possible to take a boat tour there from Ca Mau, but the timid birds can only rarely be observed at close range.

Bird sanctuaries

Vinh Long Province

Surrounded by water, encircled by boats and stilt houses, the island on which the centre of Vinh Long lies seems like a medieval fortress. The first impression is of rather hectic and loud streets, yet the esplanades, with their cafés and restaurants, provide a place to relax and take in life on the edge of the Tien Giang. Vinh Long is also known by the name Cuu Long (Nine Dragons), after which the entire ►Mekong delta is named. The new suspension bridge over the Tien Giang (upper Mekong), which resembles the Golden Gate Bridge in San Francisco, was built with Australian assistance. Vinh Long is a good base for excursions into the marvellous surrounding areas.

Vinh Long

Thick, semicircular barques full of coconuts, rambutans and rice; delicate female ferryboat pilots, in cone hats, who row powerfully; fishing barges and sampans with watchful eyes painted onto the bows

✱✱ Trips to the river islands

The narrow canals of the Mekong are crossed on these bridges

– everything flows, glides and chugs along with the Mekong River. Every ten minutes, the fishermen pull nets hanging with octopuses' spindly tentacles out of the canals. Peculiar bamboo frames (»monkey bridges«) protrude across a thousand waterways. A sleepy, dreamlike water-world exists beyond the markets and tourist spots. Don't miss the chance to visit the little islands of **Binh Hoa Phuoc** and **An Binh**, which can only be reached by boat. The tourist trail here includes a visit to experience the everyday world of Vietnam's industry, including for example a visit to a rice paper and puffed rice factory, an incense manufacturer or lychee farmers. Cai Be Market, with its »swimming« stands, is also worth a visit.

Sa Dec The former capital of Dong Thap Province, Sa Dec (23km/14mi west of Vinh Long), has become known as the location for the film of **Marguerite Duras's** novel *The Lover*. The town's many nurseries are remarkable: throughout Vietnam, cut flowers are particularly sought after, and those from Sa Dec are transported daily to Saigon.

Tra Vinh Most tourists come to Tra Vinh (67km/42mi southeast of Vinh Long) to admire the Khmer temple or to watch storks.
The thousand-year-old **Sam Rong Ek Temple** (4km/2.5mi south of the town centre) could have been brought here directly from Thailand or Cambodia, as it displays all the hallmarks of the temple architecture common there. These include the stacked roofs, the stylized Nagas on the roof ridges and the horns on the gables, which symbolize the fire bird Garuda. Inside, as is normal for Hinayana Buddhism, are depictions only of the historic Buddha. There are so many of them that no one can name the actual figure.

A couple of miles outside Tra Vinh, beyond a lotus pond and stupas and surrounded by frangipani trees, is An Vuong Pagoda (photo ► p.72). The site of the temple is said to be 1200 years old, though the existing building is considerably newer. Within the sanctuary are wall and ceiling paintings depicting scenes from the life of Buddha. The pictures that were added when the building was last renovated in 1939 can be recognized by the inclusion of uniforms worn by the French colonialists. After the harvest, rice from surrounding fields is piled up next to the altar, where it is guarded by an impressive golden Sakyamuni figure.

✳ **An Vuong Pagoda**

Over 100 storks live on the grounds of Hang Pagoda (6km/3.5mi south of Tra Vinh). They are best seen early in the mornings, when they circle above the treetops, or before sunset. An even larger group of around 300 storks can be seen near Giong Lon Pagoda (43km/ 27mi southeast of Tra Vinh).

stork watching

✳ # Chau Doc

C 7

Province: An Giang **Region:** Mekong Delta
Population: 105,000

The Mekong town of Chau Doc is home to many fish farmers: down in the »cellar« beneath the floating buildings and the houseboats flap tons of thriving fish. Visitors can venture deep into life along the Mekong River on boat tours. The broad ethnic diversity of the region means there are many different temples, mosques and churches, and Cambodia is just a stone's throw away.

What to See in Chau Doc

Chau Doc is home to the most fish farmers in Vietnam. Their houses float upon empty oil barrels on the Hau Giang River (aka: Bassac), one of the Mekong's eight arms. It is mainly **catfish** that throng in the nets beneath the houses. When the water becomes shallower during the dry season, the houses move to the middle of the river, where the piscine lodgers have enough air to breath.

Fish farmers

North of Quan Cong Temple is a ferry which brings visitors to the island of Con Tien and its pile-dwelling settlements, but the river journey is more enjoyable in a small boat, from which it is also possible to view the fish farming houseboats.

Boat trips

Between the market stands of Gia Long Street towers the imposing portal of Quan Cong Temple. The courtyard is usually very lively, as many children come here to play. Two dragon-figures watch over the

Quan Cong Temple

Life on the Mekong

site, and inside two tortoises wander around, said to look after the temple's well-being (in Buddhism, the tortoise is a symbol of immortality). On the main altar stands a bust of the red-faced General Quan Cong, clothed in a green robe and wearing a richly decorated crown.

Mosques Chau Doc also has several mosques for the Muslim Cham community, including Chau Giang Mosque on the other side of the river and Mubarak Mosque, which houses a Koran school for children and young people. Visitors should not enter during prayers, held five times per day.

✴ Sam Mountain (Nui Sam)

In the northwest of An Giang province rise a number of hilltops, the very last foothills of the Cambodian Phnom Damrei range. Among these, 3km/2mi south of Chau Doc, is Sam Mountain. In Vietnamese, »Sam« means something like **»prawn«** – which the hill does actually resemble from a distance. Only 230m/755ft in height, it is not particularly imposing, but the peak offers an extensive view over the Mekong delta, which is flat and just barely above sea level, all the way to Cambodia in the distance.

Over the course of the year, the area around the hill presents an **enchanting display of colours**: between August and December the land is covered with water as far as the horizon, with only the embankments, densely built over with wooden huts, rising up from this shimmering watery world, as if drawn with a ruler. From the beginning of the year until April the wet rice paddies finally glow a magnificent lime-green, and in May and June the ears are ripe for harvesting – an expansive, undulating sea of gold. In the evenings, the setting sun bathes everything in a fiery red light, until the sky itself appears to be in flames.

Ba Chua Xu Temple

Ba Chua Xu Temple was built in the first half of the 19th century and was continually altered until the 1970, to the point where not much of the original construction remains. The story of the person of Chua Xu and of the building of the temple is not quite clear. The most important **celebration** takes place from the 23rd to the 26th day of the fourth lunar month of each year, when pilgrims from across the land come and spend the night near the temple. On display in glass cases inside the building to the left are countless offerings in honour of Chua Xu: finely embroidered sequined clothes, head-high mother-of-pearl vases, strings of pearls, crowns and gold bars.

Chua Hang (cave pagoda)

Monks live in the lower part of the cave pagoda on the west side of Sam Mountain. The founder of the pagoda was the **seamstress Le Thi Tha**, who retreated here around 50 years ago to lead a cloistered life. The legend has it that upon her arrival, she came upon two snakes, which she tamed and then converted to a life of meditation. Upon her death, the two snakes disappeared. The grave of Le Thi Tha, as well as that of a high-ranking monk, can be found in the lower part of the pagoda. In the upper part are statues of A Di Da, the Buddha of the Past, and of the historical Buddha Sakyamuni; behind them, in a grotto, is a shrine dedicated to the Goddess of Compassion.

Ba Chuc

Very near to the border with Cambodia, just a few miles southwest of Sam Mountain, a pagoda commemorates the raids on Vietnamese soil by the Khmer Rouge between 1975 and 1978. The official justification thereof was Cambodia's historic claim on the provinces of the Mekong delta. Within just two weeks in April 1978, a total of 3157 civilians were routinely murdered. Today horrific photographs and a memorial recall the massacre. As at Cheung Ek Pagoda at the Killing Fields outside the gates of Phnom Penh, the bones of the murdered are laid out at Ba Chuc.

Ha Tien

In the middle of an attractive landscape in the province of Kien Giang, Ha Tien is located on the Gulf of Siam just 8km/5mi from the border with Cambodia. Unlike other parts of the Mekong delta,

▶ VISITING CHAU DOC

INFORMATION
**Saigon Mekong Green Tour
(Saigon Tourist)**
53 Bis, Le Loi, Chau Phu, Chau Doc
Tel. 0 76/56 23 45
www.mekonggreentours.com
Information also in hotels

EXCURSION
Boats running daily (public or with the fast boat from the Victoria Hotel) take passengers from Chau Doc to Phnom Penh in Cambodia (approx. 4 hours).

EVENTS
**Via Ba (Ba Chua Xu) –
Pilgrimage at Nui Sam**
For the Chinese New Year and the annual Via Ba Festival (May/June) thousands of believers and tourists flock to the top of the 230m/755ft-high mountain at midnight – Taoists, Caodaists, and Christians, as well as Buddhists and Muslim Cham, many travelling specifically for the occasion from outside the country, places such as Hong Kong, Taiwan and the USA.

WHERE TO EAT
▶ Inexpensive
Bassac Restaurant
32 Le Loi Street
Chau Doc
Tel. 0 76/86 50 10
daily 6am–11pm
The magnificent riverside terrace of the colonially tinged Victoria Hotel (see below) is a great place to enjoy a meal: French and Vietnamese dishes are accompanied by wines and cocktails.

Lam Hung Ky
71 Chi Lang
Chau Doc

Tel. 0 76/86 67 45
Restaurant near the market, serving the best Chinese and Vietnamese cuisine in town.

Tan Phat Restaurant
Hong Chong
Ha Tien
Tel. 0 77/85 44 04
Large restaurant built on piers with a wonderful view of the island. Guests are served extremely fresh shrimp and fish – practically »from the net to the plate«.

Xuan Thanh Restaurant
Corner of Ben Tran Hau/Tham Tuong Sam (near the market)
Ha Tien
Tel. 0 77/85 21 97
The best place in Ha Tien. Try one of the many local specialities made with coconut.

WHERE TO STAY

Baedeker recommendation

▶ Luxury
Victoria Chau Doc
32 Le Loi Street, Chau Doc
Tel. 0 76/86 50 10, fax 86 50 20
www.victoriahotels-asia.com
resa.chaudoc@victoriahotels-asia.com
Luxury in a colonial atmosphere: convincing replica of a colonial palace with French-Vietnamese flair. Located right on the bank of the Hau River.

▶ Budget
Thuan Loi
18 Tran Hung Dao Street, Chau Doc
Tel. 0 76/86 61 34, fax 86 53 80
hotelthuanloi@hcm.vnn.vn

Hovering on stilts over the Mekong, this mini hotel has 26 rooms and a small restaurant.

Khai Hoan Hotel
239 Phuong Thanh, Ha Tien
Tel. 0 77/85 22 54
Small guesthouse near the river with pleasant rooms and air conditioning or ventilators.

To Chau Hotel
4F Le Loi, Rach Gia
Tel. 0 77/86 37 18, fax 86 21 11
Even if this guesthouse doesn't appear particularly inviting from outside, the rooms are fine, with air conditioning or ventilators. Large restaurant, bicycle and boat rental for local excursions.

in addition to long sandy beaches, the area around Ha Tien features limestone formations with an extended system of **caves**, in which temples have been built. The town possesses old colonial buildings and its inhabitants live from agriculture and fish farming. Due to its proximity to Cambodia, it has become a distribution hub for smuggled goods from the neighbouring country over the recent years.

Northeast of Ha Tien, on a chain of hills known as Nui Lang (the hill of the tombs), is the final resting place of the Mac family. On the initiative of the first emperor of the Nguyen dynasty, Gia Long, the Mac family tombs were built in 1809 in thanks for their providing him with shelter during the Tay Son uprising. The tombs are in the traditional Chinese style, horseshoe shaped with depictions of dragons, lions, tigers and phoenixes. The largest tomb belongs to the **first ancestor, Mac Cuu** himself.

★
Tombs of the Mac family

Thach Dong, the »stone cave« 3km/2mi outside of Ha Tien, holds an underground temple. At the entrance stands a memorial to 130 people who lost their lives in a massacre by the Khmer Rouge in 1979. Inside are tablets dedicated to the Jade Emperor and the Goddess of Compassion (opening times: daily 7am–5pm).

A Buddha figure watches over the graves of the Mac family outside Ha Tien

Mui Nai	The beaches near Ha Tien, with their clear, warm water and fine sand, are the only ones in the entire Mekong delta. Due to their remote location and proximity to the Cambodian border, they have hardly been developed. Around 4km/2.5mi south of the city, the rocky range of Mui Nai forms a promontory, on both sides of which are beaches.
Hon Chon	Also very beautiful is Duong Beach on the Hon Chon peninsula, 20km/12mi south of Ha Tien. Here, there are long, sandy beaches with palms and clear but often very shallow water, alongside rocks that extend into the sea, the end of a limestone range which runs to the south from Ha Tien. A number of caves have formed here. One of them, the **Hang Tien Grotto**, is where the later emperor Gia Long is said to have hid during the Tay Son uprising in 1784. Close by – unfortunately unmissable – is a cement factory.
Duong Beach	Just a few miles further on, the road ends at a Buddhist cave-temple, Chua Hang. From here, it is possible to walk to Duong Beach, a real

Duong Beach, near the Father and Son Island

gem with fish restaurants and boats. The Father and Son Island (Hon Phu Tu), a few hundred metres from the coast, resembles a column with a pedestal that has been eroded by the waves.

The centre of Rach Gia, on the Gulf of Siam in the far west of the Mekong delta, stretches between two canalized arms of the Cai Lon River. Rach Gia and Long Xuyen are joined by a system of canals that resembles a rope ladder, with the main canal being the Thoai Ha. Alongside the cultivation and processing of tropical fruit, fishing also plays an important role in this port town. A walk through the streets of Rach Gia presents a chance to see splendid villas from the colonial era as well as pretty cafés, numerous shops and colourful markets. All in all, the city makes a very pleasant and prosperous impression. The **Rach Gia Museum** (27 Nguyen Van Troi Street) displays archaeological finds from the historic town of Oc Eo, the ruins of which can be visited 12km/7.5mi east of Rach Gia (opening times: Mon–Fri 7.30am–11.30am, 1.30pm–4.30pm, Sat mornings only).

North of the city centre, in Quang Trung Street, stands the 200 year-old **Phat Lon Pagoda** (Big Buddha Pagoda), which was built by the Khmer in the Theravada Buddhist style. The carved roofs and the wall paintings depicting scenes from the life of Buddha are particularly impressive. The large park, with a lotus pond and a stupa field, is a nice place to linger. Around 30 monks live in the buildings at the back of the monastery.

Rach Gia

✶ Cu Chi

D 7

Province: Ho Chi Minh City (city state)   **Region:** South

For the Vietnamese, the notorious Cu Chi tunnels are a reminder of the resistance against the South Vietnamese government and of the citizens who died in this tunnel system during the Vietnam War. School classes, former guerrillas and guests of the state come and go here, especially in Ben Duoc, the larger complex.

First of all, visitors are shown a **film on the history** of the Vietnam War and the building of the tunnel – from the point of view of those in power now, naturally. A map illustrates the magnitude of the tunnel complex and points out the positions of the Americans, the South Vietnamese Army and the Vietcong. Drawings and cross-section diagrams illustrate the construction of the tunnels, in three levels, each up to 10m/33ft deep.

Through the system of tunnels, the Vietcong soldiers could get as far as Cholon in the South Vietnamese metropolis. The brief occupation of the US Embassy (or its garden) in Saigon by Vietcong guerrillas

✶ ✶
Tunnel complex
🕐
Opening hours:
daily
7.30am–5.30pm

TUNNELS OF CU CHI

★★ At a depth of 3m/10ft the air is stifling, and sweat oozes from every pore. Your little rucksack scrapes along the ceiling, and your skin and hair are covered with crumbling earth as it falls. Even in the tourist tunnels, some places are so narrow that you can only move forward by crawling along on your front. Claustrophobics and anyone who is overweight are advised to give the visit to this system of tunnels a miss.

🕐 Opening times:
daily 7.30am–5.30pm

Creation
In the 1930s and 1940s, trenches and underground chambers served as hiding places and weaponry stores for the guerrillas who fought against the French. Gradually these were connected by means of corridors; in the war against the Americans the system of tunnels was extended further. Whole villages took part in the work, using the simplest of tools.

Extent
The concealed network eventually extended from the Vietnam-Cambodia border along the Ho Chi Minh Trail (▶DMZ) and all the way to Saigon's Chinese quarter, Cholon. At the end of the war up to 16,000 Vietkong soldiers and their families are said to have lived a total of around 250km/150mi of tunnels.

Shots from nowhere
Oblivious to their enemy under the ground, American troops established the headquarters of the 25th Infantry Division in the vicinity of the tunnels in 1966. At first they could not explain the mysterious nocturnal attacks on the military camp, which – above ground – was well defended. Then they discovered the tunnels. About 50,000 US soldiers scoured the terrain for the well-camouflaged entrances into the underground realm.

Carpet bombing
The villages surrounding Cu Chi were compulsorily evacuated and the area declared a »fire free zone«. Countless carpet bombing sorties were mounted and several million litres of poison were dropped on the region, which was eventually almost completely deforested with napalm.

»Tunnel rats«
The so-called tunnel rats, agile GIs specially trained for battle in the tunnels, forced their way singly into the tunnels, explored them, took documents, laid mines and destroyed the underground chambers. Many of them lost their lives in the course of these deployments in close combat with Vietcong soldiers or by falling prey to vicious traps.

① An underground city
The guerrillas lived on three floors up to 10m/33ft underground. The narrow shafts opened out into an underground labyrinth with sleeping and communal rooms, sick bays with operating tables, kitchens, and prayer rooms with shrines, as well as workshops, store rooms and bomb-proof chambers. Babies were even born in the tunnels, seeing the light of day only years later.

② Entrances
Tiny trapdoors, grown over with foliage and grass, led into the outside world. All were protected by means of primitive but effective traps. Some tunnel corridors are said to have ended in a river, making it easier to flee when being pursued or bombarded.

③ Perfect camouflage
Ventilation was achieved by means of inconspicuous bamboo pipes, and chilli and pepper were grown around the ventilation shafts in order to confuse sniffer dogs. Later, the dogs were unable to distinguish between the Vietnamese and the Americans, as the Vietcong had started to use American soap, aftershave and clothing, which they took from their prisoners.

④ Deadly traps
Attempts to drive the Vietcong soldiers out of the tunnels were countered with numerous tricks, for example trapdoors over ditches in which sharpened bamboo sticks, sometimes prepared with poison, lay in wait – so-called booby traps. Dummy tunnels and entrances lured intruders into such traps. In addition, bombs and mines were laid under the turf.

ll of th
vere co
rox. 80
0cm/2f
een sp
igh and
ccomm

during the Tet Festival of 1968 was possible only because of this tunnel.

It is possible to tour the complex only with a guide or in a group. Visitors pass barely perceptible tunnel entrances, around 20 x 40cm/8 x 16in in size, into which the guides disappear as a demonstration. Field kitchens and base hospitals, trap doors, captured tanks and oversized bomb craters can be seen above ground. The tourist trail finally leads through »minefields« armed with blanks.

 CU CHI

GETTING THERE

The tunnel complex can be reached from Saigon via the N 22 (approximately 60km/40mi northwest of Saigon); upon reaching the town of Cu Chi, turn right and follow the blue signs along the rice paddies for a few miles.

The Vietnamese know how to commercialize the war to the very last shell casing. Popular among Asian guests in particular is the **shooting range** – one shot, one dollar. According to information from a military expert, it is better to abstain from this questionable pastime: the weapons (AK 47s and M 16s) are thought to be old and not particularly well maintained, presenting a high risk for the user.

Ben Duoc Temple On the expansive grounds of Ben Douc, visitors can also visit Ben Duoc Temple with its 40m/131ft high, nine-storey tower, which was built on the banks of the Saigon River in 1995. Inside, the names of around 50,000 of the fallen from this region are engraved in stone.

Around Cu Chi

Handicraft village Phu Binh »Mot Thoang Viet Nam« (»a glimpse of Vietnam«) is the motto of this tourist project near Cu Chi. On a park-like area of 22ha/54ac with a small lake in the middle, visitors are given demonstrations of old Vietnamese handicrafts and traditional art. A kind of **miniature Vietnam** with famous buildings can be viewed from a platform.

Buildings characteristic of ethnic minorities and various regions – for example the clay houses in Central Vietnam – are displayed in their actual size. Also on the grounds is a small zoo housing numerous plants and animals native to Vietnam, a sugar factory, a rice wine distillery and a rice mill, an open-air restaurant, various workshops, and exhibition rooms with musical instruments and traditional clothing, as well as souvenir stands. The village is intended as both a classic tourist attraction and a training centre for typical and traditional professions. The grounds are around 5km/3mi from the Ben Duoc tunnels, in the vicinity of the village of Phu Binh.

Da Lat offers the Vietnamese an especially exotic atmosphere: cool temperatures, hills covered with forest, and plants such as strawberries and roses.

✴ Da Lat

Province: Lam Dong (capital)   **Region:** Central Highlands
Population: 187,000

Da Lat nestles between the terraced vegetable fields and the green hills of the plateau at the foot of mountains rising up to 2163m/7096ft. Even in French colonial times, this attractive mountain landscape was chosen as a holiday and resort destination, with Da Lat referred to as the »city of eternal spring«.

In past years, the Central Highlands have seen recurring guerrilla battles against the central government, as hill tribes fight for their independence in the Vietnamese, Cambodian and Laotian highlands. As increasing numbers of Vietnamese were relocated to the **»economic development zones«** around Da Lat after 1975, FULRO (»United Front for the Liberation of Oppressed Races«) came into being. With the support of western countries, the resistance movement opposed »Vietnamization« by the communist regime in Hanoi. The entire highland region was closed to tourism at short notice in 2001 and 2004, when demonstrations by the hill tribes turned violent.

FULRO

The residents of Da Lat live from the cultivation of vegetables, fruit and flowers (especially orchids for export), as well as from cattle farming and from handcrafts (silk weaving, embroidery and wood carving). The sweet, syrupy strawberry jam and strawberry wine from Da Lat are famous throughout the country.

What to See in Da Lat

Picturesque villas and dilapidated houses, which look like the witch's house from a fairy tale, ascend the hill above Xuan Huong Lake – the architectural mix in Da Lat lies somewhere between palace and tower block. The **French colonial era** has left a number of traces, for example the cathedral, the university and the Pasteur Institute, and the streets bore French names until 1975. Old, arcaded villas with terraces or country houses built with rough stone bricks are still to be found, especially along Tran Hung Dao Street – many houses have been renovated and today serve as guesthouses.

Lam Dong Museum Phan Boi Chau Street and Lu Tu Trong Street lead to the loftily situated Lam Dong Museum, which focuses on the history and culture of the province. Above all, the artisan handicrafts (ceramics, weaving, jewellery and traditional costumes) of the hill tribes, the Mon-

Da Lat Map

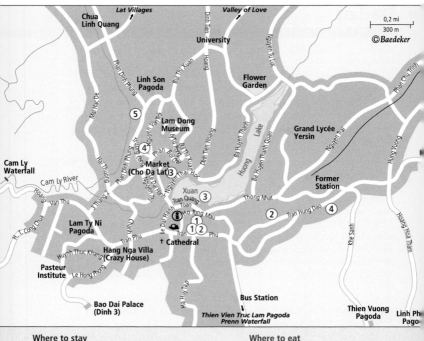

Where to stay
1. Sofitel Da Lat Palace
2. Ana Mandara Villas Dalat
3. Empress Hotel
4. Villa Hotel 28
5. Dream's Hotel

Where to eat
1. Le Rabelais
2. Larry's Bar
3. Thuy Ta
4. Thanh Thanh

The Boa Dai villa is characterized by a rather sober exterior

tagnards, is exhibited; among other pieces, visitors can marvel at the cigar case of Emperor Bao Dai(opening times: Tue–Sat 7.30am–11.30am and 1.30pm–4.30pm). The **view** of the city and its surroundings is especially pretty from here.

On the south side of the city centre stretches Xuan Huong Lake, surrounded by villas. It takes its name from a Vietnamese authoress from the 17th century. The lake, with a surface area of approximately 4ha/10ac (7km/4.3mi in circumference) was artificially dammed in 1919. **Paddleboats** can be rented near the Thanh Thuy restaurant. On the north side lies a 50ha/124ac golf course, on which Bao Dai (► Famous People) played, and beautiful gardens (opening times: daily 6am–6pm) full of roses, orchids and hydrangeas.

Xuan Huong Lake

The railway line between Saigon/Phan Rang and Da Lat was built around 1930. Today, most of the route is disused. From the station (approx. 500m/550yd east of the lake) runs an old train to Linh Phuoc Pagoda in Trai Mat. During the half-hour nostalgic journey, passengers can get to know the hill landscape and pine forests of the area. From Trai Mat an approximately 7km/4.5mi-long signposted trail runs to **Tiger Waterfall** (Thac Hang Cop). Visitors are greeted by a tiger statue – whose wide-open mouth they often climb into. It is possible to climb down the stairs that run alongside the impressive waterfall to the foot of the cascade, or relax above in one of two restaurants.

Train station

South of Tran Hung Dao Street, the main street in the south of Da Lat, two holy sites await. Heading along Hoanh Goa Tham, visitors reach the colourful Linh Phong Pagoda, the doorway of which is adorned with a baying dragon's head with threatening, protruding eyes.

Linh Phong Pagoda

● VISITING DA LAT

INFORMATION

Da Lat Tourist
10 Quang Trung, Da Lat
Tel. 0 63/81 03 24, fax 81 03 63
www.dalattourist.com.vn
dalattourist@hcm.vnn.vn

TRANSPORT

Lien Khuong Airport: approx. 30km/
20mi south of Da Lat, tel. 0 63/
84 33 74; Vietnam Airlines Shuttlebus:
0 63/82 28 95; daily flights from Saigon.

EVENTS

Da Lat Flower Festival
Every two years (2007, 2009), from 10
to 18 December, Da Lat is transformed
into a sea of blossoms: orchids, roses,
tulips as far as the eye can see. Flower
arranging competitions are held, along
with music and fashion shows, with
the climax of the festival being a
parade of colourfully decorated wag-
ons through the city.

Sa Ropu (Buffalo Feast of Sacrifice)
After a bountiful harvest, the Buffalo
Feast of Sacrifice Sa Ropu is celebrated
in honour of the rice god Ndu. The
»can« flows freely: the revellers suck
the high-proof rice wine through
bamboo straws from large clay mugs.

SHOPPING

Cho Da Lat Market
Mountains of flowers, vegetables and
fruit can be found in the alleys and on
the stairs in front of the market hall.
Inside, customers rummage through
lacquerware and typical household
goods, as well as handicrafts made by
the hill tribes.

WHERE TO EAT
► Moderate
① Le Rabelais
12 Tran Phu (Sofitel Da Lat Palace)
Tel. 0 63/82 54 44, daily noon–10pm
Elegant French restaurant with panoramic lake view.

③ Thuy Ta, »La Grenouillère«
1 Yersin
(on the edge of Xuan Huong Lake)
Tel. 0 63/82 22 88
Unsightly from outside, comfortable
inside: Vietnamese dishes with a lakeside view and piano accompaniment
or traditional folk music.

► Inexpensive
④ Thanh Thanh
4 Tang Bat Ho
Tel. 0 63/82 18 36
daily 6.30am–10pm
Tiny Vietnamese restaurant in a historic street with good service and
excellent food.

ENTERTAINMENT
② Larry's Bar
Sofitel Da Lat Palace
daily 4pm–midnight
Small bar with a good atmosphere and
a large selection of wine, beer, and
cocktails, as well as very good pizza.

Colourful Lat weavings

WHERE TO STAY

► Mid-range

③ Empress Hotel
5 Nguyen Thai Hoc
Tel. 0 63/83 38 88
Fax 82 93 99
www.empresshotelvn.com
empresdl@hcm.vnn.vn
Located on a hill, 10 of the 19 elegant rooms at this restored villa have a view of the lake; some are beautifully furnished with parquet floors, Italian terra cotta and antique telephones. Italian restaurant.

► Budget

④ Villa Hotel 28
28 Tran Hung Dao
Tel. & fax 0 63/82 27 64
Small hotel in a rustic country-house style with good rooms (shower/bath, some with fireplace), pretty garden panorama.

⑤ Dream's Hotel
151 Phan Dinh Phung
Tel. 0 63/83 37 48, fax 83 71 06
dreams@hcm.vnn.vn
This small mini hotel is in the middle of town, with large beds in only 13 rooms (nice shower/bath, TV, mini-bar, some with balcony) – a large breakfast buffet in the kitchen with the family is included.

► Luxury

② Ana Mandara Villas Dalat & Spa
Le Lai
Tel. 0 63/55 58 88
Fax 55 56 66
www.sixsenses.com/evason-ana-mandara-villas-dalat
reservations-dalat@evasonresorts.com
A journey into the past. 17 restored French colonial villas from the 1920s spread across a park. The 57 rooms are arranged with elegant, old »granny« furniture and decor; the bathtub stands on lions' paws. »In-villa-dining service« in the room's own kitchen. Heated pool, wine cellar, exclusive restaurant.

Baedeker recommendation

① Sofitel Da Lat Palace
12 Tran Phu
Tel. 0 63/82 54 44
Fax 82 56 66
www.sofitel.com
sofitel.reservations@dalatresorts.com
In a class of its own: restored colonial hotel, 43 rooms with gorgeous nostalgic furnishings – the bathroom alone makes a stay here worthwhile! Cooking courses are available on request.

The previous junction, on Khe San Street, leads to Thien Vuong Pagoda, which is visited primarily for the huge Buddha statue that sits on a throne on the hill above. Stands sell candied strawberries and artichoke tea.

Thien Vuong Pagoda

On the other side of the street stands the city's cathedral, which was built in the 1930s and dedicated to St Nicholas. The 70 colourful **glass windows** from Grenoble are noteworthy, as is an otherwise inconspicuous collage next to the altar. This was made, in honour of the Catholic martyrs of Vietnam, out of recycled paper, symbolizing the renewal of Catholicism in the country.

Cathedral

✱
**Bao Dai Palace
(Dinh 3)**

🕐
Opening hours:
daily
7.30am–11.30am,
1.30pm–4.30pm

The Dinh 3 Palace, belonging to Bao Dai (1913–97, ▶ photo p.197) in the city's southwest was built between 1933 and 1938, and bears a certain similarity to Art Deco architecture. The **last Emperor of Vietnam**, from the Nguyen dynasty, lived here with his family in the 1940s, and later only with his concubine, after the Empress Nam Phuong and the children had gone into exile in France. The two-floored, ochre-coloured palace houses 26 rooms and a large garden. The emperor also finally went into exile in France in the mid-1950s, and President Ngo Dinh Diem used the palace from then on.

On the ground floor is Bao Dai's working area, with the private chambers of the imperial family on the top floor. The reception hall is furnished with a piano, seating and hunting trophies. To the right of the entrance is a simple office with a bust of the emperor and a photo of his father, Khai Dinh. Hanging in the assembly room on the ground floor are a number of photos from his time in office.

At the end of the hallway, the visitor enters a rather modest throne room with some antique objects (including hunting lances). Here also stands the wooden bathtub of the emperor's mother. A narrow spiral staircase leads to the first floor, where rooms were once rented out to tourists. The first room was used by Princess Phuong Maiand the princes Phuong Dung and Bao Long as a living area. Adjoining it are the imperial chambers, which do not exactly leave an impression of any particular pomp. Also of note is an old wooden box by the large stairs, in which Bao Dai liked to take his steam baths.

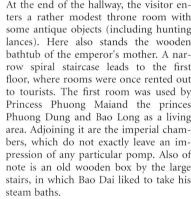
Very peculiar indeed: the Crazy House

The much vaunted Hang Nga Villa – also known as the »Crazy House« – in Huynh Thuc Khang Street is another regular attraction for groups of tourists. Under the

✱
**Hang Nga Villa
(Crazy House)**

motto »back to nature«, the Vietnamese architect and president's daughter Hang Nga created a garden out of quirky treehouses and huts without angles and corners, sometimes shaped like animals, with fantastical statues, Russian puppets, spiders' webs, stalactites and »bamboo« bridges – all made of concrete. The rather peculiarly arranged rooms are intended for various animals, and elaborately furnished with decorations and mirrors. Attached to the guesthouse are a café and an art gallery.

The area around Da Lat boasts a number of waterfalls, the nearest being Cam Ly Falls near Hoang Van Thu Street. It has been a tourist attraction for many years, also for Vietnamese visitors. Bustling on the lawns are **ponies and cowboys**, to create an exotic atmosphere – for the Vietnamese (accessible from 7am–6pm).

Cam Ly Falls

🕐

Around Da Lat – to the North

Those who want to get an impression of how the Vietnamese most like to spend their weekends should pay a visit to the »Valley of Love«. Around 5km/3mi north of the city centre lies this well attended getaway, where Emperor Bao Dai used to go hunting. Here, visitors enjoy extensive hiking in pine forests and paddling in the manmade Ho Da Thien Lake, pony rides with Vietnamese dressed as cowboys, picnics and souvenir frenzies.

★
Valley of Love

There is also a campsite on the grounds. In good weather, there is a wonderful **panoramic view** of the countryside around Da Lat, and particularly of the two peaks of the legendary Langbiang Mountain (opening times: daily 6am–5pm).

🕐

This small, artificial lake is also a popular and typically Vietnamese destination for day-trippers. It lies around 6km/4mi outside the city centre, to the east, and is surrounded by pine forests. Pony rides, hiking trails around the lake and copious souvenir stands and pubs are part of the variety of attractions on offer here. The lake is the source of many sad tales and legends.

★
Lake of Sighs

In the area around Da Lat are nine villages, which form the **Lat Village Community**, within which indeed even different dialects are spoken. Visitors require a permit in the form of a ticket. Tourists should only visit as part of a tour organized by a travel agency. The ethnic Lats (pronounced Lak) themselves live in six villages and number

> **❓ DID YOU KNOW ...?**
>
> ■ When listening closely to the lake, it is possible to hear the sighs of Hoang Tung and Mai Nuong. The happy couple lived here more than 200 years ago, until Hoang Tung was called to the war, where he was said to have fallen in battle. In her grief, Mai Nuong through herself into the lake. Yet after several years, her love did after all return home in search of his bride – to no avail. In despair, he joined her in the watery grave.

around 3000 citizens. They are mainly Catholics and live from cultivating vegetables (e.g. rice, sweet potatoes, manioc, beans), still practising slash-and-burn methods to clear the land. They also produce charcoal, which is sold at the market in Da Lat.

In a Lat village at the foot of the Langbiang Mountain, 12km/7.5mi north of the city, it is possible to see a number of private pile dwellings, the church and a tiny weaving mill with a souvenir shop. The Lat were once a **matriarchal society** and, even to this day, a man moves into the house of his wife, or that of her parents, until a cou-

Entrance to the Valley of Love

ple can afford to build one of their own. Children take on their mother's family name. The everyday life of the Lat who live here otherwise largely conforms to that of most Vietnamese: children go to Vietnamese schools; in church the hymns vary between Latin, Vietnamese and the Lat language.

The **traditional clothing** – a kind of two-piece Sarong – is only worn by the elderly or on very special occasions. Filed teeth or ears pierced with pegs are now rarely found and only among the oldest in the village.

Langbiang Mountain (Nui Ba) Close to the Lat village is the gateway to Langbiang Mountain. Accompanied by a guide from Da Lat Tourist, **walking groups** and bird lovers can climb the 2000m/6562ft peaks in around three hours. The route passes through red rhododendrons and wild orchids, and countless butterflies, rare indigenous birds and perhaps even a wild boar are to be seen. Part of the forest has already fallen victim to clearance for charcoal production, especially on the lower slopes. Evergreen forests still grow around the two highest peaks. Depending on the weather, there can be a magnificent view of Dat Lat and its surroundings.

! *Baedeker* TIP

Easy Rider, Vietnamese-style

A group of motorcyclists, who speak English, take guests on meandering (several-day) tours of Da Lat and the highlands on old Russian and East German bikes. Passengers be warned: helmets are mandatory in Vietnam, there is virtually no ambulance service to speak of outside the cities, and no insurance whatsoever (arranged verbally – haggle for the price!).

Around Da Lat – to the South

Above **Tuyen Lam Lake** (also Quang Trung) lies the popular Thien Vien Truc Lam Pagoda. The Buddhist place of worship offers a fantastic view of the neighbouring mountain and the reservoir (built in 1982). It is also possible to take the **funicular** from Robin Hill, a couple of miles south of the city (opening times: daily 7.30am–11.30am, 1.30pm–5pm).
Many Vietnamese take a motorboat trip across to the other shore, where there is a camp site and bungalows. Those who wish to can take a ride on an elephant. The meditation monastery (1993) houses a gilded Buddha as well as many woodcarvings of scenes from his life. Interested foreigners can get individual instruction on the art of meditation here – in exchange for a small donation and with prior booking. The monastery and reservoir are around 5km/3mi southwest of Da Lat (opening times: daily 6am–5pm).

Thien Vien Truc Lam Pagoda

Prenn Waterfall lies in the middle of a sort of amusement park. Visitors can walk behind the approximately 10m/33ft-high waterfall as if behind a huge, spraying curtain. At weekends there is a jostling throng of people here. It is possible to spend the night in a tent or ride a paddleboat in the forest-like park. A small zoo is also among the attractions. It seems unthinkable that even into the 1970s the tigers roaming here kept tourists away. Prenn Waterfall can be reached via the N 20, around 10km/6mi outside Da Lat.

Prenn Waterfall

The silk factories in Cu Xa can be reached via National Highways 20 and 27b (approximately 25km/15mi from Da Lat). The drive into the valley first passes coffee plantations, pineapple and vegetable fields. The many strange straw huts on the edge of the road are used to grow mushrooms, which thrive in the moist climate. Seen all around the area are mulberry trees, the leaves of which are a favourite food of silkworms.
Interested visitors can get a demonstration of the individual phases of **silk production** at the family-run businesses based here: for example the cultivation of the worms, the manufacturing of the threads and the winding by machine. The worms produce the silk fibres, wrapping themselves around in them as they pupate. The thumb-sized cocoons are boiled in a kettle until the fibres come loose and can be wound onto spools. The worms are then fried and enjoyed as a delicacy.

★
The silk-weaving village of Cu Xa

Silk cocoons are soaked

After around 30km/19mi, National Highway 20 (toward Saigon) runs past **Lien Khuong**

The trip from Da Lat to Saigon offers wonderful views of the hilly landscape. Lien Khuong Waterfall is an especially beautiful sight.

Waterfall. During the rainy season, the approximately 100m/330ft-wide waterfall is among the most beautiful in the area: the water of the Da Nhim River rushes over the rocks to cascade 20m/66ft downwards. It is nicely viewed from patio of the simple **Ngoc Hoa street café**, from where steps lead down to the riverbed.

✱
Dambri Waterfall

The road also leads to Dambri Waterfall (110km/68mi southwest of Da Lat, near Bao Loc; follow the signs along the bumpy, only partially paved country road).

The enormously loud roaring of the 50m/164ft-high waterfall can already be heard from the car park of the small amusement park. The masses of water thunder steeply down several levels of rock in a mighty cascade, spraying mist far and wide – a deafening natural spectacle!

»Chicken Village«

On the road leading toward ►Nha Trang, only 18km/11mi from Da Lat, lies the place known to travellers as »Chicken Village« (actually called Lang Con Ga), which takes its name from the 5m/16ft-high **chicken statue** on the village square. The reason for its being there is no longer really known – perhaps it was for political or religious reasons; a love story is sometimes mentioned. The inhabitants of the village are very poor and belong to the Koho ethnic minority.

✱
Bao Loc pass

If time allows, it is best to drive from Da Lat to Saigon in a car, rather than flying – the trip over the Bao Loc pass is accompanied by breathtaking landscapes: the road meanders through valleys and deep ravines, with waterfalls and giant trees shrouded in fog. Spread out across the Bao Loc plateau are vast tea plantationsand mulberry fields – an almost Tuscan, gently rolling hill-landscape with white-blossomed, intensely scented frangipani trees. Fruit stands with durian, red dragon fruit and rambutans are set up right by the side of the road. The conspicuous bricked chimneys along the road are overgrown with pepper plants.

★
Cat Tien National Park

With an area of around 80,000ha/309 sq mi, Cat Tien National Park (160km/100mi northeast of Saigon) is one of the largest in Vietnam, and is now a UNESCO Biosphere Reserve. It is famous for its rhinoceros population, this being the only incidence of **Javan rhinoceros** in mainland Asia. Alongside elephants, gibbons and buffaloes, there are at least 60 other mammalian species, around 300 bird species, 40 different reptiles and 14 amphibian species. Added to that are around 400 different plant species, including 170 medicinal herbs and 52 types of orchid..

The landscape is made up of many lakes, rivers, waterfalls, lagoons and extensive swamp areas. The terrain descends from the Truong Son Mountains in a step-like pattern southwards to the plain. Water birds and crocodiles can be seen at the many lakes and watering holes.

There are around 9000 members of ethnic groups living in the national park. They live from rice and fruit cultivation, as well as income from the harvest of coffee and cashew nuts. Relatively good places to stay can be found at **Dong Nai River**.

To get to the park from Saigon, it takes around four or five hours by car (N 20 to Madagui, then a further 23km/14mi). Admission is only allowed with an official permit from the Department of Forestry: it is easiest to book a tour with a travel agency.

La Nga Lake

The special thing about La Nga Lake is that there is a settlement on it. Along with houseboats, it consists of wooden huts built upon empty oil barrels. As in ►Chau Doc, fish are farmed here beneath the floors of the boats and huts. The boats with which the inhabitants travel from house to house, which are rowed by foot, are a local oddity.

★ Da Nang

E 4

Province: Quang Nam–Da Nang (capital)

Region: Southern Central Coast
Population: Approx. 500,000

Da Nang is considered the gateway to the three UNESCO cities of Central Vietnam (Hue, Hoi An and My Son). The city itself has little in the way of outstanding attractions, but the Cham Museum is worth seeing as is the magnificent China Beach, which is steeped in history.

History From the 4th until into the 14th century, the area around Da Nang belonged to the kingdom of the Cham. It wasn't until the end of the 15th century that the Vietnamese founded a settlement here. Due to its ideal location, the city was often beset with invaders, which is why it has a reputation as traditional **centre of resistance**. In the 16th and 17th centuries, Da Nang began to establish itself as a port town, as trade ships often had to wait here at harbour before being discharged of their cargo in Faifo (today Hoi An). From 1802, when Hue became the Vietnamese capital, all visitors to the court went ashore in Da Nang. The new Nguyen emperor Gia Long promised the French a concession for Da Nang (French: Tourane) in exchange for the help that put him on the throne. This however was granted only in 1888, after the French had shelled the harbour several times. The city grew steadily as the base of the **South Vietnamese Air Force**, but growth accelerated when US troops landed here on 8 March

Da Nang *Cham Museum*

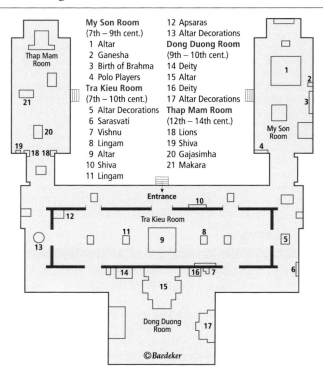

My Son Room
(7th – 9th cent.)
1 Altar
2 Ganesha
3 Birth of Brahma
4 Polo Players
Tra Kieu Room
(7th – 10th cent.)
5 Altar Decorations
6 Sarasvati
7 Vishnu
8 Lingam
9 Altar
10 Shiva
11 Lingam
12 Apsaras
13 Altar Decorations
Dong Duong Room
(9th – 10th cent.)
14 Deity
15 Altar
16 Deity
17 Altar Decorations
Thap Mam Room
(12th – 14th cent.)
18 Lions
19 Shiva
20 Gajasimha
21 Makara

Thap Mam Room
21
20
19
18 18

Entrance

10
Tra Kieu Room
12
11
9
8
5
13
14
16 7
6
15
Dong Duong Room
17

My Son Room
1
2
3
4

©Baedeker

1965. No doubt many remember the television pictures of the advance guard of Marines wading ashore at Da Nang Bay with amphibious vehicles and helicopters, to be greeted with garlands of flowers by young Vietnamese women. In no time at all, Da Nang was practically transformed into an American small town, with hospitals, cinemas, bowling alleys, parks and most of all, a whole load of bars – many GIs spent their weekends and vacations in Da Nang or at China Beach (see below). Refugees from the so-called free-fire zones flooded into service jobs, working as washers, labourers, prostitutes and drug dealers.

Yet Da Nang's role as a US military base brought not only benefits. The area surrounding the »City of War« suffered terribly from the ravages of battle: 33,000 tons of bombs were dropped, and tens of thousands died. From 1967 to 1972, the German **hospital ship** *Helgoland* was anchored in Da Nang's harbour, and, despite protests from the US, cared for the wounded from either side. In March 1975, the North Vietnamese finally began a large-scale offensive, the South Vietnamese troops fled and, without resistance, the Vietcong declared the city liberated.

✷ Cham Museum (Bao Tang Cham)

The most important attraction in Da Nang is unquestionably the Cham Museum, with a collection of Cham art that is unparalleled worldwide. It is under no circumstances to be missed, especially for those also planning to visit ► My Son. It is found on the southerly Vuong Street, near the banks of the Han. The museum is planning to expand in the near future, with further exhibition rooms. There are 1700 smaller and larger sculptures in storage, awaiting their presentation.

Unique collection of Cham artwork

On the initiative of the École Française de l'Extrême Orient, the building of a museum began in 1915. Another 24 years would pass before it is actually completed. The building itself and the meticulous presentation of the exhibits alone make a visit worthwhile. The garden, with blossoming frangipani trees and a row of superb sculptures, creates an **exceptional mood** and an impression of the epoch and reign of the Cham, who ruled for over a thousand years in southern Vietnam. Unfortunately the individual exhibits are not sufficiently explained, and the catalogue on sale at the entrance gives only

⏱ Opening hours: daily 7am–5pm; possible pause: 11.30am–1.30pm

Many people admire the sensitive depiction of a flute player immersed in his music (My Son altar)

The effective presentation...

... benefits the unusual exhibition.

a general overview and does not refer to the pieces on display.

For the most part, the art of the Cham is **religious art**; here, as in their general system of beliefs, Buddhist, Hindu and Islamic elements, as well as local influences, can be found. Recurring themes are depictions of lions, elephants and Hindu deities. Above all, Shiva, the Hindu god of destruction and reconstruction, was honoured by the Cham as the defender of their kingdom. Shiva is portrayed either as a strong man or symbolically as a lingam (phallus). Indonesian and Khmer influences can be recognized in the Buddha sculptures from the 9th century (Indrapura). The best known and most individual form of expression in Cham art is the Uroja, a kind of universal mother of the Cham kings, exemplified in the form of a breast or a nipple.

My Son Room ▶ Around 300 exhibits (altars, friezes, reliefs and statues) from the 4th to the 14th centuries are spread across ten rooms and in the garden. A tour begins with the sculptures from the temple valley of My Son (4th–11th century).

The Cham kingdoms were consolidated at the beginning of the 8th century and their own artistic style emerged. The different styles brought to light by excavations are named in accordance with the sites at which they were found. The altar, with its magnificent frieze, is considered a masterpiece of early sculptural art. The unfinished gable with the depiction of the birth of Brahma from the navel of Vishnu is especially interesting.

Tra Kieu Room ▶ The archaeological site of Sinhapura is near Tra Kieu. The splendid **capital of the Cham kingdom** of the 4th to the 8th century lies 40km/25mi southwest of present-day Da Nang. A monumental altar with scenes from the Indian epic Ramayana is very impressive. The portrayal of the marriage of Princess Sita from the 7th century displays a strong Indian influence, not just in content, but also in form.

Dong Duong Room ▶ Under the rule of King Indravarnam II, who moved the capital to the north (Indrapura), there was a move towards Buddhism. A monastery was built there at the end of the 9th century, later named Dong Duong. Scenes from the life of Buddha can be seen on the altar reliefs.

From the beginning of the 11th century, the Cham had to retreat ever further south in response to the advances of the Viet. In the Thap Mam Room, the **stylistic changes** between the 12th and 14th centuries are easy to comprehend from the exhibits. The mythical creatures and the Shiva statues seem rougher, and not as finely and elegantly worked as the examples from earlier epochs.

◄ Thap Mam Room

Further Attractions in Da Nang

Cao Dai Temple in Da Nang (35 Hai Phong Street) is the second largest in Vietnam ►Tay Ninh. Here, too, the interior is ruled by the all-seeing-eye of the highest entity, and the walls are graced with pic-

Cao Dai Temple

Da Nang *Map*

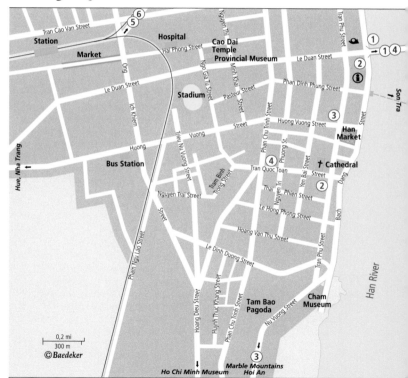

Where to stay
1. Furama Resort
2. Bamboo Green Riverside
3. Sandy Beach Resort
4. Tourane Hotel
5. Lang Co Beach Resort
6. Lang Co Hotel

Where to eat
1. Hana Kim Dinh
2. Kim Do
3. Christie's Restaurant and Cool Spot
4. Huong Viet

▶ VISITING DA NANG

INFORMATION

Da Nang Tourism
76 Hung Vuong, Da Nang City
Tel. 05 11/82 56 53 and 89 39 93
www.danang.gov.vn

Saigon Tourist
357 Phan Chu Trinh, Da Nang City
Tel. 05 11/82 70 84
info@saigontouristdanang.com

TRANSPORT

International Airport Da Nang (5km/3mi southwest): tel. 05 11/81 18 11 and 83 03 39

! *Baedeker* TIP

Da Nang Water Park

It is possible to ride the waves in the middle of town at the imaginatively designed Da Nang Water Park: young and old alike enjoy themselves in the Jacuzzi, beneath waterfalls and on huge, steep slides named »Kamikaze«. A huge restaurant with room for 500 people provides refreshment, and concerts are held regularly on the outdoor stage (2km/1.2mi south of the city centre in the direction of My Khe Beach, opening times: Mon–Wed 9am–7pm).

EVENTS

Liberation Day
Each year on the 29 March, »Liberation Day« is celebrated with traditional boat races on the Han River.

Cau Ngu Festival (Ca Ong)
The »Whale Festival« is celebrated every year (February/March) by the fishermen of the surrounding villages to honour the whales – which are believed to protect them and are considered gods – with decorated boats, sacrifices, traditional singing and music, boat regattas and other sportive competitions.

SHOPPING

Da Nang has various *markets* that are worth strolling through: the market hall on the corner Tran Phu/Hung Vuong or the Cho Con on the corner of Hung Vuong/Ong Ich Khiem, with shops offering handicrafts, especially basketwork. In addition, a lively street market is located in Hai Phong Street, east of the railway station.

Non Nuoc Fine Art Village
At the foot of the Marble Mountains (Hoa Hai, Ngu Hanh Son district) it is possible to watch the stone masons and sculptors at work and then purchase their pottery and marble figures, i.e. animals, countless Buddhas in all sizes – or how about a life-sized Ho Chi Minh for the living room?

WHERE TO EAT

▶ **Moderate**

① **Hana Kim Dinh**
15 Bach Dang
Tel. 05 11/83 00 24
daily 11am–11pm
Spacious, ship-like establishment on the esplanade near the bridge. With a view of the activity on the river, enjoy international, Japanese and local dishes (barbecue, seafood etc.) outside on the patio or in the air-conditioned interior. Beer, cocktails.

② **Kim Do**
180 Tran Phu
Tel. 05 11/82 18 46
Good Asian and European cuisine. Speciality: seafood.

► Inexpensive
③ *Christie's Restaurant and Cool Spot*
112 Tran Phu
Tel. 05 11/82 40 40
daily 10am–11pm
Popular eatery and small bar on two floors: the food is a mix of Vietnamese, Japanese and Western dishes.

④ *Huong Viet*
89 Tran Quoc Toan
Tel. 05 11/82 52 11
A small but excellent restaurant in the city centre with friendly service and Chinese-Vietnamese dishes, some Western cuisine.
In addition: There are many good-value seafood restaurants at My Khe Beach (some overcharge tourists, but the Loi restaurant is good).

WHERE TO STAY
► Mid-range
⑤ *Lang Co Beach Resort*
Loc Hai, Phu Loc (approximately 35km/22mi from Da Nang International Airport)
Tel. 0 54/87 35 55
Fax 87 35 04
www.langcobeachresort.com.vn
langco@dng.vnn.vn
Surely too good to be true! This marvellously located complex has architecture in the imperial style of Hue: 84 rooms in bungalow villas with TV, minibar and a sea view, simpler rooms up on a hill.

③ *Sandy Beach Resort*
255 Huyen Tran Cong Chua, Hoa Hai, Ngu Hanh Son District
Tel. 05 11/83 62 16, fax 83 63 35
sandybeachresort@vnn.vn
Large beach complex at the pretty Non Nuoc Beach: well-furnished rooms and bungalows, two pools, two tennis courts, convention centre.

② *Bamboo Green Riverside*
68 Bach Dang, Da Nang
Tel. & fax 05 11/83 25 91/92
riversidets@dng.vnn.vn
Middle-class accommodation right on the esplanade, offering large, pretty rooms with balconies overlooking the river. Internet and travel agency.

► Budget
④ *Tourane Hotel*
My Khe Beach (2km/1.2mi from the city centre), Phuoc My
Tel. 05 11/93 26 66, fax 84 43 28
touranehotel@dng.vnn.vn
Two-storey buildings with large, air-conditioned rooms, maybe a little too showy, but very close to the beach, some with verandas. Tennis court, pool.

⑥ *Lang Co Hotel*
Lang Co Beach, Phu Loc
Tel. 0 54/87 44 26, fax 87 35 27
codolangco@dng.vnn.vn
Small beach refuge with orderly garden rooms facing the sea (air-conditioned, shower) huge seafood restaurant.

Baedeker recommendation

► Luxury
① *Furama Resort*
68 Ho Xuan Huong, China Beach (Bac My Anh Beach)
Tel. 05 11/384 78 88, fax 384 76 66
www.furamavietnam.com
An oasis of luxury. This attractive complex was the first five-star accommodation on a Vietnamese beach, and is still top-class: the three-storey buildings are spread out across a vast landscape of gardens and lagoons, rooms with plenty of fine wood and rattan, a veranda and every comfort. Diving lessons, golf, and a huge landscape of pools and canals.

tures of religious leaders, including Laozi, Confucius, Jesus Christ and Buddha. The place of worship was closed from 1975 to 1986, but services are now held four times per day (6am, noon, 6pm and midnight). Around 50,000 believers are said to live in Da Nang.

Around Da Nang

Monkey Mountain The long Son Tra peninsula with the Monkey Mountain protects Da Nang from the winter monsoon. There really are quite a few mon-

The Huyen Khong Cave is the largest and most impressive in the Marble Mountains

keys living here. But only a small section of Son Tra can be visited, as much of it has been declared a military restricted area. A huge tourist complex is being built at Bai But.

On the side of the peninsula facing the South China Sea lies My Khe (7km/4mi southeast of central Da Nang), the legendary China Beach, where American soldiers went for recreation while away from the fighting. The beach is popular among young people and families in the evening. There are numerous hotels, beach restaurants and stands serving fresh seafood.

My Khe (China Beach) and Bac My An Beach

Around 12km/7mi southeast of Da Nang, the Marble Mountains (Ngu Hanh Son) rise up quite unexpectedly. They were named by Emperor Minh Mang (1820–40); the five individual mountains are named after the elements of fire, water, earth, metal and wood. On their peaks and in caves are **sanctuaries**, which during the war were used by the guerrillas as observation posts due to the optimal view afforded of the US airbase. The view of the coast is also impressive. Members of the Cham people came here to worship their Hindu deities, and later built Buddhist altars in the caves, which in time became significant places of pilgrimage.

★ **Marble Mountains**

After the death of Ho Chi Minh, marble from the local quarries was used to build his mausoleum.

The most visited mountain is **Thuy Son** (water). Tam Thai Pagoda, originally a Cham sanctuary, can be reached via stairs carved into the rock. Under Minh Mang, the pagoda was built on this site in 1825, where statues of the Buddha Sakyamuni (past), the Bodhisattva Quan Am (future and Goddess of Mercy) and Van Thu (wisdom) can be worshipped.

Branching off from the main path to the left, a stone arch leads to a grotto, within which stands a very beautiful Quan Am statue. Adjoined to this grotto is Huyen Khong Cave. Originally a site of animistic worship, it later became a **Buddhist place of pilgrimage**. To the left, past the Quan Am, comes a dark, somewhat slippery corridor. It takes a while until it becomes possible to make out the imposing Buddha statue carved out of the stone at the other end of the enormous hall. Four brightly painted guards watch over the entrance; holes have been broken into the high ceiling, through which shines a diffuse daylight, brilliantly illuminating the Buddha at midday. Around him are a number of altars and sanctuaries honouring Hindu, Buddhist, Taoist and Confucian gods. In addition, there are some wonderful rock formations, which can be interpreted as a stork, or a fish or an elephant. A plaque commemorates the fact that the Vietcong also used this cave as a dugout. From here, a women's unit shot down 19 US planes with only 22 rockets.

★ ★
◄ Huyen Khong Cave

Blick auf die Lagune von Lang Co

The nearby vantage point offers a magnificent view of the other mountains, Non Nuoc Beach, the Cham Islands and Monkey Mountain.

Non Nuoc Only about 500m/550yd from Thuy Son Mountain lies the so-called new China Beach, Non Nuoc Beach, which challenges My Khe for the name and the »fame«. There are already quite a few hotels and restaurants – and further touristic development is underway here, too.

Ocean Cloud Pass (Deo Hai Van) About 30km/19mi north of Da Nang lies Ai Van Son (1176m/ 3858ft), the first of three peaks of the Truong Son Mountains, which mark Vietnam's »narrow waist« in the middle of the country. This is where the country's weather divide is found. The sun may still be shining on one side while black clouds hover on the other side and the rain lashes down. Over these mountain foothills runs the Hai Van Pass, which means something like »pass of the ocean clouds«. From the south, National Highway 1 leads to the pass, at an elevation of 496m/1627ft; a **winding drive** up to the peak then follows, along with some fascinating views. Cyclists and mountain-bikers sweat their way through the challenging ascent, and there are clapped-out old buses that have broken down along the way.

The Hai Van Tunnel is probably the longest tunnel in southeast Asia (at 6.3km/3.9mi) and, since 2005, has shortened the journey between

Da Nang and Hue by an hour. But it is still possible to take the steep, now pleasantly empty, winding route over the Cloud Pass.

Driving down the other side of the pass, it gradually gets warmer again, and after a while, the aquamarine glow of Lang Co Lagoon comes into view (approximately 40km/25mi north of Da Nang). A number of huge fishing nets hang over the water from poles. **Oysters** are also farmed in the lagoon, and Vietnamese artists use the mother-of-pearl from them to create their inlays.
From between the palms emerges the village of Lang Co, which lies on a small promontory. Remains can still be seen of the bridge which spanned the lagoon until Vietminh destroyed it in 1947. Many travellers make a stop here to get something to eat, or to swim at the nearby beach.

★
Lang Co

Dien Bien Phu

B 2

Province: Lai Chau (capital)   **Region:** Northern Mountains
Population: 30,000

The journey to Dien Bien Phu is its own reward. A delightful drive over the mountains leads to the provincial capital near the Laotian border. Despite its remote location, Dien Bien Phu turns out to be a surprisingly large, but not particularly attractive city. A remarkable number of French tourists throng here – the end of the French colonial era was sealed in Dien Bien Phu.

The small town lies in an 18km/11mi-long and 6–8km/4–5mi-wide high mountain valley, through which flows the Nam Rom River. The region, whose inhabitants live from rice cultivation, is very fertile and densely populated. Mild winters and warm summers are typical of the climate of this **mountain region**. Mainly Thai and Muong people live here, along with some Vietnamese who were encouraged to do so by the government. Although the landscape has been defaced by slash-and-burn land clearance and the damage of war, there are still quite a number of very beautiful spots, particularly at higher elevations.

Fertile and densely populated

Dien Bien Phu was founded in 1841 and was continually the target of foreign invasions. The French developed the strategically located town into an important bastion. After the Second World War, however, with the strengthening of the left in France, public opinion regarding the colonial war in Indochina shifted. Although the **Geneva Conference** was already scheduled for May 1954, the French military continued to secure the plateau around Dien Bien Phu from the air.

History

● VISITING DIEN BIEN PHU

INFORMATION
Dien Bien Tourism
7A–7/5 Road, Tan Thanh
Dien Bien Phu
Tel. 0 23/82 48 41
Also in hotels.

TRANSPORT
Airport: tel. 0 23/82 49 48
Daily flights from Hanoi; 45 min.

SHOPPING
The kinsmen of the hill tribes also gather at the daily market to trade their goods, especially at weekends.

WHERE TO EAT
▶ **Inexpensive**
Lien Tuoi Restaurant
on the N 42, approximately 500m/ 550yd north of the Army Museum
Tel. 0 23/82 49 19
The only recommendable restaurant in Dien Bien Phu, menu in English and French.

WHERE TO STAY
▶ **Budget**
Muong Thanh Hotel
25 Muong Thanh
(Him Lam, east of the roundabout)
Tel. 0 23/81 00 43
Fax 81 07 13
The best hotel in town, with 70 different rooms in an old and a new building. Pool, good large restaurant with bar, many tourist groups.

Dien Bien Phu Mini Hotel
7 Be Van Dan
Tel. 0 23/82 43 19
Centrally located guesthouse, simple rooms with bath (mini hotel).

The position was meant to be invulnerable, with over 16,000 soldiers stationed here, especially the Foreign Legion. Yet the Vietnamese opposition proved to be particularly tenacious. Despite great difficulty, they were able to transport weapons into this difficult-to-access region, and gradually captured the land piece by piece. Both sides suffered thousands of casualties in these battles. On the day before the peace conference, 7 May, after a long siege, the commandant finally gave the order – contrary to the instructions from Paris – to fight to the last man. Victory was attributed to General Vo Nguyen Giap, a legendary figure ever since. This battle spelt the end of the First Indochina War.

What to See in Dien Bien Phu

Museum Today at the site of the battle is a small museum. Visitors can view charts and photographs that make the events of the time comprehensible (opening times: daily 7.30am–11am, 1.30pm–5pm).

Diagonally across from the museum, the **strategic Hill A1** with the bunker can be viewed. A memorial is dedicated to the fallen: between 3000 and 10,000 on the French side and 20,000 and 40,000 on the Vietnamese side.

The Cemetery of Dien Bien Phu across from the museum can be entered through a large archway. A white marble wall panel lists the names of the fallen Vietminh. A stairway can be climbed at the entry way, giving a good view onto the seemingly endless rows of graves with the red and black star.

Around 1.5km/1mi away, on the way to the airport, lies the bunker of the French commandant, Colonel de Castries, who surrendered on the afternoon of 7 May 1954. The rooms have been painstakingly restored, and nearby stand old French tanks and artillery.

Bunker de Castries

A child plays on a tank at a former battlefield

Around Dien Bien Phu

Tuan Chau 110km/68mi northeast of Tuan Chau, on the way from Dien Bien Phu to ► Hanoi, is a larger market town for the Black Thai and White Thai of the area. They can be seen in their beautifully worked **traditional clothing**, particularly in the early morning. Those who appreciate this kind of handiwork can find especially nice cloth here.

Son La After another 40km/25mi, at an altitude of 660m/2165ft, comes the lofty provincial capital, Son La. Visible from afar, the former French fortification is home to a small museum today. South of Son La are a number of hot springs, ideal for bathing and relaxing. A small zoo, home to bears, porcupines and tortoises, can be visited at the forestry centre (6km/4mi west of Son La).

Note Further along the way to Hanoi, it is worth stopping in Hoa Binh and Mai Chau (►Hanoi, Surroundings).

DMZ (Demilitarized Zone)

D 4

Province: Quang Tri   **Region:** Northern Central Coast

Nowhere else in Vietnam is it possible to see traces of the war so impressively as in the Demilitarized Zone along the Ben Hai River. Ruins full of holes, bunkers, military cemeteries, memorials, overgrown trenches and a range of rusting junk bear witness to the terrible battles that were once fought here.

The unfittingly named Demilitarized Zone was one of the most bitterly embattled locations of the Vietnam War. Between 1954 and 1975, the Ben Hai River, directly on the 17th parallel, was deemed the **Line of Demarcation** between North and South Vietnam. The DMZ covered an area of 5km/3mi on either side.

This separation into two provisional spheres of influence was a product of the Geneva Conference in 1954. It was created under the proviso that elections would be held in the near future, but this never came to pass. As in Germany, the Line of Demarcation then became a political border between a Communist and a capitalist state.

Places to Visit in the DMZ

The »Street without Joy« is the name by which the 60km/37mi-long section of the N 1 between Hue and Quang Tri is known. During the French colonial era there was especially heavy fighting with the Vietminh in the area, and the French subsequently called the road the »route sans joie«. In 1960 **Bernard Fall**, an American historian, wrote a book named after the street about the First Indochina War. He met his death seven years later, as a war correspondent, exactly here.

The city of **Quang Tri** (59km/37mi north of Hue) was almost totally levelled in 1972, having been captured by North Vietnamese divisions. After a battle lasting four months, South Vietnamese troops and American B-52 bombers left only more rubble. It is said that in 82 days, bombs with **seven times the explosive power of the atom bomb in Hiroshima** were dropped

Baedeker TIP

Warning

In the last 20 years, more than 5000 people, most of them poor farmers who were collecting scrap metal remaining from the war, have been critically injured or killed in this area. There are many places where live grenades, artillery rounds and land mines are still lying around. It is therefore recommended that visits to the important sites of the DMZ should only be undertaken accompanied by a guide. Day trips are offered from hotels in Dong Hoi and Hue as well as Dong Ha.

on the 4 sq km/1.5 sq mi city centre. Today there is a memorial, the remains of the once mighty citadel of Emperor Minh Mang with a small war museum, and the ruins of the La Vang Basilica, riddled with bullet holes, which all create an impression of the gravity of the battle for Quang Tri.

DMZ Map

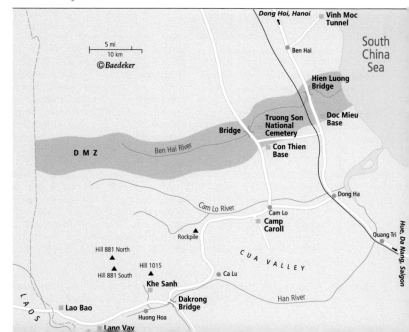

Ho Chi Minh Trail Tour

Past battlefields and bases Heading west, the journey on the N 9 runs from Dong Ha to Khe Sanh (also Huang Hoa), the site of one of the most infamous battles. Passing through an idyllic landscape of jackfruit trees, pepper plants, tea plantations and caoutchouc fields, visitors reach the battlefield of Cam Lo. A side trip to the north leads to the **Truong Son Cemetery**. Here, there are more than 10,000 gravestones and chapels (with lists of names) dedicated to the ten thousands of »martyrs« – women and men who lost their lives in the construction, transportation and defence of the Ho Chi Minh Trail. Many of the graves are purely symbolic and empty, as the mortal remains were never found after the inferno. Back on the N 9, turn after 10km/6mi to get to the former **US Base Camp Carroll**, of which little more remains than overgrown trenches with some rusty war machinery lying around. Continue on the N 9, and after crossing the Dau Mau Bridge, it is possible to see the 230m/755ft-high Rock Pile, which was used by the Americans as a sentinel, and was heavily fought. After a further 20km/12mi comes **Dakrong Bridge**, which was rebuilt in 1975–76 with support from Cuba. The Cubansalso helped with the repair of the narrow road to Aluoi (15km/9mi southwest), which was part of the legendary **Ho Chi Minh Trail**, a hidden network of routes through the jungle with a total length of 16,000km/9940mi. On these concealed paths, the North Vietnamese army and the Vietcong brought supplies to the guerrillas in the south. The Ho Chi Minh Trail is the best example of how the Vietnamese were able to overcome the supremacy of the US Army during the Vietnam War. The high-tech warfare of the American forces was met with simple means, perfect organization and flexibility.

Further south is the legendary Hamburger Hill (Ap Bia Mountain), where one of the heaviest battles took place in May 1969.

? DID YOU KNOW …?

- According to estimates by American experts, in its heyday, 5000 tons of material per month were transported on the Ho Chi Minh Trail by human carrier, bicycle, lorry etc. to the guerrillas in South Vietnam. In this way, the decisive blow against the Americans, the Tet Offensive, could be prepared.

HCM Highway Since the year 2000 work has been underway on the Ho Chi Minh Highway (also Truong Son Highway). With a total length of 3129km/1944mi, this road from Cao Bang on the Chinese border to Ca Mau in the Mekong delta is meant as an alternative to the N 1, which due to its proximity to the coast is constantly under threat of flooding and typhoons. The project costs billions, includes 314 bridges and also runs through several national parks. It will not be completed until 2010.

Khe Sanh In early 1968, the mountain fortress of Khe Sanh (65km/40mi west of Dong Ha) was the site of one of the most infamous battles of the

Vietnam War. As early as 1967, there was fighting here between US troops and the North Vietnamese infantry, who were posted in the surrounding hills. Around the end of the year, American reconnaissance noticed that tens of thousands of soldiers and masses of weapons had been transported here. Fearing a second ► Dien Bien Phu, where the French were devastatingly beaten, General Westmoreland dropped 100,000 tons of explosives, napalm and phosphorus bombs in the area around the base in only a few days – never before had a place been bombed so vehemently. Thousands, if not tens of thousands of Vietnamese died in these clashes; around 400 GIs are said to have died. But what the Americans didn't realize is that Khe San was just a **diversionary tactic** to distract from the real strike, the Tet Offensive. While the military and the media were occupied with Khe San, troops from the North Vietnamese People's Army and the National Liberation Front of South Vietnam were able to capture Hue and Quang Tri and even advance to the US Embassy in Saigon.

Today Khe San lies on a barren hill in the middle of an idyllic mountain landscape. Most of all, metal scavengers are a reminder of the events of the war; the contours of the former landing field can be readily identified, as to this day nothing will grow on the ground there. A small museum and a number of bunkers are open to visitors, displaying photos and a guest book including some poignant contributions from American veterans (opening times: daily 7am–4.30pm).

Memorial at the 17th parallel

Vinh Moc tunnels Turn eastwards near Ho Xa and after 13km/8mi comes a former supply depot and hideout (opening times: daily 7am–4.30pm). The Vinh Moc tunnels were very similar to those at ► Cu Chi, as they originated when families dug shelters near their villages in order to shelter themselves from the bombing raids. Later, the Vietcong took over the approximately 3km/2mi-long tunnel system to use as a base. A small museum shows the living conditions at the time. Many visitors find these tunnels more authentic than those at Cu Chi.

Dong Hoi

D 4

Province: Quang Binh (capital)   **Region:** Northern Central Coast
Population: Approx. 90,000

This constantly growing port city on the Nhat Le River is the best base for a visit to the UNESCO-listed caves of Phong Nha. In the north and south of the city, beautiful beaches beckon with new and attractive hotel complexes. It is only 40km/25mi over the Truong Son Mountains to Laos.

Around Dong Hoi

★★
Ke Bang National Park Due to its mile-long passageways full of stalactites and stalagmites, the Phong Nha Cave, around 50km/31mi northwest of Dong Hoi, was added to the list of **UNESCO World Heritage Sites** in 2003. In the 9th and 10th centuries, the Cham considered it to be an important shrine; inscriptions and remains of altars can be recognized in the grottoes. The 1.5km/1mi-long main path leads through 15 grottoes inside the cave, and can be seen either on foot or by boat on the underground river. The part of the cave explored so far is around

▶ VISITING DONG HOI

INFORMATION
Quang Binh Tourist (Coseco)
18 Quach Xuan Ky, Dong Hoi
(next to Hotel Phuong Dong)
Tel. 0 52/82 82 28 and 82 20 86
also in the hotels

WHERE TO EAT
Opposite the Huu Nghi Hotel on Quach Xuan Ky are *beer gardens* and *food stands* that open in the evenings. A number *of inexpensive restaurants*

can be found close to the market at the end of Quach Xuan Ky (the southern extension of Truong Phap, which leads northwards to Nhat Le Beach and the mouth of the river).

▶ Inexpensive
Anh Dao
Located at the bus station in the southwest of the city, Vietnamese dishes and various snacks are available here.

WHERE TO STAY

► Mid-range
Phong Nha Hotel
5 Truong Phap (slightly north of the city, near Nhat Le Beach)
Tel. 0 52/82 49 71
Fax 82 49 73
This hotel is somewhat outside the city centre at the mouth of the river, with 58 tidy rooms, some with sea views.

► Luxury
Sun Spa Resort
My Canh Beach, Bao Ninh
Tel. 0 52/84 29 99, fax 84 25 55
www.sunsparesortvietnam.com
sunspasm@s.vnn.vn
Magnificent beach complex with a huge pool and 234 comfortable rooms with balconies. Water sports (jet ski), spa with a massage pavilion at the beach, Jacuzzi and tennis court.

19km/12mi in extent (opening times: daily 6am–4pm; in November and December the cave can be closed due to flooding). Around 85 mammalian species live in the **Ke Bang National Park** adjoined to the cave complex (e.g. a total of ten ape species, some indigenous, including langurs and gibbons, of which four species are in danger of extinction).

★ Dry Ha Long Bay

C/D 2

Region: Red River Delta

The fairytale landscape of Tam Coc is anything but dry. Like dark guardsmen, karst mountains and rocky outcrops watch over the charming region around the provincial capital of Ninh Binh and the village of Tam Coc. They rise up from the paddy fields and are only described as dry because they do not stand directly in the sea, in contrast to their geological cousins further north in Ha Long Bay.

Boats depart from a landing stage at Tam Coc into the incomparable landscape. They make their way past high cliffs and paddy fields before finally gliding into the dark world of Tam Coc, the **Three Grottoes** (2–3 hours).

Tam Coc

Just 2.5km/1.5mi from the jetty stands Bich Dong Pagoda, hewn into the rock of the cliff on two levels. At its foot lies the main hall, whilst a second room higher up contains some wooden statues of Buddha. Steep steps lead up to the Green Grotto with the three Buddhas of the Past, Present and Future, as well as representations of the Goddess of Mercy (Quan Am). The sound of the bells and the aroma of incense in the temple transport visitors into the spiritual world of Buddhism. From the summit of the mountain, unparalleled views of the Dry Ha Long Bay may be savoured.

Bich Dong Pagoda

▶ VISITING DRY HA LONG BAY

INFORMATION
Ninh Binh Tourist
Tran Hung Dao Road, Hoa Lu,
Ninh Binh
Tel. 0 30/87 12 63
Also in hotels.

SHOPPING
Several handicrafts villages await your custom: Van Lan close to Tam Coc offers embroidered goods such as tablecloths and serviettes.

WHERE TO EAT
On Le Hong Phong in Ninh Binh City (before the bridge over the River Van) al fresco establishments serve fresh Vietnamese beer on draught and light snacks.

▶ Inexpensive
Van Long Restaurant
Gia Van (15km/9mi northwest of Ninh Binh, adjacent to Van Long Hotel)
Tel. 0 30/64 12 48
Open-air restaurant with houses on stilts (some air-conditioned). Excellent menu with many tasty Vietnamese dishes.

WHERE TO STAY
▶ Mid-range
Thuy Anh Hotel
55 A Truong Han Sieu,
Ninh Binh City
Tel. 0 30/87 16 02, fax 87 69 34
www.thuyanhhotel.com
thuyanhhotel@hn.vnn.vn
Modern hotel in town with friendly staff and 37 bright, reasonable rooms. Bar on the 5th floor, rooftop restaurant on the 7th floor. Travel agency. Car and bicycle hire. Small eatery next door: Thao Son Tuu (the menu features rather amusing »translations«).

Van Long Eco Hotel
Gia Van, Gia Vien (approx. 20km/12mi
northwest of Ninh Binh)
Tel. & fax 0 30/64 12 90
www.thaoson-vanlong.com.vn
info@thaoson-vanlong.com.vn
Large, modern hotel complex at Van Long Pier: elegant rooms (satellite TV, telephone), open-air bar in garden pavilions, pool, tennis court, spa with various massages on offer. Comfortable for the price, although no »ecological« elements.

▶ Budget
Anh Dzung Hotel
Tam Coc (opposite the ticket office; approx. 10km/6mi west of Ninh Binh)
Tel. 0 30/61 80 20, fax 61 80 37
anhdzung_tamcoc@yahoo.com
Good hotel with several storeys and vast »suites«. Good value for money.

The Long Hotel
Tam Coc (approx. 10km/6mi west of Ninh Binh)
Tel. 0 30/61 80 77, fax 61 81 33
Small, pretty hotel with excellent panorama over the Dry Ha Long Bay from the terrace: good rooms on three floors, some small, some air-conditioned (satellite TV, telephone). Large restaurant.

Hoa Lu

At the heart of Dry Ha Long Bay is Hoa Lu, once the capital of imperial Vietnam. Idyllic minor roads lead the way there, across dams between paddy fields, past lotus and palm trees and via overgrown, green limestone rocks – a fine journey to undertake by bicycle. After the yoke of Chinese central government had been cast off in the year 939, the country initially fragmented into a mass of small principalities. In the year 968, the Governor Dinh Bo Linh shifted the capital from Co Loa to his home town of Hoa Lu, which was better protected against possible attacks by the Chinese, due to its »hidden« location at the heart of the limestone mountains and karst cliffs. As Emperor Dinh Tien Hoang he seized power and established his royal household in Hoa Lu. During two short-lived dynasties, Hoa Lu maintained its new status. In 1009 the rulers of the Ly dynasty seized power and relocated the capital to Thang Long (Hanoi). Not a great deal remains of the old capital's Citadel, which housed its temples, shrines and the emperor's seat of government. **Two temples** have survived, however, to serve as a reminder of the two main rulers of Hoa Lu.

Relics of an ancient imperial capital

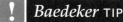

> ## ! *Baedeker* TIP
>
> ### Watch out for the sun!
> A sun hat or parasol is an essential accessory on a boat trip through Dry Ha Long Bay, as the sun beats down mercilessly between the limestone mountains.

Dinh Temple (11th century) was erected in honour of Emperor Dinh Tien Hoang. The room to the front is adorned with beautiful carvings and inscriptions celebrating the glory of the king. In the hall behind this room stands one of the oldest statues of a Vietnamese ruler. It represents Dinh Tien Hoang, accompanied by his three sons: the eldest son, Dinh Lien, is on his left, whilst the two younger sons, Hang Lang and Dinh Tue, are on his right.

Den Dinh Tien Hoang

Le Dai Hanh Temple is very similar to the neighbouring Den Dinh, although of a more simple design. It is around 600 years younger and was built in honour of Le Dai Hanh, the first emperor of the early Le dynasty. Statues of the emperor and his wife Duong Van Nga, who had already been married to his predecessor Dinh Tien Hoang, can be found in the hall to the rear of the temple.

Alongside stands the statue of his son Le Ngoa Trieu, who became emperor in the year 1005 whilst his father was still alive. The tombs of

Figure from the Dinh Temple

Verdant limestone rocky outcrops rise out of the paddy fields of Ninh Binh

both rulers can be found behind the temples at Ma Yen Mountain: Le Dai Hanh's tomb is the lower of the two, with that of Dinh Tien Hoang on the knoll. From the top, there is a splendid view of the landscape of Dry Ha Long Bay.

✱ Cuc Phuong National Park

Vietnam's oldest national park

🕐 Opening hours: daily 9am–11am, 1.30pm–4pm

Cuc Phuong National Park (25,000ha/61,775ac) is situated in the far northwest of Ninh Binh province (approx. 50km/31mi from Ninh Binh City, approx. 140km/87mi from Hanoi). Established in 1962, it is the oldest national park in Vietnam. The region boasts impressive karst mountains and **primary forest**, one of the last surviving in North Vietnam. Some of the giant trees, up to 50m/164ft high, with buttress roots as tall as a man, are centuries old, forming a dense roof of leaves which allows little light to penetrate through to the climbing plants and moss on the forest floor (one of the colossi has a circumference of a phenomenal 25m/82ft).

Flora and fauna

The national park is home to almost 2000 species of tree and plant, as well as some 90 varieties of mammal (including around 40 different types of bat). More than 320 bird species and 40 types of amphibian and reptile have been counted. Delacour's langur, endemic to Vietnam, is a rare breed of ape which was rediscovered in the national park in 1987, having previously been considered extinct. To aid their conservation, in 1993 the **Endangered Primate Rescue Center** (www.primatecenter.org) was opened, a non-profit organization in which some 140 animals live in 15 groups, subsequently to be released into the wild (including six unique to this institution, namely the grey-shanked douc). Almost wiped out in the wild, the

! *Baedeker* TIP

Hiking in the national park

Hiking trails lead to the hitherto accessible attractions (max. 18km/11mi). Excursions last from one to three days (overnight accommodation in a Muong village). Some of the guides speak English. The best times to visit are from October to December and March–April. Those seeking some peace and quiet should avoid weekends, Vietnamese holidays and holiday periods in general (tel. 030/84 80 06, dulichcucphuong@hn.vnn.vn).

Vietnamese sika deer (axis deer) are kept in enclosures. Other residents of the Cuc Phuong National Park include the Asian black bear, clouded and common leopard, serow and muntjac – although these are not likely to be spotted on a tourist excursion. Countless butterflies can be seen, however, especially in April/May.

Large herds of axis deer used to roam the national park. A breeding centre now strives to return them to the wild

Poaching There are many caves, such as the Nguoi Xua, inside the karst mountains, which are up to 600m/1960ft high. Prehistoric stone tools, bone remnants and ceramics at least 7000 years old have been discovered in the grottoes. Sadly, there are repeated incidents of poaching and illegal felling in the national park. The onrush of some 80,000 tourists each year (mostly Vietnamese) also has adverse effects on the park and its ecological balance: the access road has been tarmacked and an artificial lake created with hotels and bungalows, some comfortable (10–25 US$), a campsite and restaurant. Moreover, the new N 2 (the so-called Ho Chi Minh Highway, a second connecting route between Hanoi and Saigon) in the valley of the Buoi River cuts right through the national park.

✳ Keo Pagoda

Traditionally carved wooden building Standing on the bank of a lake, in the shade of trees, is the Buddhist Keo Pagoda (approx. 50km/31mi east of Ninh Binh), a remarkable example of traditional Vietnamese timber construction and wood carving.

It was established in the 12th century and dedicated to the monk Khong Minh Khong, who cured Emperor Ly Than Tho of leprosy.

Under the rulers of the Ly dynasty (11th and 12th centuries) Buddhism received its greatest support from the state. As this waned, many of the temples fell into disrepair, as did the original buildings of Keo Pagoda. It was only in the 16th and 17th centuries that Buddhism experienced a renaissance, and most of the buildings of the Keo Pagoda complex visible today date back to this era. At the same time, a new architectural style emerged, which became known as **Tam Quan** (named after the entrance portal with its three wings) and also found favour in China. This is a 17th-century original, adorned with carved clouds, suns and dragons.

The low-lying roof of the vestibule gives the room the impression of being very wide and squat; statues of guards and the Earth God can be seen here. The central hall is almost square and features altars for sacrificial offerings and incense sticks. Finally, the main hall is broad in appearance, a **pantheon**

The bell tower is a masterpiece of Vietnamese woodcarving

with Buddhas and Bodhisattvas. Almost all of the statues date from the 19th century, with the exception of the Goddess of Mercy, a 17th-century figure.

Keo Pagoda departs from the usual trinity of structures, with an additional hall behind the main one dedicated to the monk Minh Khong. His sanctuary is only opened for the temple festival (see below). The final structure on the north-south axis is a three-storey bell tower with two bronze bells dating back to 1687 and 1796. The columns and beams display a fantastic variety of unique. The heavy construction is supported by massive pillars.

Minh Khong

Every three years, on the 15th day of the 9th lunar month, a **temple festival** is staged. **Boat races** form a part of the festivities. The boats are stored in the courtyard's covered galleries.

Further Places to Visit in the Region

An **idyllic boat trip** through the reeds of the canals of Van Long Nature Reserve (approx. 23km/14mi northwest of Ninh Binh) offers the opportunity to glide between the limestone mountains, listening to birdsong as the boatsmen stand and punt their vessels through green waters. Vietnam's last great population of Delacour's langurs lives here and, with luck, they may be spotted (the chances are higher in the early morning or late evening, when the tourist groups have left).

Van Long Nature Reserve

Harvest in the paddy fields commences at the break of day

**Phat Diem /
Kim Son**

The area to the south of Ninh Binh was traditionally a bastion of Catholicism in Vietnam. Although over 100,000 Christians fled to South Vietnam when the Communists seized power in 1954, around half of the inhabitants today are still Catholic, as demonstrated by the fact that almost every community has a church, the spires rising between the paddy fields. Phat Diem Cathedral (28km/17mi south of Ninh Binh) is particularly impressive. Having been badly destroyed in the war, it was reconstructed thereafter. It was built in the 1880s and 1890s under the guidance of the Vietnamese priest Tran Luc, also known by the name Père Six, whose grave can be found in the courtyard between the nave and bell tower. In 1933, the **first Vietnamese Bishop** was ordained here. The persecution of the Catholics (1954–75) led to the arrest of the priests and closure of the seminary, yet as a result of the doi moi policy, the situation grew more relaxed in the mid-1980s. Today, the imposing complex of buildings is again the centre of Catholicism in Vietnam.

✹

Cathedral ▶

🕑
Opening hours:
daily
7.30am–11.30am
and 2.30pm–5pm,
Mass: Mon–Fri 5am
and 5pm,
Sat and Sun 5am,
10am and 4pm

The complex consists of several buildings which unify eastern and western styles of construction, as well as featuring both Buddhist and Christian elements. Hence the free-standing bell tower does not only contain a huge bell, but also a Buddhist drum. Statues of the Four Evangelists surround the bell tower. Alongside, two large stone slabs served as seats for the mandarins of the region from which to observe the church services. Perhaps this was their way of dismantling reservations with regard to Christianity.

The interior is dominated by gold lacquered ironwood columns and a number of altars. Most impressive of all is the **high altar at the back**, fashioned from a single block of granite. Representations of six martyrs serve as a reminder of the persecution of Christians during the Nguyen dynasty in the 19th century. Alongside the main building are several small chapels – the most spectacular being that of St Peter, with splendid carvings – and behind them three artificial caves and another bell tower. Living accommodation and seminary buildings for the aspiring priests completing their training here stand among the gardens.

The Hanoi History Museum boasts an admirable collection of Dong Son drums

At the excavation site of **Dong Son**, some 8km/5mi northwest of Thanh Hoa, bronze ritual drums were unearthed, thereby lending their name to the Dong Son culture (8th–13th centuries). Some fine examples can be inspected in the history museums of Saigon and Hanoi.

The meaning of the stellar inscriptions in the centre of the drum skin remains a mystery until today. Images of ships and seabirds on the bronze drums suggest that their owners travelled overseas from the Malayan-Indonesian islands and intermingled with the Sino-Tibetan inhabitants of North Vietnam. As well as these unique relics, other items found at the dig included axes, daggers and belt buckles. Dong Son culture is now perceived as the **cradle of Vietnamese civilization**. It stretched across the Song Ma and Song Hong regions and, for the Vietnamese, is on a level with the mythological Hung kings (►Hung Temple) and their kingdom of Van Lang.

The white sandy beaches of Sam Son (16km/10mi southeast of Thanh Hoa) are some of North Vietnam's finest places to bathe. The French held these beaches in high regard, building their colonial villas here. Subsequently, an increasing number of tourists found their way here from the countries of the Eastern Bloc. Today, there are many western visitors here as well. Sam Son is also a favourite destination of the wealthy Hanoi crowd. The range of accommodation on offer is suitably broad, from old French colonial villas to hotel blocks dating back to the socialist era and on to modern bungalows. **Sam Son**

The village of Kim Lien, where Ho Chi Minh grew up as a child, lies a mere 14km/8.5mi northwest of Vinh. He was born on 19 May 1890 in Hoang Tru, just 1km/0.6mi away, where his mother came from. After his family moved out, the simple house increasingly fell into disrepair. In 1955, however, the villagers began to rebuild it and today the attractive renovated home is open to visitors, with writing desk, books and toys which belonged to little Ho. Nearby, a museum has photographs of Ho Chi Minh's many travels on display. **Kim Lien**

★ Ha Long Bay

D 2

Region: North   **Area** 1500 sq km/580 sq mi

This is a landscape in which legends come true: the approximately 2000 islands of Ha Long Bay inspire the imagination of every visitor, who might expect to come across dragons, sleeping giants or a caravan of camels here. The magnificent scenery of wildly overrun limestone mountains, where junks with rose-red sails float by, was created over the course of millions of years.

Ha Long means »descending dragon«, in contrast to Than Long (»ascending dragon«), the old name of the capital, Hanoi. As **legend** has it, aeons ago a huge dragon came down from the mountains into the valley, in order to assist the Vietnamese in the fight against their ene- **Formation**

Tower Karst Formation

Surface water seeps into the porous subsoil. Dissolution creates hollow areas.

Progressive karst formation causes these hollow areas to cave in. Star-shaped sinkholes form between the karst cones.

The forces of erosion lead to the holes expanding not only side but also downwards. Karst tower created.

☐ Vegetation cover   ☐ Water-permeable limestone   ▨ Water-permeable rock layer

mies. He furiously smashed around with his tail, and in doing so, split the mountains and cut huge notches and valleys into the landscape. When he finally disappeared into the sea, he displaced so much water that the land was flooded, leaving only the steep crags jutting out.

A **second legend** tells of the heavenly dragon mother and her children, who lived here and protected the fishermen. When one day pirates attacked the bay and its inhabitants, the dragons spat fire at the invaders. The fireballs fell back into the sea as grey clumps of ash, and so created the jagged islands of rock that stand today. Exhausted, the baby dragons lay down in the easterly Bai Tu Long Bay, which is therefore named after them.

★ ★ Places to Visit in Ha Long Bay

Ha Long City   Most tourists begin their exploration of the spectacular Ha Long Bay in Ha Long City – previously two idyllic fishing villages, today an emerging holiday destination with an amusement centre (including an overpriced water-puppet show), dolphin shows, casino, luxury resorts and dingy karaoke bars. In the **Bai Chay district** to the west lies the pier for the approximately 300 tourist boats, barges, junks and paddle-steamers that navigate Ha Long Bay. Among the boats are some real eye-catchers with bright red ribbed sails and temple-like superstructures on the upper deck (e.g. the *Annam Junk*, www.annamjunk.com; the *Huong Hai Junk*, tel. 033/84 50 42, huonghaijunk@hcm.vnn.vn; or the *Jewel of the Bay*). The two districts of Ha Long City, the more tourist-oriented Bai Chay with its hulking hotels towering into the sky and **Hon Gai** with its coal-loading harbour, were only recently joined by a bridge. Neither district is particularly well suited to bathing, even though Bai Chay recently received a light sandy beach and the sun chairs with colourful umbrellas stand in rank and file on the promenade – the water here is not especially appealing.

Canoe trip

In a canoe, it is possible to paddle into a number of the caves through their small entrances and explore the emerald-green lagoons behind (e.g. in Hang Luon). Alternatively, row over to the **floating fishing villages**, e.g. Van Gia, where even the school floats. Sometimes there is an opportunity for a chat with the villagers and an invitation for tea on the veranda of a rickety little floating house. Most inhabitants live from fishing and fish farming: beneath the planks of the veranda, the fish flap noisily in their cages when the lady of the house feeds them – with leftover food and fellow members of their own species, finely chopped.

★ ★
Journey through the wondrous limestone scenery

The excursion boats chug past the magnificently green oversized limestone giants, many of which take their name from the similarity of their characteristic form to animals (tortoise, elephant, buffalo), or have simple names such as »nose«, because the island resembles the human profile.

For many, a journey through the mystery-shrouded, fairy-tale landscape of Ha Long Bay is the highlight of the trip to Vietnam

Ha Long Bay Map

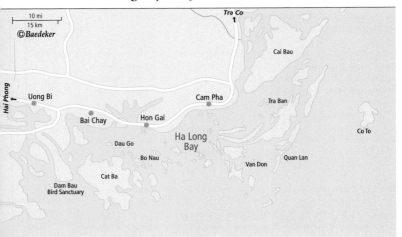

It is not only the limestone rocks leave plenty to the imagination; so too do the **stalactites and stalagmites** in the caves, which can be interpreted as fairies, ghosts and goblins. It is possible to be dropped off on some of the islands to view one of the many caves there.

Hang Dau Go ▶ The »Grotto of Wooden Stakes« on the French-named Ile des Merveilles takes its name from the bamboo stakes that aided the commander Tran Hung Dao in sinking the Mongolian fleet at the **Battle of Bach Dang** in 1288. Some of them are preserved in a dripstone cave which is reachable by way of 90 steps and consists of three domes, one behind the other.

✸
Hang Thien Cung ▶ The Thien Cung Cave is a very pretty cave full of unusual stalagmites and stalactites, from which there is a good view of the calm bay, strewn with small islands and jagged coral reefs. Colourful light reflections enhance the wondrous impression.

Hang Trinh Nu ▶ In the Trinh Nu Cave, all kinds of interestingly formed stalagmites and stalactites are to be seen. Some of them are said to resemble the face of a young girl, and as the story goes, a Mandarin kidnapped a young maiden from a poor fisher family and made her his mistress. Because any attempt to flee would put her family in danger, the maiden decided to end her own life. Since then, the isle has been known as the **Virgin Island**.

✸
Hang Dong Tien/
Dong Me Cung ▶ After worming your way through the sometimes narrow corridors of the Dong Tien Cave, there comes a larger hall full of stalagmites and stalactites from which a path leads into the open. Suddenly a wonderfully calm, turquoise-blue sea appears, surrounded by a few shrubs and bushes. The little visited Me Cung Cave is just as enchanting.

▶ VISITING HA LONG BAY

INFORMATION
Tourist Service Center
Bai Chay Pier (new tourist pier)
Ha Long City
Tel. 0 33/84 65 92
www.halong.com

TRANSPORT
Getting there: travel to Ha Long City by tourist bus or public bus (approx. 3½ hours), train or ferry from Hai Phong (or on the hydrofoil from China); journey to Cat Ba Island and to Bai Tu Long Bay on (fast) boats from Hai Phong or (tourist) boats from Ha Long City (Hong Gai).
In Ha Long City: get around by bicycle, moped and taxi.

EXCURSIONS
Tickets and boats for trips on the bay and to Cat Ba Island can be found at the new tourist pier (starting from around 25 euros per boat and day, depending on the type of boat). Tours of Ha Long also start from Cat Ba.

SHOPPING
Night market in Bai Chay (Ha Long City, daily 6pm–11pm): stroll past the souvenir stands between the esplanade and the beach, where chopsticks, bathing suits, shoes, toys and bric-a-brac are piled high on the stalls and a small funfair magically attracts children.
Gold Hand Silk (Ha Long Road, Bai Chay): boutique on the esplanade with chic silk dresses and silk shirts, pillowcases, ties, embroidered bags.
Hong Ngoc Humanity Center (halfway between Hanoi and Ha Long City, Sao Dao, Hai Duong, tel. 03 20/88 29 11): this huge handicrafts centre offers shoes, ties and silk clothes, tea services and vases, jewellery, sculptures, books, paintings etc. Customers can wait for half an hour in the cafeteria for smaller made-to-measure goods. Good quality, but it is still possible to haggle a bit. The proceeds go to an education project for people with disabilities.

WHERE TO EAT
▶ Inexpensive
Kim Hang Restaurant
Ha Long Road, Bai Chay (approximately 4km/2.5mi outside the centre of Ha Long City)
Tel. 0 33/84 68 09
daily noon–10pm
A five-storey building, with a restaurant on each floor. Excellent Vietnamese food at bargain prices. The delicious seafood menus with crab, fish filet, prawns and fried squid are a speciality.

Phuong Oanh Restaurant
Ha Long Road, Bai Chay (across from the post office and the Thong Nhat Hotel)
Tel. 0 33/84 61 45
daily 6am–10pm
Small restaurant with good Vietnamese food (rare: menu in English with prices!), lots of seafood, also breakfast.

Green Mango
1/4 Road (eastern esplanade near the Holiday View Hotel), Cat Ba City
Tel. 0 31/88 71 51
daily 6.30am–open end
Modern restaurant-bar with »fusion-food«: variations on tapas and salads, vegetarian dishes and seafood, Vietnamese classics and pasta, as well as sweets.

Duc Tuan
Promenade (around the middle),

Cat Ba City
Tel. 0 31/88 87 83
daily 6am–11pm
Vietnamese restaurant with a balcony on the first floor from which diners can watch the sunset. Large selection on the menu with seafood, chicken and pork dishes, hotpots and breakfast.

ENTERTAINMENT
Ever tried karaoke?
In all of Ha Long City, karaoke is*the* way to have fun in the evenings, and has been for years. Everyone should give this typically Asian amusement a try at least once. There are karaoke machines in every mini hotel and in the huge, open-air restaurants on the esplanade – plenty of opportunity for a sing-along!

Trung Nguyen
Ha Long Road, Bai Chay,
Ha Long City
Tel. 0 33/84 43 38
daily 10am–11pm
Vietnamese coffeehouse chain whose open-air patio restaurants are meeting places for well-heeled young people and tourists: strings of fairy lights, loud disco music, fruit juices, beer, whiskey, ice cream and iced coffee, snacks.

Blue Note
Nui Ngoc Street, Cat Ba City
(in a cross street behind the post office and the Sunflower Hotel)
Tel. 0 31/88 89 67
daily 5pm–2am
Small bar with dirt cheap, good cocktails, beer and other alcoholic beverages.

Flightless Bird
Promenade, Cat Ba City
Tel. 0 31/88 85 17
daily 6.30pm – open end

Nice small bar on two floors with games, darts, newspapers and books – the boss is from New Zealand.

WHERE TO STAY
► Luxury
Heritage Hotel
88 Ha Long Road (esplanade)
Bai Chay, Ha Long City
Tel. 0 33/84 68 88
Fax 84 69 99
www.heritagehalong.com
The best establishment in town (4 stars): 100 small rooms, some with rocking chairs, marble baths, balcony. The pool is a pure oasis, where dining is also possible. Karaoke-disco, massage, sauna.

Au Lac Resort
Tuan Chau Peninsula, Ha Long (approx. 5km/3mi outside Ha Long City)
Tel. 0 33/84 21 15, fax 84 21 66
www.tuanchauresort.com.vn
tuanchauresort@hn.vnn.vn
53 beautifully decorated villas and rooms on a private beach or on the hill (large baths, some with Jacuzzi). Pool, karaoke, fitness room, golf course, helicopter flights over the bay, many Asian guests.

Baedeker recommendation

Sunrise Resort
Cat Ba, Cat Co 3 Beach,
Ha Long Bay
Tel. 0 31/88 73-60/-64/-66
Fax 88 73 65
catba-sunriseresort@vnn.vn
There are worse places to spend a week (ideally between May and November – from December on, it can be cold and wet) than at the best beach hotel in Ha Long Bay! This marvellous small villa-like complex is situated on a tiny 100m/110yd-wide bay. Jacuzzi pool, three restaurants, water sports.

View from the Dau Go Cave

▶ Mid-range

Halong 1 Hotel
Bai Chay, Ha Long City
Tel. 0 33/84 63 20, fax 84 63 18
Magnificent old colonial villa (don't be frightened away by the lobby!). Airy balcony-corridors, old lamps, man-sized vases, four-poster beds, folding doors and a balcony patio (with the suite).

Thang Long Hotel
Bai Chay, Ha Long City
Tel. 0 33/84 64 58, fax 84 57 44
www.bmc-thanglonghotel.com
bmc-tlonghotel@vnn.vn
Hulking new building across from the new tourist-boat pier, with nicely decorated rooms.

Atlantic Hotel
Tuan Chau peninsula, Ha Long
Tel. 0 33/84 28 42, fax 84 20 48
www.atlantichotel.com.vn
atlantichotel@vnn.vn
The lime-green hotel boasts Bauhaus-like style with a snappy-looking roof, airy lobby and patio restaurant: 52 well-furnished rooms on five floors (satellite TV, phone, some with balcony).

Holiday View Hotel
Road 1/4 (at the eastern end of the esplanade), Cat Ba City
Tel. 0 31/88 72 00, fax 88 72 08-9
holidayviewhotel@vnn.vn
Excellent mid-range hotel: 14-storey building with balconies, restaurant (with terrace) with panoramic view on the 2nd and 13th floors, friendly and professional service.

Viethouse Lodge
Tuan Chau Peninsula, Ha Long
Tel 0 33/84 22 07, fax 84 22 08
www.viethouselodge.com
One of the most original guesthouses

in Vietnam: a rustic brick building on a slope with a great view, 23 rooms with old roof beams and pillars, nice folding doors, done up to look old-fashioned, and plenty of rattan, terracotta and wood (satellite TV, internet). Patio restaurant, sauna, friendly staff, tours.

▶ Budget

Than An Hotel
Vuon Dao, Bai Chay
Ha Long City
Tel. & fax 0 33/84 69 59
Mini hotel with 20 simple but air-conditioned rooms and heavy, ornate wooden furniture (satellite TV, fridge, shower/bath), fantastic view from the balcony, quietly located on a slope above the town.

! *Baedeker* TIP

Sleeping on the water

A night away from the hoards of tourists on board a boat in the middle of Ha Long Bay, enjoying the changing of the light on its striking rocky islands, is a very special experience. In the evening the scenery is bathed in a soft pink light, and at night, in the moonlight, the limestone giants surround the boat like ghostly sentinels.

Sunflower Hotel
Nui Ngoc Road, Cat Ba City
Tel. 0 31/88 84 29, fax 88 84 51
www.sunfloweronehotel.com
10-floor hotel on the esplanade with good rooms and a view of the bay and harbour from the balcony.

Rong Bien Hotel
Nui Ngoc Street (small cross street), Cat Ba City
Tel. 0 31/88 87 30

For the price-conscious: this simple mini hotel with a communal balcony is by no means first rate, but the 24 rooms are fine for this absolute bargain price (in single figures!).

Mai Quyen Hotel
Van Don, Bai Tu Long Bay
Tel. 0 33/79 31 88, fax 87 44 29
Modern hotel above a long beach in an original style with little Russian-or-thodox cupolas: nice rooms with tessellated floors, a bathtub and a small balcony with a marvellous panorama.

Bai Tu Long Eco Resort
Bai Dai Beach, Van Don,
Bai Tu Long Bay
Tel. 0 33/79 31 56, fax 79 36 74
in Hanoi: tel. 04/7 54 85 24
Fax 7 54 75 68
www.atiresorts.com
ati-baitulong@atiresorts.com
Nice complex situated in front of an impressive rock formation with 46 relatively simple rooms (air-conditioned, parquet floors, Vietnamese TV) on stilted bungalows (longhouses) of various sizes spread throughout the garden. The beach is approximately 100m/110yd away.

Quan Lan Eco Resort
Quan Lan (approx. 2km/1mi from pier),
Bai Tu Long Bay
Tel. 0 33/87 73 71, fax 87 72 57
in Hanoi: tel. 04/78 94 00
Fax 7 54 94 04
www.atiresorts.com
ati-quanlan@atiresorts.com
Seven rustic stilted huts covered with palm leaves, dirt cheap (cold water shower, fan) and right on the beach and in the dunes on a small, clean bay, very idyllic and solitary (though extensions are planned). Open-air restaurant.

Hang Sung Sot is effectively illuminated with electric light, which is not actually necessary. The vault is massive, and even entire tourist groups can spread out within the three rooms, which are full of stalactites and stalagmites. The circular path reveals almost mystical views of the dripstone in the shimmering haze.

◄ Hang Sung Sot

✱ Cat Ba Island and National Park

Cat Ba is the largest island of an archipelago that has been a nature reserve since 1986. Cat Ba National Park takes up approximately half of the mostly rocky island (around 28,000ha/69,200ac). Most of the approximately 7000 islanders live in **Cat Ba City** in the south, which has transformed itself into a small Asian version of St Tropez. There are regular traffic jams in the overflowing town, especially in summer and at weekends. An esplanade runs around the bay and the harbour with high-rise hotels, discotheques and puny little trees. The old town in the west is somewhat calmer, and here colourful little houses still crouch along the promenade, a small Taoist temple awaits visitors, and a market hall offers fresh goods all day long. From the eastern end of the esplanade in Cat Ba City it is possible to walk, partly along the cliffs, to the three numbered **Cat Co Beaches**. Day trips set out from Cat Ba to islands and caves in the nearby Lan Ha Bay, e.g. to »Monkey Island«.

Asian St Tropez

A drive across the island gives an impression of its wild karst landscape. The road snakes along through the rice fields or the rugged coastline with its shrimp farming ponds. The **limestone formations** typical of the area are remarkable, and they are covered with subtropical evergreen trees which hold on to the jagged rocks as if with tentacles. As late as 1893, seafarers gave reports of **pirates** who retreated to this at-the-time wild island after their forays. Among the ecosystems deserving protection are swamps and mangrove forests, small freshwater lakes, beaches and the coral reefs off the coast.

The karstified limestone walls and their caves (e.g. the Trung Trang Cave) offer shelter to various types of macaque and gibbon, as well as mountain goats and bats. A rare subspecies of langur, the golden-headed langur, has also been found here. On archaeological digs, traces of the primitive **Cai Beo culture**, which thrived here around 5600 years ago, as well as of the **Ha Long culture** (2000 BC) have been found. On the coast the karst is surrounded by mangrove forests, forming a unique habitat: migratory birds from the north gather here in winter. In addition, an unusually high number of reptiles (including

Flora and fauna

? DID YOU KNOW ...?

- In Cat Ba National Park is a type of tree known colloquially as the »chopstick tree«. Apparently, the wood reacts to poisonous substances by becoming darker in colour, why is why the emperor had his chopsticks made of this wood.

geckos, water snakes, pythons) congregate in the area of the national park, as well as dolphins. Around 700 plant species, many of pharmaceutical use, can be found on Cat Ba.

Bai Tu Long Bay The neighbouring Bai Tu Long Bay is much quieter than Ha Long Bay. The caves here are less spectacular, but the beaches larger.

Quan Lan ▶ On the sleepy little island of Quan Lan, tiger prawns and fish are farmed. The people here still enjoy ancient traditions such as the boat race during the village festival. A regional speciality is xa sung, a sand worm from the sea, which is put in some noodle soups. The ferries from Cam Pha on the mainland run several times daily to Quan Lan, as they also do from Hon Gai (Ha Long City).

Van Don ▶ From Quan Lan there is a ferry running twice per day to the northern-lying island of Van Don (or take the hydrofoil from Ha Long City) – a larger island, marvellously located between two limestone giants. At Dai Beach, at the eastern end, Van Don still seems sleepy and rural. Beyond the beach and the magnificent setting of hunched, rocky islands runs an endless stream of freighters, ships, old boats and ferries – around 1000 years ago Van Don was the first commercial fishing harbour under the rule of the Ly dynasty.

✳ Hai Phong

D 2

Province: Hai Phong (city state)   **Region:** Red River Delta
Population: 1.6 million

Vietnam's third-largest city, the industrial centre of Hai Phong surprises visitors with a pretty, old colonial centre, where wide avenues are lined with flame trees and surrounded by canals and streams. Some travellers use the town as a base for the boat trip to Cat Ba Island or Ha Long City.

History Close to Hai Phong, Bach Dang has repeatedly been the site of battles against the Chinese and Mongols since the second century before Christ: in the year 938 the Vietnamese general Ngo Quyen found himself confronted with the overpowering Chinese fleet, whereupon he ordered that stakes fortified with iron points be anchored in the riverbed. When the Chinese appeared at the estuary of Bach Dang, he sent a small fleet of agile boats out as a lure. The enemy launched their attack, but when they reached the ebb, their heavy ships were pierced by the stakes (▶see also p.51). More than half of the Chinese drowned in this battle. This strategy was similarly repeated in 1288, when 400 Mongolian ships approached with the intention of invading Vietnam. In both cases the victories were so overwhelming and the losses of the enemy so immense that any further plans for invasion by the Chinese and the Mongols were put to rest.

⏵ VISITING HAI PHONG

INFORMATION
Hai Phong/Vietnam Tourism
60A Dien Bien Phu, Hai Phong
Tel. 0 31/84 29 57 and 84 32 90
also in the hotels

EVENTS
Do Son Buffalo Fighting Festival
Every year, in the middle of September, a festival with bullfights is held in Do Son in honour of the resistance fighter Nguyen Huu Cao. These bear little similarity with those held in Spain: the first one to run away is the loser. Afterwards the bulls are canonized and distributed among the participating villages as Loc, a gift of the spirits.

SHOPPING
Commercial centre
North of Tam Bac Lake, between Tran Thinh Street and Cho Sat, is the commercial centre of Hai Phong, full of street markets, flower stands, grocer's shops and hardware stores. A local feature is the Siamese fighting fish offered for sale on many street corners.

WHERE TO EAT
► Inexpensive
① Sai Gon Café
107 Dien Bien Phu
Tel. 0 31/82 21 95
daily 7am–11pm
Beef steaks and fried rice, spaghetti, sandwiches and other snacks, »bia«, whiskey and cocktails are served in this large, air-conditioned restaurant and bar with a TV projector on the main street, and sometimes live bands.

WHERE TO STAY
► Luxury
① Harbour View Hotel
4 Tran Phu
Tel. 0 31/382 78 27
Fax 382 78 28
www.harbourviewvietnam.com
This luxury hotel with colonial flair is located at the harbour, of all places. Pool, vintage car tours through town.

► Mid-range
② Huu Nghi Hotel
60 Dien Bien Phu
Tel. 0 31/82 32 44, fax 82 32 45
www.huunghi-hotel.com
huunghihotel@hn.vnn.vn
Modern city hotel with pool and comfortable, sometimes elegant four-star rooms with a balcony. Piano accompaniment in the tenth-floor bar in the evenings (open 24 hours).

► Budget
③ Ben Binh Hotel
6 Ben Binh Street
(near ferry pier)
Tel. 0 31/84 22 60
Fax 84 25 24
Quiet, in an old building located in a garden. On three floors are 22 relatively basic, reasonable rooms.

Hai Phong Map

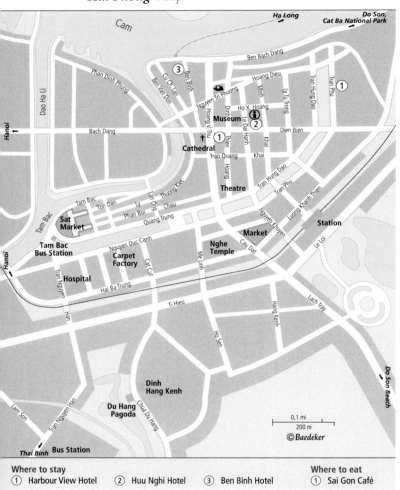

Where to stay
① Harbour View Hotel ② Huu Nghi Hotel ③ Ben Binh Hotel

Where to eat
① Sai Gon Café

During the 17th century there were first attempts to turn the small fishing village and military post into a **port city** – yet the natural conditions were not the best: the village lay in a swamp area around 20km/12mi from the sea. It was not until 1874, when the French took over Hai Phong, that the area could be drained and a city built. A few years later the colonial rulers set up a supply base, which is the foundation for the present-day use of the harbour.

What to See in Hai Phong

Somewhat to the south is the recently restored cathedral, which was built at the end of 19th century.

Cathedral

On the same street a few blocks further south, across from a lavish avenue, stands the salmon-coloured theatre, the materials for which were shipped over from France at the beginning of the 20th century. The broad square in front is where 40 Vietminh died in a skirmish with the French in November 1946.

Theatre

The Den Nghe, around 10 minutes on foot to the east, is also particularly impressive. The small, somewhat hemmed-in temple was built at the beginning of the 20th century and dedicated to Le Chan, a comrade of the Trung sisters (► Famous People). Sacrifices are offered at the main altar, especially on the 8th day of the 2nd lunar month, the annual **temple festival**, when plates of shrimp with rice noodles are laid here. The Den Nghe is also known for its pretty woodcarvings.

Den Nghe

The origin of the Le Chan district was the village of Kenh, the old Dinh of which is found on Duong Hanh Kenh Street. In general, the

Dinh Hanh Kenh

Finely crafted wood carvings decorate Nge Temple

Hai Phong's wonderful carpets are made here

village gods are usually honoured in these congregation houses, but this one is dedicated to King Ngo Quyen, the conqueror of South China (938). The short building with the curved roof was built opposite an artificial lake, in the shape of a boat. Great attention to detail was put into the façade and the astonishing **carvings**. More than 500 wooden reliefs, portraying scenes from everyday life, are found here. Despite being over 200 years old, most of them are still in their original condition.

Around Hai Phong

Do Son Around 20km/12mi south of Hai Phong, surrounded by lush green forests and palm-lined beaches, the Do Son peninsula juts out into the Gulf of Tonkin. The approximately 4km/2.5mi-long sandy beach is divided into three sections and protected by a chain of hills. Day trippers from Hanoi or Hai Phong like to flee from the heat of the city to the peninsula to enjoy the cool sea breeze beneath the palms and casuarinas. For the many visitors, 40 more or less confidence-inspiring hotels line the 4km/2.5mi beach. Since 1994 there has also been a casino, the first one in Vietnam. A walk to the **Spring of the Dragon** can be recommended, and to **Ba Da Temple** at the northern end of the peninsula. This is dedicated to a young maiden who killed herself after a night of love with a courtier.

✶ Hanoi

Province: Ha Noi (city state)   **Region:** Red River Delta
Population: Approx. 3.5 million

**»The city between the rivers« – that is what the Vietnamese call
their capital. The Red River delta, where dragons and Mongols
once ruled, is today home to one of the most beautiful cities in
Asia – with French charm and typical Vietnamese chaos. In the historic old town beats the somewhat lived-in heart of Hanoi – increasingly between chic boutiques and cafés.**

The area around Hanoi is referred to as the cradle of Vietnamese culture. Even if, in the consciousness of the Western world, Saigon
played the lead role in colonial history and the wars of the 19th and
20th centuries, Hanoi, with its 4000 years of history, is undoubtedly
the more important city. Here, in the Red River delta and the nearby
mountains, is the source of the early **ancestral legends** of the Vietnamese people. There are numerous mythological tales, too, about
the city itself and its foundation.

**Cradle of Viet-
namese culture**

Hanoi's atmosphere is characterized by the various epochs and their
representative figures like no other place in Vietnam. Kings and Confucius, colonial rulers and military recruits, and, more recently, even
capitalists have made their mark on the cityscape: hundreds of temples and pagodas alternate with colonial façades and Art Deco villas,
socialist prestigious buildings, mirror-glassed high-rises and department stores. The highly modern Hanoi can best be seen in the **West**

Highlights *Hanoi*

**Tai chi, jogging and aerobics at
Hoan Kiem Lake**
Get up early to witness this huge sporting
spectacle. The best thing to do is join in!
▶ page 248

Water Puppet Theatre
Drama in the damp: the Vietnamese bring
their puppets to life.
▶ page 255

**Stroll through
the old town**
Drift along through the tangle of streets,
follow the scents or buy something exotic.
▶ page 257

Temple of Literature
The highest officials of the land were once
trained at this important Confucian sanctuary.
▶ page 261

Ho Chi Minh Mausoleum
Be prepared to wait in line for quite a
while before paying respects to the father
of the country.
▶ page 264

Ethnological Museum
Those who wish to learn about Vietnam's
people, their history, culture, customs and
traditions, are in the right place here.
▶ page 272

Lake district: villas, mini hotels and luxury accommodation have appeared on the banks. The many parks, lakes and tamarind-shaded avenues lend Hanoi a pleasantly green countenance.

Close to Hanoi, archaeological finds have revealed traces of significant early cultures such as the Dong Son epoch 2500 years ago or the prehistoric Hoa Binh culture. Under various names over the last two millennia, Hanoi has served as the **residence of princes and kings** and the centre of the administration and the military, of Confucian teachings and science, but the city was also often the setting for power struggles between competing dynasties. Particularly in the 18th and 19th centuries, many palaces were razed to the ground, while remnants of old fortresses such as Co Loa (3rd century BC) and Dai La (9th century) remained intact.

History		
7th century	The Chinese construct the Dai La fortress.
1010	The Ly dynasty moves its seat to Dai La.
18th century	The Chinese are finally expelled from the city.
around 1882	French occupy Hanoi.
1945	In Hanoi, Ho Chi Minh declares the Democratic Republic in the north.
1976	Hanoi becomes the national capital of the unified Vietnam.
1986	Economic reforms, enacted at the National Party Congress in Hanoi, mark the turning point in Vietnamese politics.
1996	US Embassy opens in Hanoi.

1010, when the Vietnamese **Ly dynasty** moved their residence to the fortress of Dai La, is considered the year that Hanoi was founded. Under the rule of the Ly dynasty in the 11th century, the One Pillar Pagoda and the Temple of Literature, the first academy in Vietnam, were built, as was the civil service. Over the course of the following centuries, Hanoi was repeatedly conquered by invaders (China, the Nguyen dynasty), from time to time lost its function as capital and was renamed several times. Only since the beginning of the 19th century has the city been called Hanoi. Beginning in 1862–63, the French were able to bring large portions of Vietnam under their influence, starting from the south and moving up. Eventually, in 1882, they captured Hanoi. They declared the city the capital of their northern protectorate of Tonkin and of the entire **colony of Indochina**.

After the Second World War, on 2 September 1945, Ho Chi Minh declared independence from Ba Dinh Square and proclaimed the

The bridge to the Jade Mountain Temple is also known as →
»the place where the morning sun rests«

Morning Tai Chi exercises at Hoan Kiem Lake

Democratic Republic of Vietnam (DRV) in the north. The French colonial rulers initially recognized this independence in a treaty, but shortly afterwards reoccupied Hanoi and Saigon. It was not until 1954, after eight years of the Indochina War, that the Communist Vietminh was able to emerge from the underground to re-enter Hanoi and take over power in the north of the now partitioned country – around one million people fled to the southern republic in the time that followed. After the end of the **Vietnam War** – the bombs fell on Hanoi until December 1972 – Vietnam was reunited as the Socialist Republic of Vietnam (SRV) on 2 July 1976, with Hanoi the capital of the unified nation for the first time. The turning point in Vietnamese politics came at the Sixth National Party Congress of the Communist Party in Hanoi (1986), at which far reaching economic reforms were enacted. A further decade passed before the US Embassy was opened in Hanoi in 1996. Finally, in 2000, President Clinton visited Hanoi. Today, national leaders from across the world come and go regularly, as Vietnam ranks high on the list of countries attracting **foreign investment**, and trade with the Americans in particular has doubled several times in a row over recent years. Tourists no longer neglect Hanoi either. The Vietnamese capital is just as much a part of the sightseeing itinerary as its southern sister metropolis, Saigon.

Around Hoan Kiem Lake

★★
Hoan Kiem Lake

At first sight, Hoan Kiem Lake in the centre of Hanoi seems rather small – it is possible to walk around it in a hour without hurrying.

Yet it is still the soul of Hanoi. Even early in the morning, there is already plenty going on. Joggers do their laps, walkers stroll around, and aerobic dancers move to disco rhythms. In the northwestern corner of the lake a small community of mostly older people practise **tai chi**. At midday, many who work in the nearby offices and shops take their breaks in the park at the lake. In the afternoons, old men play Chinese chess and children scramble around. There is also plenty going on in the evenings: couples meet, families enjoy a stroll and many tourists head from here to the streets of the old town again.

In the middle of Hoan Kiem Lake, which means »lake of the restored sword«, a three-level pavilion, the **Tortoise Tower**, stands on a little island. An old legend tells of Le Loi, the national hero who led the uprising against the Chinese occupiers in the 15th century. It is said that while fishing in this lake, Le Loi caught a shining sword, with whose help he was able to defeat the Chinese after ten years of battle. When he returned, he wished to thank the spirit of the lake, but while he was preparing his offering there was a loud roll of thunder and the sword flew out of its sheath directly into the mouth of a golden tortoise, who brought it back to the gods. The story is one of the most popular in Vietnam to this day, and it is often presented at water puppet theatre performances (►Baedeker Special p.358).

Across the red-lacquered The Huc Bridge is another small island on which stands Jade Mountain Temple. The pretty setting makes the bridge seem very romantic, so it is called »the place where the rising sun rests«. Next to the crossing is a 9m/30ft-high obelisk with Chinese ideographs which label it as »a pen to write on the blue sky«. Jade Mountain Temple (Den Ngoc Son, opening times: daily 8am–5pm) is beautifully situated between two ancient trees. It was built here in the 14th century and dedicated to a very select group: General Tran Hung Dao, who defeated the Mongols in 1288, the God of Literature Van Xuong, the physicist La To and the warrior Quan Vu. The building that stands today dates from the 19th century and displays a number of elements typical of the Nguyen dynasty, such as the remarkable **dragons' heads**. The real highlight, and the reason most tourists come here, is not found in the main altar room, but in another room outside: it is the shell of a gigantic tortoise, caught in 1968.

Huc Bridge and Jade Mountain Temple

In the main altar room of the Jade Mountain Temple

Hanoi Map

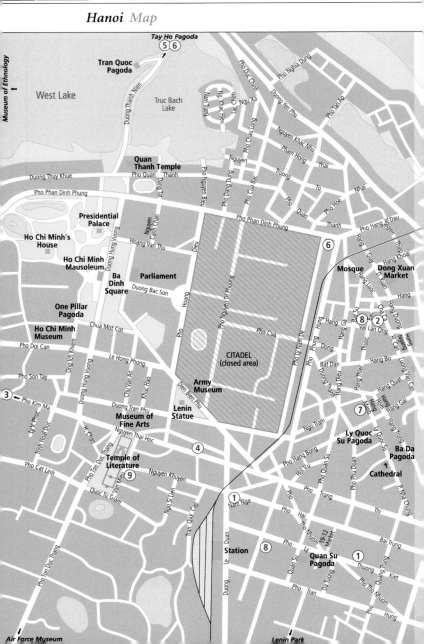

Tay Ho Pagoda

Tran Quoc Pagoda

West Lake

Truc Bach Lake

Museum of Ethnology

Quan Thanh Temple

Pho Quan Thanh

Duong Thuy Khue

Pho Phan Dinh Phung

Presidential Palace

Ho Chi Minh's House

Ho Chi Minh Mausoleum

Ba Dinh Square

Parliament

Duong Bac Son

One Pillar Pagoda

Ho Chi Minh Museum

Pho Doi Can

Chua Mot Cot

Le Hong Phong

Pho Son Tay

Pho Kim Ma

Duong Tran Phu

Museum of Fine Arts

Nguyen Thai Hoc

Temple of Literature

Quoc Tu Giam

Nguyen Khuyen

Pho Cat Linh

Pho Phan Dinh Phung

CITADEL (closed area)

Army Museum

Lenin Statue

Mosque

Dong Xuan Market

Hang

Ngo Tram

Ly Quoc Su Pagoda

Ba Da Pagoda

Cathedral

Pho Hang Bong

Pho Quan Su

Nam Nga

Pho Hai

Station

Quan Su Pagoda

19-12 Market

Bai Trung

Pho Ton Duc Thang

Air Force Museum

Lenin Park

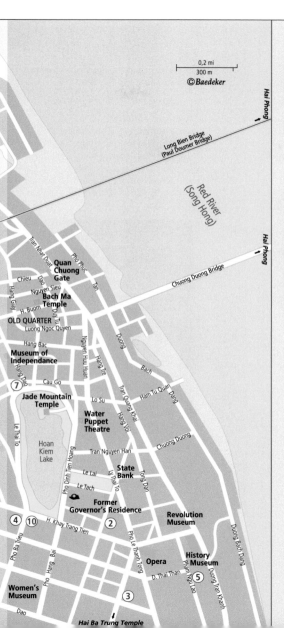

0,2 mi
300 m
©Baedeker

Where to stay
1. Sol Meliá Hanoi
2. Sofitel Metropole
3. Daewoo Hotel
4. Zephyr Hotel
5. Army Hotel
6. Chains First Eden Hotel
7. Hong Ngoc
8. Continental Hotel

Where to eat
1. Indochine
2. Cha Ca La Vong Restaurant
3. Nam Phuong
4. Brother's Café
5. Highland Coffee
6. Sen Restaurant
7. Kim Quy
8. Quan An Ngon
9. KOTO
10. Bobby Chinn

▶ VISITING HANOI

INFORMATION
Vietnam Tourism Hanoi
30A Ly Thuong Kiet,
Hoan Kiem, Hanoi
Tel. 04/ 8 26 40 89
www.vn-tourism.com
www.vietnamtourism.com

Saigon Tourist
55B Phan Chau Trinh,
Hoan Kiem, Hanoi
Tel. 04/8 25 09-23
www.saigontouristhanoi.com

Better information can sometimes be
found at travel agencies or hotels.

TOUR OPERATORS
Asiatica Travel
Suite A1203
Building M3-M4
91 Nguyen Chi Nhanh
Tel. 04/266 28 16
Fax 266 28 18
www.asiaticatravel.com
info@asiaticatravel.com
City tours, walking tours, excursions
to Ha Long Bay, kayak tours etc.
English and French-speaking guides.

TRANSPORT
Noi Bai International Airport (approx.
30km/19mi away): tel. 04/8 86 65 27;
Vietnam Airlines shuttle buses starting
in the old town, public bus lines 7 and
17.
Main railway station: 120 Le Duan,
ticket reservations tel. 04/8 25 39 49
and 8 25 27 70; information tel. 04/9
42 36 97 (for tourists: desk 2 – beware:
in the past, not all trains have departed
from here).
In the city: the best way to get around
is on foot, by moped-taxi (as pillion
passenger) or by Cyclo (always negotiate beforehand!) or the inexpensive
taxameter taxis (around 30 cents per
km; only the new, very good public
buses are cheaper, there is a map for
sale showing the bus lines).

EVENTS
National Holiday
On 2 September independence is
celebrated more enthusiastically here
than in other places, with a military
parade (traditionally-clothed attendees
and women marching along), a fireworks display at Hoan Kiem Lake and
boat races.

SHOPPING

In the *old town*, the best streets for
shopping and a stroll are: Hang Gai,
Hang Bong, Hang Trong (silk goods,
tailors); the chic and expensive Pho Na
Tho; Bao Hung and Hai Van (T-shirts
with likeness of HCM) as well as Hang
Bong (handicrafts).

Shop until midnight: in the *Dong Xuan market hall*, the largest market in Hanoi, there is fresh fish, sweets, lacquerware, karaoke machines and much more (Hang Khoai, corner Dong Xuan, old town).
Craft Link (43 Van Mieu) and *Hoa Sen Gallery* (51 Van Mieu): both of these handicrafts shops at the Temple of Literature funnel their proceeds into projects for street children or ethnic minorities in the mountains. *Craft Collection* (39A Ly Quoc): handicrafts of the hill tribes and a nice selection of souvenirs are available at this well-known chain.

CULINARY SPECIALITIES

Nom bo kho is the name of a tasty beef salad with green (unripe) strips of papaya and peanuts which attracts locals to the food stall next to the Thang Long Theatre on the Hoan Kiem Lake.
Bun cha, the North Vietnamese speciality with grilled meat and rice noodles, fresh herbs, chilli and cabbage, is best enjoyed in the old town street of Hang Manh.
Inexpensive seafood restaurants line the bank of West Lake on *Thuy Khue*: earthy atmosphere, great view, huge selection of living sea creatures.

WHERE TO EAT
► Expensive
① *Indochine*
16 Nam Ngu
Tel. 04/9 42 40 97
daily 11.30am–2pm, 5.30pm–10pm
A classic: excellent Vietnamese cuisine in an elegant atmosphere, traditional music in the evening.

► Moderate
② *Cha Ca La Vong Restaurant*
14 Cha Ca
Tel. 04/8 25 39 29

For many, this is a must in Hanoi. Famous for its speciality: fish with rice noodles, herbs, fish sauce and peanuts.

③ *Nam Phuong*
19 Phan Chu Trinh
Tel. 04/8 24 09 26
Elegant restaurant in a wonderfully restored French villa. South Vietnamese dishes, traditional music performances.

④ *Brother's Café*
26 Nguyen Thai Hoc,
Tel. 04/7 33 38 66
Mon–Sat 11.30am–2pm,
daily 6.30pm–10.30pm
Marvellous old temple ruin with columns and a calm, courtyard oasis. Vietnamese buffet, bar in evening.

⑤ *Highland Coffee*
34 Thanh Nien, West Lake
Tel. 04/8 29 21 40
daily 7am–11pm
Trendy two-floor floating restaurant on the bank of West Lake, with seating outside beneath sun shades or in the air-conditioned interior, with music. Small Asian and international snacks, soups, salads, wine and inexpensive cocktails.

⑥ *Sen Restaurant*
10 Ngo 431, Au Co, West Lake
Tel. 04/9 13 52 35 and 7 19 92 42
daily 11am–2pm, 6pm–11pm
Some distance from the city centre, but worth the trip. Dine in pagoda-like pavilions with a lakeside view (open-air or in the historic building, 500 seats in total) with traditional live music (Mon and Fri) or piano accompaniment. Buffet with around 60 Vietnamese specialities and classics à la carte or set meals.

▶ Inexpensive

⑦ *Kim Quy*

3 Le Thai To, Hoan Kiem
Tel. 04/9 28 78 68
Pleasant restaurant and bar, narrow balcony on the first floor overlooking Hoan Kiem Lake. Vietnamese and international cuisine, set meals in the evening.

⑧ *Quan An Ngon*

18 Phan Boi Chau
Tel. 04/9 42 81 62
A huge selection of freshly prepared dishes are offered at different stands and eaten in the large courtyard beneath potted trees and canvas marquees or in the rooms of the adjacent villa.

⑨ *KOTO (know one, teach one)*

59 Van Mieu (right of the Temple of Literature)
Tel. 04/7 47 03 37,
www.koto.com.au
daily 8am–11pm
Tiny restaurant belonging to an Australian project for street children, who are trained as cooks, barkeepers and waiters here. Small Asian, western and vegetarian dishes, sandwiches, fruit juices, milkshakes, cocktails etc. are served on two floors.

ENTERTAINMENT

⑩ *Bobby Chinn*

1 Ba Trieu, Hoan Kiem (southwestern corner of the lake)
Tel. 04/9 34 85-77/-78
daily 11am–midnight or later
Chic restaurant and novel club-bar with an Arabian touch (hookahs in an extra room) between colourful silk curtains – award-winning for the large selection of wines and spirits. Take off your shoes and snuggle into the cushions!

WHERE TO STAY

▶ Luxury

① *Sol Meliá Hanoi*

44 B Ly Thuong Kiet, Hoan Kiem
Tel. 04/9 34 33 34, fax 9 34 33 44
www.solmelia.com
melia.hanoi@solmelia.com
Five-star high-rise hotel near Hoan Kiem Lake with every luxury. Famous guests included Fidel Castro.

Baedeker recommendation

② *Sofitel Metropole*

15 Ngo Quyen, Hoan Kiem
Tel. 04/8 26 69 19, fax 8 26 69 20
www.sofitel.com
sofitelhanoi@hn.vnn.vn
Hanoi's traditional hotel from 1911 has been praised by authors such as Graham Greene and Somerset Maugham. Comfortable rooms and excellent service, French restaurant, bar, swimming pool and conference rooms.

③ *Daewoo Hotel*

Daeha Centre
360 Kim Ma Street

Ba Dinh District
Tel. 04/8 31 50 00
Fax 8 31 50 10
www.hanoi-daewoohotel.com
reservation@daewoohotel.com
This modern hotel is a joint venture with South Korea, a 15-storey building in the west of the city with plenty of extras: swimming pool, nightclub, fitness centre, restaurants and conference rooms are just some of them.

► Mid-range

④ *Zephyr Hotel*
4 Ba Trieu, Hoan Kiem
Tel. 04/9 34 12 56
Fax 9 34 12 62
www.zephyrhotel.com.vn
Elegant hotel, central and quiet, with 40 rather small rooms, some with large balconies and a panoramic view of Hoan Kiem Lake.

⑤ *Army Hotel*
33c Pham Ngu Lao
Tel. 04/8 25 28 96 and 8 26 55 41
Fax 8 25 92 76
armyhotel@fpt.vn
Don't be put off by the name! This hotel (84 rooms) is central yet quietly located in a side street near the Historical Museum. The decor – in a former military guesthouse – is plain but quite acceptable. Good service, large pool.

⑥ *Chains First Eden Hotel*
2 Phung Hung
Tel. 04/8 28 38 96
Fax 8 28 40 66
cfeden@hn.vnn.vn
Business hotel (42 rooms) with health centre, sauna, conference rooms and restaurant. Situated in the north of the Old Quarter close to the Long Bien Bridge.

► Budget

⑦ *Hong Ngoc*
34 Hang Manh, Hoan Kiem
Tel. 04/8 28 50 53
Fax 8 28 50 54
hongngochotel@hn.vnn.vn
Mini hotel with large rooms, beautiful furniture with carved wood and mother-of-pearl inlays, TV, air conditioning, some with balcony (meanwhile, nearly every district in Hanoi has a hotel from this very good chain).

⑧ *Continental Hotel*
24 Hang Vai, Old Town
Tel. 04/8 28 28 97
Fax 8 28 29 89
continental@fmail.vnn.vn
Comfortable and central hotel with 15 super-cheap and well equipped rooms (bathtub, small balcony). Travel agency.

For more than 1000 years, an art form that is unique worldwide has held its own in Vietnam in the face of MTV, soap operas, Gameboys and the rest: in water puppet theatre (mua roi nuoc), people and stories from everyday life in Vietnam play the lead role. The colourful wooden puppets and figures rise from the water as in a **real water ballet**. To this day, the puppeteers stand behind a curtain, up to their hips in water and, by means of metre-long, invisible bamboo poles and strings, they get the puppets to glide across the water as if by magic (57B Dinh Tien Hoang, tel. 04/8 24 94 94, daily 4pm, 6.30pm and 8pm; also in Hanoi Water Park, 614 Lac Long Quan, Tay Ho).

★ ★
Kim Dong Water Puppet Theatre (Thang Long Ensemble)

Pagoda accessories are found at the Hang Quat in the Old Quarter

Ba Da Pagoda When walking around the southern part of the lake, there is the chance to take a detour to the cathedral in Nha Tho Street. On the way is Ba Da Pagoda, its entrance decorated with arcades. The pagoda contains an impressive collection of Buddha figures.

Cathedral ▶ In order to build the Cathedral of St Joseph in the 1880s, the French colonial rulers sacrificed the most significant pagoda in Hanoi (Chua Bao Thien) with its ten-floor tower. Particularly notable are the colourful glass windows and the many votive tablets in the Lady Chapel in the northern nave. A black marble grave lies on the opposite side – this is where the last Vietnamese cardinal was laid to rest after his death in 1990. The main entrance to the cathedral is only used during Mass, otherwise it is possible to enter through the side door in Nha Chung Street (closed 1pm–2pm).

Ly Quoc Su Pagoda Follow Ly Quoc Su Street heading north to reach the little Ly Quoc Su Pagoda (13th century), named after a Buddhist healer, teacher and royal adviser. He is said to have cured the hallucinating king Ly Thanh Tong of his mad belief that he was a tiger. The healer's likeness crowns the altar, with three Buddhas behind it. He is flanked by a number of interesting statues: four female figures on one side and three mandarins on the other. Walking around the various altars, a number of old stone figures, which date from around 1500, can be seen opposite the rear wall.

✳ Old Quarter

The narrow streets of the old commercial district of Hanoi call to mind a beehive. The shops are overgrown with climbing plants and bird cages are hung outside, their occupants tweeting and chirping away. The pavements are crowded with street stands and food stalls, from which pleasant-smelling soups are offered. Any space left over is filled with bicycles and mopeds, or populated with playing children and gossiping neighbours. Still pottering about are the scattered descendants of the **earlier trades people**, like in the street for bamboo goods (Hang Tre) or Hang Quat, in which religious devotional objects are sold. Anything to do with paper is found in Hang Ma, and jewellery can be purchased in Hang Bac. Those interested in tin objects should head for Hang Thiec, and enthusiasts of traditional healing methods will find what they need in Lan Ong.

In recent years, designer boutiques and souvenir shops, galleries, travel agencies and smart restaurants have been competing for space with the stores belonging to long-term residents, who often live on the premises and just pull down a metal lattice in the evenings. Visitors can explore the streets confidently – getting lost is almost impossible, as train tracks border the district to the north, as do the large streets Phung Hung and Tran Nhat Duat to the east and west. The many cafés are ideal for watching the hustle and bustle in peace.

Among all the distractions that present themselves in these streets, it is easy to overlook one of the architectural features of the quarter, which, alongside ► Hoi An, boasts Vietnam's only trading houses from the 15th century. These buildings in the Old Quarter are, however, not so exquisitely decorated, but are nevertheless striking, primarily for their form. They are known as »tube houses« because from the street only a small shop can be seen, often only 2m/7ft wide, but this is attached to a workshop and then several living, sleeping and storage rooms, so that in the end the buildings often reach lengths of 60–80m/200–260ft! This kind of house arose because **taxes** were once calculated based on the size of the shop front, and businesses were divided accordingly upon inheritance. The entire building features courtyards at regular intervals, letting in light and air, and where rain water can be collected and vegetables planted; there are also often pens for small animals.

Atmospheric quarter with narrow, noisy streets

Baedeker TIP

Typical tube house

A typical tube house can be viewed at number 87 Ma May Street (put slippers on!). The former inhabitants were members of the bamboo-makers' guild (ma may) and three generations of them lived in this marvellously restored wooden house. Note the finely carved folding doors and windows with the four mythological animals, and the real gem on the second floor in the form of a bed with mother-of-pearl decoration (opening times: daily 8am–5pm).

✳
Tube houses

The outer façades of some of the »tube houses« were changed during the colonial era, and received balconies when the streets were widened to build walkways. Yet some of the owners were wealthy or influential enough that exceptions were made for their houses, and to this day they stand out in the streetscape, as can be seen in Hang Ba and Ma May Street.

Museum of Independence

The building at 48 Hang Ngang is where Ho Chi Minh drafted the Declaration of Independence of the Democratic Republic of Vietnam of 1945. The building, in which he lived at the time, today houses the Museum of Independence (opening times: Tue–Sun 8am–5pm). In the upper rooms, the original furnishings can be seen, while downstairs there is a small photo exhibition.

Bach Ma Temple

Bach Ma Temple on Hang Buom Street is the oldest and most visited sanctuary in this district. Founded in the 9th century, it was later dedicated to the White Horse (Bach Ma), the guardian spirit of Thang Long. The building that stands today dates from the 18th century, and its most valuable possession is the **copper Bach Ma statue**, represented here in its original form as the earth god, Long Do. On either side of the altar a replica of a horse and two guard figures, which are blessed with gold-painted rows of teeth, catch the eye (opening times: daily 7.30am–11am 2pm–6pm.

Modelled on the one in Paris – the Hanoi Opera

✶ French Quarter

A stark contrast to the busy bustle in the narrow streets of the Old Quarter can be found in the generously proportioned boulevards of the French Quarter, south and east of Hoan Kiem Lake. The first French settlement was established in 1874, close to the site of the Opera today. Many unique Vietnamese buildings were razed to the ground at this time. The attractions in this area are not as close to one another as they are near Hoan Kiem Lake and in the Old Quarter.

Colonial legacy on broad boulevards

It is easy, even at the first glimpse, to see that the Hanoi Opera is modelled on an important building, namely the Paris Opera. For its construction, the land near the Red River was first reclaimed; after ten years of construction, it was finally inaugurated in 1911. For many years, the Opera was the pride of French Hanoi, its cultural and commercial heart – until 1945, when the Vietminh proclaimed the **August Revolution** from its balcony. It is located on the corner of Trang Tien and Le Thai To. Unfortunately, it is not possible to visit its interior.

✶ Opera

The History Museum is located only one block further east (1 Pham Ngu Lao Street). The building can be found a little hidden behind trees, a mixture of a Vietnamese palace and a French villa.
The first room wastes no time in teaching about the Dong Son culture (1200 to 200 BC). The most significant relics from this time are the large **bronze drums**, which were beaten at ceremonies, at funerals, to summon the monsoon or to perform fertility rituals. An especially beautiful piece with finely worked figures (game, people, ships) is found in the next room: the Ngoc Lu Drum. Further important exhibits on this level are the meditating Buddha from Phat Tich Pagoda (11th century), a gold-inscribed lacquered tablet (11th century) with a poem by King Ly Thuong Kiet, which is considered to be Vietnam's first declaration of independence, and a group of five wooden posts originating from the glorious battle at Bach Dang River (1288).
The upper floor is dominated by the 3m/ 10ft-high **stele in praise of Le Loi**, who led the resistance movement against Chinese occupation (15th century). Some interesting exhibits refer to the Nguyen dynasty and their life at the court of Hue as well as the time of French colonial rule. The last section of the room is dedicated to the struggle for independence under the leadership of Ho Chi Minh.

✶ History Museum
🕐
Opening hours:
Tue–Sun
8.30am–5pm

Meditating Buddha (11th century)

Revolution Museum

Those wishing to learn more about the Vietnamese independence movement should pay a visit to the Revolution Museum, one block further north (216 Tran Quang Khai Street). The colonial building was once the headquarters of the customs supervision. Today, the history of the liberation is shown, from the beginning of the 20th century until 1975 (opening times: Tue–Sun 8am–11.30am, 1.30pm–4.30pm).

Residence of the Governor of Tonkin

The **prettiest colonial building in Hanoi** was built in 1918 and is used today by the government as a guesthouse for high-ranking visitors of state. Unfortunately, it is not possible to visit this pretty estate on Ngo Quyen Street. The terrace my seem familiar to film buffs, as a number of scenes from the film *Indochine* were shot here.

Trang Tien Street

Trang Tien Street, the main street of the French Quarter, runs south of Hoan Kiem Lake directly to the Opera. On this lively commercial street are all kinds of book shops and galleries, cafés and hotels.

On the corner of Hang Bai stands the eight-storey »Hanoi Plaza« with shops, apartments and offices. South of Trang Tien is the start of the actual **villa district** of the French Quarter, through which run cool, shady boulevards. As in the Old Quarter, these genteel buildings have survived primarily due to a lack of money. There are many European influences from the early 20th century exhibited here, from the elegant neoclassicism of the 1920s to Art Deco with a particularly oriental note.

Women's Museum

36 Ly Thuong Kiet Street is home to the Women's Museum, opened in 1994. The exhibits are very nicely presented on three floors and also explained in English. The purpose of the collection is to present the role of women in Vietnamese society, in doing so not overlooking the world of the gods and ethnic minorities. Of particular interest are the **handcrafted works** by women of the, Khmer, Hmong, Ede, Cham and Dao peoples (opening times: Tue–Sun 8am–5pm).

Hanoi Hilton / Hoa Lo Prison

The legendary »Hanoi Hilton«, which attained worldwide notoriety in the 1960s, stood just one block further west at the crossing of Hai Ba Trung and Hoa Lu. This was under no circumstances luxury accommodation; rather it was a prison in which American soldiers were held and also tortured.

Since 1997, an exclusive hotel and conference centre has been here, a modern high-rise has jutting skywards (»Hanoi Tower«). A **museum** was established in a remaining part of the old building to commemorate the prisoners – both Americans and also Vietnamese, who were held here under French colonial rule (opening times: Tue–Sun 8am–11.30am, 1.30pm–4.30pm).

Ambassador's Pagoda (Chua Quan Su)

Turn leftat the next crossing into Quan Su Street to reach the Ambassador's Pagoda (Chua Quan Su, opening times: daily except Sat

8.30am–11.30am and 1.30pm–4pm). As the name suggests, it was built in the 15th century to provide accommodation for ambassadors from neighbouring Buddhist countries. However, the building which stands today is not so old, having been constructed in 1942.

To this day, Quan Su Pagoda is one of the most significant and **most-visited cult sites** of the city. In the large prayer room, old ladies sit beneath the smoky lanterns, reciting sutras. On the 1st and 15th days of the 5th lunar month, pilgrims and beggars crowd the forecourt, while inside a huge iron lamp seems to hover over the believers, lighting the crimson Buddhas through a misty shroud of incense smoke.

✳ Temple of Literature (Van Mieu)

Van Mieu Pagoda is not only the most lavish and beautiful temple complex in the city, but primarily the main sanctuary of Confucianism and the first university in Vietnam. The Temple of Literature was built in 1070 under Emperor Ly Thanh Tong, and the National Gallery was founded six years later by King Ly Nhan Tong and dedicated in honour of Confucius, who had a large and wealthy legion of followers in Vietnam. It is said that the design of the temple complex

Confucian sanctuary and first university in Vietnam
🕐
Opening hours:
daily 8am–5pm

The interior of the Temple of Literature glows red-gold

Hanoi Temple of Literature

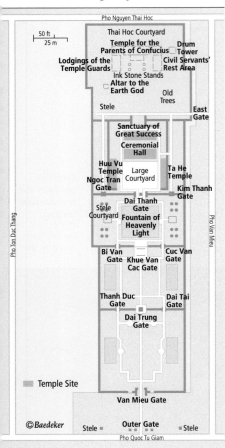

Pho Nguyen Thai Hoc

50 ft
25 m

Thai Hoc Courtyard
Temple for the
Parents of Confucius
Drum
Tower
Lodgings of the
Temple Guards
Civil Servants'
Rest Area
Ink Stone Stands
Altar to the
Earth God
Old
Trees
Stele
East
Gate

Sanctuary of
Great Success
Ceremonial
Hall
Huu Vu
Temple
Large
Courtyard
Ta He
Temple
Ngoc Tran
Gate
Kim Thanh
Gate
Stele
Courtyard
Dai Thanh
Gate
Fountain of
Heavenly
Light

Bi Van
Gate
Cuc Van
Gate
Khue Van
Cac Gate

Thanh Duc
Gate
Dai Tai
Gate

Dai Trung
Gate

Pho Ton Duc Thang

Pho Van Mieu

■ Temple Site

Van Mieu Gate

©Baedeker

Stele ■
Outer Gate
■ Stele

Pho Quoc Tu Giam

is based upon a sanctuary at Confucius's birthplace in Qufu (China). Today the Temple of Literature is interpreted as a symbol of the diminishing significance of Buddhism during the Ly dynasty, which the religious teachings of Confucius began to supersede. In time, Van Mieu became the intellectual and spiritual centre of the kingdom, whereby education took on a new status at the court, under the mandarins and among the people. But the place serves not only as a venue for exams; as at other pagodas, the poor and the sick are fed. The complex, aligned from north to south, built as a series of walled courtyards, is entered from Quoc Tu Giam Street.

On both sides of the outer gate, an inscription on the **stelae**, »ha ma«, orders the visitor to descend from his horse. This is to remind even the highest of dignitaries that they must continue along the path on foot from here. It leads to the large **Van Mieu Gate** (15th century), which is decorated with dragons and only opened on special holidays. Pass through it to arrive at a small, meticulously laid out park with lawns and trees. Through the plainer **Dai Trung Gate** is a second, similarly designed garden and the Khue Van Cac Gate (1805), the two-storied pavilion, which leads to the third courtyard. Its upper section is decorated with four shining suns; the roof is covered with yin-yang tiles.

★ ★
Stelae courtyard

The stele courtyard comes next. In the middle is a pond bordered by walls: the Fountain of Heavenly Light. It is flanked on both sides by rows of stone tortoises, which carry stone stelae. These are the **most valuable pieces in the sanctuary**, for they carry the results of the examinations of the Confucian academy as well as the names of 1036 successful graduates. The 82 remaining stelae – 30 are no longer there – originate from the years 1442 to 1779.

Each one stands vertically on the back of a tortoise, the symbol of strength and long life. There is no recognizably consistent order, but the two oldest stelae (1442 and 1448) are each found in the middle of the first row. The 14 smallest, dating from the 15th and 16th centuries, carry floral motifs and yin-yang symbols, but no stately dragons. The portrayal of dragons was first allowed in the 17th century, as can be seen on the 25 stelae from this period. The remaining 43 were made in the 18th century. They are the largest and most imposing, decorated with two stylized dragons and flames.

Stelae carried by tortoises

The fourth yard is entered through the Gate of Great Success (Dai Thanh Gate)and leads to the actual temple buildings. The pavilions on both sides once held altars and statues, which were dedicated to the 76 students of Confucius. Today books and souvenirs can be purchased here, and an exhibition can be viewed.

✳ **Gate of Great Success (Dai Thanh Gate)**

The Ceremony Hall, a low building with a curved roof, is crowned by two dragons supporting a full moon. The red-gold altar room is where the king and his mandarins made their offerings to the sound of drums and gongs. Two bronze cranes, standing on tortoises, guard the genealogical table of Confucius. The beautiful **carvings** showing dragons, phoenixes, lotus flowers, fruit, clouds and yin yang symbols are striking. These portrayals stand for the Confucian concept of the order of the universe and for the god-given hierarchy of society – both principles which the Communist rulers hardly welcomed, but did tolerate. Sometimes there is an opportunity to attend traditional concerts.

✳ **Ceremony Hall**

Directly behind the Ceremony Hall lies the sanctum that was once even forbidden to the king. In the middle of the darkened room stands a statue of Confucius, surrounded by his four most important students. To the side on two altars are the genealogical tables of a total of ten further important students.

✳ **Sanctuary of Great Success**

The fifth and last courtyard (Thai Hoc Courtyard) was once the seat of the National Academy, the first university in the land. It was founded in 1076, originally to educate the heirs to the throne, and

Fifth courtyard / Thai Hoc Courtyard

later also the sons of the mandarins and high officials. This procedure was practiced almost without interruption until 1802, when

Emperor Gia Long moved the capital to Hue. Then a temple to the parents of Confucius was established. However, in 1947 French bombs destroyed the building, which was restored some years ago. In the former National Academy, a small **museum** on the ground floor shows a model of the Temple of Literature, historic garments, wooden printing plates and old writings, as well as writing utensils belonging to the former students.

On the second floor are three altars in honour of the kings Ly Nhan Tong, Ly Thanh Tong and Le Thanh Tong.

Ho Chi Minh Mausoleum and Its Surroundings

Ba Dinh Square

The lavishly arranged Ba Dinh Square is the political and ceremonial centre of the Vietnamese capital. The mausoleum of Ho Chi Minh dominates the west side of the square, and the National Assembly stands opposite. This is where, on 2 September 1945, Ho Chi Minh read the **declaration of independence** in front of half a million people, and a military parade has been held here every year in commemoration ever since.

★ ★
Ho Chi Minh Mausoleum

🕐
Opening hours: April–Sept daily except Mon and Fri 7.30am–10.30am, Nov–Mar daily except Mon and Fri 8am–11am; usually closed Sept and Nov for restoration of the body

In the tradition of great communist leaders, the corpse of Ho Chi Minh was embalmed – against his will, however. The instructions he left were as follows: »Divide my ashes into three parts and keep them in three ceramic urns, representing the north, the centre and the south«. The body was not displayed publicly until 1975, but today the mausoleum is one of Hanoi's main attractions – for Vietnamese and tourists alike. The masses throng here, especially at weekends and on holidays, to pay their respects to »Uncle Ho«. Even if the building seems gloomy and hulking, a visit is not to be missed. The escort by soldiers in white uniforms, the ceremonial silence and the effective lighting of Ho Chi Minh's face and hands make the passage through the hall a unique experience.

Foreign visitors must leave their bags and cameras at reception in Hung Vuong Street before proceeding to the assembly point. From here, visitors are escorted into the mausoleum. There is no admission for those in shorts, miniskirts or shoulder-baring tops.

Presidential Palace

After leaving the mausoleum, the path continues to the former Presidential Palace and the house of Ho Chi Minh, which is also located on this premises. The Residence of the Governor General of Indochi-

No home is without his image, no city without his statue, and no political speech fails to invoke his name – Ho Chi Minh

UNCLE HO

Although little is known about the private life of Ho Chi Minh, today most Vietnamese refer to him familiarly as Bac Ho (Uncle Ho). His life is inextricably bound up with the history of his country and its struggle for independence.

He left hardly any personal writings for posterity and in the course of his life lived under about **50 different names**, mostly as a disguise. What is known about him? Only that he was extremely cultivated – an aesthete who remained unmarried all his life and dedicated himself completely to his family, the whole Vietnamese people.

Early career

Under the name Nguyen Sinh Cung he was born on 19 May 1890 in a small village near Ninh, the son of a low-ranking official. His father, who set great store by education, sent him to the **French grammar school** at Hue in 1905, even though he rejected the French colonial rulers and their local mandarins – an attitude that his son adopted. In 1911 Ho left the country and travelled to America and Europe as a cabin boy. He worked in the docks at Brooklyn and as a pastry cook at Escoffier in the Carlton Hotel in London. Finally in 1917 he reached Paris, where he took on the name Nguyen Ai Quoc (Nguyen the Patriot) as a sign of his commitment to the nationalist cause.

Even at that time he attracted attention by presenting a **petition** during the Versailles Conference demanding a democratically elected government in Indochina. For a time he supported the French Socialists, but when this group broke up, he became a founding member of the French Communist Party, impressed by Lenin's unequivocal rejection of imperialism. This was the start of Ho Chi Minh's career as a revolutionary.

Liberation movement

In 1923 the Communist International (Comintern) called him to **Moscow** and appointed him secretary for

colonial questions. In the following years he travelled to China, Western Europe, Thailand and Hong Kong on behalf of Comintern. The first Vietnamese liberation movement, which he organized in Guangzhou (Canton) in 1924, attracted many young supporters. However, when Chiang Kai Shek, leader of the Chinese nationalists, turned against the Communists three years later, Ho was forced to flee the country.

For a time he lived in Thailand in the guise of a Buddhist monk, but back in Hong Kong in 1930 he founded the Vietnamese Communist Party, which he was forced to rename the Communist Party of Indochina a short time later on the instructions of Comintern. The French **condemned him to death** for incitement to rebellion. Ho was arrested on forged evidence and taken to hospital due to the poor state of his health. However with the help of the medical staff, who managed to convince the French police that he had died, Ho succeeded in escaping. He went underground for a few years, most of the time in Moscow, and did not reappear in the border area of south China, where he organized anticolonial resistance, until the late 1930s.

Foundation of the Vietminh

After 30 years abroad he finally returned to Vietnam early in 1941. His only possessions were the clothes and sandals he was wearing, a bamboo cane and his typewriter. He was 51 years old, and suffering from dysentery, malaria and tuberculosis. Home again, he adopted the name by which he is known today, Ho Chi Minh (»he who strives for enlightenment«), and kept it until the end of his life.

Ho Chi Minh's house in Hanoi

In accordance with Confucian tradition, »Uncle Ho« is present throughout the land even in death, by means of statues, busts, portraits or as altarpieces. He himself rejected all forms of personality cult.

In the mountains of northern Vietnam, he was joined by Vo Nguyen Giap, Pham Van Dong and other young soldiers with whom he established the League for the Independence of Vietnam (Vietminh), a union of anti-colonial groups under the leadership of the Communist Party of Vietnam. Its aim was to fight for independence from French colonial rule and Japanese occupation.

However, once again events did not go his way. On a journey to China in 1942 he was arrested on suspicion of being a **Franco-Japanese spy** and had to spend more than a year in a succession of prisons. During this period he wrote his legendary prison diary, which is in fact a collection of poems.

Partisan fighting

By now the situation in Vietnam was becoming more and more volatile, and the end of Japanese occupation in August 1945 created a power vacuum. The Vietminh were in a position to rule the country, but only for a short time. The French regained power in 1946 and the government fled to the jungle of Cao Bang, from where Ho Chi Minh led a partisan struggle that was not to end until **Dien Bien Phu** in 1954. At the Geneva Conference on Indochina the 17th parallel at Dong Ha was agreed as a provisional line of demarcation. However, the »provisional« partition of the country was to last more than 20 years.

In the next 15 years, as president of the Democratic Republic of Vietnam, Uncle Ho led his country along a socialist path that was often stony, always endeavouring to achieve reunification. His fight against South Vietnam, which was supported by the United States, made him a **symbolic figure** for the protest movements in Europe and America against American involvement in Vietnam. However, he did not live to see Vietnam reunited. He died on 2 September, 1969, the Vietnamese national day. The day of his death was therefore moved to 3 September.

The myths about Ho and his real life have now blended into a kind of cult which places him at the pinnacle of the gallery of Vietnamese national heroes – something he undoubtedly would not have wished.

na was built from 1900 to 1908; today guests of state are received here. The palace is closed to the public.

Ho Chi Minh House

After independence in 1954, Ho Chi Minh officially moved into the former royal residence, but said that it was now the property of the people. He had a more modest house built nearby. When it got too hot for him in summer, he designed a small **stilted hut**, which was built at an idyllic site on a small lake. The rooms on ground level are furnished with a desk, telephone and table; his study and bedroom upstairs are kept just as he left them.

Ho Chi Minh lived here for the last 11 years of his life (from 1958), as well as during the Vietnam War. What looks like a guest room to the left is the entrance to his bunker. It is said that Ho was very attached to his garden and his carp pond (opening times: daily 8am–11.30am).

One Pillar Pagoda

In the immediate vicinity is the One Pillar Pagoda (Chua Mot Cot). Like the Tortoise Tower at Hoan Kiem Lake, it is an emblem of Hanoi. Among the hundreds of pagodas that the Ly kings donated in the

Visitors wait in line outside the Ho Chi Minh Mausoleum

11th century, this one is surely the most unusual. The wooden Quan Am sanctuary has an area of only around 3 sq m/32 sq ft and is supported only by a single pillar, which juts out from the middle of the lake. The form is intended to represent a lotus flower, the Buddhist symbol of enlightenment. As can easily be seen, the structure in question is not actually the original, and the concrete pillar, poured in 1954, detracts from the scene immensely.

Little is known about the origins of the pagoda, but a **folk legend** says that it was built in 1049 under King Ly Thai Tong. Quan Am appeared to him in a dream, sitting on her lotus throne and holding a baby boy out toward him. Shortly thereafterthe queen gave birth to a boy,

Another of Hanoi's landmarks: the One Pillar Pagoda

and Ly Thai Tong had the pagoda built in thanks. In actual fact, he had already had a son in 1022, six years before he ascended the throne, making a less romantic version of the story slightly more believable: the king dreamed that Quan Am had invited him to sit with her on the lotus throne. The royal advisor saw this as a bad omen and persuaded him to build a pagoda in the form of a lotus in order to obtain a long life.

Behind the pagoda is a Bodhi tree, a cutting from the tree under which Buddha found enlightenment. Ho Chi Minh was presented with the sapling in 1958 during a trip to India.

🕐 Opening hours: daily 8am–6pm

The large, modern building around 100m/110yd west of the One Pillar Pagoda was built with Soviet help for the 100th birthday of Ho Chi Minh on the 19 May 1990. The museum honours the man and the special role he played for the country. Small exhibits describe his life, the Vietnamese revolution and the development of socialism throughout the world. Also to be seen are personal objects such as documents and photographs, as well as the clothes he wore when he fled Hong Kong (opening times: Tue–Sun 8am–11.30am, 1.30pm–4pm).

✱ **Ho Chi Minh Museum**

🕐

Heading east of the Ho Chi Minh Museum via Ba Dinh Square, visitors reach Dien Bien Phu Street, a road with gnarled old trees and pretty colonial buildings. Around 500m/550yd from the square, a statue of Lenin stands in front of the white, arcaded Army Museum. It is worth a visit, even for those who are not especially interested in all things military, as it gives an informative overview of the history

✱ **Army Museum**

Opening hours: daily 8am–11.30am and 1pm–4.30pm, closed Mon and Fri

of Vietnam – also in English. The yard of the museum is full of weapons, including a Russian MiG 21, artillery from Dien Bien Phu, antiaircraft guns from the Vietnam War and wreckage from American planes, among them a B52 bomber. The exhibition begins on the second floor. A feature is the **diorama of the Battle of Dien Bien Phu**. In addition, a video in English can be viewed. In comparison, the exhibition on the war is relatively drab, with mostly medals on display.

Cot Co Flag Tower

In the grounds of the Army Museum stands the 33m/108ft-high Cot Co Flag Tower, one of the few remnants of the citadel built by Emperor Gia Long in the early 19th century. There is a nice view over the city from the top, though climbing the tower is not always allowed.

West Lake and Its Surroundings

West Lake

The district around West Lake, also known as »Hanoi's Beverly Hills«, recently came into fashion as a villa district. Around the lake there are nice hotel buildings and conference centres, parks and clubs. This is also the site of **Chua Tran Quoc**, Hanoi's oldest pagoda. In the 17th century the village inhabitants built a dam at the southeastern end of the lake, creating a small lake that was rich with fish (Truc Bach).

The attractions of West Lake are on the south side, only around 500m/550yd away from Binh Dinh Square, making it easy to combine seeing the sights there with a detour to the lake (or vice versa).

The name Truc Bach refers back to a summer palace, which was built in the 18th century under the Trinh rulers and later served as a

? DID YOU KNOW ...?

■ ... how West Lake is said to have been created? A long time ago, a monk had a bell cast in bronze from the imperial Chinese treasury, in which there lived a golden calf. The calf heard the bright ringing and followed it, believing it to be his mother calling. When the ringing stopped, the calf became disoriented and in his despair he turned around and around on his own axis. This created a trough, which filled with water. It is said that the golden calf still lives at the bottom of the lake.

Truc Bach Lake

kind of asylum for concubines and other »fallen« women, who were employed here for the weaving of fine white silk (truc bach). It is splendid to ride around Truc Bach Lake on a bike, as there is barely any traffic on the very quiet, narrow streets here.

Quan Thanh Temple

The palace no longer exists, but on the southeast bank of the lake stands Quan Thanh Temple, which was built under King Ly Thai To and dedicated to the Guardian of the North (Tran Vo). The 3m/10ft-high statue of Tran Vo on the main altar is made out of black bronze (1677) and shows the Taoist god with his two animal symbols: a snake and a tortoise. In the altar room are tablets with poems and

Opening hours: daily 8am – 4.30pm

BAN THỜ TỔ

A group of sculptures in Tran Quoc Pagoda

parallel sentences (words of wisdom written in pairs hanging on neighbouring columns). Some of them are decorated with elaborate mother-of-pearl inlays. On the way back to the main street, a large bronze bell, also from the year 1677, makes itself noticeable at the entryway.

Directly opposite lies a small park with a monument to the anti-aircraft gun assistants who were stationed here during the Vietnam War. In particular, the landing of **Field Officer John McCain** comes to mind here. He landed with a parachute in Truc Bach Lake in October 1967 and was held prisoner at the notorious »Hanoi Hilton« (▶ p.260) for more than five years. Afterwards he returned to the United States of America, where he became a Senator for Arizona, and did much to normalize relations between Vietnam and the USA. He was defeated by Barack Obama in the presidential election of 2008. This little park is today a popular meeting point, where families picnic and many drinks sellers and Cyclo drivers await their customers.

Monument

The street along the shore (Thanh Nien Street) is lined with Royal Poincianas and leads to Hanoi's oldest sanctuary, Tran Quoc Pagoda, which lies upon a small island in West Lake. It is believed to have been founded as early as the 6th century during the early Ly dynasty,which for a short time interrupted the 1000-year rule of the Chinese. On a stone stele (1639) at the entrance is an inscription saying that the pagoda was brought here from the Red River in the early

✴
Tran Quoc Pagoda

17th century, when Buddhism regained prominence. The temple complex is reached via a dam. The interior of the temple appears very grandiose, with many Buddhas and various sentinel figures between red-gold columns. The garden and the yards, especially the stupa garden and the eleven-floored pagoda tower, are very impressive (opening times: Mon–Sat 7am–11.30am and 1.30pm–6pm, Sun, holidays 7am–6pm).

★★
Museum of Ethnology

Opening hours:
Tue–Sun
8.30am–5pm

TheMuseum of Ethnology in Nguyen Van Huyen Street was opened in April 1998. It impresses with its lavish premises – the building was designed based upon a bronze drum. With the help of good, explanatory plaques, charts and overviews (also in English), much is explained about the life and diverse culture of the ethnic minorities, who are often still seen as underdeveloped in Vietnam itself.

The first section is concerned with the largest and dominating group of the Viet, the actual Vietnamese. Further along is the section on the Muong, Tho and Chut, in which scenes (e.g. a burial) and tools from everyday life are shown. The first room on the upper floor focuses on the Thai, Tay and Nung peoples, mainly upon various models of buildings and traditional garments.

Because the Museum of Ethnology lies in an area that is only partly developed, it is advisable to take a taxi there and have the driver wait until the visit is over (agree on the fee in advance!).

✔ DON'T MISS

- Water puppet theatre and cult of ancestral spirits in the Viet department
- Dao frames that were used to keep special wedding hairstyles in place
- Batik and dying work of the Hmong women
- Khmer calabashes

Around Hanoi – Near Vicinity

Even if Hanoi itself does have so much to offer, it is still worth taking at least one **excursion** out of the city. The pretty ► delta landscape of the Red River is strewn with dykes, villages with old community houses, and tomb groups in the rice fields, as well as temples and other sanctuaries. Some of the most beautiful pagodas in the country are actually found in the near vicinity of the capital. Those interested in handicrafts also have an opportunity to visit a number of handicraft villages and observe how carvings or pottery are made there. All of the following destinations can be visited on a day trip. The best solution is to book the appropriate tour directly from Hanoi or to rent a car and a driver.

Hung Temple and Co Loa Citadel

History and mythology seem to intertwine here – the very **origins of Vietnam** can be found at the temples of the legendary Hung kings. For it is said that the capital of Van Lang, the legendary first kingdom of Vietnam, was founded not far from the intersection where the Red, the Black and the Clear rivers meet. Just 12km/7mi west of the industrial city of Viet Tri, near the village of Phong Chau, an almost conical hill rises straight up from the plain of the Red River. At its foot lie two idyllic little lakes. The special beauty of this place alone explains why a temple to the Hung kings was built here.

✷ **Hung Temple**

Although the actual existence of the Hung dynasty remains disputed by scientists to this day, most Vietnamese still consider the kings to be the creators of their country. **Ho Chi Minh** even assembled his troops here before the liberation of Hanoi to recall these forebears and to defend their legacy.

Hung Temple Map

The simple temple complex is spread over three levels. There are nearly 500 steps to be climbed in order to reach the highest temple, where once stood the assembly hall of the rulers, who made offerings to the earth god here. Approaching from the car park, visitors first reach a small **museum**, in which finds (13th–10th century BC) from the area such as arrow heads, ceramics and jewellery can be seen, as well as bronze drums from the Dong Son epoch (3rd–5th century BC).

Just as Ho Chi Minh would have wished, pilgrims come to the temple all year round to remember their forebears. But it is especially lively here during the temple festival on the 10th day of the 3rd lunar month. Hawkers, jugglers, stalls and snack bars offer every kind of diversion. **Boat races** are held on the swan lake.

Temple festival

The northern hill country of the province is characterized by tea plantations, bamboo groves and fan palms. At the beginning of the 20th century the French built their first holiday resort here at Tam

✷ **Tam Dao**

Dao (930m/3050ft, approximately 35km/22mi east of Hung Temple), with a backdrop of up to 1400m/4600ft-high mountains. The place was badly damaged during the various wars, leaving only few colonial era buildings intact. In the meantime, work has begun on restoration and the building of new spa and leisure facilities.

Co Loa Citadel The earliest Vietnamese kingdoms had their origins in the plain of the Red River – the legendary Van Lang of the Hung kings, as well as Au Lac (258–207 BC), which was ruled by King An Duong from the imposing Co Loa Citadel (»snail-shaped citadel«, 16km/10m north of Hanoi). Little of its former splendour remains today, but if passing through is worth a stop to see two temples and a 1000-year-old banyan tree. At the entrance stand statues of King An Duong and his daughter. The pond in front is said to have magical powers. There are plans to build a National Tourism Park next to Co Loa Citadel. The three fortification rings, canals and the grave of My Chau are to be restored. The park is planned to be opened in 2010, in time for Hanoi's 1000th birthday.

✱ ✱ But Thap Pagoda (Chua But Thap)

Home of the most beautiful Quan Am figure The most beautiful temple statue in Vietnam is found in the pagoda of the small village of Dinh To, around 25km/16mi east of Hanoi. Founded by monks in 1647, the pagoda lies in the middle of the fields, right behind a dyke.

✱ ✱ Quan Am statue The altar room contains an abundance of ornate statues, but one overshadows all the others: the portrayal of the **Goddess of Compassion** (3.7m/12ft high) decorated with gold and lacquer. Springing from the richly ornamented pedestal is a monster with a lotus flower, from which Quan Am rises up in a meditation position. One pair of arms rests in her lap, the other is crossed in front of her chest; the 16

others growing from her back once held her attributes. Further, smaller-scale arms – each with an eye in the palm of the hand – surround the figure like a fan. It is said that Buddha gave them to her in order to defeat the monster at her feet. On her head Quan Am wears a crown of Buddha heads with an Amitabha in the middle. She is accompanied by Kim Dong, the Golden Child, and Ngoc Nu, the Jade Daughter. Uncharacteristically, there is an inscription on the pedestal of the statue giving the name of the do-

Chua But Thap Plan

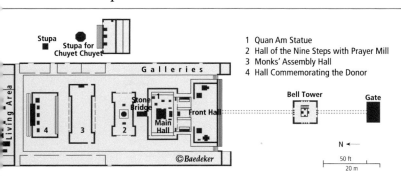

1 Quan Am Statue
2 Hall of the Nine Steps with Prayer Mill
3 Monks' Assembly Hall
4 Hall Commemorating the Donor

nor and the year (1656). Through the interplay of light and shadow, it seems as if the hands of the figure are moving. Also remarkable are the depiction of the Fasting Buddha on the left side of the altar and the figures of the 18 arhats (La Han, ►Baedeker Special p.42) along the side walls.

Hall of the Nine Steps

The passageway to the three following buildings, which are not otherwise common in the design of Vietnamese pagodas, is made up of a richly decorated stone bridge. The first is the Hall of the Nine Steps, in which a 6m/20ft-high 13th-century wooden prayer mill stands. During the pagoda festival on the 24th day of the 3rd lunar month, the mill is put into motion in a festive ceremony through which all of the prayers written on slips of paper inside are considered to have been spoken.

Tip

It is a good idea to combine the trip to Chua But Thap with a visit to the handicraft villages (►p.275). Dong Ky is close to the N 1a, while Bat Trang and Dong Ho are not far from the N 5.

✱ Perfume Pagoda (Chua Huong)

Sights along the way

There are two other interesting stops along Highway 6 on the way to the Perfume Pagoda: around 10km/6mi southwest of Hanoi is the **silk village of Van Phuc**, where of course visitors can also purchase silk clothes and fabric.

About 13km/8mi southwest of Hanoi is the **Ho Chi Minh Trail Museum**, which offers an impressive overview of the network of jungle paths in the border regions of three countries. The trail played a decisive role in the outcome of the war.

On the road to the Perfume Pagoda is another specialized handicraft village, **Chuong** (also Phuong Trung), where the famous hats are made and sold in all variations.

Around Hanoi Map

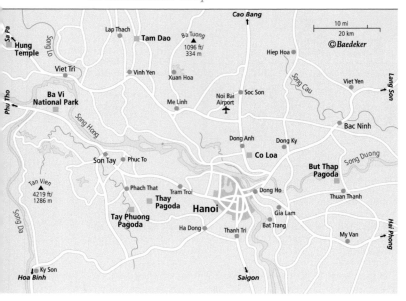

Pilgrimage site at the »Mountain of the Fragrant Traces«

Hardly any other attraction in Vietnam is so idyllically and mysteriously hidden away as the Perfume Pagoda, the most famous pilgrimage site in northern Vietnam. Huong Tich Son, the »Mountain of the Fragrant Traces« (60km/37mi southwest of Hanoi), home to the sanctuary dedicated to Quan Am, can only be reached by boat. The trip runs through a flooded valley between karst mountains, where fishermen and farmers work in the flooded fields. Visible on the shore and a little further into the valley are little temples, which are also related to the legend surrounding the Perfume Pagoda.

Legend

Once upon a time there was a king with a beautiful daughter. She did not wish to marry any of the suitors her father had presented, but instead wished to devote her entire life to Buddha. She hid herself away in a temple, and when threats and promises would not change her mind, the king ordered his soldiers to kill her. A white tiger rescued the princess and brought her to a secluded mountain cave. But then her father became sick with leprosy, went blind and lost his hands. None of the doctors or healers could help him. However, a Buddhist sage told him that he could be saved if one of his subjects would give him his hands and eyes. Yet no one came forward. When the news finally reached the princess in her cave, she decided to make the sacrifice. After he was saved, the king wished to visit the donor with a reward. He was brought to the cave, where he

Pilgrim boats on the way to the Perfume Pagoda

recognized his daughter, who had in the meantime become a Buddha and regained her eyes and hands. The king subsequently realized the error of his ways and also devoted his life to Buddhism.

After leaving the boat, the difficult part of the journey begins, unless the choice is made to take the funicular. A steep, only occasionally shaded path leads up to Chua Thien Tru, a 15th-century sanctuary (approximately 2 hours). There is a **stone statue of Quan Am** here, made in 1793 after the Tay Son rebels stole its bronze predecessor and melted it down to make cannon balls.

Thien Tru Pagoda

A path leads further on into a wide open cave, which the Vietnamese see as a giant dragon's mouth. It is found on the edge of a large hollow, which is grown over with trees and bushes. A member of the Trinh family had this inscription chiselled into the rock: **»The most beautiful grotto under the southern sky.«** Steps lead downward to the interior of the over 50m/164ft-high cave. The gilded Buddha can be glimpsed in the darkness, shrouded in billows of incense smoke; pilgrims mumble the magical greeting »Nam mo A Di Da Phat« (»Praise Amitabha Buddha«). In addition to pilgrims, ever since its foundation in the 17th century, the pagoda has attracted poets and scholars, whose verses are engraved in the stelae. The scenery is very impressive here, even despite the masses of visitors and peddlers. The Vietnamese pilgrims visit the sanctuary in March and April in particular. The peak provides a stunning view.

★ ★
Perfume Pagoda

Tay Phuong Pagoda (Chua Tay Phuong)

Simple building in Tam Quan style

Located in the village of Thac Xa (42km/26mi west of Hanoi), Chua Tay Phuong (Pagoda of the West) is one of the oldest pagodas in Vietnam (8th century). Moss-covered steps lead up the hill to the temple complex, built in the Tam Quan style. The pagoda has been destroyed and rebuilt several times since its establishment, but today the basic structure of the building mostly dates back to the 16th century.

✻
Collection of unusual wooden sculptures

The pagoda is famous for its unique collection of more than 70 man-sized sculptures, made from the wood of jackfruit trees. Today some of them can be marvelled at in the Museum of Fine Arts in Hanoi. Particularly worth seeing are the **18 arhat figures** (18th century), extremely lifelike portrayals of monks and ascetics, which can be found behind the main altar. Their realistic, individualized features are meant to emphasize the status of Arhats, who are about to enter nirvana, as human beings and students of Buddhism. Also known throughout the land are the imposing guard figures. (photo ►p.42).

✻ ✻ Thay Pagoda (Chua Thay)

Ideal setting for water puppet theatre

The long Thay Pagoda (6km/4mi east of Tay Phuong Pagoda) looks as if it is snuggled up against the limestone rocks, before which spreads the picturesque Dragon Lake. The 11th-century sanctuary lies in the village of Sai Son, just 40km/25mi southwest of Hanoi.

The pagoda at Dragon Lake with the little temple to the guardian spirit is the setting for one of the nicest water-puppet theatres in the land

The name of the pagoda means »Pagoda of the Master«, though it is also called Thien Phuc Tu, or »Pagoda of the Heavenly Blessing«.
It was built in honour of the **healer Tu Dao Hanh**, the master who lived here in the village and is said to have performed many miracles.

Yet he was not just a monk, he was also a declared lover of water puppet theatre (► Baedeker Special p.358), for which he had an attractive lake pavilion built. According to legend, Tu Dao Hanh had three incarnations: as a master (monk), as King Ly Nhan Tong and as a Buddha.

The dark prayer halls are full of statues – nearly 100 of them. The oldest ones date back to the establishment of the pagoda, but the most striking are the two huge guard figures from the 15th century, made out of clay and papier maché. Each of them weighs 1000kg/1.1 tons, and they are said to be the **largest of their kind in Vietnam**. On the first altar stand a Buddha and a likeness of the master in a yellow robe. To the right, the tomb of the master is held inside a shrine, which is only opened for viewing during the temple festival (5th to 7th day of the 3rd lunar month). A water puppet festival is also held at this time.

! *Baedeker* TIP

Snake village Le Mat

Those who aren't afraid of snakes should take a trip to Le Mat in the Gia Lam district. A number of families here have specialized in the breeding of snakes and the production of snake liquor. Restaurants serve snake meat and the corresponding alcoholic drinks. It even has therapeutic value: snake products are said to be good against joint pains and bronchitis, and to increase potency.

★
Guard figures

Handicraft Villages

Dong Ho is known in North Vietnam as the »village of the new year's pictures« (►also p.83). The new year's Tet Festival is the most important festivals of the year, the time when the kitchen god Tao Quan goes up to heaven to report on how the family has behaved (► Baedeker Special p.112). The colourful **wood carvings** that are hung up on the day, depicting old stories and legends or showing good-luck motifs such as well-fed children, pigs, fish or chickens, are made here. Dong Ho lies on the right bank of the Song Duong, just a few miles from the centre of Hanoi.

Dong Ho

On the other side of the Red River in the Gia Lam district (approximately 7km/4mi east of Hanoi) lies Bat Trang, which specializes in ceramics and pottery. Bricks and stoneware were produced here as early as the 15th century. Today about 2000 families live in Bat Trang, predominately producing the traditional **blue and white ceramics**. Everything can be found at the street stands and in the showrooms here, from small figurines and chopstick holders to huge animal sculptures and cachepots.

Bat Trang

Browse for the nicest one right on the street...

Around Hanoi – Further Afield

It is possible to get to know other facets of Vietnam on excursions of two or three days. Nature lovers will appreciate the wonderful landscape of ►Dry Ha Long Bay, with the old capital of Hoa Lu and Cuc Phuong National Park, as well as Ba Vi National Park (see below). Those interested in art should pay a visit to Keo Pagoda, a masterpiece of woodcraft. To get a sense of the mountainous region of the north and the various ethnic groups, it is worth a making a trip to Hoa Binh, ►Sa Pa or ►Dien Bien Phu. Tours to all of these destinations are available from Hanoi. It is recommended to book a tour or rent a car with a driver from here.

Ba Vi National Park Countless lakes, streams, waterfalls and grottos are the attractions of the area where the Black River converges with the Red River (65km/40mi west of Hanoi). Including the surrounding nature reserves, Ba Vi Park has a total area of around 7000ha/27 sq mi. The highest elevation is the **Dinh Vua Mountain** (1296m/4252ft). Day trippers from Hanoi like to visit the three pagodas at up to 1200m/3937ft in altitude. 38 mammalian species are said to live here: easiest to spot are gibbons and macaques, mountain goats and bats. There were nearly 5000 subtropical plant species counted here at the end of the 19th century, only half of which probably exist today. This has to do with the slash-and-burn land clearance practiced by the Muong and Dao who live here. The national park is also famous for its **myths**, which tell of earth and water spirits and play a big role in the perception of the hill tribes. There are a number of simple guesthouses for tourists here (bring a passport!). From Hanoi, the national park can be reached on the N 11 via Son Tay.

When visiting the park, a trip to the cult house of Tay Dang at the foot of the Ba Vi is a must. The wood carvings inside depicting scenes from country life are particularly worth seeing.

Dinh Tay Dang

The nearby Dong Mo Lake and its surroundings has become a popular bathing and hiking area, even featuring an 18-hole golf course.

Dong Mo Lake

Hoa Binh and Its Surroundings

The landscape around Hoa Binh (74km/46mi southwest of Hanoi, 2½ hours) is like a prehistoric Garden of Eden with its karst cones rising suddenly from the plain and expansive bamboo thickets. The scenery and the atmosphere seem symbolic of Vietnam. Hoa Binh is known as the location of Vietnam's largest hydroelectric power station, which was built with Soviet help and to this day is still not in service.

Hoa Binh

From Hoa Binh it is possible to visit a number of Muong villages, including Xom Mo, Ban Dam and Giang, all of which are less than 10km/6mi away. Here the families live in large pile dwellings (longhouses) and small farm animals and poultry amble around the lanes. The inhabitants live mainly from rice and vegetable cultivation. Boats run about 25km/16mi upstream from Hoa Binh to the **Dao villages of** Duong and Phu.

Villages in the area

The village and the valley of **Mai Chau**, located around 40km/25mi south of Hoa Binh, are well known for their marvellous setting of rice fields and distant mountain ranges. This is where the White Thai live in their beautifully decorated stilt houses, in which families also offer accommodation to tourists. The village market sells all kinds of products from the area.

In order to visit the Thai, it is worth travelling further west to the plateau of **Moc Chau** (approximately 70km/43mi southwest of Hoa Binh). The Thai villages are beautifully located in an enchanting mountain landscape.

Muong woman with child

Ho Chi Minh City

►Saigon

✶✶ Hoi An

E 5

Province: Quang Nam – Da Nang   **Region:** Southern Central Coast
Population: Approx. 80,000

A hint of China is perceptible in the old harbour town of Hoi An, with its narrow streets and low houses that seem to crouch beneath their curious tiled roofs. The area around Tran Phu Street in particular, where the pretty trading houses, temples and pagodas are found, seems like an Asian open-air museum.

History The one-time Cham harbour of Hoi An had long been situated on the trade routes between east and west before, in the 16th and 17th

Depiction of a carp transforming into a dragon

centuries, the Chinese from Fujian – and later also Japanese, Dutch and Indians – set up bases here, making the place an important-**centre of commerce**. Ships from around the world headed into this harbour to participate in the important fairs and exchanges held here. The trade with China led to a decrease in influence for the city, then called »Hai Pho« (place on the sea), and then the mouth of the Thu Bon silted up. During the Tay Son uprising (1771–88), the city of foreign merchants was nearly destroyed.

Unlike the Japanese, the Chinese rebuilt their quarter. Under the Nguyen emperor and the French colonial rulers, who gave Hoi An the name »Faifo«, Da Nang was favoured for its better transport conditions. This led to the remote and neglected Hoi An becoming a **hideout for resistance movements** against the French and later also against the Americans, which led to heavy attacks on the city.

The old Hoi An is relatively small and easy to get to grips with. Because the centre has been preserved, with its unique concentration of residential and trading houses, assembly halls, pagodas, shrines and temples, the fountain, the central market and the wharf, it vividly recreates the image of a Southeast Asian town of the past.

★ ★
Old Town

The historic centre is for the most part made up of three streets, which extend parallel to the riverbank, with sections closed to cars and motorcycles. To this day **Tran Phu Street**, the oldest of these streets, is the main thoroughfare of Hoi An boasting the main points of interest as well as a whole host of shops, galleries and restaurants. One block further south is **Nguyen Thai Hoc Street** with its pretty shops and traditional pharmacies. Running directly along the riverside is the lively **Bach Dang Street**; here there are a number of pleasant cafés and restaurants, from which the comings and goings on the river and the street can be watched in peace. The old town of Hoi An was declared a UNESCO World Heritage Site in 1999. East of the three streets is the market, with a large hall and many street stalls. When following Phan Boi Chau Street in the same direction, there are numerous relics of French colonial architecture.

◄ Architectural highlights

The special system by which the **roof tiles** are interlocked is interesting. This style of tiling is known as »yin-yang« after the way the alternating concave and convex-shaped tiles are slotted into one another. The rows are usually then closed off with decorative, often colourfully glazed Chinese coins.
Another detail typical of Hoi An are the **»eyes«** (mat cua) that guard the entrances to houses or religious buildings. In addition to this are

The Japanese Covered Bridge once connected the Chinese and Japanese Quarters

two thick wooden spikes with a diameter of 20cm/8in hammered like nails into the door lintels in order to protect residents and visitors from dark forces. At the Phuoc Kien Assembly Hall they are found in form of yin-yang symbols with two dragons who pay homage to the sun; alternatively, at the Tan Ky House they take the form of flowers or often simply an octagonal amulet.

Seen again and again during a visit to Hoi An, on weather vanes, lantern holders or roof beams, is a mythical creature with the body of a fish and the head of a dragon. The **carp** (cá chép) is a symbol for wealth and success, and in this form, showing its transformation into a dragon, is meant to remind that nothing in this life happens all by itself. In order to become a dragon, thereby attaining immortality, the fish must pass through three gates, much like a scholar must pass three examinations before becoming a mandarin, requiring a great deal of patience and hard work.

Places to Visit in Central Hoi An

★
Japanese Covered Bridge

The modest Japanese Covered Bridge at the west end of Tran Phu Street once joined the Japanese quarter of the city with the Chinese quarter. At the western exit are two simple dog statues; on the eastern side, two monkeys can be seen. It is therefore assumed that the construction of the bridge took two years, beginning in the year of the monkey and ending in the year of the dog. According to legend, the bridge was built following heavy **earthquakes** in Japan, which geomancers (►also p.67) attributed to a huge dragon. His head was said to be located in India, his tail in Japan and his heart in Hoi An. Because of this, the crossing was built on stone abutments meant to symbolically pierce his heart – and at the same time provide a protective, covered bridge over the muddy current. The first bridge was built crossing the small arm of the Thu Bon at the end of the 16th century. It was destroyed and rebuilt several times. It is assumed that during the work in 1763, the **bridge pagoda** (Chua Cau) was also built, attached to the north side and dedicated to the Taoist god Tran Vo Bac De (the Emperor of the North), to whom power over the wind, rain and other bad influences is ascribed.

Opening hours:
daily 8am – 6pm

A few hundred yards north of the bridge, at the western end of Phan Dinh Phung Street, is a mysterious shrine beneath an old banyan tree. The Emperor of the North is also honoured here, in order that he protect the bridge from harm.

Hoi An Map

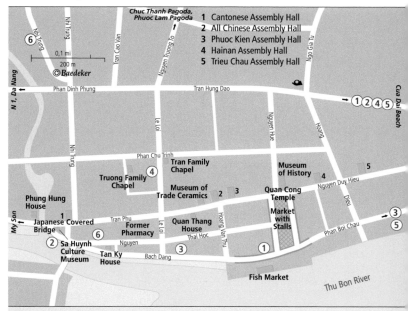

1 Cantonese Assembly Hall
2 All Chinese Assembly Hall
3 Phuoc Kien Assembly Hall
4 Hainan Assembly Hall
5 Trieu Chau Assembly Hall

Chuc Thanh Pagoda, Phuoc Lam Pagoda

0,1 mi
200 m
© Baedeker

N 1, Da Nang
Nhi Trung
Nhi Trung
Tran Cao Van
Nguyen Tuong To
Ngo Gia Tu
Cua Dai Beach

Phan Dinh Phung
Tran Hung Dao

Le Loi
Nguyen Hue
Hoang

Phan Chu Trinh
Nhi Trung

Tran Family Chapel
Truong Family Chapel
Museum of History
Museum of Trade Ceramics
Quan Cong Temple
Nguyen Duy Hieu
Dieu

Phung Hung House
Japanese Covered Bridge
My Son
Tran Phu
Former Pharmacy
Le Loi
Quan Thang House
Thai Hoc
Market with Stalls
Phan Boi Chau

Sa Huynh Culture Museum
Tan Ky House
Nguyen
Bach Dang
Hoang Van Thu

Fish Market
Thu Bon River

Where to stay
① Life Resort Hoi An
② Victoria Hoi An Resort
③ Ha An Hotel
④ Dong An Beach Hotel
⑤ Ancient House Resort
⑥ Thanh Xuan Hotel

Where to eat
① Café des Amis
② Han Huyen
③ Hong Phuc
④ Good Morning Vietnam
⑤ Brother's Café
⑥ Tam Tam

▶ VISITING HOI AN

INFORMATION

Hoi An Tourist Service
Tran Hung Dao 6
(in the Hoi An Hotel)
Tel. 05 10/86 13 62, fax 86 16 36
Also in hotels and travel agencies
(especially Tran Hung Dao opposite
the Hoi An Hotel)

TRANSPORT

Da Nang International Airport
(approx. 25km/16mi north of Hoi
An):
Tel. 05 11/81 18 11 and 83 03 39.

COMBINATION TICKET

Combination tickets are sold for the
main attractions of the city, which are
each valid for one museum, one
assembly hall, one old house and the
Japanese Bridge or Quan Cong Temple.

EVENTS

Hoi An Legendary Night
Each month on the evening before the
full moon (14th day of the lunar
calendar) the old town is illuminated
with the light from silken lanterns and
fairy lights, light balloons ascend into
the evening sky, and traditional music
and theatre are performed in the lanes
and old buildings.

SHOPPING

Hoi An – Shopping Paradise
The many souvenir shops in the centre
welcome customers to browse and buy
their wares. The goods on offer range
from inlayed ornaments, wood carvings and embroidery to T-shirts and
puppets, opium pipes, Vietnamese
ceramics and on to beautifully decorated chopsticks (don't forget to
haggle!).
Tran Phu Street Market: inside the
market hall and at the numerous

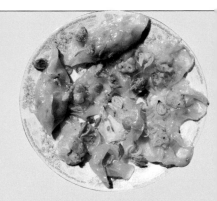

*Tasty: Hoi An's speciality »white rose« is
a delicious little cake made with maniok
flour and finely chopped shrimp or crab.
It is served with crispy roast onions and a
dip made with lime, sugar and fish sauce.*

stands around it, everything from fruit
and vegetables, poultry and fish,
basketry and medicinal herbs, kitchen
appliances and ceramics are available.
Hoi An Handicraft Workshop (9
Nguyen Thai Hoc, daily 8am to
around 7pm): a large selection of nice
souvenirs and handicrafts, daily performances of traditional music.
Somewhat further on: **Reaching Out**
(103 Nguyen Thai Hoc, daily
8am–9pm).
Tailors offer their services in **Le Loi
Street**. It is possible to have clothes
made overnight for low prices, including suits, pyjamas, kimonos,
blouses and skirts in western or Asian
designs.
Be careful when buying silk: »Vietnamese silk« is artificial, »Thai silk« is
the name for real, raw silk. In order to
be certain, it is best to test by setting
fire to a thread: if it melts, it's
polyester. Real silk smells like burnt
hair.

COOKERY COURSES

Those wishing to enjoy typical Vietnamese flavours and dishes such as Cao Lau or Hot Pot at home, and who want to use the herbs correctly and not to overcook the vegetables, can take part in a Vietnamese cooking course – the latest trend in Hoi An. Many restaurants offer more or less complicated taster courses e.g.: *Vy's Cooking School* in the Cargo Club, 107 Nguyen Thai Hoc, tel. 05 10/91 04 89. *Red Bridge Cooking School*, Thon 4, Cam Thanh, tel. 05 10/93 32 22 (visit the market with an English-speaking guide, a boat trip to the restaurant, cooking with a view of the river, 3–4 hours, cost including ingredients approx. 15 US$).

WHERE TO EAT
▶ Moderate
① *Café des Amis*
52 Rue Bach Dang
Tel. 05 10/86 16 16
No menu, but guests can decide between seafood or vegetarian and be surprised with a tasty five-course meal. Nice location with a view onto the water.

▶ Inexpensive
② *Han Huyen*
Bach Dang
Tel. 05 10/86 14 62
Small floating restaurant at the river bend near the Japanese Bridge. Cuisine with a Chinese emphasis and excellent specialities such as prawns grilled on sugar cane, rolled in rice cakes with fresh herbs.

③ *Hong Phuc*
86 Bach Dang
Tel. 05 10/86 25 67
Magnificently located on the esplanade, this restaurant in an old trading house offers many fish specialities (e.g.

wrapped in banana leaves) and the regional delicacy: Cao Lau noodle soup.

④ *Good Morning Vietnam*
34 Le Loi
Tel. 05 10/91 02 27
Tasty Italian dishes and wine are served at this pizzeria chain, which meanwhile is found in many tourist areas.

ENTERTAINMENT

⑤ *Brother's Café*
27 Phan Boi Chau
Tel. 05 10/91 41 50
daily 10am–10pm
Excellent Vietnamese dining at a colonial villa in a tropical garden right on the riverbank, also cocktails, wine and beer.

⑥ *Tam Tam*
110 Nguyen Thai Hoc
Tel. 05 10/86 22 12
daily 10am–1am
Popular café-restaurant and bar in the old town, on two floors with a narrow balcony from which to watch the

Clothes can be tailored inexpensively

activity on the street below, or on comfy sofas in the corner, Vietnamese and international dishes (from tapas to steak to pasta), good wine selection, cocktails.

WHERE TO STAY

► Mid-range

③ *Ha An Hotel*
6 Phan Boi Chau, Cua Dai Beach
Tel. 05 10/93 31 77, fax 91 42 80
A calm oasis with a pretty garden, lovingly furnished rooms (rose petals, CD player), courteous service. Complimentary bicycle rental.

④ *Dong An Beach Hotel*
Cua Dai
Tel. 05 10/92 78 88, fax 92 77 77
www.donganbeachhotel.com
donganbeachhotel@dng.vnn.vn
Two-storey beach complex of the better middle class arranged around a pool: 81 rooms, some with balconies (with a panoramic view of the sea, lagoon, river or city) and parquet floors.

⑤ *Ancient House Resort*
377 Cua Dai (beach road, approx. 1km/1000yd outside Hoi An on the road to the beach)
Tel. 05 10/92 33 77, fax 92 34 77
www.ancienthouseresort.com
hoangthinhha@dng.vnn.vn
Pretty, somewhat convoluted two-storey complex with tile-roofed houses grouped around a traditional villa with 42 middle-class rooms, veranda with a view of the river or the garden. Large pool.

Le Domaine de Tam Hai
Tam Hai, Nui Thanh (island approximately 45km/28mi from Hoi An, 15 minutes by boat)
Tel. 05 10/54 51 03, fax 54 51 05
www.domainedetamhai.com

info@domainedetamhai.com
A small island paradise: twelve palm-leaf-covered bungalows, quaint Vietnamese-style decor (air-conditioned, minibar, telephone) on the beach beneath the palms, some with large, airy baths. Pool, French restaurant and cocktail bar.

► Budget

⑥ *Thanh Xuan Hotel*
22–23 Nhi Trung
Tel. 05 10/91 66 96
Fax 91 66 97
www.thanhxuanhotel.com
sales@longlifehotels.com
Modern, three-storey city hotel somewhat detached from the old town, with 30 nice rooms, some bright and with a good bathroom. In-house restaurant.

► Luxury

① *Life Resort Hoi An*
1 Pham Hong Thai
Tel. 05 10/91 45 55, fax 91 45 15
www.life-resorts.com
hoian@life-resorts.com
Highly praised hotel on the riverbank: stylish colonial replica with 94 spacious, smart rooms on two storeys, small patios, pool, spa section.

Baedeker recommendation

② *Victoria Hoi An Resort*
Cua Dai Beach
Tel. 05 10/92 70 40
Fax 94 70 41
www.victoriahotels-asia.com
victoriahoian@dng.vnn.vn
Pure elegance at the best beach hotel in Hoi An (10 minutes from the city centre): 4-star luxury under French management, with gorgeous bungalows and rooms with balconies. View of the sea or the estuary. Everything arranged in the style of a fishing village.

At the western end of the bridge stands the nearly 200-year-old Phung Hung Old House (4 Nguyen Thi Minh Khai Street), which has been in the same family for eight generations. The carved shutters and the free-floating ancestral altar on the upper floor are particularly pretty. The book shop is a nice place to browse around, and there is a ceramics exhibition here to admire (opening times: daily 8am–7pm).

Phung Hung Old House

The Sa Huynh Culture Museum (149 Tran Phu) located diagonally across from the eastern exit of the bridge, houses a number of archaeological finds, giving an impression of the time before the Cham rulers.

Sa Huynh Culture Museum

Just a bit further on is the impressive portal of the Cantonese Assembly Hall (176 Tran Phu). The Chinese immigrants organized themselves according to their region of origin and built five assembly halls, which serve as a meeting point as well as a **religious centre**. Even today it is quite clear that the atmosphere here is not one of a museum, but of everyday life.

★
Cantonese Assembly Hall
Opening hours: daily 6.30am–6pm

The portal is decorated in great detail: Phuoc Kien Assembly Hall

The halls are all similar from the basic set up, with the main buildings and the altars all arranged on one axis. However from the entrance the view of the godly figures is blocked, as walls or »blind« doors have been built in between to mislead evil spirits and keep them out. First comes a small forecourt, which leads to a gatehouse with just such a door, as well as memorial plaques and inscriptions. Next is a courtyard, usually adorned with a miniature stone landscape, trees and other plants. It is adjoined on either side by assembly and business rooms. Now comes the **temple area**, the size and features of which correspond with the wealth of the community. In general the rooms are characterized by lacquered and painted wooden columns and finely carved altars with figures of gods and ancestral charts. The roof ridges also stand out, embellished with almost excessive reliefs and mosaics made with shards of porcelain.

Small home altar

The Cantonese hall, built only in 1884, has nothing to show in the way of old, valuable treasures, but has a particularly nice courtyard with plants. The elaborate fountain immediately catches the eye, with its colourful dragons and carp decorated with ceramics. The red-faced Quan Cong, a Chinese general from the days of the Han dynasty is honoured at the main altar. The design of the building is unusual in its combination of granite pillars and supports with carved wooden beams.

Quan Than House

✺

🕐

Opening hours:
daily 8am – 6pm

The Old House of Quan Than (no. 77) is among the oldest and best preserved buildings in the city (from 1690). The layout of the house – actually two buildings joined by a courtyard and a covered passageway – is **characteristic of southern China** and Hoi An. From the street, all that is visible is a dark, wooden-panelled shop front. There follows a light and airy courtyard, and finally the living quarters, with the furthest end housing the kitchen, toilet and fountain. The fine wood carvings and green ceramic tiles at the roof ridge are marvellous, as are the various home altars.

Ceramics Museum

Diagonally opposite is the Keramik Museum of Trade Ceramics (80 Tran Phu). It holds a small collection of ceramics from various places with which Hoi An had trading relations during the 16th and 17th centuries. In addition, it is possible to learn more about the **typical**

roofing techniques (yin-yang) in Hoi An. At least as interesting as the exhibition itself is the chance to stroll around the building and enjoy the view across the town and the rooftops (opening times: daily 6.30am–6pm).

To visitors to thePhuoc Kien Assembly Hall (46 Tran Phu) it is soon apparent that this facility belongs to the largest and most influential Chinese community of Hoi An. A relatively new gateway leads into the impressive complex with its green yards and exuberantly decorated halls. The origins of this sanctuary are said to date back to the late 17th century, when a valuable Buddha statue was found on the riverbank, and a pagoda was built in its honour. But over time it was neglected, so the Chinese from Phuoc Kien rededicated the temple to Thien Hau. At the main altar is a 200-year-old gilded **papier mâché statue**. It is flanked by two helpers, the green-faced Thien Ly Nhan (who can hear from over a thousand miles away) and the red-faced Thuan Phong Nhi (who can see for over a thousand miles). A striking wall painting at the entrance shows the goddess in a storm, as she watches protectively over a junk.

★ ★
Phuoc Kien Assembly Hall
⊙
Opening hours: daily 8am – 6pm

Visited by many childless couples

The altar room behind the **main sanctuary** is a destination for many childless couples and pregnant women. This is where three heavenly women are honoured who are believed to have a great influence over the fate of children. It is said that the middle one decides if a woman is to become pregnant, the right one influences the gender of the child, and the left one watches over the birth itself. They are flanked by twelve midwives, each of whom teaches the newborn something during its first year, for example to feed, to smile or to roll over. To the left stands the actual main altar of the room, paying homage to six ancestors who left Phuoc Kien in the 17th century to settle in Hoi An (then called Faifo). Standing in a small display case is a figure of the famous Vietnamese doctor Le Huu Trac.

Those wishing to get to know an entirely different facet of Hoi An should pay a visit to **Phan Boi Chau Street**. This was once the site of the French Quarter, with town houses decorated with plaster work, colonnades and balconies. The private house of Tran Duong is open to visitors (no. 25, opening times: daily 9am–6pm).

French Quarter

⊙

In front of Quan Cong Pagoda

Quan Cong Temple (Chua Ong)

Back in Tran Phu Street, opposite the entrance to the market is the eye-catching colourful façade of Quan Cong Temple (Chua Ong) from the 17th century. Originally built as the religious centre for the immigrants from the Chinese province of Quang Nam, it is now dedicated in honour of Ong Quan Cong, a legendary general (3rd century). To his right and left are the military mandarin Chau Xuong and the administrative mandarin Quang Binh. His red and white horses are also standing guard. The carp, a symbol of patience commonly seen in Hoi An's Chinese buildings, is found here in a particularly appealing form: as colourfully glazed dragon figures and water spouts (opening times: daily 6.30am–6pm).

Museum of History

Through the rear exit of the temple or via the entrance in Nguyen Hue Street is Hoi An's Museum of History, which is also housed in a former pagoda. A number of old maps showing details of the previous city of Faifo are very interesting. The **tranquil courtyard** with its many plants and wooden ornamentation is also particularly pretty (opening times: daily 6.30am–6pm).

★ Trieu Chau Assembly Hall

Further along the road (from the market onwards it is no longer called Tran Phu Street, but Nguyen Duy Hieu) is the Trieu Chau Assembly Hall, which was built by merchants from Chaozhou or Trieu Chau in 1776. For those who have not already seen enough beautiful ornaments and decorations, there are some very special **wood carvings** to discover here. Ong Bon, a Chinese marine general who is said to have power over the wind and waves, is honoured here. Running alongside his statue is a frieze full of birds, insects and small animals – so realistic that it almost seems as if chirping and rustling should be audible. The altar itself depicts scenes from life on land and at sea, and at the doors before it are two Chinese ladies who are trying out the latest Japanese hair fashions (opening times: daily 6.30am–6pm).

On the return trip, the cross street Le Loi is slightly more than half-way back; follow it to the right for one block further to reach Phan Chu Trinh Street. At exactly this corner stands the 200-year-old Tran Family Chapel. Like those of the other Chinese clans, the chapel was originally built as a **merchant's house** (see below), but over time the religious meaning of the place became more significant for the family. The focal point here is the large altar room honouring the ancestors. The Tran, who once became rich and influential through trade and whose ancestors include mandarins, still meet here once per year to this day. On these occasions, family matters are discussed and the ancestors are remembered.

Tran Family Chapel

The small but also very pretty chapel of the Truong family is slightly hidden next to the Pho Hoi Restaurant at 69 Phan Chu Trinh. A visit here is not included as part of the ticket (►p.286), but it is possible to enter and look around on request. The house is full of family mementos and carvings.

Truong Family Chapel

The prettiest and most-visited of the old merchant's houses is the Old House of Tan Ky (101 Nguyen Thai Hoc). The English and French-speaking guides at this two storey house relate quite a bit about its architecture and history, which makes it popular among tour groups. The nearly 200-year-old building with its exquisite carvings and inlay work is very well preserved and is viewed by the city as a showpiece. It was built by a member of the second generation of the Tan Ky family, who fled China for political reasons in the late 16th century.

✶✶ Old House of Tan Ky

Through a narrow, slightly spooky store and the richly decorated living room is the courtyard. From here it is possible to continue to the rear section with the kitchen and an exit to the river. It was possible to bring goods directly into the warehouse on the upper floor from here, protecting the goods from flooding. The use of the dark **jack-fruit wood** for the main pillars, which is resistant against termites, is an interesting feature. The filigreed carvings are imaginative and playful, and the abundance of mother-of-pearl inlays is especially elegant (opening times: daily 6.30am–6pm).

Outside the City Centre

Following Nguyen Truong To Street (the northern extension of Le Loi) and passing numerous market stalls leads directly to the gate of the Tiger Temple, which is easily recognized by its brightly coloured statues. The sanctuary itself is modest and decorated only with Chinese calligraphy.

Tiger Temple

The good life on Cua Dai Beach

Chuc Thanh Pagoda

Turn left before the Tiger Temple onto a rather dusty road, bordered by small houses with attractive gardens and burial sites, to reach two pagodas in idyllic surroundings. This perfectly tranquil, isolated spot is a pleasant contrast to the hustle and bustle in the centre of Hoi An. Some 700m/770yd further on stands Chuc Thanh Pagoda. It was founded as early as 1454 by Minh Hia, the first Buddhist monk of Hoi An. The present building is somewhat younger, but some of the older cult objects, including bells and a gong in the form of a carp, can still be seen. Trees, bougainvillea and other flowers decorate the pagoda grounds. To the left is a small area with coloured stupas and mossy tombs (photo ►p.71).

Phuoc Lam Pagoda

Follow the well-worn path another 500m/545yd (crossing a small canal) to Phuoc Lam Pagoda, erected in the mid-seventeenth century. According to legend, the young monk An Thiem reported for military duty instead of his brothers at the end of the century and rapidly rose to the rank of general. After the war he returned to the monastery, where, in order to be cleansed of his sins, he would sweep the market of Hoi An for the next twenty years. On completing this penance, he was nominated as the highest figure of Phuoc Lam Pagoda, the holy ground of which is surrounded by frangipani trees and flowerbeds. To one side, moss-covered memorial stones, adorned with ceramic mosaics, stand in a small field.

! *Baedeker* TIP

Boat trips

Excursions by boat along the Thu Bon lead to islands on the river and artisan settlements, such as the potters' village of Thanh Ha or the woodcarvers' Cam Kim Island, where boats and furniture are manufactured. Somewhat further in from the coast lie the Cham Islands: the Cu Lao Cham archipelago has been sustained for centuries by trade in swallows' nests.

Around Hoi An

Following a healthy round of sightseeing, some time to relax on the beach is in order. Follow Tran Hung Dao Street eastwards, cycling for some 20 minutes through paddy fields and a residential area before arriving at the white Cua Dai Beach. The broad expanses of the beach are spotlessly clean, dotted with refreshments stalls and traders. Here, sun and sea can be savoured in peace. The presence of numerous new hotels and restaurants is indicative of efforts to **develop the area further as a tourist centre**.

Cua Dai Beach

✶ Hue

D 4

Province: Thua Thien–Hue   **Region:** North Central Coast
Population: 280,000

The former imperial city of Hue nestles between the foothills of the Annamite mountain range and the sea. As early as the 18th century, poets paid romantic tribute to its gardens, lakes and canals and its charming location on the »Perfume River«. Today, the complex of Hue monuments is on the UNESCO World Cultural Heritage list. The city retains a certain courtly flair and a hint of the Francophile lifestyle.

Essentially, the town can be divided into three parts, each with its own distinctive character. The Citadel complex with the Imperial Enclosure on the north bank of the Perfume River really is a must-see. To the east of the Dong Ba Canal lies Phu Cat, an erstwhile trading post, now an overcrowded district packed with shops, pagodas and Chinese union halls; on the south bank of the Perfume River the European town has developed, the modern administrative centre of Hue and home to many of the town's hotels and restaurants, graced with beautiful streets and villas. The landscape to the south of the town is marked by pine forest hills interspersed with tombs and pagodas. This is where the Nguyen emperors built their mausoleums. The Perfume River winds its way through the scenery, its name a legacy of the blossoms and tree gum it carries with it. An excursion with a **dragon boat** through the romantic river valley is an unforgettable experience. The famous Thien Mu Pagoda and Thuan An Beach are just a bicycle ride or boat trip away.

A town in three parts

Until 1306 Hue belonged to the Cham dynasty, before the land north of Da Nang was handed over to the Vietnamese as a condition of a peace treaty. However it was **Emperor Gia Long** (1802–20), founder of the Nguyen dynasty, who bestowed such significance on Hue as the capital of his empire. His reign not only witnessed the construc-

History

tion of the Citadel, but also of dykes, bridges and canals, as well as the Mandarin Road, which connects Hue to Saigon and Hanoi. Hue would subsequently become an important centre for Buddhism, the arts and scholarship.

City map p.309

In 1885, the **French** conquered Hue. The colonial rulers allowed the Nguyen to continue as masters by name, but without the corresponding influence. So it was that Hue was stripped of its status as capital city and fell into a slumber of almost *Sleeping Beauty* proportions, which lasted for almost 20 years. When the Geneva Conference of 1954 split Vietnam in two, Hue was allocated to the south.

Thousands died on both sides in the **Vietnam War** and the Citadel was almost completely reduced to rubble and ash.

Meanwhile, the gargantuan task of rebuilding Hue has spanned a period of over 20 years. Thanks to UNESCO, which designated the Imperial Enclosure and Royal Tombs as **World Heritage Sites** in 1993, these initiatives have gained immense support, proving not only beneficial to the historical buildings, but also helping to revive the traditional craftsmanship required.

> ## ❗ *Baedeker* TIP
>
> ### Culinary specialities
> The most famous delicacy in Hue is banh khoai, small, crispy pancakes with shrimps, pork and bean sprouts, served with peanut-sesame sauce and star fruit, green bananas, salad and mint leaves.
> Noodles are also very popular in Hue, above all as a specially spiced rice noodle soup called bun bo, bun ga or bun bo gio heo – depending on whether beef, chicken or beef and pork is used.

★ Citadel

The glorious days of Hue began when Emperor Gia Long ordered the construction of the Citadel in the year 1802. It was to be more than just a fortress; it would be a home for the imperial family and the officials, a kind of idyllic **»town within a town«** with small villages, paddy fields, artificial hills, temples, gardens, lakes and alleys. It was conceived as a square in shape, with three concentric defences behind a Flag Tower rising high into the sky. Behind the walls lay the Imperial Enclosure with its administrative buildings, gardens, and dynastic temples, yet the imperial palaces of the Forbidden Purple City were the actual heart of the Citadel. The English traveller George Finlayson was utterly fascinated by what he saw. He wrote in 1821–22 that the Imperial Enclosure was of such sheer elegance, grandeur and perfection, that all other Asian cities seemed in comparison to be the work of children.

What remained of the former Imperial Enclosure

🕐 Opening hours: daily 7am–5pm

Today, only around 80 of the original 300 buildings can be seen – and these too are in ruins. Battles, fire, typhoons and floods have all played their part, but it was primarily the **bombing attacks** of the Vietnam War (Tet Offensive, 1968) that left the complex, completed in 1833, in its present state. The ancient magic can still (or again) be

← *Outside the citadel walls*

Official guests entered Hue Palace through the Noontime Gate

sensed here and there, but, for the most part, Hue's most important landmark is a disconsolate place.

Geomantic guidelines

Inspired by Peking, Hue was destined to become the most magnificent city of the region. Geomancy was the defining rule for even the smallest of planning details. A long time was spent looking for the ideal place to build, to establish the crucial harmony between emperor and his subjects, man and nature. Hence the entire complex would face southeast, towards the mountain of **Nui Ngu Binh** (the »emperor's shade«), which would repel evil spirits. Two small islands in the Perfume River symbolize the benign spirit of the Blue Dragon in opposition to the aggression of the White Tiger. If this were not protection enough, the 520ha/1285ac complex is surrounded by a 7m/23ft-high and 20m/65ft-wide wall and a 23m/75ft-wide, 4m/13ft-deep moat. In accordance with geomantic principles of construction, the Citadel's ground plan is almost square, as this was the symbol of authority over the earth – the perception of earth itself was that of a quadratic plane.

Flag Tower and Holy Cannons

Before entering the Imperial Enclosure, small pavilions can be seen on the river. In former times, edicts were read out here. Behind them, the 21m/69ft-high, three-storey Flag Tower rises upwards. For 25 years during the Tet Offensive the yellow star of the Vietcong flag fluttered here. To either side stand the Nine Holy Cannons, representing the four seasons and the five elements (earth, fire, metal, wood and water). Like the Dynasty Urns outside the Pavilion of Famous Souls, they also symbolize the empire.

Of the four gates that lead into the Imperial Enclosure, the most impressive is the Noontime Gate **Noontime Gate**. At the zenith of the Nguyen dynasty visitors must have been overwhelmed as they cast their gaze over the yellow and green tiled rooftops, entered the pavilions, resplendent in red and gold, and wandered amongst the lotus pools. After 1945, however, the entire complex was neglected and the acts of war contributed further to its state of disrepair. Nevertheless, the buildings that remain standing have been carefully restored and are deeply impressive, particularly the Palace of Supreme Harmony and the Temple of Generations.

Imperial Enclosure

The majestic Noontime Gate (Ngo Mon), built under Minh Mang in 1833, leads into the Imperial Enclosure. The portal has five entrances, with only the emperor permitted entry through the central one. The smaller two on each side were for the military and official mandarins, whilst the two giant openings in the wings were intended for the **imperial elephants**.

★ Noontime Gate

Hue Citadel

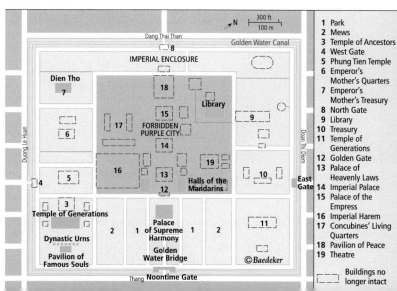

1	Park
2	Mews
3	Temple of Ancestors
4	West Gate
5	Phung Tien Temple
6	Emperor's Mother's Quarters
7	Emperor's Mother's Treasury
8	North Gate
9	Library
10	Treasury
11	Temple of Generations
12	Golden Gate
13	Palace of Heavenly Laws
14	Imperial Palace
15	Palace of the Empress
16	Imperial Harem
17	Concubines' Living Quarters
18	Pavilion of Peace
19	Theatre

- - - Buildings no longer intact

The lower part of the Noontime Gate was built out of vast blocks of ashlar stone. An elegant pavilion stands regally on top of it, scene of important ceremonies held in the presence of the emperor. It was here that the last Nguyen ruler Bao Dai (▶ Famous People) announced his abdication in 1945. The middle section of the roof is decorated with painted tiles in royal yellow; the sides are in green – the colour of the nobility. The wonderfully ornate roof ridges also catch the eye, featuring symbols of good fortune such as dragons, bats, gold coins, orchids and chrysanthemums.

Golden Water Bridge

Countless lotus blossoms float on the two pools bisected by the Golden Water Bridge (Cau Trung Dao), which was also exclusively for the use of the emperor, and leads to the Great Rites Court.

Great Rites Court

This broad courtyard is where the mandarins would assemble for official events. 18 stone stelae mark the exact points according to the nine ranks, divided into civilians (on the left) and military (on the right).

★ ★
Palace of Supreme Harmony

Miraculously, the Palace of Supreme Harmony (Dien Thai Hoa, 1805) has survived all military onslaughts. It has been restored several times and stands glittering in all its former glory today. In the red and gold finery of the **Throne Room** the emperor would receive envoys and attend important festivities. His elevated seat was placed beneath a heavy golden canopy and he wore a golden tunic and crown, decorated with nine dragons. Events of this nature were, however, extremely few and far between and the ruler seldom showed himself to his officials, thus feeding the aura of mystery so closely associated with imperial power. The emperor would get ready for his grand appearances in the room behind the throne, where nowadays people come to purchase souvenirs.

The bronze urns symbolize the emperors of the Nguyen Dynasty from Hue

The crumbling walls to the north of the Palace of Supreme Harmony surrounded the Forbidden Purple City (Tu Cam Thanh) with the palaces of the emperors and empresses. The only persons allowed to reside here, apart from the imperial family, were concubines and eunuchs – and, of course, the

Forbidden Purple City

many members of staff whose job it was to maintain their well-being and the estate's splendour. A great effort of the imagination is required to conjure up an image of life in days gone by when confronted with the barren field of dry grass and rubble visible today.

Dragons – symbols of imperial power – adorn the roof ridges of the Palace of Supreme Harmony

Only a few buildings have survived here, the Halls of the Mandarins, for example, where imperial robes may be hired out for a photographic pose. In the centre once stood the **Palace of Heavenly Laws**, to which the emperor would retreat to consider political decisions. The right-hand hall is now a souvenir shop.

★
Library

The Imperial Library, an attractive building with a garden and pond, has been lovingly restored. It was constructed during the reign of Minh Mang and redesigned on the orders of Khai Dinh, who had it decorated with mosaics. Inside, historic scenes of Hue can be viewed, souvenirs purchased and a flautist's music admired.

pavilion

The octagonal pavilion close by is the only other remaining building (reconstructed) of the Forbidden Purple City. It was originally one of two such buildings and a favourite retreat of emperors, who are said to have come here to listen to music.

Trieu Temple

At the southwest perimeter of the Imperial Enclosure there are more buildings that are worth seeing, collectively known as Trieu Temple (Temple of the Ancestors). The easiest way to reach them is by returning through the Noontime Gate and then turning right.

Famous Soul Porch

The three-storied Famous Soul Porch (Hien Lam Cac, 1821), with its interesting carvings, leads onto the courtyard where the momentous Nine Dynastic Urns (Cuu Dinh) stand.

★ ★
Nine Dynastic Urns

Some 2m/6ft high, these bronze urns represent the finest examples of local craftsmanship and were cast at the behest of Minh Mang between 1835 and 1837. Each of them features intricately engraved details (mostly landscape scenes), eulogizing the beauty and uniqueness of Vietnam. Traces of bullet impact can still be seen on some of them. The largest and **most ornate urn** (approx. 2600kg/5730lbs) stands in the middle of the line. It is dedicated to the founder of the Nguyen dynasty, Gia Long.

The Temple of Generations

Across the courtyard stands the Temple of Generations (The Mieu), built on the orders of Minh Mang in 1821 to honour his father. A row of **ten altars** bearing the genealogical trees of the rulers and their wives can be found inside the memorial. Officially, there were 13 emperors between the years of 1802 and 1945, but some are neither recognized nor represented in the temple. On each Holy Table lie a sleeping mat, blankets and other personal belongings. On the anniversary of each one's death, a small ceremony is held in The Mieu Temple. To the north is the **Temple of the Resurrection** (Hung Mieu, 1804) dedicated to the worship of the parents of Gia Long.

Dien Tho

In the northwest corner of the Forbidden Purple City stand the restored chambers of the emperor's mother, latterly the residence of the last emperor, Bao Dai. Today the palace houses antique furniture and valuable royal robes, whilst an exhibition of photographs in the reception hall helps visitors to visualize the courtly life of the past.

On the Banks of the Perfume River

Dragon boat cruises

A trip on one of the colourful dragon boats on the Perfume River is not to be missed. It is not only a lovely way to enjoy the idyllic landscape, but also an opportunity to take in some of the unique sights away from the main streets. As a rule, organized boat trips stop at Thien Mu Pagoda, Hon Chen Temple or one of the more interesting mausoleums, usually Tu Duc, Khai Dainh or Minh Mang (► Royal Mausoleums, see below).

Thien Mu Pagoda

The history of Thien Mu Pagoda (Linh Mu Pagoda or the Pagoda of the Heavenly Lady) is closely associated with two legends. In one, an old woman appears before Prince Nguyen Hoang at Song Huong, telling him to light a torch and follow the river eastwards until the flame goes out. At this point he should build his town. He later had a pagoda constructed in honour of the old woman, believing her to be a messenger of God. The second legend has the old lady appearing on a mountain in the form of a dragon's head and prophesying that one will come and build a pagoda here, bringing eternal prosperity to the land. Either way – it was, indeed, Nguyen Hoang who ordered the construction of the pagoda in 1601, making it the **oldest pagoda in Hue**. The pagoda's tower can be seen from a great distance, standing on a bank above the river, around 4km/2mi upstream on the former site of a Cham sanctuary. The Phuoc Duyen Tower (1844) has seven storeys, each

*Dragon boats are a relaxing means of progressing along the
Perfume River to the Thien Mu Pagoda and the Royal Mausoleums*

representing an incarnation of Buddha; at its peak a basin collects
rainwater, as water is seen as the source of happiness. Pavilions stand
on both sides, housing a large bell (1710) and a turtle (1715) carrying a stele. The stone tablet relates the tale of the pagoda and the history of Buddhism in Hue. The platform to the front of these buildings provides a wonderful panoramic view of the romantic river valley.

★
◀ Panorama

An archway, protected by six colourfully painted guards, leads to the
main sanctum, with a laughing bronze Buddha at the front.

★ Royal Mausoleums

Along with the Citadel, the tombs of the emperors, which lie south
of the city in the vicinity of the river, are Hue's main attraction. The
acclaimed resting places of seven of the thirteen Nguyen rulers are
all similar in design, yet each has something of the taste and preferences of each individual emperor. They were built whilst their future
occupants were still alive; Tu Duc (1847–83) actually spent several
years of his life here.

Park of Death

Opening hours:
of all tombs:
daily 7am–5pm

It could sometimes take years to find the right location, as the
courtly geomants and astrologers also had their say in the matter.
The ideal scenario entailed sheltering mountains to the north, if pos-

sible to the east and west as well, and an opening southwards down to the water. If these conditions were not naturally available, the terrain was landscaped accordingly. Artificial lakes, waterfalls and hills were added to meet the geomantic requirements on the one hand, and to create the most picturesque park environment possible on the other, as can be seen at the **tombs of Tu Duc and Minh Mang**.

They may differ in some respects, but each mausoleum comprises the following three elements: a temple dedicated to emperor and empress, containing the reliquary of the imperial family, a stele pavilion as an encomium of the ruler, watched over by stone elephants, horses, soldiers and officials, and finally – on a hilltop, ideally – the tomb itself, enclosed by thick walls. It was customary to keep the actual location of the tomb a secret to guard against grave robbers and enemies of the state; in extreme cases, for this reason, all those who attended the burial were subsequently executed.

The best way to reach the tombs is by car or bicycle. Alternatively, the mausoleums of Tu Duc, Dong Khanh and Minh Mang can also be reached on foot from the boat jetties.

★★
Tomb of Minh Mang (Lang Hieu)

The tomb of Minh Mang (1820–41) is the only one situated to the west of the Perfume River (12km/7.5mi from Hue). Many consider it to be the most beautiful, inspired by Chinese design and blending harmoniously into the landscape. Architecture was a passion of the second Nguyen emperor Ming Manh. He also completed the Citadel in Hue after the death of Gia Long, and planned his mausoleum on a symmetrical axis running east to west. The tomb was built between 1841 and 1843 under his successor.

The tall main gate leads onto the Honour Courtyard where stone mandarins and elephants stand guard and on to the Stele Pavilion

Hue Tomb of Minh Mang

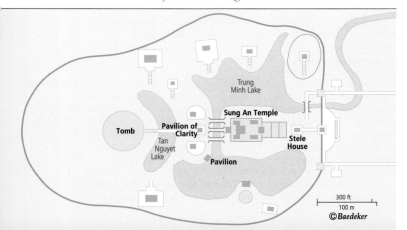

Trung
Minh Lake

Sung An Temple

Tomb   Pavilion of
Clarity

Tan
Nguyet
Lake

Stele
House

Pavilion

300 ft
100 m
©Baedeker

The Mingh Mang Mausoleum is based on Chinese design

with the eulogy written by his son Thieu Tri. Beyond several more courtyards stands the red and golden **Sung An Temple**, dedicated to Minh Mang and the empress. The columns and beams are intoxicatingly beautiful, as are the many antique pieces decorating the room. Three bridges span Trung Minh Lake, the central one reserved for the emperor's use alone. On the other side stands the elegant **Minh Lau Pavilion** (Bright Pavilion), offering a wonderful view across the crescent-shaped Tan Nguyet Lake. Adjacent is a small garden where the flowerbeds were once painstakingly planted to spell out the Chinese characters for a long life. Past sweet-smelling frangipani trees, steps bordered by dragon pillars point the way to the actual tomb of Minh Mang on a pine-covered hill, surrounded by a round wall.

Lang Khiem attracts the most visitors and is an especially beautiful site (7km/4mi from Hue), built from 1864 to 1867. Tu Duc (1847–83) was not only emperor during a period in which the independence of Vietnam was greatly threatened, but also, indeed above

★ ★
Tomb of Tu Duc (Lang Khiem)

Hue *Tomb of Tu Duc*

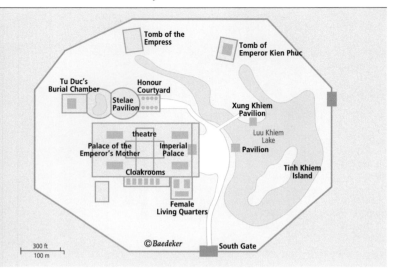

Tomb of the Empress

Tomb of Emperor Kien Phuc

Tu Duc's Burial Chamber

Honour Courtyard

Stelae Pavilion

Xung Khiem Pavilion

theatre

Luu Khiem Lake

Palace of the Emperor's Mother

Imperial Palace

Pavilion

Tinh Khiem Island

Cloakrooms

Female Living Quarters

300 ft
100 m

©Baedeker   South Gate

all, a **Romantic poet**, who liked nothing better than to hide away from the world in his garden. Thus he lived for 16 years in this artificially created landscape protected by a wall, spending his time in a boat, fishing, meditating, writing poetry and drinking tea.

On entering through the southern gate, a path leads the way past a pond filled with water lilies and lotus flowers to a prettily decorated pavilion. Across the lake stands the **Xung Khiem Pavilion**, restored courtesy of UNESCO. Where once Tu Duc would retire to write, Vietnamese families come today to enjoy a picnic. The steps leading up from the lake end at a portal with three entrances. The central one, painted yellow, was reserved for the emperor. Continuing onwards through an enclosure, **Hoa Khiem Temple** is reached, used by Tu Ducas as the imperial palace. Following his death, the funerary tablets were displayed here, with Tu Duc's being noticeably smaller than that of the empress. A theatre stood behind the temple to the left, with the clothing stores opposite and the living quarters of the emperor's wives and concubines close by.

Continue along Luu Khiem Lake to reach the emperor's tomb. Before entering, however, visitors must pass the stone elephants, horses and guards standing watch on the Court of Honour. The military mandarins can be identified, on closer inspection, by their swords, whilst each of the mandarin officials holds a sceptre. Moving on to the **Stele Pavilion**, this is a chance to see the largest stele in Vietnam (weighing 20 tons and inscribed with almost 5000 characters). Traditionally the sons of the emperor would write their father's epitaph, yet the childless Tu Duc had no option but sorrowfully to compose his own. A small crescent lake is situated immediately behind the pavilion, and behind the lake lies the walled tomb of the emperor. In actual fact, however, Tu Duc is said to be buried elsewhere. His adopted son Khien Phuc, who reigned for a mere seven months, and the empress are buried in a small pine wood on the opposite side of the lake.

The magnificent resting place of Emperor Khai Dinh (1916–25) is the last mausoleum of the Nguyen dynasty to have been built and serves as an example of the downfall of Vietnamese culture in the colonial era. Khai Dinh was a **puppet of the French**, dazzled by the French lifestyle and its architecture. Instead of bricks, the European-influenced structure was built with concrete. Even the faces of the mandarins in the Court of Honour reveal a mixture of Vietnamese and European traits.

✳
Tomb of Khai Dinh (Lang Ung)

The mausoleum sits majestically on Chau Chu Mountain (10km/6mi from Hue) looking towards a white Quan Am statue. Before construction commenced, Khai Dinh had the graves of Chinese nobility removed. The Chinese nobles had selected the place for its excep-

The Khai Dinh vestibule is opulently adorned with maiolica and porcelain

tionally beautiful and geomantically favourable location. Steep, broad steps, bordered by imposing concrete dragons, lead the way up to the Court of Honour, with its obligatory statues of mandarins, elephants and horses, and on to the octagonal Stele Pavilion. Higher still is the **actual tomb**, consisting of three connecting rooms. Mosaics of coloured glass and ceramic chips decorate the walls and ceilings, depicting, amongst other scenes, the four seasons. The actual tomb is situated approximately 9m/30ft beneath the throne where the bronze statue of the emperor sits, a jade sceptre in his hand. In the third and final room stands the altar dedicated to Khai Dinh.

Tomb of Dong Khanh (Lang Dong Khanh) The tomb of Dong Khanh (1885–89) lies just 500m/550yd from that of Tu Duc. Constructed in 1889, it is the smallest of the royal mausoleums, but has its own individual note. Although Dong Khanh was the first Nguyen ruler to be installed by the French, the rumour persists that he was also disposed of by them. The mausoleum is notable for its »double architecture«, with a walled-in part containing temples, pavilions and courtyards, and a second part some 100m/110yd away, an open arrangement of terraces featuring the Guard of Honour, Stele Pavilion and tomb.

Tomb of Thieu Tri (Lang Xuong) Thieu Tri's tomb is a smaller version of the resting place of his predecessor Minh Mang. Unusually, it faces northwest, considered unfavourable then as now, indeed seen by many as the reason that Vietnam fell under French rule just a few years after its construction (1847–48). Few visitors venture this far, although the temples and pagodas are well worth inspecting.

Further Places to Visit in Hue

Hue Museum Hue Museum (3 Le Truc, opening times: daily 7am–5pm) presents a variety of exhibits from the collection of the Nguyen emperors, including furniture, robes, porcelain and much more besides. The building itself, the beautiful Long An Palace, is certainly worth a look. It was originally built inside the Imperial Enclosure in 1845 and later moved to its present location. In 1923, Emperor Khai Dinh had the palace converted into a museum.

Provincial Museum Directly opposite stands the Provincial Museum. It is housed in the Di Luan Pavilion (1808), formerly a school for princes and the sons of senior mandarins. Three different exhibitions can be witnessed here: in the central portion, archaeological and ethnological collections with impressive burial statues of the Ede are on display. In the western building there is an interesting section dealing with regional architecture, industry and agriculture, whilst the eastern building is dedicated to more recent history, particularly the war against the USA (opening times: daily except Thu 7am–11am and 1.30pm–5pm).

Hue Map

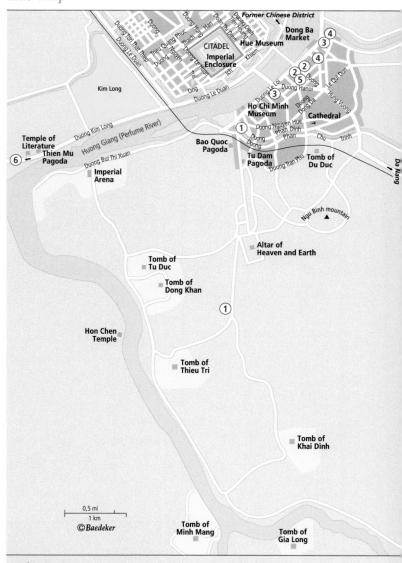

Former Chinese District
Dong Ba Market ④ ③
CITADEL   Hue Museum
Imperial Enclosure   ② ② ④
⑤
Kim Long   ③
Ho Chi Minh Museum   Cathedral
Duong Nguyen Hue
Temple of Literature   Huong Giang (Perfume River)   Bao Quoc Pagoda
Thien Mu Pagoda ⑥ ←   Duong Bui Thi Xuan   Tu Dam Pagoda   Tomb of Du Duc
Imperial Arena   Da Nang

Ngu Binh mountain ▲

Altar of Heaven and Earth

Tomb of Tu Duc
Tomb of Dong Khan
①

Hon Chen Temple

Tomb of Thieu Tri

Tomb of Khai Dinh

0,5 mi
1 km
©Baedeker

Tomb of Minh Mang   Tomb of Gia Long

Where to stay
① Pilgrimage Village
② Saigon Morin
③ Century Riverside
④ Huong Giang Hotel
⑤ Indochine Hotel
⑥ Morin Bach Ma Hotel

Where to eat
① An Dinh Palace
② Song Huong Floating Restaurant
③ Banh Khoai Thuong Tu
④ Why Not

▶ VISITING HUE

INFORMATION

Hue Tourist
18 A Le Loi, Hue
Tel. 0 54/82 16 26

Vietnam Tourism
14 Nguyen Van Cu, Hue
Tel. 0 54/82 83 16
Also in the Huong Giang Hotel

TRANSPORT

Phu Bai Airport (approx. 15km/9mi southeast of Hue): tel. 0 54/82 32 49.
International Airport Da Nang:
Tel. 05 11/81 18 11 and 83 03 39.
Seaport at Thuan An Beach and pier at Hotel Huong Giang

EVENTS

Hue Festival
Hue Festival, with classical court music and dances, is held over several days in June in even-numbered years (2010, 2012...). Exhibitions, fashion shows, folklore and kite-flying competitions are just some of the highlights.

Wrestling Festival
In January and February, thousands of young men congregate for the traditional wrestling championships in the village of Sinh, on the south bank of the Huong (Perfume River).

*Hon Chen
Temple Festival*
Twice a year in the third and seventh lunar months (February/March and July/August): on the Perfume River, west of Hue and in the village of Cat Hai, worshippers gather to perform plays and take part in processions, with lighted rafts and boats illuminating the river.

SHOPPING

Dong Ba Market is several storeys high and it is said that the finest conical straw hats in all of Vietnam can be found here. They are decorated with delicate silhouettes which shine through the virtually transparent hats in the light. The usual market wares of fruit, vegetables, meat and fish are also on offer.

WHERE TO EAT

▶ Moderate

① *An Dinh Palace*
78A Nguyen Hue and 97 Phan Dinh Phung (entrances)
Tel. 0 54/83 30 19
daily noon–2pm, 5pm–10pm
Eat like a king in the former villa of Emperor Bao Dai's mother: typical regional fare served in two dining halls (many groups) decorated with stucco and ornate pillars, ceiling frescoes and shrines of honour.

▶ Inexpensive

② *Song Huong Floating Restaurant*
3 Thang 2 Park, Le Loi Street
Tel. 0 54/82 37 38
daily 8am–9pm
Built on stilts on the riverbank next to the Trang Tien Bridge. Hue cuisine

can be sampled here, along with international dishes.

③ *Banh Khoai Thuong Tu*
6 Dinh Thien Hoang
(close to the Phu Xuan Bridge)
Tel. 0 54/52 73 48
Speciality of the establishment is banh khoai: pancakes with shrimp, meat, soya beans and nuoc leo, a peanut-sesame sauce.

ENTERTAINMENT
④ *Why Not*
21 Vo Thi Sau
Tel. 0 54/82 47 93
Enjoy a game of pool or darts in this small bar offering Western and Viet-namese classics, pizza, snacks, fresh fruit juices and cocktails, wine or beer.

WHERE TO STAY
► Luxury
① *Pilgrimage Village*
130 Minh Mang Road
(approx. 3km/2mi in the direction of the Royal Tombs)
Tel. 0 54/88 54 61, fax 88 70 57
www.pilgrimagevillage.com
A village for pilgrims. Designed in traditional style, rustic yet elegant: two-tier brick houses with 50 rooms, each with two balconies, peaceful exotic garden, pool with a small waterfall and bar.

② *Saigon Morin*
30 Le Loi
Tel. 0 54/82 35 26, fax 82 51 55
www.morinhotel.com.vn
sgmorin@dng.vnn.vn
Splendidly ostentatious colonial con-struction from the year 1901: 130 restored rooms (»extended« in some cases) with balcony (facing a main street, unfortunately), whilst the courtyard is a veritable oasis with a fountain, a beautiful café by a mini-

pool, three restaurants and rooftop bar. Following the Royal Cemetery marathon, relax with a foot massage (good offers available via the internet).

► Mid-range
③ *Century Riverside*
49 Le Loi
Tel. 0 54/82 33 90, fax 82 33 94
cenhuevn@dng.vnn.vn
Modern but hulking 4-star block on the bank of the Perfume River, with 158 different rooms, some unexpect-edly elegant. Small, attractive pool, massage facilities, fitness centre, disco. Five restaurants and bars.

④ *Huong Giang Hotel*
51 Le Loi
Tel. 0 54/82 21 22, fax 82 31 02
www.huonggiangtourist.com
hghotel@dng.vnn.vn
Renovated hotel in the upper middle class. Quaint garden close to the Dap Da Bridge on the main crossing of the east bank. Excellent restaurant, pool, travel agency.

► Budget
⑤ *Indochine Hotel (Dong Duong)*
2 Hung Vuong
Tel. 0 54/82 38 66, fax 82 60 74
indochine-hotel@dng.vnn.vn
Hotel combining old and new build-ings, located close to the river. Indi-vidually appointed rooms (air-conditioned, satellite TV).

⑥ *Morin Bach Ma Hotel*
Km 19, Bach Ma National Park, Phu Loc (approx. 30km/19mi from Hue Airport)
Tel. 0 54/87 11 99, fax 87 11 77
French-style villa hotel with twelve simple, but well-equipped rooms (satellite TV, minibar, telephone) and small balconies. Night club and res-taurant.

European quarter

The main street of the French quarter is Le Loi Street, running parallel to Song Huong. This is also where the Quoc Hoc High School can be found, its illustrious pupils including not only Ho Chi Minh, but also General Vo Nguyen Giap, victorious at Dien Bien Phu, and the former president Ngo Dinh Diem. A few steps further on is the **Ho Chi Minh Museum**, with the obligatory photographs and souvenirs (opening times: Tue–Sun, 7.30am–11.30am, 1.30pm–4.30pm). The **Cathedral** of Notre Dame on Nguyen Hue Street looks like a cross between a church and a pagoda. It was erected in 1962–63 at the instigation of the Archbishop of Hue, Ngo Dinh Thuc, brother of President Diem.

Bao Quoc Pagoda / Tu Dam Pagoda

At the western perimeter of the European quarter, there are two pagodas worth visiting: Chua Bao Quoc is up on Ham Long Hill and can be reached by taking Dien Bien Phu Street away from the town and turning right immediately after the railway tracks.

Just 500m/550yd further south, on the corner of Dien Bien Phu and Tu Dam Street, stands Tu Dam Pagoda (1690–95).

Around Hue

Thuan An Beach

Roughly 13km/8mi northwest of Hue (4km/2.5mi from the road to Da Nang), the Perfume River opens out into a vast lagoon, protected by a long sandbank. Across the lagoon lies the village of Thuan An

The city's cathedral stands in the southern part of the European Quarter

and beyond the village is the beach. Past the refreshments stalls and small seafood establishments, the sunloungers and parasols peter out after a few hundred yards and the atmosphere becomes appreciably more peaceful. The route to the beach is dotted with countless tombs and formidable burial temples of Vietnamese families who fled into exile as »boat people«. Approximately 6km/4mi further on, the **village of Duong No** is reached, where Ho Chi Minh (► Baedeker Special p.265) lived for some years as a child. The simple wooden house with a grass roof is open to visitors.

> ### ! Baedeker TIP
>
> **A walk in the park**
> Six walking trails lead through the rainforest of the national park, none of them particularly long. The best time to visit the park is after the rainy season from March to June. Six rustic, restored brick villas from the colonial period are today again in service as guesthouses. There is also a campsite and jeeps are available for hire (information: Phu Loc, Hue, tel. 054/87 13 30, www.bachma.vnn.vn).

Bach Ma (Hai Van) National Park (22,000ha/54,000ac) extends from the Central Highlands to the coastal region and is the wettest of Vietnam's rainforests with over 8000mm/315in of precipitation per annum, most of which falls between September and December (leeches included). On a clear day, the mountains of Bach Ma (1450m/4750ft) and Noc (1259m/4130ft) offer a spectacular panorama towards the coast. Streams and rivers flow through steep and narrow gorges, numerous waterfalls plunge from a height into idyllic bathing pools, such as Do Quyen Waterfall, whose cascades total 300m/985ft in height. The scenery is especially impressive in February when the red rhododendrons are in bloom. The park's fauna includes over 330 species of bird and at least 55 different mammals. In 1992, a **breed of antelope named saola**, thought to be extinct, was discovered here. Another rare and exotic inhabitant is the muntjac, a deer species. A few tigers, and perhaps some leopards as well, move back and forth in the dense borderlands between Vietnam and Laos. Automatic cameras are positioned at locations where the deer pass is at its busiest, as natural scientists seek to plot their movements. One thing seems certain: the local herd of elephants has retreated to Laos. Illegal felling and poaching have taken their toll on the national park. A kilogramme (two pounds) of rhinoceros horn can fetch as much as 60,000 US dollars according to the WWF, and the antlers of a particular species of deer around 3000 US dollars. The national park lies approximately 45km/28mi southwest of Hue (N 1, exit at Truoi).

Bach Ma National Park

The hot springs of Thanh Tan (approx. 30km/18mi northwest of Hue) are a popular destination at weekends for the Vietnamese, although women will only enter the 60°C/140°F hot, bubbling water in shorts and T-shirts. The thermal baths consist of several basins, private areas and a restaurant (towel required).

Thanh Tan

Phu Cam (Phuoc Vinh) The hat-making village of Phu Cam lies on the south bank of the An Cuu River. For several hundred years and many generations, the women here have been painstakingly making the intricate conical hats for which the region is so famous from (ironed) palm leaves. Their dexterity is essential in fashioning the wafer-thin hats, decorated with silk threads, painted landscapes or poetry.

Lang Son

D 2

Province: Lang Son (capital)
Population: 70,000

Region: Northern Highlands

Lang Son, the provincial capital, is an excellent base from which to tour the mountainous north, e.g. ▶Dien Bien Phu, ▶Sa Pa or the Ba Be National Park. The town itself has been thriving since the resumption of border traffic to China (1992), but can hardly be termed attractive.

Frontier town to China Following the Vietnamese invasion of Cambodia, China retaliated in 1979 with a form of **punitive campaign** which had a severe impact on Lang Son, which along with Lao Cai (▶Sa Pa) is the most important border crossing to China. Since the border was reopened in 1992, trade has flourished – both legally and illegally – as Lang Son enjoys good road and rail connections to Hanoi. The train journey from Hanoi to Lang Son takes approximately 8 hours, by bus about 6 hours, although the poor state of the roads make this something of

 VISITING LANG SON

INFORMATION

Lang Son Tourist Service
41 Le Loi, Vinh Trai, Lang Son
Tel. 0 25/87 20 36

SHOPPING

Close to town, on a rocky granite outcrop visible from some distance, the daily market of Kya Lu is held. The Tay, Nung and Dao womenfolk can be seen here selling fruit, vegetables and craftwork from the early hours of the morning.

WHERE TO EAT

In Lang Son, the inns of the Le Loi and Tran Dang Ninh Street serve good food, but the hot food stalls and market stands are not to be dismissed, with noodle dishes, suckling pig and duck all especially worth sampling.

WHERE TO STAY

▶ **Budget**
Mao Son Hotel
Tran Dang Ninh
(at the Ky Lua Market)
Tel. 0 25/87 68 18
The best of a number of quite basic hotels on the main street, some rooms with an attractive view overlooking Phai Loan Lake.

an ordeal. At least the beautiful mountain scenery offers a compensatory distraction.

Around Lang Son

Roughly 1km/1100yd down from the market at Kya Lu, by the river, stands the small **Ky Cung Temple**, tucked under the bridge on the north bank. It was dedicated to Quan Tuan Tranh, who fought bravely against the Chinese, over 500 years ago. Inside the temple is a picture of Ho Chi Minh, who paid a visit to Lang Son in 1960.

Around 2km/1mi further north, two beautiful caves wait to be explored. The **Tam Than Cave** boasts a deep pool and an impressive vantage point in the form of a natural window in the rock offering a vista of the neighbouring paddy fields. The enchanting features of **Nhi Thanh Cave** include beautiful stalactites and stalagmites and a small cave stream.

The highlands of the north

Dong Dang Market, at the border gate some 14km/8.5mi away, is also frequented by Tay and Thai people. The most popular items on sale here are water buffalo, groceries, Russian motorbikes and cheap goods from China. On the hills between Lang Son and Dong Dang some **Japanese fortifications** from the Second World War can be looked over.

Dong Dang

✶ ## Ba Be National Park

Vietnam's largest natural lake, the Ho Ba Be, forms the heart of the eponymous national park to the north of Lang Son in the province of Cao Bang. At the heart of evergreen rainforest and karst limestone mountains, which seem to grow out of the lowlands and reach up to 1800m/5900ft high, the 9km/5.5mi-long lake extends across three valleys. The hills, the habitat of apes, flying squirrels, Asiatic mountain goats and bats, are awash with orchids in bloom, flamboyants and palms. The flora encompasses around 450 species, including many varieties of bamboo and rattan. There are probably still tigers and leopards in the region, as well as some macaque troops. Boat trips can be undertaken to the neighbouring villages of Tay and Hmong and

Flamboyant in bloom

the Puong Cave (north bank of the lake). The imposing **Dau Dang Waterfall**, crashing down from a height of 45m/145ft, is also close by. Guesthouses offer overnight accommodation, whilst the entrance to the park is situated between Nha Phac and Cho Ra.

Cao Bang

Cao Bang, the capital of the province of the same name, lies some 40km/25mi northeast of the national park, on the border to China. Almost completely destroyed by the Chinese in 1979, Cao Bang now profits from the border traffic with its great neighbour.

✷ ✷ Mekong Delta

C/D 7/8

Region: South	**Area:** 70,000 sq km/27,000 sq mi

The Mekong delta is Southeast Asia at its most authentic: few large towns but a deeply rich, rural terrain. Its warm, sultry climate and lush vegetation make the Mekong delta the ultimate example of a tropical landscape. A certain somnolence pervades the region, inspiring a veritable holiday feeling in visitors, perhaps more so than in other regions of Vietnam.

»Nine Dragon River«

The Mekong is one of the largest rivers in Asia, its final 200km/125mi of a total of 4800km/2980mi coursing through South Vietnam. It rises in the highlands of Tibet, flows as Lancang Jiang through Southwest China, forms the border between Burma and Laos, continues through Laos and demarcates a further frontier between two states, namely Laos and Thailand. Thereafter it enters the lowlands of Cambodia, dividing into two currents at Phnom Penh, the Tien Giang (Upper Mekong) and the Hau Giang (Lower Mekong, Bassac). In Vietnam these two rivers fan out into **eight main tributaries**, one canal and numerous other distributaries, forming a vast delta as they progress to the sea at different points. Although it only has eight estuaries, the Mekong is also called the Song Cuu Long in Vietnam: »Nine Dragon River«, due to the Chinese mythological attachment to the number nine.

Flooding

Every 2–5 years, the delta is subject to serious flooding. Thanks to the sand and mud which is swept along by the Mekong and its tributaries, the **fertility of the soil** is maintained. Furthermore, the Mekong delta is advancing at an annual rate of some 80m/87yd into the sea. Thus the remains of the ancient port of Oc Eo, which belonged to the Funan Empire, and surrendered in the 7th century, today lies 30km/18mi inland.

Colonization

As the delta region in the north runs seamlessly into the Cambodian lowlands, it is virtually the only area of Vietnam to which neighbouring peoples had unhindered access. This is the reason for the influx of diverse ethnic groups in the past and the high contingent of **ethnic minorities** in the Mekong delta today. From the 1st century it formed part of the Funan Empire, and following that regime's demise (7th century) it fell to the various Khmer dynasties over the next 1000 years. In the 17th century it ultimately became a catch basin for Chinese refugees who had been forced out of their homeland under the Qing dynasty. The Cham also retreated here, taking flight from the Vietnamese. The latter did not assume control of the region until the 18th century as they ventured south and integrated the area into the empire of the Nguyen dynasty. As Cambodia offered ample opportunities for rice cultivation, the Mekong delta was, at this time, an overgrown swampland, rife with malaria. It was not until the French took possession of the Mekong delta from 1861 and added Cochinchina to their colonial empire that the land was reclaimed and drained to create the **largest »rice bowl« in the country**. With 19 million inhabitants, the Mekong delta is now one of the most densely populated and economically successful regions in Vietnam.

The delta is riddled with canals and tributaries

Both the Cambodians and the Vietnamese live in villages in the middle of their agricultural areas. In contrast to the otherwise compact huddles of villages in the rest of Vietnam, **more loosely scattered settlements** dominate the picture here. The houses are often built on stilts. Homes of this type, commonly found in Laos, Cambodia and Thailand, feature a living area mounted on twelve round supports accessed by a ladder with five, seven or nine rungs – an even number is considered unlucky. The room below is reserved for pets. This design improves air circulation and serves as protection against floodwater.

Economy

With the exception of the mangrove swamps near the coast, the region is intensively farmed and is, along with the Red River delta, one of the two largest rice bowls in the country. Although the Mekong delta covers less than 10% of the surface area of Vietnam, approximately half of the country's rice harvest is yielded here. This is a major contributing factor to Vietnam's status as the **second largest ex-**

Mekong Delta *Map*

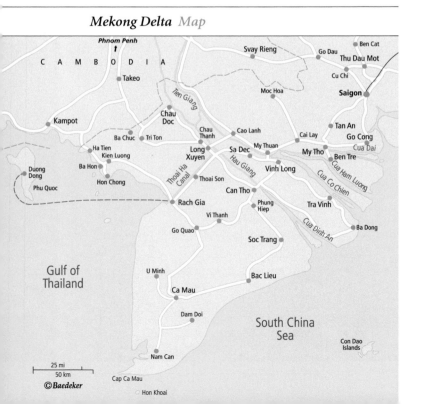

The inhabitants of the Mekong delta live by the water, and make their living from it

porter of rice in the world after Thailand. Even so, the monoculture of rice, as propagated primarily by the French, has given way to a wider variety of tropical fruit crops, including sugar cane and coconut palms. Recent years have also seen a significant increase in shrimp and fish farms.

The Mekong delta has a relatively good road transport system and a number of huge, new bridges. Progress can be slow, nevertheless, as larger and smaller ferries criss-cross the tributaries and estuaries of the Mekong. Variations in water level mean that not all rivers are navigable throughout the year, whilst the dry months of March and April present the boats with their own problems of sandbanks. A **network of canals** with an aggregate length of 5000km/3100mi is therefore used to transport goods independently of the river levels.

Transport

The Mekong delta is one of the regions most severely afflicted in the war. Dense primeval forest provided ideal cover for the Vietcong, enabling them to overrun enemy troops in jungle warfare. It comes as little surprise that this area was uncompromisingly targeted in the **Americans' deforestation strategy**, depriving the Vietcong of their natural hideouts. The devastating consequences for the tropical for-

Consequences of war

Rice and more rice: a huge variety is on sale at the markets

Rice kernels hang on the long panicles before they are harvested

RICE – NO PAIN, NO GRAIN

Green, in all its nuances, is the dominant colour of the Vietnamese countryside. The two »rice bowls« of the land, the Mekong delta in the south and the Red River delta in the north, seem to be a mosaic made up of patches of varying green, from the tender shades of young shoots to a range of strong, intense colours as the plants ripen and the greenish-yellow brown tones of fields that are ready to be harvested.

Foraging water fowl and heavily treading water buffalo with their constant companions, white cattle herons, complete an idyllic picture that does nothing to betray the endless labour involved in cultivating rice, from sowing the grain until harvest time.

Strenuous work

The grains of rice from the last harvest have to be soaked overnight before they are sown over muddy seeding beds, farmland of especially good quality which must be **irrigated at a constant level**. After a month, when the shoots are about 20cm/8in tall, they are individually uprooted and planted in carefully prepared rice fields. The fields have to be ploughed

beforehand, flooded and harrowed in order to make the heavy clay earth into an ideal soil for growth. Traditionally the fields are worked using **water buffalo** and oxen. Today tractors can be seen here and there, but the sight of rice farmers following

their buffalo through the fields remains one of the eternally unchanging images of Vietnam.

Before the shoots are planted in bundles in the muddy rice fields, the upper ends of the stalks are pulled apart. This is intended to improve the yield. They are then pressed into the earth in **closely spaced rows**, unbelievably strenuous work for people standing in water with their backs permanently bent and exposed to the scorching sun. To relieve the pain somewhat, a little marijuana is sometimes added to the workers' lunch.

The water level has to be monitored daily and kept as constant as possible so that the young rice plants neither dry out nor rot during the phase of growth that follows. In order to gain a rich harvest it is necessary to ensure consistent irrigation that matches the stage of growth of the plants. In areas where the farmers are dependent on rain, they have no choice but to hope and pray that not too much and not too little falls. In order to keep the favour of the **Goddess of Rice**, they carry out elaborate and carefully prepared ceremonies. If this does not produce the desired results, every drop of water has to be fetched in buckets carried on a yoke. The situation of the farmers is better in regions where rice is grown with artificial irrigation. Usually water can be taken from the main canals which flow around the fields. By this means it is possible to harvest rice two or three times per year in some places.

The rice is often laid out at the side of the road. The kernels are easily separated from the stalks when vehicles and carts ride over them. They also dry well here.

However, the effort involved in allocating labour and monitoring this system, which operates over large areas, usually exceeds the capacity of a single family or clan. It requires the **cooperation of a whole village** or district. A dyke inspector decides when to let in water and how much, manages the labourers who repair and

There are over 100,000 different kinds of rice worldwide ...

clear the dykes and also determines which fields are given water first.

While waiting for the rice to ripen, the only activity apart from irrigation is **weeding**. In this phase the farmers and their families sometimes move into huts by the fields in order to keep an eye on the rice at all times. The old practice was to use fish and ducks to fight pests in the rice fields, but nowadays the farmers sometimes employ pesticides to protect their rice and ensure a good yield. Finally, shortly before harvesting, after a period of between 90 and 130 days, the field is dried out so that the grain

can ripen fully. The **harvest**, too, involves extremely hard labour. Mechanical aids are hardly used, as the grains, which grow on long panicles, are not suitable for harvesting by machines. The stalks are therefore bunched to be cut with a sickle. The farms help each other by supplying labour. After harvesting the rice is threshed, sometimes straight away using small machines on the field. However, village women can also be seen **threshing with flails**. Sheaves of rice are often also left lying on roads, as the grains are separated from the stalk when a car runs over them – thus saving labour in one part of the process. The grains are then left to dry for a while by the roadside. Finally they are taken to the village and sold or stored in barns. The great harvest festival is held only when all the rice is in a safe place.

Now the never-ending cycle of sowing, planting, watering, harvesting and threshing, which has marked the rhythm of life in Vietnam since time immemorial, can begin all over again.

ests can still be seen today – the decimated natural woodland is compounded by the deformities in the growth of trees and leaves. Today, however, the greatest threat to the woods is the economy, as ever increasing areas of forest stand and mangroves are cleared to make way for fresh arable land.

From ► My Tho a **boat trip** along the northernmost branch of the Mekong, the Tien Giang, to the lush fruit orchards at Ben Tre is recommended. Cau Lanh is the perfect destination for ornithologists. It can be reached via Vinh Long (► Can Tho), where those interested can venture to the Khmer pagodas at Tra Vinh. Pleasant hotels and restaurants await in ► Can Tho, along with floating markets and fruit plantations. To the south lies the **primeval swampland** of Ca Mau (► Can Tho). Boats depart from the coastal town of Rach Gia (► Chau Doc) to Phu Quoc Island and its unique beaches. Those wishing to penetrate deeper into the western area of the delta should visit Ha Tien (► Chau Doc) and ► Chau Doc close to the Cambodian border.

What to see in the delta

✳ My Lai

E 5

Province: Quang Ngai   **Region:** South Central Coast

The name of My Lai is surely familiar even to those whose knowledge of Vietnam is otherwise limited. Located 12km/7.5mi north of the provincial capital Quang Ngai, the village gained tragic notoriety through the brutal actions of the US Army on 16 March 1968, going down in history as the My Lai Massacre.

The district of Son My was known as the Vietcong stronghold. Some American soldiers were injured and killed in the area in March 1968, stinging the US Army into an **act of reprisal**. During the course of a so-called Search and Destroy operation the village was razed to the ground and the entire population – more than 500 people, the majority of them women, children and the elderly – abused and slaughtered in the most gruesome manner imaginable. A year later, one »traitor« in the American ranks found himself unable to keep his memories to himself any longer and the atrocities were made public. He told the press what had really happened

My Lai Massacre

 MY LAI

GETTING THERE

Located approx. 170km/105mi north of ► Qui Nhon and approx. 110km/68mi south of ► Hoi An

To reach the memorial, take the N 1 eastbound from the provincial capital Quang Ngai and cross the Tra Khuc River. A signposted path branches off eastwards after the bridge.

and presented photographic evidence to back up his statement. In this way the world came to learn that defenceless people had been

Memorial for victims of the massacre

herded together and gunned down with automatic weapons into ditches. Women and girls had been mutilated and gang-raped, babies and children butchered. America was deeply shaken. Nobody could fathom that the young men sent to Vietnam as protectors of peace and human rights had revealed themselves to be murderers of babies and the elderly. Media pressure did lead to an **investigation**, but the commission seemed intent on perpetuating the cover-up – especially when it became apparent that My Lai was not an isolated incident.

Only one single participant, Lieutenant William Calley, was tried in court. Initially sentenced to life imprisonment, he found vehement support from one element of the public and was portrayed as a martyr. Ultimately, he was given an early reprieve by President Nixon, tantamount to an illegal interference in the jurisdiction of the United States.

✱ Memorial

Lest we forget

🕐 Opening hours: daily 7am–6pm

My Lai was only one of four villages in the Son My region where massacres occurred simultaneously. Today the hamlets again nestle idyllically between paddy fields and palm groves. Dedicated to the victims of the events on 16 March 1968, the Son My Memorial stands on the original site of the massacre. The first impression of a peaceful park landscape is challenged by the **monumental war memorial** in its midst. On the few remaining palm trees, notices inform visitors where particular families' huts once stood in their shade, still scorched and riddled with bullet holes. Small pathways wind through the meadows past the gravestones, with incense sticks in memory of the dead. On each an inscription notes whose house stood at this point and how many members of the family (with names and ages) lost their lives in the massacre. Nearly all of them were either children or old people. Mass graves are also noted.

The **museum** shows images captured by an American military photographer and presents detailed information about the war and the events that unfolded at My Lai in particular. Personal effects of the victims, found in the rubble, can also be seen. A documentary filmed by Dutch television for the 30th anniversary of the massacre can be viewed on request in the adjacent building.

✳ My Son

E 5

Province: Quang Nam–Da Nang   **Region:** South Central Coast

Standing before the temple ruins of My Son in the hills of Song Thu Bon, the erstwhile grandeur of the religious and cultural centre of the Cham (4th–13th centuries) can only be imagined. The transient nature of an ancient civilization is strikingly apparent – and provides a vivid contrast to the sprawl of vegetation, forcing its way into every nook and cranny.

A good 20km/12.5mi from the capital Tra Kieu, in a basin almost entirely surrounded by mountains, the Cham king Bhadravarman (4th century) built a sanctum dedicated to **Shiva**, the Hindu god. Around three hundred years later, the original wooden temples were replaced with brick constructions. Ensuing generations extended the site continuously and added further sacral buildings. Today it is thought that the temple complex was considered to be the realm of gods and divine kings, populated by many priests, dancers and servants. French scientists divided the buildings into groups based on

History

Temple ruins of the Cham shrine: green shoots find their way through every nook and cranny

their findings and ordered them alphabetically. Within these groups, the individual buildings were sorted numerically. When the Vietcong used My Son as their hideout in the late 1960s, the American Air Force **carpet bombed** the area. Most of the unique temple towers were destroyed, including the legendary Kalan A1, declared by the French to be the most beautiful **brick construction** in Asia. Bomb craters can still be seen here today, especially in groups E and F, where they have evolved into harmless looking pools filled with water lilies. Since 1981, this unique historical site has been restored. In 1999 the sanctuary was added to the UNESCO World Heritage list, and UNESCO along with the World Monuments Fund and other sponsors provide funds to protect the site.

✸ ✸ Relics of the Temple Site

Site

🕐
Opening hours: daily 6.30am–4.30pm; dance and musical performances daily except Mon 9:30am and 10.30am.

Although the site of My Son was built upon over centuries, the only temple buildings grouped here consist of a tower (kalan), library, meditation hall (mandapa) and auxiliary buildings – none of the three-tower sanctuaries typical of later Cham architecture. The temple towers symbolize the **Hindu mountain realm of Mehru**, home of the gods. Inside, the sanctum is plain and simple, with an iconic image of the revered god at its centre. Usually this was the phallic symbol of Shiva, a lingam. South of the kalan stood the library, housing objects of ritual. The mandapa, a rectangular hall to which the priests would retreat in preparation for ceremonies, was located outside the temple walls. Temple dances were also held here. It remains a mystery just how the highest towers on site could be built with fired bricks, **yet without mortar**. One theory suggests that the Cham used a kind of resin instead of mortar, mixed with ground shells and brick dust. A contrasting theory posits the idea that unfired bricks were first built up, the building was covered with earth and then completely fired.

 MY SON

GETTING THERE
Located approx. 40km/25mi southwest of ►Hoi An.

As the heat tends to accumulate in the temple valley, it is advisable to set off to My Son early in the morning. This is the only way to explore the terrain at a bearable temperature.

SECURITY NOTICE
It is strongly recommended that visitors keep to the marked pathways as a number of (live) mines and bombs are still thought to be in the area.

The entrance leads directly onto the **B, C and D groups**, still relatively intact and offering an idea of how the site may once have looked. The religious centre is thought to have been located in Kalan B1, of which only the foundations have survived. A few years ago, the **lingam** was discovered in the earth below and now stands in front of the building. Stone inscriptions found close by reveal that this lingam was erected

My Son Map

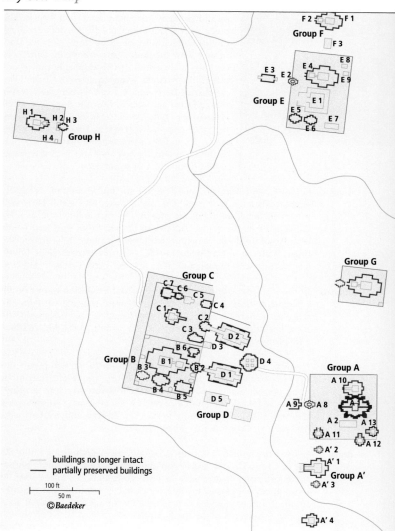

buildings no longer intact
partially preserved buildings

100 ft
50 m
©Baedeker

in the 11th century in honour of the god Bhadresvara, a descendant of Shiva and King Bhadravarman. The two smaller temples (B3 and B4) on the south side of B1 were dedicated to Shiva's offspring, Skanda and Ganesha. Fortunately, B5, with its roof in the form of a

Uroja plinth

boat, is better preserved. Ritual objects and sacred scriptures were kept here in former times. The outer walls feature not only ornate stonemasonry, but also bullet holes resulting from Vietcong skirmishes with the Americans. Above the entrances on both sides, reliefs of two elephants can be admired, their trunks wrapped around a palm. The interior of B6 contains a basin where **holy water** was collected and poured over the lingam in sacral ceremonies. It is particularly noteworthy, being the only one in existence in Cham culture. Between B5 and B6, a ruined gate listed as B2 leads to the D1 group, a prayer hall in which the priests would meditate prior to services.

Group C   Group C (8th century) was designed in similar fashion, originally separated from B by a wall. The main tower, C1, is still fairly well preserved. Small statues of the gods and an ornate lintel can be marvelled at here. The statue of Shiva in human form, however, which once stood inside the sanctum, has long since been relocated to the Cham Museum in Na Dang. Outside, a Garuda, a mythological bird-like creature with human and feline features, can be seen.

Group D   In the former meditation halls D1 and D2, **exhibition rooms** house Cham sculptures. French archaeologists were the first to name the space between the buildings the Stelae Court. As time has passed, the most beautiful stelae, altar relics, divine statues, rods and columns have been placed here.

Group A   Heading further east, a path crosses a stream to the completely destroyed Group A, once the pride of the entire temple site. Judging by what can be seen today, the magnificent **Kalan A1** (10th century) must have folded like a house of cards when attacked. Unusually, it is the only Cham construction to have an eastern and western gate. The ruins of Group A are completely overgrown.

Group G   Leaving the remains of group A behind, the neighbouring hill is the site of Group G. The main kalan is no longer in good condition but some interesting figures with devilish expressions can still be seen. At its southeastern corner is a bizarre character resembling a gargoyle. At the front of the site is a plinth, its foundation bordered with breasts, the symbol of the Earth-Mother Uroja.

Groups E and F   Groups E and F (7th century) lie at the end of a small trail to the north. This area was almost completely destroyed. The pools are, in actual fact, bomb craters. A few stelae and lingams are dotted around the temple remains, along with a circular lingam base, a Nandi and a decapitated statue.

★ My Tho

D 7

Province: Tien Giang (capital)   **Region:** Mekong Delta
Population: 120,000

The small market town of My Tho on the Tien Giang River is surrounded on three sides by water. What better way to delve into the everyday life of the Mekong delta than by boat, sampling such delicacies as rice wine, coconut candy and »Elephant Ear Fish«?

What to See in My Tho

On the eastern bank of the canal lies My Tho, the Chinese quarter, still the scene of assiduous trading. Piles of sugar cane, dried fish and watermelon stand outside the narrow shops, awaiting transport to Saigon.

Chinese quarter

Around 1km/1100yd northeast, Vinh Trang Pagoda was built in 1820 and boasts a wealth of Buddha and Bodhisattva figures. Constant alterations and renovations have left the temple looking like an indulgently decorated palace. On entering the pagoda, the dining hall and dormitory of the monks living here can be seen on the right hand side. In the **main sanctuary**, behind the courtyard with its notable miniature mountain, the ornately carved columns are resplendent in gold. The 60 statues, including 18 arhats, are also worth inspection. Ponds, gardens and tombs surround the temple complex (opening times: 7.30pm–noon and 2pm–5pm daily).

Vinh Trang Pagoda

On the way to the pagoda, smaller enterprises proffer their wares (sweets, for example). On the corner of Anh Giac and Nguyen Trung there is an opportunity to see **incense sticks being manufactured**: bamboo shavings are dipped into a perfumed mixture of sawdust and paste, then painted yellow. They are subsequently dried in front of the house.

Around My Tho

Tan Long Island is just a five-minute boat trip away, the vessels departing from Le Loi Boulevard in My Tho. The palm-covered »Dragon Island« offers lovely walks through fruit plantations and the island restaurant offers refreshment.

Gods of Nature are also worshipped on the miniature pagoda mountain

My Tho Map

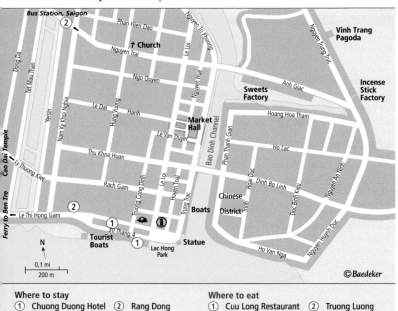

Bus Station, Saigon
Phan Hien Dao
Nguyen Tri Phuong
Vinh Trang Pagoda
Dong Da
† Church
Nguyen Trai
Le Loi
Nguyen Trung Truc
Tet Mau Than
Ngo Quyen
Anh Giac
Incense Stick Factory
Nam Ky Khoi Nghia
Le Dai
Hung Vuong
Hanh
Nguyen Hue
Sweets Factory
Hoang Hoa Tham
Yersin
Market Hall
Bao Dinh Channel
Phan Thanh Gian
Ho Lac
Cao Dai Temple
Thu Khoa Huan
Le Van Duyet
Hoai Duc
Nguyen An Ninh
Ly Thuong Kiet
Rach Gam
Truong Cong Dinh
Le Loi
Huyen Toai
Trung Trac
Dinh Bo Linh
Doc Binh Kieu
Ferry to Ben Tre
Le Thi Hong Gam
②
Chinese District
Trinh
Nguyen Huynh Duc
30 Thang 4
Boats
① Tourist Boats
① Lac Hong Park
Statue
Ho Van Nga
N
0,1 mi
200 m
©Baedeker

Coconut Monk's Island

🕐 Opening hours:
daily
8am–11.30am,
1.30pm–6pm

A few miles outside My Tho lies the so-called Phoenix Island, Phung, the refuge of the Coconut Monk Ong Dao Dua, who died in 1990. The story concerns one of the many **sects** found in the Mekong delta, which experienced their heyday during partition. In 1945 Nguyen Tanh Nam, the founder of the sect, left his family and became a monk. He developed his own doctrine (Tinh Do Cu Si), preaching a union of Christianity and Buddhism and advocating the peaceful unification of North and South Vietnam, leading to his repeated imprisonment by the government of the south. Like other faiths, the Dao Dua sect was fought by the Communist leadership, but nevertheless maintained a community on the island into the 1980s. At their **peak** in the 1960s, the sect had as many as several thousand members. The buildings of the erstwhile sect, with their dragon columns and a multistage throne where the Coconut Monk would hold audience, are rather like a cross between an amusement park and a spaceport. They no longer look well cared for and the earlier prosperity of the island can barely be recognized. Although it is in such close proximity to My Tho, the Coconut Monk's island belongs, in administrative terms, to the neighbouring province of Ben Tre.

Approximately 10km/6mi to the west of My Tho, cobras and pythons are bred at the Dong Tam Snake Farm. Their **uses** are manifold: serums are extracted from snake venom, snakeskin is worked into leather and, last but not least, snake meat is considered a delicacy by many a connoisseur. The snake farm also features a section with mutant turtles and fish, their genetic deformities probably a result of the spraying of Agent Orange in the Vietnam War (opening times: daily 7am–6pm).

Snake farm

? DID YOU KNOW ...?

■ The founder of the Dao Dua sect earned the name »the Coconut Monk« by virtue of his apparently having lived for years on an exclusive diet of coconuts.

There is also a ferry from My Tho to Ben Tre (12km/7.5mi south), on an island between the Cua Dai and Co Cien branches of the Mekong. During the Vietnam War, Ben Tre was seen as the **stronghold of the Vietcong**, already established here at the end of the 1950s; the town would later become an American military base. Nowhere else were the battles between government troops and the Americans against the insurgents as fierce as here, nowhere else were such quan-

Ben Tre

Unloading freight

▶ VISITING MY THO

INFORMATION

Tien Giang Tourist
No. 8, 30 Thang 4
(also at: 30/4, Bank Street), My Tho
Tel. 0 73/87 31 84 and 87 34 77
7am–5pm

Ben Tre Tourist
16 Hai Ba Trung, Ben Tre
Tel. 0 75/82 23 92 and 82 21 97
9am–6pm
Both cater for boat trips as well as car
and bicycle rentals.

SHOPPING

In keeping with its status as an
important trading centre for the
surrounding region, My Tho hosts a
turbulent market between the Bao
Dinh Canal and Nguyen Hue. Heaps
of exotic fruits, rice sacks, stalls with
freshly plucked chickens, marinated
fish delicacies and various types of
noodles jostle for position alongside
little shops selling fishing nets and
household goods.

CUISINE

Hu Tieu My Tho – a tasty local
speciality, not to be missed: served
piping hot everywhere in town, this
hearty noodle soup is enriched with
seafood, chicken and pork.

WHERE TO EAT
▶ Inexpensive
① **Cuu Long Restaurant**
28–30 Thang 4

Tel. 0 73/87 07 79
A nice place to sit and watch the
activity on the Mekong. The food is
good, if a little pricey.

② **Truong Luong**
Tel. 0 73/85 54 41
Attractive garden inn on the N 1 at the
approach to town. Former German
chancellor Helmut Kohl once dined
here!

WHERE TO STAY
▶ Mid-range
① **Chuong Duong Hotel**
10–30 Thang 4
(beach promenade)
Tel. 0 73/87 08 75, fax 87 42 50
Best hotel in town, situated on the
river with air conditioning, some
rooms with balcony and river view.
Attractive terrace bar on the promenade.

▶ Budget
② **Rang Dong**
25–30 Thang 4
Tel. & fax 0 73/87 44 00
Mini hotel with spacious rooms, some
overlooking the Mekong.
An increasing number of private
families can be contacted through the
local tourist offices for simple, often
traditional accommodation in the
area and in Vinh Long at Can Tho
(double room 5–8 euros).

tities of napalm and Agent Orange deployed and nowhere else were
civilian casualties higher. Thus Ben Tre became the »Island of a
Thousand Widows« and the neighbouring Luong Hoa became
known as »Widows' Village«, inhabited only by women.

At the heart of the town of Ben Tre lies the **Vien Minh Pagoda**, dedicated to the Goddess of Mercy. The central market and the rice wine distillery in the southern part of town are also worth seeing. By car, the journey to Ba Tri in the southeast, with its charming Nguyen Dinh Chieu Temple, takes less than an hour.

Thap Muoi stork sanctuary

The marshy environs of Cao Lanh (approx. 95km/60mi west of My Tho) are ideal for studying wildlife. A small bird sanctuary here is largely populated by **white storks**, the heraldic animals of the Mekong delta, who do not seem in the least troubled by visitors.

Tam Nong Nature Reserve

Another nature reserve is situated close to the small town of Tam Nong (barely 50km/30mi north of Cao Lanh) and can be reached on land or by boat, if somewhat laboriously.
The area offers refuge to hundreds of species of bird, including **cranes and purple herons**. Great patience is required to watch them as these birds are not used to people and rarely come into view. Hence the region remains the domain of genuine bird-watching enthusiasts.

✱ Nha Trang

E 6

Province: Khanh Hoa (capital)
Population: Approx. 300,000

Region: South Central Coast

There can be no place more cosmopolitan in Vietnam to take a dip than the port of Nha Trang. French colonial masters, the former emperor Bao Dai, US soldiers and Russian labourers on holiday have all ambled along the 6km/3.5mi-long beach with turquoise waters, a ring of mountains in the distance. The famous Cham towers, over 1000 years old, offer an alternative to lounging around on the beach.

International bathing resort

Nha Trang is a hotbed of international activity and nightlife, with backpackers, package holidaymakers and Vietnamese families all congregating here. The culinary palette stretches from fried rice and German sausage to excellent seafood in the beachfront beer gardens. An armada of hawkers pampers vacationers at the beach with massages, fresh coconut juice, dragon fruit and iced beer, even fingernail manicures, without having to leave the deck chair.
For those seeking more lively pursuits, Nha Trang has a wealth of **water sports** on offer, boasting a higher concentration of diving schools than anywhere else in Vietnam. Around 70 islands off the coast are perfect for boat trips and 25 diving spots wait to be explored.

The fish market at the harbour is lively and colourful

What to See in Nha Trang

Alexandre Yersin Museum

Following a sunny spell on the beach, a walk along Tran Phu Street heading north leads to the Pasteur Institute with the Alexandre Yersin Museum. The exhibition centres on the Swiss doctor who settled here in 1893. Yersin is something of a hero in Nha Trang. Not, however, for his major achievement – his discovery of the microbe that causes bubonic plague – but primarily as a result of his meteorological knowledge, enabling him to predict **typhoons**, thus saving the lives of many fishermen.

Some of his laboratory equipment such as telescopes and barometers are on display, whilst the library illustrates the broad spectrum of his fields of interest – from medicine to horticulture and from bacteriology to astrology. The Pasteur Institute, which houses the museum, was founded by Yersin himself in the year 1895 (opening times: Mon–Fri 8am–11am, 2pm–4.30pm, Sat 2pm–4.30pm).

Cathedral

Heading southwest, Thai Nguyen Street leads to two further sites of interest. The cathedral on the corner of Nguyen Trai Street was built in 1933 and features beautiful stained glass windows.

Hard to miss, the great, white Buddha who seems to watch over the town can be seen from afar. He is seated on a lotus throne above Long Son Pagoda, just a few hundred yards from the cathedral. This temple was built in 1930. An impressive bronze Buddha is enthroned above the main altar, and the walls are decorated with paintings of Jataka scenes. Behind the central columned hall, steps lead past hawkers and beggars up the hill. At the top stands an **imposing statue of Buddha**, erected in 1963 as a symbol of the Buddhists' struggle against the repressive Diem regime. Its plinth bears images of monks and nuns who burned themselves in protest, their number including Thich Quang Duc (►Famous People). The hilltop offers a wonderful panorama of Nha Trang and the coast.

✷
Long Son Pagoda

On the south side of town stands Bao Dai Villa, five houses at the heart of a beautiful park. Today, the Art Deco building that stands regally on the cliffs above the sea has been converted into a hotel. The garden restaurant provides a fascinating vista of the coast, harbour and offshore islands.

Bao Dai Villa

▶ VISITING NHA TRANG

INFORMATION
Khanh Hoa Tourist
1 Tran Hung Dao, Nha Trang
(next to the Vien Dong Hotel)
Tel. 0 58/82 22 57
Also in various hotels and numerous travel agencies

TRANSPORT
Cam Ranh Airport, 60km/37mi
south, tel. 0 58/82 67 68 and 98 99 18.
There is a second airport in the town
(tel. 0 58/82 37 97)

EVENTS
Merian/Po Nagar Festival
The tutelary goddess of the town, Yang Ino Po Nagar, is taken each year from the Cham temple down to the beach in a procession (March to May) where she is bathed and her robes changed – all accompanied by oblations, music, theatre and dances.

ENTERTAINMENT
② **Nha Trang Sailing Club**
72 Tran Phu, Nha Trang
Tel. 0 58/82 65 28
daily 7am–2am
The city's hottest club in recent years, a place to see and to be seen in: predominantly a meeting place for foreigners on the beach terrace, with Italian-Vietnamese cuisine on offer. Beach parties and campfires, dancing and cocktails.

WHERE TO EAT
▶ Moderate
① **Ngoc Suong**
16 Tran Quang Khai, Nha Trang
Tel. 0 58/82 70 30
daily 11am–11pm
Excellent dining establishment close to the yachting club, all manner of seafood swimming in the tanks. Guests have only to choose what they want – whether mussels, shrimps, lobster or jellyfish.

▶ Inexpensive

③ *Dua Xanh Restaurant*
(also: Coco Verde, Green Coconut)
Nguyen Binh Khiem, Nha Trang
(close to the beach lane, at the
northern end)
Tel. 0 58/82 36 87
Air-conditioned restaurant with garden. Excellent seafood and fish served
in all varieties, either inside or on the
terrace.

④ *Cyclo Café*
5A Tran Quang Khai, Nha Trang
Tel. 0 58/52 42 08
daily 7am–11pm
Attractive little eatery with Vietnam-
ese-Italian menu, vegetarian options,
Western breakfast, muesli and snacks.

WHERE TO STAY

▶ Luxury

*Evason Hideaway & Spa
at Ana Mandara*
Van Ninh, Ninh Hoa (approx. 50km/
30mi north of Nha Trang)
Tel. 0 58/82 98 29, fax 72 82 23
www.sixsenses.com/six-senses-hide-
away-ninh-van-bay
Island oasis with natural materials in
abundance. 50 rustic, yet extremely
comfortable villas, typical for the
region, situated between the rocks or
on the hill above a quiet bay: rocking
chairs, small, individual pools and
personal wine cellar!

Sofitel Vin Pearl Resort & Spa
Hon Tre (»Bamboo Island«, ▶p.339)
Tel. 0 58/59 81-46/-88, fax 59 81 99
info@vinpearlresort.com
Vietnam's largest luxury hotel on an
island: five-storey beach complex with
232 rooms and a few small houses on
the beach. Pool, several restaurants,
club for children, tennis court and
nightclub. Exclusive Shiseido spa.

Baedeker recommendation

① *Ana Mandara Resort & Spa*
86 Tran Phu, Nha Trang
Tel. 0 58/52 22 22, fax 52 58 28
www.sixsenses.com/evason-ana-mandara-
nha-trang/index.php
Splendid first-class beach complex:
17 bungalows (some with sea view) with
74 luxurious rooms, delightful decor and
»canopy beds«.
Two restaurants, pool, water sports.

Ana Mandara resort

► Mid-range

② Nha Trang Lodge Hotel
42 Tran Phu, Nha Trang
Tel. 0 58/81 09 00, fax 82 88 00
www.nt-lodge.com
Good value, middle-class hotel (approx. 100 rooms) in the city centre, palm beach lies across the main street. Tennis and water sports, pool.

③ Vien Dong Hotel
1 Tran Hung Dao, Nha Trang
Tel. 0 58/82 16 06, fax 82 19 12
viendonghtl@dng.vnn.vn
Hotel with prettily appointed rooms, pool, restaurant, shops.

► Budget

Whale Island Resort
Hon Ong, Van Ninh (island approx. 60km/37mi north of Nha Trang)
Tel. 0 58/84 05 01 and 81 16 07
Fax 82 22 51
www.whaleislandresort.com
Stay on the veritable Robinson Crusoe island of the same name in one of 23 original, stylish and yet rustically appointed bamboo bungalows on the beach (mosquito nets, ventilator fans). Lots of wood, rattan and terra-cotta, with the chief attraction being the bamboo beds, along with hammocks outside (some less expensive rooms). Seafood inn (full board including transfer from Nha Trang).

Paradise Resort
Doc Let Beach, Ninh Hoa
(approx. 50km/30mi north of Nha Trang)
Tel. 0 58/67 04 80, fax 67 04 79
www.vngold.com/doclet/paradise/
paradise_doclech@hotmail.com
Simple, rustic bungalows with sea view right on the beach. Guests are catered for with full board, including fish and an all-inclusive around-the-clock service offering fruit and non-alcoholic drinks. Kajaks, angling, pool table.

A small gallery is dedicated to the works of Long Thanh, a famous Vietnamese photographer. Marvellously atmospheric black and white pictures from the everyday life of his fellow countrymen are on display. Long Thanh is celebrated far beyond the borders of his hometown and has also exhibited his photographs in Europe (126 Hoang Van Thu, opening times: daily 7am–7pm).

Long Thanh Gallery

🕒

From the harbour of the fishing village Cau Da (5km/3mi south of the city centre), boat trips leave for the **karst islands** off the coast. Small, round wicker boats ferry passengers to the coloured barges, where hearty meals of seafood and fish are prepared and served. There is plenty of opportunity to go bathing or snorkelling in the pretty bay. A floating bar is a common sight, offering refreshments to those lounging in the water. Different itineraries are available, with some tours visiting the fish farm on the island of Tri Nguyen, better known as Hon Mieu. The islands, Hon Yen (Swallow Island) in particular, are famed for the **bird's nests** from which »bird's nest soup« is made. Twice a year, when the young have flown, the nests, which largely consist of saliva, are collected from the cliffs. They are considered a delicacy throughout Asia and thought to enhance po-

**✱ ✱
Boat trips**

Nha Trang Map

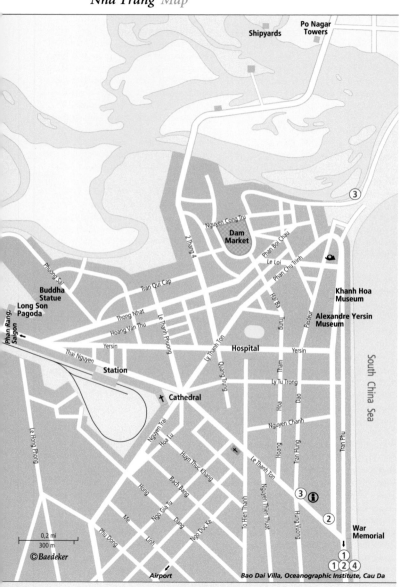

Po Nagar Towers
Shipyards

Nguyen Cong Tru
Dam Market
2 Thang 4
Phan Boi Chau
Le Loi
Phan Chu Trinh

Phuong Sai
Tran Qui Cap
Buddha Statue
Long Son Pagoda
Khanh Hoa Museum

Phan Rang; Saigon
Thong Nhat
Hoang Van Thu
Le Thanh Phuong
Hai Ba
Trung
Pasteur
Alexandre Yersin Museum

Yersin
Thai Nguyen
Ly Thanh Ton
Quang Trung
Hospital
Yersin
South China Sea

Station
Ly Tu Trong
Hoa
Tham
Dao

✝ Cathedral
Nguyen Chanh

Le Hong Phong
Nguyen Trai
Hoa Lu
Huyn Thuc Khang
Bach Dang
Hoang
Tran Hung
Tran Phu

Hong
Ngo Gia Tu
Dang
Le Thanh Ton
Nguyen Thien Thuat
Hung Vuong
③ ⓘ
②

Me
Phu Dong
Linh
Ngo Duc Ke
To Hien Thanh
War Memorial

0,2 mi
300 m
①
① ② ④

©Baedeker
Airport
Bao Dai Villa, Oceanographic Institute, Cau Da

③

Where to stay
① Ana Mandara Resort & Spa
② Nha Trang Lodge Hotel
③ Vien Dong Hotel

Where to eat
① Ngoc Suong
② Nha Trang Sailing Club
③ Dua Xanh Restaurant
④ Cyclo Café

tency. On Hon Lao (Monkey Island) lives a family of apes who are happy to let themselves be fed by day trippers. As the monkeys are also happy to bite, however, visitors are advised to keep their distance. Hon Tam (Silkworm Island), with a hotel and parasailing, and the smaller islets of Hon Mun and Hon Mot, Hon Thi and Hon Heo (the last with waterfalls) await snorkellers and sunbathers.

★ The Towers of Po Nagar

On the way to the towers of Po Nagar (Thap Ba, 1.5km/1mi north of the city centre), the Xom Bong Bridge crosses the Cai River, passing a small harbour with its colourful fishing fleet, red and blue canoes and round wicker boats. At their very heart, a huge rocky outcrop reaches up out of the water. A **Chinese shrine** has been erected on the rock and the local fisherman leave small offerings here before they set sail. The temple hill presents a fabulous view of the scenario.

The sanctuary was dedicated to Po Nagar, the Mother Goddess of the Cham, who, in Hinduistic ritual, became Bhagavati, wife of the god Shiva. Over the centuries, the temples of Kauthara, as they were known under the Cham, were repeatedly attacked by the Malays, the Khmer and the Chinese. So it is that, of the eight Cham towers or kalan which were built between the 7th and 12th centuries on Cu Lao Hill, only four remain today.

The complex has since developed into a well-frequented Buddhist place of worship, as made apparent by the variety of oblations and incense.

Visitors ascend a flight of steps up the hill past beggars and traders, whereas the pilgrims of old would have passed through the mandapa (a meditation hall), of which some column fragments remain. From here, steps lead directly to the main temple (opening times: daily 6am–6pm).

Mandapa

Three storeys and 23m/75ft high, the northern tower, built by Harivarman I in the year 817, is one of the finest examples of Cham architecture. Reaching up from its base, decorated with double pilasters and lotus-embellished arcades, this is a mighty work of construction. Above the portal, the many-armed Shiva (Nataraja) dances, his foot resting on the head of the bull Nandi, framed by musicians. The lintel and walls of the vestibule bear Sanskrit inscriptions, telling of sacrifices to the goddess. The vestibule tapers to a

★
Northern tower with Po Nagar statue

> ! **Baedeker** TIP
>
> ### Eco-boom in Vietnam
> The island of Hon Tre (Bamboo Island) is developing its »eco theme«, although, in practical terms, the Vietnamese version includes concrete tree facsimiles, gigantic luxury resorts with golf courses and jet skis shooting across the water. Since 2007, a 3km/2mi-long cable car has connected Hon Tre to the mainland. The journey time is around nine minutes.

Opening hours:
daily 8am–5pm

pyramidal ceiling and into the **sanctum**, where the shadows take a little getting used to. A golden lingam originally stood here, stolen by the Khmer in the 10th century and later replaced by the Po Nagar statue still seen here today. Admittedly, the head has been replaced, as the French removed the original. There is something doll-like about the new head, an image accentuated by the yellow cloak which covers her ten arms. Two ironwood elephants stand guard alongside the 8th–9th-century figure, the only surviving Cham sculptures of this type. On the rear wall, a garderobe contains the various different robes that Po Nagar dons during elaborate ceremonies three times a year (Tet, 30 March and 15 July). She is still honoured as the protectress of the town and her statue is bathed in the river during the Merian Festival in March.

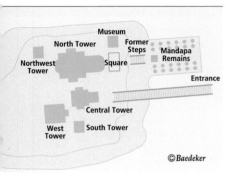

Po Nagar Plan

©Baedeker

Central tower The three smaller towers are less intricate and in poorer condition than the northern tower. Especially worse for wear is the middle ka-lan (12th century). Childless couples come here to pray for fertility at the lingam.

South tower The southernmost kalan (12th century) contains an impressive lingam. The tower itself comprises two sections, a vaulted roof and an almost square construction with vestibule.

Northwestern tower The northwestern tower dates back to the late 10th century and is no longer accessible. It was formerly dedicated to Ganesha, Shiva's son with the head of an elephant. Still visible on its outer walls are representations of animal gods: Garuda on the south façade, a lion on the north side and a human form with elephant's head to the west.

Museum On display in the small adjacent museum are photographs of restoration work and fragments of the foundations.

Around Nha Trang

Hon Chong Bay For a quiet life on the beach, Hon Chong Bay is the place to go, just 500m/550yd north of Po Nagar. This stretch of coastline may not be quite as well groomed as the town's beach, but the water is crystal clear, glistening turquoise as the sun catches its surface. On the south side, smooth boulders can be seen, one bearing an imprint that is said by locals to have been made by a giant.

Travelling north, the white sands of Doc Let (50km/30mi from Nha Trang) on Hon Khoi peninsula are a good place to break the journey. Casuarina and palm trees provide shade; in addition, two simple beach resorts, a restaurant, changing facilities and refreshments stalls can also be found here. Basket boats from the neighbouring fishing village can be seen bobbing along off the coast.

Doc Let

A small peninsula and a paradise for divers, Hon Ong inspires dreams of Robinson Crusoe. Jaques-Yves Cousteau dived off »Whale Island« back in the 1930s, exploring the underwater fauna of the depths. With luck, the whales and whale sharks who give the island its name may pass by during a dive, along with rays (the best period is from April to July). Indulge in a spot of surfing, snorkelling, catamaran sailing, diving, sunbathing – or do none of the above and just relax (the island, which lies approximately 60km/ 37mi north of Nha Trang, is just a short boat trip away, via the peninsula of Hon Gom).

Hon Ong (Whale Island)

Phan Rang

E 7

Province: Ninh Thuan (capital)
Population: 140,000

Region: South Central Coast

Phan Rang and Thap Cham are sister cities a few miles from the sea on the Chai River. The place itself holds little attraction, so move swiftly on to the famous Cham towers of Po Klong Garai and the beautiful white beach. Cacti, dunes and flamboyants are the distinctive features of the region along with, surprisingly, grape vines.

✷ Po Klong Garai Towers

On National Highway 20 to Da Lat (8km/5mi west of Phan Rang), the four imposing towers of Po Klaung Garai rise up from the xeric landscape. In the late 13th century, during the reign of Jaya Simha-varman III, these Hindu temples were built on top of a granite hill. The sanctuary is dedicated to the legendary Prince Po Klaung Garai, who, in Cham mythology, was the equal of the Hindu god Shiva. Together with the mother goddess Po Nagar, he was superior to the divine king of the dynasty.

Best preserved example of Cham architectural art
🕐
Opening hours:
daily 7.30am–6pm

Steps lead up to the complex, which is surrounded by cactus scrub. Entrance to the **main kalan**, with its distinctly structured three-level roof, is through a 21m/69ft-high stone archway. The lotus-shaped corner towers and the divine images in the niches are noteworthy. The tower opens to the east onto the meditation hall, the original foundations of which are still standing. To the south is the library, whose saddle-like roof has two bullhorns at its extremities. A similar

● VISITING PHAN RANG

INFORMATION
Phan Rang Tourist
Thong Nhat, corner of Nguyen Trai,
Phan Rang
Tel. 0 68/83 64 05

TRANSPORT
Cam Ranh Airport (approx. 80km/
50mi north of Phan Rang):
Tel. 0 58/82 67 68 and 98 99 18

EVENTS
Kate Festival
A three day festival in the seventh
lunar month (September/October) of
the Khmer calendar, marking the
beginning of the Cham New Year for
the Muslim minority; a celebration of
traditional singing and dancing, a
procession and ritual ceremonies in
the temple towers.

CUISINE
If tasting roasted gecko (ky nhong)
has been a lifelong ambition, the time
to fulfil it has arrived. This crispy
regional delicacy is savoured with
(unripe) green mango.

WHERE TO EAT
▶ Inexpensive
Hiep Thanh
18 A Le Hong Phong
Pleasant eatery with tasty dishes such
as chicken with lotus sprouts and
lemon juice.

WHERE TO STAY
▶ Mid-range
Den Gion Ninh Chu Resort
Ninh Chu Beach, Van Hai (6km/4mi
outside Phan Rang)
Tel. 0 68/87 40-47/-48, fax 87 44 31
www.dengionninhchu.com
dongthuantourist@hcm.vnn.vn
Modern hotel on the lengthy beach
with pleasant rooms in brick bungalows (TV, satellite television), some
with sea view, terra-cotta decor in
ancient Cham style, tennis court, pool
and camping tents on the beach.
Open-air bar with seafood and barbecue. Reservation recommended at
weekends.

Saigon Ninh Chu Hotel
Khanh Hai, Ninh Hai
Tel. 0 68/87 39-00/-01,
fax 87 30 23
www.ninhthuanpt.com.vn/
ninhchutourist
ninhchuhotel@hcm.vnn.vn
Three-storey beach hotel belonging to
Saigontourist, the reputable travel
group: 48 spacious, individual rooms
(air-conditioned, telephone) and bungalows. Two restaurants, karaoke bar.

▶ Budget
Thong Nhat Hotel
99 Thong Nhat 343, Phan Rang
Tel. 0 68/82 72 01, fax 82 29 43
thongnhathotel_pr@hcm.vnn.vn
Renovated four-storey hotel
(16 rooms), good location.

form can be seen on the windows. Due to Po Klaung Garai's affinity
to Shiva, the sanctuary contains many symbols and representations
of the god: the dancing, six-armed Shiva (Nataraja) above the entrance to the main tower, Shiva as the bull (Nandi) in the vestibule

and the Mukha lingam (stylized phallus), symbolizing creativity and virility, in the sanctum sanctorum. The latter features the face and insignia of Po Klong Garai. In former times, it is said that the Nandi was regularly »fed« to ensure a good harvest. This custom is still practised today during the **Kate Festival** (October), the New Year celebrations of the Cham.

! *Baedeker* TIP

Cham Museum

Those interested in learning more about Cham culture can visit the small Cham Museum in Phan Rang, 17 Ngyuen Trai. Pottery fragments, jewellery, some statues and other relics from excavations can be inspected (opening times: Mon–Fri 8am–11am, 2.30pm–4.30pm).

Further Places to Visit around Phan Rang

6km/3.5mi east of Phan Rang, the splendid sweeping crescent of Ninh Chu Beach stretches out with its yellow sands and clear waters. A few quite bizarre hotels with bungalows and a handful of snack bars are sprinkled along the beach, which is generally empty during the week.   **Ninh Chu Beach**

The towers of Po Klong Garai rise up on a small hill

Towers of Po Ro Me The towers of Po Ro Me (15km/9mi south of Phan Rang), built on a hill in the 17th century, are regarded as the **last Cham constructions of significance**. Sadly, the sanctuary dedicated to Po Ro Me, the final ruler of the independent Champa, is practically in ruins. Some interesting features of the late architectural style can still be recognized, such as the distinctive corner towers on the roof of the central tower.

Dragon fruit is cultivated primarily in the regions of Phan Rang and Nha Trang

A captivating bas-relief presents Shiva as the bearded King Po Ro Me, flanked by two Nandis. West of the complex – in the direction of the deceased forefathers, according to the Cham – stands a roughly hewn memorial stone (kut) for the king. Having been forced to flee their capital Vijaya in 1471, the Cham saw their empire crumble and were no longer able to maintain the high standards of their sculpture. As a consequence they emulated their ancestors and their veneration of natural deities, represented in the form of simple stones. This temple site is also considered to be a Cham sanctuary. The annual Kate Festival is also celebrated here.

Cham villages Wearing their turban-like headgear, many Cham can still be seen living in the region. Like Muslims all over the world, they celebrate the Ramadan month of fasting. Many living here earn their livelihood from **handicrafts**: to the east of the N 1, the weaving village of My Ngiep produces woven goods and clothing in the traditional manner. In Bau Truc village, pottery wares can be purchased, and the production process of the goods in the ovens may be observed. At the Cham village of Tuan Tu (approx. 5km/3mi south of Phan Rang) the beautiful Nam Cuong dunes stretch out.

✷ Ca Na A fine, white beach, turquoise-blue water and a charming coral reef await sunlovers and snorkellers at Ca Na (32km/20mi south of Phan Rang). Refreshment can be found at the few small restaurants and beach huts, albeit rather close to the busy N 1, along with the hitherto basic places to stay and a Korean diving resort. Eucalyptus groves and fields line the route, as do fruit orchards with cactus-like, tendrillar plants bearing exotic. The produce in question is **dragon fruit** (thanh long), approximately the same size as a mango. Crimson on the outside with green shoots, they can be sliced open to reveal white flesh with black pips. Some roadside stalls offer them for sale and tropical fruit fans should definitely give them a try. Their taste is a little reminiscent of kiwi fruit.

✳ Phan Thiet · Mui Ne

E 7

Province: Binh Thuan (capital)   **Region:** South Central Coast
Population: 170,000

It took just a few years for word of this »insider tip« on the south coast near the port of Phan Thiet to spread. That should come as no surprise, as Mui Ne is truly a gorgeous peninsular with a long, broad, sweeping bay laced with coconut palms. Nevertheless, the beautiful beach is still dominated by fishermen with their cutters, baskets and nets, apart from when surfers and kitesurfers breeze in for the »Fun Cup«.

What to See in and around Phan Thiet

Around 16km/10mi long, the peninsula's beach, reaching as far as the dunes at Kap Ne (Mui Ne), is paradisiacal and has become a real competitor to Nha Trang as an international bathing resort. The local inhabitants earn their living from **fishing**: the entire village help to drag the shimmering nets onto the beach, and no sooner have the villagers done so than the catch is sorted into baskets and prices negotiated. Under cover of coconut palms, the beach road passes small fishing settlements and an increasing number of bungalow resorts and numerous restaurants.

✳ ✳
Beach and dunes

The small settlement of **Mui Ne** boasts a vibrant harbour and is home to a number of small factories making fish sauces. At the end of the Mui Ne peninsula, sand hills casting a reddish-orange and yellowish-white glow wait to be conquered on foot or by Jeep. In Mui Ne, surfers ride the sand as well as the waves – »surfing« down the sand dunes on plastic boards. Immediately behind the palm grove, the South China Sea beckons to those wishing to cool off overheated feet. An alternative is the **»White Lake«** (Bao Trang): actually three small and picturesque lakes at the heart of snow-white sand dunes close to Hon Hghe Bay in which the dunes are reflected amongst the lotus leaves. As marvellous as the panorama of palms and coastline may be, the rubbish depot is unfortunately also in the vicinity.

Road 706 follows the coastline northeast to the peninsula of Hon Gom, growing progressively quieter with just the herdsmen shooing their cattle and goats across the new highway northeast of Mui Ne.

> ! *Baedeker* TIP
>
> **Nuoc mam fish sauce**
> No Vietnamese meal is complete without a dip. The basis is nuoc mam – a salty, spicy sauce made from fermented anchovies and used in cooking and seasoning like salt. Every cook has her own recipe for nuoc mam and varies it according to the dish in question, using it as a dip or salad sauce with lime juice, garlic, chilli and sugar.

**Suoi Tien
(Fairy Springs)**

A very popular walk (approx. 1 hour) leads from the sea at Ham Tien village (shortly before Mui Ne) along a stream and through the dunes, past the glowing red rock of the little **Red Sand Canyon** to the well at Suoi Tien with its cascading waterfall.

On the way to Phan Thiet, not far from Mui Ne Beach, the southernmost Cham sanctuary can be seen rising up on Ngoc Lam Hill: the three small **Po Shanu Towers** (8th century), restored in 1999. Less ornate than the famous Po Nagar or Po Klong Garai Towers at ▶Phang Rang, they were dedicated to Queen Po Shanu. A wonderful **panoramic view** of the coast and the town of Phan Thiet may be enjoyed from up here.

**Khe Ga
Lighthouse**

Built by the French in 1897, the lighthouse of Kap Khe Ga stands some 25km/15mi southwest of Mui Ne. Vietnam's tallest and oldest lighthouse stands on a small island and continues to light up the coastline of Binh Thuan province at night. **Tien Thanh Beach** on the mainland seems to go on forever. Free of shade, the otters spotted here are not the only ones tempted to its shores – construction work for new accommodation is underway.

Ganh Son canyon ▶

The impressive mini canyon of Ganh Son can be seen from the road leading to Khe Ga (tourists are advised only to venture further with

The peninsula entices with beaches from paradise

The dunes of Mui Ne are reminiscent of the Sahara

official guides due to the dangers of quicksand and old mines – an American military base named LZ Betty was once located here).

The town of Phan Thiet lies approximately 20km/12.5mi from the sun-drenched peninsula of Mui Ne and is famous for its **nuoc mam fish sauce**, which is distributed to all parts of Vietnam and is a must on every dining table. This is one of Vietnam's largest fishing regions. A good vantage point from which to observe the early morning hustle and bustle in the harbour of Phan Thiet is the Tran Hung Dao Bridge. When the colourful barges of the municipal fishing fleet return, the fish market (southern end of the Trung Trac) is also a hive of activity to behold. The old **water tower** of the town is a little gem: its triple-gabled roof, curving upwards to the heavens, rises above the Ca Ty River. Van Thuy Tu Temple on Ngu Ong (Fisherman Street, Duc Thang district) was erected in 1762 and is a national monument. A 22m/72ft-long whale skeleton is on display here.

Phan Thiet

? DID YOU KNOW ...?

■ Vietnamese fishermen worship the whale as a god who will protect them at sea. In Phan Thiet, beached whales are buried in their own graveyard at Van Thuy Tu Temple.

Ong Pagoda on Tran Phu Street is frequented by childless women who come here to pray for offspring. The room to the right contains a large mask for the dragon dance.

▶ VISITING PHAN THIET · MUI NE

INFORMATION

Binh Thuan Tourist
82 Trung Trac, Phan Thiet City
Tel. 0 62/81 68 21
www.muinebeach.net

Vidotour Travel
65 Nguyen Dinh Chieu, Mui Ne,
Ham Tien, Phan Thiet
Tel. 0 62/84 76 99, fax 84 77 27
www.vidotourtravel.com
Also in hotels.

TRANSPORT

Daily direct rail connection between
Saigon and Phan Thiet (departs
7.30am from Saigon, 1.45pm from
Phan Thiet, shuttle bus service to Mui
Ne Beach).

EXCURSIONS

Binh Thuan Tourist organizes excursions to the islands off the coast, such
as the tiny local island of Lao Cau
and, approximately 100km/62mi east

of the coast, Phu Quy, home to 20,000
Vietnamese.

EVENTS

The three-day Kate Festival of the
Cham is held annually in September/
October with traditional costumes
and dishes, singing and dancing at the
Po Shanu Towers.

WATER SPORTS

Ideal wind speeds for kitesurfers and
surfers of 18–30 knots can be expected between November and early
April on the Mui Ne coast, attracting
the international kiting and surfing
community.
February sees surfers gather here for
the annual »**Fun Cup**«, when the
boards glide over the waves and the
kites fly high in the sky.
Several *kite schools* can be found here;
Jibe's is a cool place to meet in the
middle of the beach
(90 Nguyen Dinh Chieu, km 13,
www.windsurfing-vietnam.com,
www.surf-vietnam.de, www.kite-
boarding-vietnam.com).

WHERE TO EAT

▶ **Moderate**
Forest Restaurant
67 Nguyen Dinh Chieu,
Ham Tien, Phan Thiet
Tel. 0 62/84 75 89
daily 10am–3pm, 6pm–11pm
Large, rustic establishment with
Cham decor, classic Vietnamese cuisine as well as tapas, pasta and salads,
grilled dishes, lobsters, steaks, wine
and cocktails. Traditional music with
folkloristic accompaniment, cookery
courses.

Jibe's Club

Paradise Beach Club
in the Coco Beach Resort
Tel. 0 62/84 71-11/-12
Very good Vietnamese and international cuisine, relatively broad selection of beer and wine.

► Inexpensive
Luna d'Autunno
km 12, Nguyen Dinh Chieu, Ham Tien, Mui Ne
Tel. 0 62/84 73 30
A genuine Italian restaurant with wood-fired pizza oven, antipasti, pasta and salads.

WHERE TO STAY
► Luxury
Cham Villas
32 Nguyen Dinh Chieu,
Ham Tien, Mui Ne
Tel. 0 62/74 12 34, fax 74 11 47
www.chamvillas.com
reservations@chamvillas.com
Lush green complex on the beach with 14 bungalows decked in palm leaves, king-sized canopy beds, restaurant also serves European dishes.

► Mid-range
Coco Beach Resort
km 12,5/7.5mi, 58 Nguyen Dinh Chieu,
Ham Tien, Mui Ne
Tel 0 62 / 84 71 11, fax 84 71 15
www.cocobeach.net

paradise@cocobeach.net
Delightful wooden houses on stilts, air-conditioned, at Mui Ne Beach with Franco-German management. Pool and great food.

Palmira Resort
km 11, Mui Ne
Tel. 0 62/84 70 04, fax 84 70 06
www.palmiraresort.com
cocogarden@palmiraresort.com
20 two-storey, Mediterranean-style villas dotted around a vast pool.

Bamboo Village Resort
km 11.8, Mui Ne
Tel. 0 62/84 70 07, fax 84 70 95
www.bamboovillageresortvn.com
bamboo-village@hcm.vnn.vn
Beautiful site featuring around 40 closely knit, octagonal bamboo and rattan huts and stone houses with palm leaf roofing, some with sea view, delightfully furnished with carved wooden beds. Pool and open-air bar.

Baedeker recommendation

Victoria Phan Thiet Beach Resort
Binh Thuan, Phan Thiet
Tel. 0 62/81 30 00, fax 81 30 07
www.victoriahotels-asia.com
Rambling four-star complex with 60 palm-thatched cottages, sea view from the terrace, pool landscape and golf course.

On the 694m/2275ft-high Ta Cu (Takou) Mountain in the **nature reserve of the same name** lies what is probably the longest Buddha statue in Vietnam: the reclining Sakyamuni Buddha measures a full 49m/160ft from illuminated head to toe and has a shoulder height of 18m/59ft. A cable car ride is the swiftest way to the site; otherwise a hike takes some two hours. At the top, the Linh Son Truong Tho Monastery, over a century old, welcomes pilgrims and visitors (Ta Ku is not far from Tan Lap, approx. 30km/18mi southwest of Phan Thiet, small guesthouse on site).

Ta Cu
(also: Takou)

✷ **Phu Quoc** (Island)

Province: Kien Giang   **Region:** Mekong Delta
Population: 80,000

Tranquility and solitude on a total length of 40km/25mi of beaches against a background of coconut palms and jungle scenery: that is Phu Quoc (pronounced Fu Wok), Vietnam's largest island, close to the Cambodian border. The holiday islander can enjoy idyllic sunsets on the west coast from small hotels and bamboo huts.

Virtually all communities in Phu Quoc are located on the coast; the jungle terrain of the island interior is almost entirely free of people. Most settlements lie on the flatter, west side of the island, the largest being Duong Dong with around 10,000 inhabitants. Fishing and processing of fish have hitherto been the chief sources of employment for its inhabitants. One major source of income is the famous **fish sauce** of Phu Quoc, favoured all over Vietnam (annual production: approx. 10 million litres/2.5 million gallons).

What to See in and around Phu Quoc

Beaches   The Vietnamese government has big plans for the island and aims to attract between two and three million holidaymakers by 2020 – that's per year, as many as in all of Vietnam today! There is no doubt that the island has potential: unpopulated beaches to the west and south, the finest bathing bays are often hidden and can only be reached via dusty paths or by climbing tour (Khem Beach in the south is still a restricted military zone, as the Cambodian neighbours also lay claim to the island). **Bai Truong** (Long Beach) south of the main resort Duong Dong boasts a good 20km/12mi of golden sands under palm trees, the beach stretching as far as the small fishing port of An Thoi at the southern tip of the island, punctuated only by rocks and fishing villages. Some 3km/2mi have already been developed with groups of bungalows and hotels (some several storeys high). The beautifully sweeping **Bai Ong Lang** (north of Duong Dong) promises several

 VISITING PHU QUOC

INFORMATION

Information in Saigon Phu Quoc Resort
Tel. 0 77/84 86 24 and 84 85 42
(cash machine also on site)
www.phuquoc.info
www.vietnamphuquoc.com

TRANSPORT

Phu Quoc Airport: a minimum of five flights a day from Saigon in the main holiday season and some flights during the week via Rach Gia (tickets tel. 0 77/84 63 44 and 84 60 86).
By boat: three fast hydrofoil crossings

per day from Rach Gia (2½ hours) and an uncomfortable ferry (6–8 hours); dependent on weather conditions in the rainy season.
(Extremely irregular, slow ferries from Ha Tien).

WHERE TO EAT
► Inexpensive
Tropicana Resort
Idyllic terrace inn and bar at Bai Truong with good seafood, Vietnamese and European dishes.

Phu Quoc Resort Thang Loi
Bai Ong Lang is the place to go for those keen on hearty European fare, served on an atmospheric open-air restaurant terrace.

Rainbow Bar
Bai Truong, close to Saigon Phu Quoc Resort
Open-air beach bar serving snacks, salads, sandwiches and hamburgers.

WHERE TO STAY
► Mid-range
Saigon Phu Quoc Resort
1 Tran Hung Dao, Bai Truong (Long Beach)
Tel. 0 77/84 69 99 and 84 65 10, Fax 84 71 63
www.sgphuquocresort.com.vn, www.vietnamphuquoc.com
The best address on »Pepper Island«: tasteful rooms in bungalows and small houses with sea views: »Presidents« can luxuriate in a private Jacuzzi, while »Tarzans« and »Robinsons« are mid-range, equipped with bath and TV. Pool on the slender palm beach, two bars, large restaurant. Sauna, steam bath, karaoke and diving school.

Tropicana Resort
Tran Hung Dao, Bai Truong

(Long Beach)
Tel. 0 77/84 71 27, fax 84 71 28
www.vietnamstay.com/hotel/tropicana
Small, pleasant beach complex with nine air-conditioned bungalows and some cheaper rooms in the garden. Pool, sea view restaurant, bicycles and motorbikes available for hire, windsurfing, boat excursions to the islands.

► Budget
Phu Quoc Resort Thang Loi
Bai Ong Lang, P.O.Box 73
Tel. 0 77/98 50 02, fax 0 77 84 61 44
www.phu-quoc.de
thangloiresort@hotmail.com
15 bamboo huts under palm trees with sea view from the small veranda (some with hot shower, mosquito nets, electricity in the evenings only). Basic but friendly, under German management.

Beach Club Resort
Bai Truong
Tel. 0 77/98 09 98
www.beachclub-vietnam.com
Simple rooms, palm-thatched bungalows at the beach, nice, family atmosphere. Yoga courses.

Children playing on the beach

miles of splendid isolation, with cliffs at intervals. **Bai Sao**, close to An Thoi in the deep south, is quite beautiful and a popular destination for the Vietnamese at weekends and on holidays.

Excursions Both the fishermen of An Thoi and pleasure boats from Bai Truong bring tourists looking for diving or snorkelling opportunities to the **offshore islands** such as Turtle Island (Hon Doi Moi) in the north and the tiny An Thoi archipelago in the south, with its coral reefs in crystal clear waters. The diving grounds are amongst the best in Vietnam, with visibility touching 50m/160ft. Staying dry is also an option, however, by trekking to smaller waterfalls and springs in the dense, mountainous hinterland of the **Phu Quoc National Park**, and exploring caves and pepper plantations, as well as pearl farms on the coast. There is a very good reason why the island is called »99 Mountains«. Some are as high as 603m/1978ft, although most of them lie within the military restricted zone in the north. The best time to visit the islands is the dry season in winter.

Duong Dong The main town of Duong Dong holds few tourist attractions. Everything worth seeing is concentrated around the harbour basin: a small fishing fleet, stalls serving Vietnamese snacks, the fish sauce factories and Dinh Cau: a temple with a lighthouse dedicated to Thien Hau, Goddess of the Sea. A temple festival is celebrated here in October.

Qui Nhon

E 6

Province: Binh Dinh (capital)   **Region:** South Central Coast
Population: 230,000

A good place to break a coastal journey is the port of Qui Nhon (also: Quy Nhon). The peninsula (between Nha Trang and Hoi An) can serve as a base for excursions to Cham towers, the ▶ My Lai Memorial and into the highlands. Alternatively, just lie on the beach under palm trees, watch the fishermen in action and dine on fresh seafood.

The provincial capital Qui Nhon can trace its origins back to the ancient Cham harbour, Shri Banoi, and lies around 10km/6mi east of the N 1 on a peninsula at the mouth of the Song Cai. In the 1960s, one of the biggest American military bases was located here, and the tip of the headland is still off limits for military reasons. Due to the **severe humidity** – the town is often subjected to typhoons and heavy rainfall – many houses are covered in moss and look rather unkempt.
Vietnam's finest Tuong theatre group is based in Qui Nhon.

Colourful tombs in the Buddhist part of the cemetery

What to See in Qui Nhon

The focal point of the town is the lively and colourful Lon Market, where fruit and vegetables from the region are sold.

Lon Market

Just a short walk away, between the market and the stadium, the 300-year-old Long Khanh Temple stands in Tran Cao Van Street. Its 17m/55ft-high statue of Buddha (1972) can be seen from a distance, rising out of a lily pond. The temple dates back to the year 1700, yet has suffered damage time and again, explaining its current state of disrepair. The last renovation work took place in the late 1970s.

Chua Long Khanh

A vast cemetery is located in the northern part of town, consisting of a military cemetery as well as Buddhist and Catholic burial grounds. If time allows, there is much to be discovered here: old and relatively new gravestones, some simple, some ornately decorated with pictures and ornaments – all colourfully painted. The Buddhist sites can be recognized by the lotus blossom placed on top or by a swastika, a symbol of good fortune.

Cemetery

Around Qui Nhon

Many relics of Cham culture can be found in the environs of Qui Nhon, as the former Cham capital, Vijaya, lay just 35km/21mi to the north, close to Dap Da village. After the fall of Indrapura in the year 982, the Cham settled here and, in spite of repeated attacks by the Khmer and the Vietnamese, held firm over a long period of time. It was not until 1471 that Vijaya was captured and destroyed as the Vietnamese further extended their empire and advanced into the south. In the area surrounding the **former stronghold**, a number of

Cham towers

towers were erected in the 11th and 12th centuries, named after materials (such as silver), although the names had no bearing on the actual construction.

At the edge of the town of Qui Nhon (approx. 1km/1100yd north of the town centre), close to the N 1, stand the 11th-century **Thap Doi** twin towers. In contrast to the terraced roofs commonly seen in Cham architecture, the towers of Thap Doi feature curved, pyramidical structures. Garuda figures sit at their corners. With support from UNESCO, the towers have been reconstructed and restored in recent years.

Pleiku
A wonderfully scenic road (no. 19) leads into the highland region to the town of Pleiku (Plei Ku), 163km/101mi to the west. Roughly half

 ## VISITING QUI NHON

INFORMATION

Binh Dinh Tourist
10 Nguyen Hue
(on the beach road)
Le Loi, Qui Nhon
Tel. 0 56/89 25 24

Saigon Tourist
24 Nguyen Hue, Qui Nhon
Tel. 0 56/81 99 22 and 82 82 35
Information also in the hotels.

TRANSPORT

Qui Nhon Phu Cat Airport
(36km/22mi north of Qui Nhon):
Tel. 0 56/82 29 53

WHERE TO EAT

In the Tha Doi on the northwestern edge of town by the canal (close to the Thap Doi Cham Towers) simple, good value eateries serve seafood dishes.

▶ Inexpensive

Seaview Café
25 Nguyen Hue (Beach road, adjacent to tourist information)
Tel. 0 56/89 17 91
Simple open-air establishment with snacks and refreshments.

WHERE TO STAY

▶ Luxury

Life Wellness Resort & Spa
Ghenh Rang, Bai Dai, Qui Nhon
(16km/10mi south)
Tel. 0 56/84 01 32, fax 84 01 38
www.life-resorts.com
quynhon@life-resorts.com
Wonderful complex on a beach interspersed with cliffs: 63 rooms with maximum comfort and panoramic views of the sea from the terrace or the bath. Pools, spa with Tai Chi and Yoga classes.

▶ Mid-range

Hai Au Hotel
489 An Duong Vuong, Qui Nhon
Tel. 0 56/84 64 73, fax 84 69 26
ks.haiau@dng.vnn.vn
Middle-class hotel at the beach, close to town, with pool and good international restaurant.

▶ Budget

Yaly Hotel
89 Hung Vuong, Pleiku
Tel. 0 59/81 48 58, fax 81 76 19
Centrally located mini hotel with 35 pleasant rooms, some with air conditioning, some without.

of the journey twists and turns over the An Khe Pass and it is worth looking across the lowlands, where the Ha Giao River winds its way to the coast. The Giang Pass is also part of the route, as are numerous Bahnar villages, where examples of their traditional communal longhouses can be seen. Rubber plantations, woods and slopes covered in coffee trees point the way to the plateau of Pleiku in the Central Highlands of Vietnam. In this sparsely populated area, the South Vietnamese Army once had their command post for the entire mountain region. Agent Orange was sprayed liberally here, and bombing raids were carried out on a number of occasions – especially in the year 1972. Today, sober, unembellished buildings dominate the townscape, often seen through a misty veil of rain. The **market** is the sole site of interest, filling up rapidly in the early hours of the morning as the inhabitants of surrounding villages arrive to sell aubergines, shallots, parsnips and garlic. Tourists tend to combine a visit to Pleiku with a trip to Buon Ma Thuot to explore the highlands and visit settlements of the minority peoples (Jarai, Bahnar, Ede).

Baedeker TIP

Sensibility required

Visiting the villages of ethnic minorities requires a degree of sensibility. It is advisable to come with a guide, who can explain certain alien aspects.

Jarai villages

A number of Jarai villages lie on the road to Kon Tum. First, however, comes the Bien Ho Tea Company after 14km/8.5mi; another 1km/1100yd further on are Yaly Falls. The Jarai can already be seen here in the paddy fields and rubber plantations or carrying huge baskets of goods from village to village. Above all, the women's garb catches the eye: it is awash with colour and horizontal stripes. Just a few miles from the waterfall lie the villages of Plei Mrong and Plei Mun, complete with longhouses. The carved wooden statues on the burial grounds are also of interest.

Thap Bac (Banh It)

Close to the junction (N 19) at An Nhon (approx. 20km/12mi north of Qui Nhon), four richly ornate 12th-century towers (Thap Bac) rise up amidst the hills. The so-called Silver Towers were one of the first kalan groups to have been erected on a hill – which later became common practice. From these heights, a wonderful view across the landscape can be savoured, taking in the other Cham towers of the area.

Sa Huynh

The quaint fishing village of Sa Huynh appears in a crescent-shaped bay of golden sands around 115km/71mi north of Qui Nhon. Fringed with palm trees, its beautiful beach is an inviting place to take a break on the way to ► My Lai or ► Hoi An. The small hotel restaurant serves fine fish. Fruit and drinks merchants are also on hand. Boat trips to the neighbouring island of Genh Nhu are a possibility here.

✳ Red River Delta

Region: North   **Area:** 15,000 sq km/5800 sq mi

Although the northern Red River delta lies only a few meters above sea level, it has been canalized and cultivated for hundreds of years. Today the landscape is a network streaked with old dykes and dams, strewn with temples, pagodas, churches, family tombs and community houses.

River network

The Red River (Song Hong) begins in the southwest Chinese Yunnan province and flows across North Vietnam for the last 500km/310mi of its total 1200km/750mi length. Adjoining the Red River are other large tributaries such as the **Black River** and the **Clear River**, with which it joins above Hanoi upon entering the lowlands. Here, the Red River spreads out into many arms before flowing into the South China Sea south of the port of Hai Phong.

The Red River delta is considered the cradle of Vietnamese culture

It is worth taking a trip out to the delta area from Hanoi, even though apart from the unique Perfume Pagoda, there are only a few real attractions. Among all of the historic buildings, Thay Pagoda and Tay Phuong Pagoda, (all three ►Hanoi, Surroundings) located far inland, are the nicest examples of classical Vietnamese architecture. Many cities still heavily bear the signs of destruction from the Vietnam War., but it is worth paying a visit to the villages of Bat Trang and Dong Ky, in which handicrafts are produced. Among the scenic highlights on the other hand are ►Dry Ha Long Bay and Cuc Phuong National Park.

Colouration from varied sediments

The rugged mountains and the relatively steep slopes here mean that the watercourses carry off a lot of sediment. The Red River contains mostly iron-rich sediments, which lead to its reddish-brown colour; the Black River in turn carries mainly dark, humus-based material, and the Clear River comes from an area where there is little erosion, so that little colouration is noticeable. Heavy **flooding** is not uncommon. As a result, life on the Red River has always had to go with and against the flow. In order to keep the effects of the summer monsoon floods in check, dams and dykes have been built here since before

Red River Delta Map

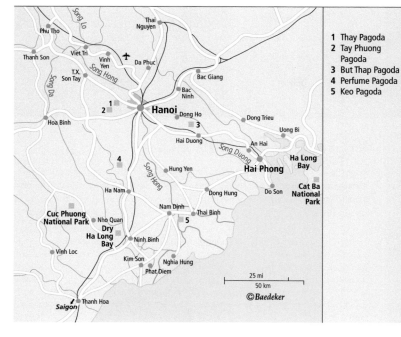

1 Thay Pagoda
2 Tay Phuong Pagoda
3 But Thap Pagoda
4 Perfume Pagoda
5 Keo Pagoda

the Common Era. Their combined length today totals more than 3000km/1870mi. They succeed in taming the masses of water, but this also means that a large amount of the contained sediments no longer reach the fields, but are washed straight into the sea. Through this, the ground is robbed of its natural richness, making the use of artificial fertilizers inevitable.

The fertile alluvial lands of the Red River are considered the core country and **heartland of Vietnam**. Settlement of this area dates back to the Bronze-Age Dong Son culture. Today nearly 40% of the Vietnamese live in the delta region, which amounts to a population density of nearly 2000 inhabitants/sq km or 5180 inhabitants/sq mi. A characteristic of the region is the close proximity of the rice fields to villages built on hilltops, dunes and dams, protected by bamboo fences. This allows the continuing extensive self-sufficiency of Vietnamese villages. Buildings are constructed on the ground rather than on stilts, as is typical in Laos and Cambodia.

Settlement

With 15,000 sq km/5800 sq mi, the agriculturally-oriented Red River delta has only a third of the surface area of the Mekong delta, but is

Economy

The characters of the water-puppet theatre make an impressive entrance...

... and the puppeteers of the Thang Long Ensemble in Hanoi

VIETNAMESE PUPPETS

Rivers and canals criss-cross the broad deltas of Vietnam. Monsoon rains dominate the lives of the inhabitants, and the festivals, too, usually revolve around water. The water-puppet theatre mua roi nuoc, unique in the world, is no exception.

Loud detonations from fireworks welcome the audience with a musical greeting. The members of a small **orchestra** give the puppets their voices. They dress in glowing, colourful robes and sit next to the »stage«, which in this case is the water. Usually a lake or the village pond is chosen. In cities such as Hanoi, Saigon and Hue special water-puppet theatres have been built with a pool as the stage. Two balustrades of wooden stakes bound the stage area to left and right. Colourful flags are raised here at the start of the performance – as if by a ghostly hand. The brownish water is calm, and clouds of white smoke slowly drift across the surface of the water as the fireworks fall silent.

A peasant hosts the programme

Then Teu comes on stage. He is the **showmaster**, comedian and link between the public and the actors. This white-painted puppet with a wry expression, a figure without whom no roi nuoc is complete, represents a young peasant. He opens the performance and greets the audience. Then the sound of a bamboo flute is heard, and a female voice starts to sing.

As if pulled by strings, a brown **water buffalo** glides onto the water. With its broad muzzle it keeps diving into the waters and makes great splashes all around. Puffing and snorting, it makes its way through the water, pulling a plough and a farmer behind it – a scene that is as much part of the landscape in Vietnam as the conical hats of the women. Before long peasants ploughing, women labourers planting rice and fishermen in their little boats populate the pool to the strains of a folk melody.

Scenes from real life ...

Most motifs of water-puppet theatre are taken from the everyday life of Vietnamese rice farmers, which is represented with all its joyful and sad incidents in short entertaining scenes: herding ducks, hunting foxes, boat races or the perils of fishing. The fish hop around merrily as the fishermen with studied clumsiness thrust their nets in the wrong places. The

audience roar with laughter, of course, when the nimble fish escape and the fishermen catch nothing, especially when, to cap it all, the nets are thrown over a cheeky little boy instead of the fish in the heat of the action.

... or from history

Other episodes are based on **fairy tales, legends** or other forms of theatre whose heroes are usually taken from Vietnamese history. A famous and highly popular historical tale relates to the mythical king Le Loi, who expelled the Chinese from Vietnam in the 15th century.

According to the legend he was victorious with the help of a magic sword that the gods gave him. The performers of water-puppet theatre like to recount the story of how Le Loi took a boat trip on Hoan Kiem Lake in Hanoi after a war. There he encountered an enormous turtle, which grabbed the sword from him and disappeared into the depths of the lake, in order to return it to its divine owners.

A damp profession

At the end of the performance, drums and cymbals sound once more. To a beat that gets faster and faster, the **four holy animals** glide, hop and jump through the water: the wondrous phoenix, the mythical unicorn Kylin, the magnificently coloured dragon and the golden tortoise. When they dance together, peace and happiness reign in Vietnam.

After performing, the figures disappear into a water pavilion that has been constructed at the back of the stage. The requisites, puppets and puppeteers are housed under its curved pagoda roof. The puppeteers, unseen by the public, do their work behind a curtain of woven bamboo. To do this they stand up to their waists in water! The puppets, by contrast, seem to hover above the water. They are moved on bamboo poles 3 to 4 metres (10 to 13 feet) long and can be turned and manipulated by means of rudders and strings so that spectators have the impression they have come on stage straight from the rice fields and villages.

of comparable importance to the economy of the country. The alluvial soil ensures **high yields**, and the climate is also conducive to farming. As in the Mekong delta, the high precipitation rate is caused by the summer monsoon. However, winter temperatures of the Red River delta are considerably lower than in the Mekong, leading to fog formation with a constant drizzle, which keeps the ground sufficiently moist even in the dry season. This means that a second harvest can be brought in without artificial irrigation. Nevertheless, the region does not export rice, as the high population density means that the harvest barely covers local requirements.

✶ ✶ Sa Pa

B 1

Province: Lao Cai
Population: 38,000

Region: Northern Highlands

Situated idyllically between the Tonkinese Alps (Hoang Lien Mountains) and paddy fields on endless terrace slopes, populated by hill tribes in colourful costume and with wondrous walking trails, Sa Pa was bound to attract a flow of tourists sooner or later, no matter how far off the beaten track it lies.

The stepped hills of Sa Pa

Dauntless trekkers start out from this pretty town

The French developed the mountain village as a climatic spa as early as the 1920s. Today the place is booming; indeed, particularly at weekends, it threatens to buckle under the weight of incoming tourist groups. Not that the hill-tribe traders are complaining.

Originally, various ethnic minorities lived around Sa Pa, above all the diminutive Hmong, clothed in indigo blue, and the taller Red Dao, whose women wear impressive red turbans. Since time immemorial, they have cultivated fruit, vegetables, tea and cinnamon in the cool region. Apart from the bustling, colourful markets, Sa Pa has little of interest to offer; visitors are attracted by its location in a thoroughly charming landscape and as a base for undertaking **mountain tours**. The ascent of Fan Si Pan, for example, at 3143m/10,311ft the highest peak in Vietnam, offers a particularly strenuous challenge (allow 3 days). Sa Pa is the coldest place in Vietnam: winter visitors (Dec to Feb) are well advised to pack warm clothing, especially for night time (also in springtime and from August onwards).

Tours into Surrounding Areas

Sa Pa is a good base from which to take a tour by either moped taxi, Jeep or horse and trap. This can be an expensive undertaking, however, which is all the more reason to choose the more attractive alter-

Moped, car or horse

▶ VISITING SA PA

INFORMATION
Sa Pa Tourism
28 Cau May, Sa Pa
Tel. 0 20/87 19 75
www.sapatourism.com

TRANSPORT
The beautiful »Victoria« Express, from the luxury hotel chain of the same name, runs between Hanoi and Lao Cai several times a week, whilst trains belonging to the state-owned railway run every day (7–10 hours, reasonable sleeper cars, varying standards for the same price!); public and tourist buses continue from Lao Cai to
Sa Pa.

SHOPPING
Hill tribe markets
Every Saturday, countless tourists converge on Sa Pa for the legendary weekend market. The market also takes place during the week (albeit in smaller form) with the hill tribes in attendance; it is less crowded then. There are other similarly colourful markets in neighbouring villages on different days. Worth noting: indigo clothes dye tends to run.

WHERE TO EAT
▶ Moderate
Top Mountain View Bar
24 Dong Loi
Tel. 0 20/87 12 45
On the fourth floor of the Chaulong Sapa Hotel, fine selection of drinks and splendid mountain panorama.

▶ Inexpensive
Mimosa
Cau May
Tel. & fax 0 20/87 13 77
daily 8am–11pm

A little removed from the main street, hidden at the top of some steps: a small inn serving Vietnamese and vegetarian dishes, seafood or wild boar, pasta or pizza, even Nutella for breakfast!

The Gecko
Ham Rong
Tel. 0 20/87 15 04
daily 7am–10pm
Nice little bar with cosy sofas in the corners (for non-smokers as well) and »La Petite Bouffe« restaurant. French management (five reasonably priced rooms with bath also available).

Baguette & Chocolat
Tha Bac
Tel. 0 20/87 17 66
daily 7am–10pm
Charitable project and school (www.hoasuaschool.com) for disadvantaged children, plus restaurant, bakery, café, bar and small hotel: small dishes and bakery products can be enjoyed in cosy corner seating by the fireplace downstairs, whilst the first floor has four lovely, if basic, rooms with shower and small balcony.

WHERE TO STAY
▶ Mid-range
Chaulong Sapa Hotel
24 Dong Loi
Tel. 0 20/87 12 45, fax 87 18 44
www.chaulonghotel.com
info@chaulonghotel.com
Once the best hotel in the town centre, now somewhat overpriced, combining a new building (large rooms with balcony and mountain panorama) with an older, castle-like house (ask to see the rooms first!).

Bamboo Sapa Hotel
Cau May
Tel. 0 20/87 10 75, fax 87 19 45
www.sapatravel.com
trekkingsapa@hn.vnn.vn
New three-storey hotel with most
attractive and comfy rooms, some
with decorative fireplace, chaise lon-
gue and balcony (satellite TV, telephone, heating), marvellous view of
the mountains, good travel agency.

ATI Sapa Rose Valley Resort
Muong Hoa Road (1km/1100yd outside Sa Pa)
Tel. 0 20/87 10 56, fax 87 22 35
www.atiresorts.com
ati-sapa@atiresorts.com
Spread out on a steep slope just before
the town, these large bungalows on

stilts boast excellent views: the rooms
are quite simple, but spacious and
quiet (satellite TV, some rooms with
bath).

Auberge Hotel
Cau May
Tel. 0 20/87 12 43, fax 87 16 66
auberge@sapadiscovery.com
Pleasant guesthouse from the colonial
period, reminiscent of a Swiss chalet.
Rooms on the top floor have a
wonderful view of the mountain
scenery.

Ham Rong Hotel
Ham Rong
Tel. 0 20/87 12 51, fax 87 13 03
www.vietnamhotels.biz/hamronghotel
hoanglienhotelsp@hn.vnn.vn

A colourful market of the hill tribes around Sa Pa

On the way to Lao Cai

Striking hotel in colonial style with 30 very cheap, some extremely large, rooms. Minibar, satellite TV, bath.

Vuong Hoan Guesthouse
79 Phan Dinh Phuong (Pho Moi),
Lao Cai Stadt
Tel. & fax 0 20/83 53 71
Simple hotel in Lao Cai with tiny rooms and tiled bathroom. For good Vietnamese food, cross the street to the Hiep Van corner inn immediately opposite.

Baedeker recommendation

Visitors stay in one of two old French villas, spacious rooms with fireplace. Restaurant is recommended, renowned for its snakemeat dishes.

► Budget
Hoang Lien Hotel
8 Cau May
Tel. 0 20/87 11 78, fax 87 11 76
hoanglienhotelsp@hn.vnn.vn

► Luxury
Victoria Sapa
Tel. 0 20/87 15 22
Fax 87 15 39
www.victoriahotels-asia.com
resa.sapa@victoriahotels-asia.com
First-class hotel on the edge of town, country house style with very comfortable rooms, some with canopy bed and balcony. Tennis and badminton courts, heated in-

native of exploring the region on foot, following narrow, often steep trails. It makes sense to take a guide along. Should the path seem too long, there is always the chance of flagging down one of the moped taxis on the main road (as far as the next valley turn-off).

✳ Cat Cat Several Hmong villages are within trekking distance of Sa Pa, the most popular of which is undoubtedly Cat Cat in the Muong Hoa valley (approx. 3km/2mi away). Take the street to the west of the marketplace as far as a turreted French villa (National Park office), then turn left onto a path leading down into the valley.
Before long, the wooden huts come into view amongst fruit trees and bamboo thicket. Beneath the village, follow the steps and cross a rope bridge to reach a waterfall, a pleasant spot for a breather. From here, it is another 4km/2.5mi to the larger Hmong settlement at Sin Chai.

Lao Cai Another hike leads south through the Hmong village of Lao Cai to Ta Van (approx. 11km/6.5mi), where Giay and Dao people live. The route passes through pretty villages and wonderful scenery, past baskets of indigo leaves, used by the Black Hmong to dye their clothes, and herdsmen riding water buffalo. At the side of the road, stones are engraved with symbols, thought to be an ancient **Hmong script**. The streams click-clack to the sound of the »coi gia gao«, wooden contraptions which process rice through water power. It is a good idea to carry a stick at all times to guard against snakes and the many wild dogs barking in the villages. The villagers themselves are more attuned to tourists and the majority of them, both old and young, seem to sell souvenirs – with more or less persistence.

Ta Phin

Northeast of Sa Pa on the road to Lao Cai lies the Red Dao settlement of Ta Phin. After roughly 6km/3.5mi, take a left-hand branch of the road through a wonderful valley with rice terraces to reach Ta Phin some 5km/3mi further on. The inhabitants of Ta Phin have concentrated their efforts on **handicrafts** (hats, bags, etc.) and sell their wares through the Craft Link as far afield as Hanoi and Saigon. A small cooperative with a souvenir shop can be visited in the village.

Fan Si Pan

Trekking tours (3–5 days) up Fan Si Pan are also offered. Vietnam's highest mountain (3143m/10,311ft) rises up from the heart of Hoang Lien Son Nature Reserve, 9km/5.5mi from Sa Pa. The trek is not to be taken lightly, however: to cover the roughly 14km/8.5mi-long trail, it is first necessary to descend to 1200m/3937ft and traverse a rickety bamboo bridge. The real ascent then begins (difference in height approx. 2000m/6561ft), following sometimes overgrown paths through pine forests and bamboo thickets. A breathtaking panoramic view of the mountains of northwest Vietnam is the reward for the endeavour – it extends as far as the province of Son La in the south and the peaks of Yunnan in China to the north. A critical factor to bear in mind for the Fan Si Pan tour is the weather: it is prone to change swiftly and many a trekker has been obliged to turn back due to

> ## ! *Baedeker* TIP
>
> ### Rules of conduct amongst the hill tribes
>
> When paying a visit to the homes of one of the hill tribes, under no circumstances touch, photograph or point at their altar. Houses with a bundle of bamboo, chicken feathers or leaves hanging above the entrance should not be entered – its occupants are having a marital row, are sick or have had a family bereavement and do not want to be disturbed. Children should not be photographed, at least not without permission, as the Dao believe that their soul will be captured by a snapshot.

mist, rain or cold. Under no circumstances is this an expedition to be undertaken alone! A guide who is familiar with the trails, can negotiate a path through the undergrowth and can find water is essential. Competent guides can be booked through the »Auberge« and »Mountain View« hotels.

★ ★ Saigon (Ho Chi Minh City)

D 7

Province: Ho Chi Minh City (city state)   **Region:** South
Area: 2000 sq km/772 sq mi   **Population:** 3.5 million
     (metropolitan area)

Every visitor falls under Saigon's spell: the South Vietnamese metropolis on the river of the same name impresses with colonial buildings in soft shades of ochre and shady boulevards lined with tamarind trees, Chinese temples and a host of sites made famous through literature and film.

Three districts   Saigon's appeal lies in the mix of districts, each having retained its own distinctive character: the former **French town centre**, the real Saigon, is outstanding, as is Cholon, the old **Chinese quarter**. Gia Dinh was the third and most Vietnamese of the three districts that grew together to make up the city of Saigon. Even though the Communists gave the city and the neighbouring rural lands the name Ho Chi Minh from 1975 onwards, none of its inhabitants stopped calling the old heart of town on the harbour by the name by which it had been known for centuries: Saigon.

Upwardly mobile metropolis   In recent years, the cityscape has been evolving more and more, with mirror glass hotels and office blocks shooting up. The old Saigon of crumbling façades, colonial villas graced with arcades and greying prefabricated concrete blocks weathered by monsoons, street traders with fruit carts and countless food stalls all seem to be fading somewhat into the background as the upwardly mobile metropolis takes centre stage with a modern veneer as can already be found in the neighbouring countries and so-called tiger states of Asia.

The people of Saigon are generally considered to have an **easygoing lifestyle**, in contrast to the inhabitants of the political centre which is Hanoi, who are perceived as more reliable and broader in their vision. Modern Western influence is particularly evident in architecture, restaurants and fashion. Behind the new scenes, however, old traditions persevere right in the middle of the street. Vietnamese daily life unfolds, as ever, in the open air: men ponder their next move as they hunch over board games, oblivious to the cacophony of bi-

! Baedeker TIP

Overview

To obtain a first overview of Saigon, the panoramic bar on the 33rd floor of the Saigon Trade Center (37 Ton Duc Thang) is recommended, permitting a look at the chaos from a safe distance.

Hectic traffic amidst office blocks and modern façades – →
Saigon is very much on the move

cycle bells and horns. Shoeshiners wave at passers-by as they stroll under the tall trees of the boulevards, and a woman carrying tasty snacks in her shoulder baskets cleans empty rice bowls on the kerb.

History

17th cent.	Vietnamese Nguyen rulers conquer the region.
1862	Saigon becomes the capital of the French colonial empire Cochinchina.
Second World War	Japan occupies Saigon.
after 1945	The French defend Saigon against Ho Chi Minh's forces.
1954	Saigon is named as capital of the Republic of South Vietnam.
30.4.1975	Communist troops march into Saigon.
from 1986	Doi moi reforms
1994	Lifting of the US embargo

Over 1000 years ago, Khmer villages stood where the metropolis of Saigon stands today. The Vietnamese first settled here in the late 17th century, when the Nguyen rulers advanced from Hue further into the south.

The first contact with the French in South Vietnam and in Saigon came through missionaries, but French troops were not far behind the monks. From 1859 to 1975, South Vietnam stood under **foreign rule**. Saigon became the capital of the French colonial territory of Cochinchina. The marshy land on which the town was built was drained and canals were converted into broad streets such as Nguyen Hue Boulevard. An era of French plantation owners, opium-smoking colonialists and elegant coffee houses had begun. The first railway lines were laid. The Governor's Palace, Notre Dame, the Opera House, the Central Post Office and grand villas were all built in this period. Travellers of the age arriving in far-off Vietnam found a place which reminded them of a French provincial town, as Somerset Maugham recorded. During the Second World War the Japanese occupied the city and were thereupon attacked by Viet Minh units from the north. On 2 September 1945 in Hanoi, Ho Chi Minh declared Vietnam an **independent republic**. The French ignored this and returned as a colonial power to Saigon, reinstalling the former emperor Bao Dai as head of government and defending the town against Ho Chi Minh's soldiers.

Following the First Indochina War and the subsequent partition of Vietnam (1954), Ngo Dinh Diem, the first president, initially supported by the United States, declared Saigon the capital city of the South Vietnamese Republic. Saigon's population grew rapidly in this era (up to one million). The skirmishes of war encroached ever closer to the town. On 31 January 1968, during the **Tet Offensive**, Vietcong militants scored their biggest coup to date – forcing their way into the garden of the US Embassy. Far more fundamental changes came with the accession to power of the Communists, who

marched into Saigon on 30 April 1975. Countless businesses, workshops and restaurants were forced to close and disappeared overnight. Dispossessed shopkeepers found themselves reduced to penniless boat people by the following day. The pulsating lightness of daily life was surrendered to bureaucracy and five-year plans. In the wake of the so-called doi moi economic reforms (from 1986), a more liberal investment law (1988) and the lifting of the US embargo (1994), some two to three million Vietnamese expatriates invested in or returned to Saigon, which has become a »boom town« today.

The economic boom in Saigon also has its disadvantages. Many Vietnamese from the surrounding areas want to grab a share of the business yet fall short of the mark. An estimated figure for the number of **homeless people** in Saigon exceeds half a million, including a significant number of orphaned children from the rural provinces. Tourists cannot evade the young traders on the street – they stick to potential customers like glue. In spite of compulsory school attendance, child labour is prevalent, as many impoverished parents opt to have their offspring on the streets earning money rather than sending them to school, which is subject to a fee from the sixth grade upwards. It is not uncommon for entire families to set up camp on woven mats at the kerbside, close to the boulevards and large hotels.

Downside of the boom

Highlights Saigon

History Museum
Vietnam's past is evoked by art relics from the relevant periods in history.
► page 385

Thien Hau Pagoda
If a boat trip is on the agenda, a trip to the most beautiful pagoda of Cholon offers the opportunity of asking the Goddess of the Sea for her protection. This may be followed by a wander through the alleyways of the Chinese district.
► page 389

Binh Tay Market
Few go home empty-handed from a visit to the market and the surrounding alleyways.
► page 391

Jade Emperor Pagoda
Immerse yourself in a world of timbals and swathes of incense.
► page 392

Giac Lam Pagoda
The oldest place of worship in Saigon and the most beautiful in the city.
► page 397

Saigon Map

Vinh Nghien Pagoda
Airport

④

Station

Truong Dinh

Nguyen Thong

Ly Chinh Thang

Ba Huyen Thanh Quan

Women's
Museum

Tran Quoc Toan

3 Thang 2

Chua Bo

Dien Bien Phu

Cach Mang Thang Tam

Vo Thi Sau

Tu Xuong

ⓘ

Pasteur

Dien Bien Phu

Pham Ngoc Thach

Ngo Thoi Nhiem

Le Qui Don

Nam Ky Khoi Nghia

⑨

Xa Loi Pagoda

Cao Thang

Nguyen Dinh Chieu

Truong Dinh

**War Remnants
Museum**

Nguyen Dinh Chieu

Vo Van Tan

⑩

Cach Mang Thang Tam

Nguyen Thi Minh Khai

Nam Ky Khoi Nghia

Nguyen Thi Minh Khai

Pasteur

⑩

Cong Quynh

Bui Thi Xuan

Le Thi Rieng

H.T Cong Chua

**Reunification
Palace**

Le Duan

**Notre Dame
Cathedral**
✝

**Thai Binh
Market**

Nguyen Trai

Nguyen Du

Nguyen Du

Cong Quynh

Ly Tu Trong

Le Lai

Pham Ngu Lao

Le Thanh Ton

Truong Dinh

**Mariamman
Temple**

Nguyen Trung Truc

⑦ **Revolution
Museum**

Town Hall

⑥

Bui Vien

⑪

⑫ **Ben Thanh
Market**

ⓘ ⑧

⑤

Chuon

Tran Hung Dao

Le Loi

Nam Ky Khoi Nghia

① **Opera**

⑧ ③

De Tham

Co Bac

Nguyen Thai Hoc

Yersin

Nguyen Thai Binh

**Art
Museum**

**Thendayyutthapani
Temple** ⑥

Pasteur

② ⑪

Mac Thi Buoi

Co Giang

Calmette

Pho Duc Chinh

**Phung Son Tu
Pagoda**

Ham Nghi

⑦

Ton That Dam

Nguyen Hue

Ngo Duc Ke

②

Ben Chuong Duong

Ben Nghe Channel

Ben Van Don

Nguyen Cong Tru

Ben Chuong Duong

Nguyen Tat Thanh

Ben Van Don

**Ho Chi Minh
Museum**

Ton Duc Thang

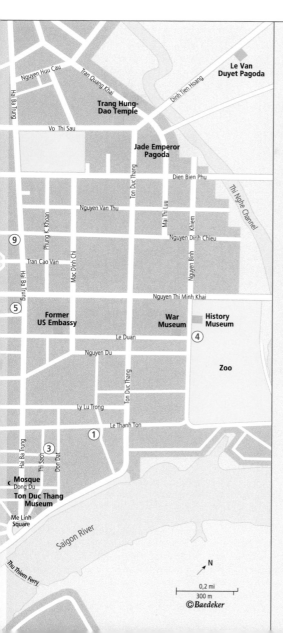

Where to stay
1. Rex Hotel
2. Hotel Majestic
3. Caravelle Hotel
4. Omni Saigon Hotel
5. Continental Hotel
6. Kim Do Royal City Hotel
7. Duxton Hotel Saigon
8. Asian Hotel
9. Liberty 1 Que Huong Hotel
10. Saigon Boutique Hotel
11. Le Le Hotel

Where to eat
1. Restaurant Hoi An
2. Vietnam House
3. Camarque
4. Tell
5. Thanh Nien
6. Chu Bar
7. Quan An Ngon
8. Café Brodard
9. Canh Buom
10. Lang Nuon Nam Bo
11. Dong Du Restaurant
12. Pho 2000

Map labels:
Nguyen Huu Cau
Tran Quang Khai
Dinh Tien Hoang
Le Van Duyet Pagoda
Hai Ba Trung
Trang Hung-Dao Temple
Vo Thi Sau
Jade Emperor Pagoda
Ton Duc Thang
Dien Bien Phu
Thi Nghe Channel
Nguyen Van Thu
Mai Thi Luu
Khiem
Phung K. Khoan
Nguyen Dinh Chieu
Nguyen Binh
Tran Cao Van
Mac Dinh Chi
Hai Ba Trung
Nguyen Thi Minh Khai
Former US Embassy
War Museum
History Museum
Le Duan
Nguyen Du
Ton Duc Thang
Zoo
Ly Lu Trong
Le Thanh Ton
Hai Ba Trung
Thi Sach
Don Dat
Mosque
Dong Du
Ton Duc Thang Museum
Me Linh Square
Saigon River
Thu Thiem Ferry

N
0,2 mi
300 m
©Baedeker

▶ VISITING SAIGON

INFORMATION

Vietnam Tourism
234 Nam Ky Khoi Nghia, District 3, Saigon
Tel. 08/9 31 67 76 and 8 29 07 76
also in the Dong Khoi, 18 Nam Quoc Cang and Pham Ngu Lao
www.vietnamtourism.com

Saigon Tourist
49 Le Thanh Ton, District 1, Saigon
Tel. 08/8 29 89 14 and 8 23 01 00
www.saigon-tourist.com
www.saigontourist.net

TOUR OPERATORS

Far East Tourist
158 Le Lai, District 1, Saigon
Tel. 08/9 25 60 99, fax 9 25 61 00
www.fareasttourist.com
fareasttour@hcm.fpt.vn

Trails Of Indochina
10/8 Phan Dinh Giot, Tan Binh district, Saigon
Tel. 08/8 44 10 05, fax 8 44 33 50
www.trailsofindochina.com
phong@trailsofindochina.com
toi@fmail.vnn.vn

Focus Asia
70 Pham Ngoc Thach (Green Star Building, 4. St.), District 3, Saigon
Tel. 08/8 20 77 87, fax 8 20 77 86
www.focus-asia.biz
info@focus-asia.biz
Long-established in Saigon, this tour operator offers trips to neighbouring countries as well.

TRANSPORT

Tan Son Nhat International Airport
(7km/4mi outside the centre): Visitors Information and Service Center, tel. 08/8 48 67 11 and 8 48 53 83, www.saigonairport.com (daily 9am to 11pm; Vietnam Airlines shuttle bus and public bus no. 152)

Saigon Main Railway Station: 1 Nguyen Thong, tel. 08/8 46 65 28 and 8 36 01 05, tickets from Saigon Railway Tourist Center: tel. 08/8 36 79 70 and 08/8 36 76 40.

In the city: on foot or by cyclo, also: xyclo (not at night, and be prepared to haggle over the price. Cyclos are banned on many streets, so do not be surprised if they are forced to take a detour); moped taxis (price negotiable!) or regular taxis with meter, modern municipal buses (timetable on sale at Ben Thanh Market, for example, see below).

Tip for pedestrians: Saigon traffic resembles a rumbling dodgem car ride at the fair, on both two wheels and four – nobody would dream of applying the brakes on a moped or cyclo at an intersection unless a traffic light is unmistakeably red. Tourists aiming to cross the street are advised to »grab the coat tails« of a Vietnamese pedestrian and dodge the motorized chaos in his »slipstream«.

EVENTS

Magazines such as *Time Out* and *Metro* are packed with tips for events and can often be found in bars and hotels.

New Year's Festival

For the Tet new year's celebrations, a part of Saigon is transformed into a sea of flowers, particularly on Nguyen Hue Boulevard and Tran Hung Dao Boulevard. The flower markets prosper as the people of Saigon stock up on popular apricot and peach branches and little orange trees to decorate their homes in festive fashion (►Baedeker Special p.112).

Cyclo Race

An annual event in March is the Saigon Cyclo Race, a charity event which makes an exception to the usual traffic policy by allowing the vehicles to be driven along the boulevards of the city centre.

SHOPPING

Most of the souvenir shops, galleries and silk boutiques are located in the *Dong Khoi* and *Hai Ba Trung*; *Le Loi* is also renowned for leather goods.
Authentic and replica Asian antiques can be found in *Le Cong Kieu*, close to the Art Museum.
Thanh Tuy (125 Le Thanh Ton, next to the Norfolk Hotel, District 1, daily 8am–6.30pm): long-established, small silk shop, good quality tailored clothes.
Factories: visitors to Lam Son can not only purchase leather goods but also watch them being made, with a variety of handicrafts on display (106 Nguyen Van Troi, opposite Omni Hotel) also at Tay Son: leather goods, furniture etc. (198 Vo Thi Sau).
Ben Thanh Market: Ben Thanh Market in the southwest of the town is housed in several halls and proffers the complete range of Vietnamese goods and merchandise.
Road 22 to Tay Ninh passes through the district of *Tan Binh*, famous for its many handicrafts and wood carving workshops. Furniture, basketry, ceramics and toys are on sale at *Dong Duong*, 28/3 A Cach Mang Thang Tam Street, Ward 15 (tel. 08/8 64 03 28).

CUISINE

Ben Thanh Night Market: from 6pm in the evenings, the streets to the east and west of Ben Thanh Market present an opportunity to tuck in to some seafood or other regional specialities with the local Vietnamese at one of the many little stalls selling set-price dishes.
A number of *seafood establishments* can be found on Thich Sach and Le Thanh Ton in District 1.
Very popular with the people of Saigon for special occasions and with travel groups are the *restaurant boats* and *dining excursions* on the Saigon River: Chinese, Vietnamese and international menus with orchestral accompaniment, sometimes vocalists as well, though the latter take a little getting used to (trips lasting one hour depart daily from around 7.30pm from the Bach Dang promenade, e.g. with the triple level Saigon Tourist boat: tel. & fax: 08/8 23 03 93).

WHERE TO EAT

▶ Expensive

① Restaurant Hoi An
11 Le Thanh Ton
Tel. 08/8 23 76 94
Gourmet restaurant with refined colonial atmosphere, elegant interior, delicious food. Popular with businessmen.

② Vietnam House
93–95 Dong Khoi
Tel. 08/8 29 16 23
daily 10am–10pm
Nice, peaceful ambience. Tasty Vietnamese dishes, a good introduction to the national cuisine.

▶ Moderate

③ Camarque
16 Cao Bat Quat
Tel. 08/8 24 31 48
11.30am–2pm, 6.30pm to midnight
Garden restaurant under palm trees, French and international fare, plus the trendy »Vasco's Bar«, live music on Fridays and Saturdays.

④ Tell
5 Nguyen Binh Khiem (at the zoo)
Tel. 08/8 29 88 69
For those who would like to take a break from noodles and rice, typical German and Swiss cuisine in a pleasant, tranquil eatery with garden.

⑤ Thanh Nien
11 Nguyen Van Chiem
Tel. 08/8 21 59 09
daily 7am–10.30pm
Lovely open-air location with live band, air-conditioned rooms, Vietnamese and vegetarian dishes.

⑥ Chu Bar
158 Dong Khoi
Tel. 08/8 21 39 07
6pm to midnight all week
Establishment with modern flair overlooking Dong Khoi Street. A place to enjoy a good wine or cappuccino, also with smaller dishes on the menu.

⑦ Quan An Ngon
138 Nam Ky Khoi Nghia, Quan Mot
Tel. 08/8 25 71 79
The queue outside indicates that this lively and noisy eatery has become quite an institution. Patrons can see a wide variety of very tasty dishes being prepared.

▶ Inexpensive

⑧ Café Brodard

131 Dong Khoi
Tel. 08/8 21 39 66
daily 6.30am–10.30pm
Legendary café bar and restaurant with opulent breakfasts. Cakes a speciality of the house, there is also ice cream and an extensive wine list.

⑨ Canh Buom

127 Pasteur Street
Tel. 08/8 22 20 00
daily 10am–11pm
How about some wild boar, turtle or salmon? »Normal« dishes are also on the menu in this popular Vietnamese al fresco restaurant, e.g. fiery seafood curry (lau cari hai san) for two to three people. Send back the hors d'oeuvres if not ordered, as they will otherwise be charged to the bill.

⑩ Lang Nuon Nam Bo

209 Cach Mang Tam
Speciality of the house is bo tung xeo – »execution in slices«. This is, in fact, a Vietnamese barbecue: thin slices of marinated beef fried with ginger and onion.

⑪ Dong Du Restaurant

57 Dong Du
Tel. 08/8 29 50 45
daily 8am–2pm, 5pm–10pm
Excellent Vietnamese and French cuisine. Pleasant atmosphere with »tropical rain«, friendly service and discreet music.

⑫ Pho 2000

Phan Chu Trinh
Tel. 08/8 21 27 88
daily 6am to midnight
Soup kitchen where in the year 2000 Bill Clinton ate what was probably his first bowl of pho.

ENTERTAINMENT

Saigon Saigon Bar

19 Lam Son Square (Caravelle Hotel)
Tel. 08/8 23 49 99
Live music daily from 11pm
When the house band reel off pop and rock classics at the Caravelle roof bar on the tenth floor, the five-star priced cocktail (inevitably called »Good morning Vietnam«) tastes a great deal better.

Sax n'Art

28 Le Loi
Tel. 08/8 21 84 72
daily 6pm to midnight and later
Jazz club under the auspices of Vietnam's leading saxophonist Tran Manh Tuan: very much the place to be, with lively activity on two floors, featuring many well-known local bands and vocalists.

Baedeker recommendation

Q Bar

7 Lam Son Square (in the Municipal Theatre opposite the Caravelle)
Tel. 08/8 23 34 79
daily 6pm to midnight and later
Legendary bar in the right wing of the Municipal Theatre: earthy, vaulted cellar, chic and cool crowd, good cocktails, often live music. The adjacent Qucina bar is also worth a visit.

WHERE TO STAY

▶ Luxury

① Rex Hotel

141 Nguyen Hue
Tel. 08/8 29 60 43 and 8 29 21 85,
Fax 8 29 65 36
www.rexhotelvietnam.com
rexhotel@hcm.vnn.vn
Luxurious establishment (227 rooms) with an exhaustive range of services:

beauty salon, massage, acupuncture, tailor, gift shop, swimming pool and much more. The rooftop terrace is also an attraction for non-residents – taking a drink amongst small trees and sculptures to the sound of birdsong from bamboo cages.

② *Hotel Majestic*
1 Dong Khoi
Tel. 08/8 29 55 17, fax 8 29 55 10
www.majesticsaigon.com.vn
majestic@majesticsaigon.com.vn
On the promenade of the Saigon River. One of the city's most beautiful hotels (175 rooms), some rooms rather dingy and noisy (onto Dong Khoi). A drink on the attractive rooftop terrace overlooking the river on a warm summer's evening is something that can be savoured by residents and non-residents alike.

③ *Caravelle Hotel*
19 Lam Son Square (next to the Municipal Theatre)
Tel. 08/8 23 49 99, fax 8 24 39 99
www.caravellehotel.com
rsvn@caravellehotel.vnn.vn
Renovated five-star tower block from the 1960s, equipped with every luxury, several restaurants, nice pool, spa & fitness centre.

④ *Omni Saigon Hotel*
253 Nguyen Van Troi, Phu Nuan Bez.
Tel. 08/8 44 92 22, fax 8 44 91 98
www.omnisaigonhotel.com
info@omnisaigonhotel.com
One of the city's best hotels, a short distance outside the centre.

Baedeker recommendation

⑤ *Continental Hotel*
132–134 Dong Khoi
Tel. 08/8 29 92 01
Fax 8 29 09 36
www.continental-saigon.com
Colonial classic from the year 1880: bask in the historical surroundings where Graham Greene and Somerset Maugham were residents, amongst precious wood and marble (e.g. Greene's room 214). The »regular« rooms are no less attractive (and are somewhat cheaper), some with a tranquil view of the garden. Marvellous bar oasis under the frangipani trees in the courtyard.

▶ Mid-range
⑥ *Kim Do Royal City Hotel*
133 Nguyen Hue Avenue
Tel. 08/8 21 59 14, fax 8 21 59 13
www.kimdohotel.com
kimdohotel@fmail.vnn.vn
In the heart of the city, comfortable and friendly. Lovely view of Saigon life from the terrace restaurant on the 4th floor.

⑦ *Duxton Hotel Saigon*
63 Nguyen Hue
Tel. 08/8 22 29 99, fax 8 24 18 88
www.duxton.com
enquires@saigon.duxton.com.vn
Chic, centrally located business hotel
with 200 rooms, Japanese and American grill restaurant, spa, karaoke,
pool.

⑧ *Asian Hotel*
150 Dong Khoi
Tel. 08/8 29 69 79, fax 8 29 74 33
asianhotel@hcm.fpt.vn
Right at the centre of activity: small,
familial hotel with pleasant rooms of
varying size (some with balcony), top
floor with terrace offering a wide, airy,
view of the proceedings below.

► **Budget**
⑨ *Liberty 1 (Que Huong) Hotel*
167 Hai Ba Trung
Tel. 08/8 29 41 27, fax 8 29 09 19
www.libertyhotels.com.vn
quehuong1@quehuonghotel.com.vn

Good hostel with 50 rooms, run by the
Liberty chain in the quiet diplomatic
and residential district.

⑩ *Saigon Boutique Hotel*
57 Pham Viet Canh
Tel. 08/8 33 05 40
Fax 8 32 24 70
www.saigonboutiquehotel.com
info@saigonboutiquehotel.com
Only 20 modern, variable rooms, on
four floors. Small business centre and
adjoining art gallery with »Bar 57«.

⑪ *Le Le Hotel*
171 Pham Ngu Lao
Tel. 08/8 36 86 86
Fax 8 36 87 87
www.vngold.com/hcm/lelehotel
lelehotel@hcm.fpt.vn
Comfort in backpacker territory: 40
bright and attractive rooms are fine,
with balcony and minibar (hot showers, air-conditioning or fan, satellite
television, telephone).

Colonial Saigon (Centre)

The French bequeathed a rich architectural legacy to Saigon, inspiring 19th-century visitors to describe it as the **»Paris of the East«**.
Some of the colonial structures in today's tourist centre (District 1 in particular), such as the town hall and the cathedral, are among the city's genuine landmarks. The remaining villas still convey something of their Mediterranean flair, even though they are mirrored in the neighbouring tower blocks. All of the main tourist sites in the centre of Saigon are less than half an hour's walk from the cathedral.

Colonial villas and mirrored modern buildings

Hôtel de Ville and Its Surroundings

The Hôtel de Ville is one of the main attractions in Saigon and pulls in innumerable visitors – tourists by day and Saigon locals by night.
Located at the northern end of Nguyen Hue Boulevard, this marvellous example of **French colonial architecture**, in yellow and white with a red tiled roof, was built between the years of 1901 and 1908.
Columns, ornate gables, balconies and decorative stucco, along with

★
Hôtel de Ville (town hall)

One of the main attractions: the richly decorated town hall

a small bell tower, all lend the official building a dignified air. Some visitors may find it a little strange that this Baroque house, of all places, houses the **People's Committee** of the city. Lined with bonsai trees, the square in front of the Hôtel de Ville features Ho Chi Minh (►Baedeker Special p.265) with a child on his lap – Uncle Ho thus poses patiently for photographs with hundreds of Vietnamese every evening. A seemingly endless stream of mopeds, above all at weekends, flows through the neighbouring boulevards. Parents stroll across the square with their spruced up little ones, buying them all manner of tooting toys, balloons and plastic pistols. But beware: pickpockets also tend to make up the numbers in this bustling scene.

✱ Rex Hotel

The building which houses the Rex Hotel today – identified by the gold crown twinkling on its rooftop – has been standing at one of Saigon's major crossroads (on the corner of Nguyen Hue/Le Loi) for around four decades. The hotel enjoys a legendary reputation, with the rooftop terrace, adorned with kitsch accessoires, a **popular meeting place** for tourists and rich Saigonese. Bonsai trees draped with fairy lights, bamboo cages with birds in full song, elephant sculptures and even a miniature replica of the One Pillar Pagoda compete for attention. During the Vietnam War, the US Army used the banqueting hall for its press conferences. At 5pm each afternoon, the officers of the JUSPAO (Joint United States Public Affairs Office) would invite war reporters from all over the world to take note of the latest successes of their war effort. Graham Greene describes the events of just such a press conference in his novel *The Quiet American*.

Thendayyutthapani Temple

One block south of the Rex Hotel stands Thendayyutthapani Temple, the most beautiful of the three Hindu temples of Saigon (entrance: 66 Ton That Thiep). Colourful tiles and lamps decorate the interior, with pictures of Hindu gods, Nehru and Gandhi adorning the walls. To the right of the sanctuary, a staircase leads up to the roof terrace, crowned by a tower featuring intricately sculpted statues of the gods.

Along Dong Khoi Boulevard

The famous Dong Khoi Boulevard – once known as Rue Catinat, the **elegant strollers' promenade** bordered by splendid colonial houses and lined with tamarinds, street cafés and shops, stretches from Notre Dame Cathedral to the bank of the. In spite of all the construction work going on, and the many hawkers on the street, its charm can still be sensed today.

Dong Khoi Boulevard (formerly Rue Catinat)

At the northern end of Dong Khoi stands the Cathedral of Notre Dame. Saigon's interesting Christian place of worship is hard to miss, rising as it does from a large square at the centre of a busy roundabout. This Neo-Romanesque church was built from reddish bricks in 1880. Its two quadratic towers in Neo-Gothic style dominated the town's skyline for many years. Today they stand in the shadow of plate-glass office blocks and the adjacent Diamond Plaza shopping centre. The cathedral is open to visitors on weekdays from 7am to 11am and 3pm to 4pm. It is worth inspecting the **altar** with blue

✱ Notre Dame Cathedral

The red-brick cathedral rises up amongst mirror glass tower blocks

Ave Maria lettering and gloriole – both in neon! Notre Dame Cathedral is very popular with Vietnamese Catholics, hence the many wedding parties encountered here.

Paris Commune Square

A statue of the Virgin Mary graces the square in front of the cathedral (Paris Commune Square). Saigonese locals gather here of an evening for a chat and a snack. Stalls selling toy helicopters and cars made from old drinks cans can be found amongst the refreshments and postcard stands.

Central Post Office

Another building from the colonial era stands opposite the cathedral. The Central Post Office (1886–91) boasts an impressive **dome-shaped roof** with cast-iron supports. The high-ceilinged hall is decorated with copious glass, old maps, ceiling fans and chandeliers. An outsized portrait of Ho Chi Minh watches over the nostalgic postal business in the refurbished hall (opening times: daily 6.30am–9.30pm).

Hotel Continental

The Hotel Continental (Lam Son Square, 132–143 Dong Khoi) found fame through Graham Greene's ***The Quiet American*** (►Literature). His fictional characters sat at the veranda bar on the kerb to discuss the latest events of war, watching Franco-Vietnamese life come and go, admiring the charming ladies in their long, slit ao dais. It was here that, in the early 1950s, the hero of the novel, the British journalist Fowler first met the »quiet American« and secret agent Pyle, who would poach his Vietnamese girl.

Vaulted ceiling in the main post office

Just a few steps further on is the **Municipal Theatre**, a striking white building standing between two hotels steeped in tradition, the Continental and Caravelle.

Designed by the French architect Ferré as an opera house, it was festively inaugurated in 1899. Up until 1975 the South Vietnamese National Assembly sat here. Under the Communists, it reverted to a municipal theatre in 1976. Today, both Vietnamese and Western pieces are performed in the beautiful building, and fashion shows and pop concerts are also staged here.

On the Banks of the Saigon River

The warrior Tran Hung Dao, who defeated the Mongolians under Kublai Khan is remembered with a statue standing tall over Me Linh Square, gazing peacefully into the distance across the Saigon River. Early in the morning, mostly elderly men and women can be seen practising their **Tai Chi exercises** along the river promenade. After sunset in the evenings, the Saigonese come here to chat with one another, drink green tea, play or read the newspaper. Couples cuddle up in the miniscule deck chairs. Some stroll through the mild evening air in glittering outfits, others wear comfortable silk pyjama suits. The restaurant boats are moored in a row behind colourful chains of lights on the quay, and love songs are crooned on board.

History lesson at the Ho Chi Minh Museum

✴
River promenade (Bach Dang/Ton Duc Thang)

At the southern end of the street along the river bank, a bridge crosses the water to the Ho Chi Minh Museum. Erected in 1861–62, the administrative building was once the seat of the French Shipping Company. It was here that, on 5 June 1911, a young man by the name of Nguyen Tat Thanh boarded the ship that would take him around the world. Approximately three decades later, he returned to his homelands and ultimately became the unanimously revered President Ho Chi Minh (▶Baedeker Special p.265).

The five exhibition rooms contain many photographs, documents, newspaper articles, models, sculptures and everyday personal possessions of Ho Chi Minh on two floors; on display in Room 4, for example, are articles of Ho Chi Minh's clothing, his rusty typewriter and a walking stick. Activity in the harbour can be well observed from the terrace or the small café in the courtyard.

Ho Chi Minh Museum
🕐
Opening hours:
Tue–Sun
7.30am–11.30am,
1.30pm–4.30pm

The striking clock tower of Ben Thanh Market by night

Ben Thanh Market and Its Surroundings

Ben Thanh Market is situated at the opposite end of Le Loi, in the southwest of the city centre. The market hall is characterized by its distinctive clock tower, a veritable emblem of the city. The halls were built on the traditional market square in 1914. Both the market hall and the square out front, with its lively and chaotic roundabout, have sadly become a popular meeting place for **pickpockets**, so take care in the market crowds!

Art Museum The Art Museum (Bao Thang My Thuat, 97A Pho Duc Chinh) is housed in a quite lovely cream-coloured building. One of the most interesting national collections can be seen here: from Oc Eo culture via works of Socialist Realism to contemporary trends. Some works ⏲ are available for purchase. The garden attached is very attractive (opening times: Tue–Sun 7.30am–11.30am and 1.30pm–4.30pm).

Reunification Palace and Its Surroundings

★
Reunification Palace (Thong Nhat) West of the cathedral, all roads lead to Reunification Palace (visitors' entrance: 106 Nguyen Du Street). In complete contrast to the magnificent colonial architecture, the three storeys of Reunification Palace, which served as presidential residence until 1975, seem rather sober. The modern building was constructed in 1966, designed by the Vietnamese architect Ngo Viet Thu. Previously, in 1868, the

Norodom Palace had been erected on this site for the French Governor General. In the 1950s the **dictator Ngo Dinh Diem** lived in and ruled from the colonial building with his family. On 27 February 1962, the structure was badly damaged by bombs, as rebel soldiers of the South Vietnamese Army attacked the presidential residence from the air. Diem survived the offensive and had the ruins demolished. Four years later, the new, larger building, with over 100 rooms and a helicopter pad on the roof, was opened. It was to become the centre of the battle for Saigon: on the morning of 30 April 1975, viewers around the world were able to witness on television how a North Vietnamese T-54 tank crushed the iron gate and Communist soldiers occupied the building. On the roof, the flag of the Democratic Republic of Vietnam was hoisted. In the winter that followed, the negotiations for reunification were held here – hence the present name. Inside, the style is dominated by a Western, functional aesthetic with cavernous assembly and conference rooms. The banqueting halls, however, are rich in pomp. On the first floor, the former reception rooms and living quarters of the president can be found. Also open to visitors are ballrooms, a small cinema and countless rooms with red carpets and flowing curtains, leather armchairs and antique chairs. The cellar leads on to subterranean **escape tunnels** and a form of command centre. As well as being a museum, the palace also hosts international congresses and receptions.

⏱ Opening hours:
7.30am–11.30am,
1pm–4pm daily

★ ★
**War Remnants
Museum**

The former »Museum of American War Crimes« (28 Vo Van Tan Street) awaits with many facts and figures, documentation and photographs from the Vietnam War. A few years ago, the place was renamed the War Remnants Museum so that the many visiting US veterans did not feel insulted. The museum was opened as early as September 1975 and expanded to incorporate six exhibition rooms and an open space with tanks, war planes and gun defences from the Americans. Visitors should steel themselves to witness images (largely by US photographers) illustrating all conceivable **horrors of war**.

The first two rooms, entitled »Historic Truths« and »War Victims« contain the bulk of the horrific war images, e.g. from ► My Lai, where, on 16 March 1968, a total of 504 villagers were shot dead. Display boards also describe the struggle for recogni-

Vietnam War relic

Opening hours:
7.30am–11.35am
and
1.30pm–4.30pm
daily

tion of US veterans as »Agent Orange victims« in the USA. Foetuses deformed by the chemical agent are conserved in preserving jars which, until just a few years ago, were stored in a Saigon hospital. Various weapons can be seen in the third room, while the final room is dedicated to Vietnamese war heroes. At the end of the site, an iron door set in a mighty wall leads the way to an exhibition concerning the **Con Dao Island Prison** (► Vung Tau). In three sections of the building, models of the so-called »tiger cages« (cells measuring 2.7m/9ft x 1.5m/5ft x 3m/10ft), some instruments of torture and a guillotine from French colonial times can be inspected. The guillotine was used as a means of execution as late as the year 1960. Souvenir shops sell war memorabilia (ostensibly genuine cigarette lighters, watches, shell cases) and all manner of handicrafts. Diagonally opposite, a water puppet theatre awaits an audience.

Xa Loi Pagoda

Xa Loi Pagoda, a modern Buddhist structure from the year 1956, is of interest primarily for its historical significance. In the early 1960s, the sanctuary (89 Ba Huyen Thanh Quan Street, close to Dien Bien Phu Street) was seen as the **centre of the resistance** against the dictatorial president Ngo Dinh Diem.

A single Buddha dominates the empty space of Xa Loi Pagoda, a sanctuary of Hinayana Buddhism

Some 400 Buddhist monks and nuns congregated here to find sanctuary from the reprisals of his regime. Some even went as far as self-immolation by burning to underline their protest, among them the monk Thich Quang Duc (►Famous People), to whom a monument now stands, close to the pagoda at the crossroads of Nguyen Dinh Chieu/Cach Mang Thang Tam Street.

Opening hours: daily 7am–11am and 2pm–5pm

The pictures of his spectacular act of desperation were seen all over the globe and weakened the reputation of the Catholic president considerably. Finally, in August 1963, soldiers stormed Xa Loi Pagoda, arresting the monks and nuns. Today the temple is a popular destination for Buddhist

? DID YOU KNOW ...?

- The swastika symbol seen on Xa Loi Pagoda is often encountered in Vietnam and originated as a sign of good fortune in Indian Buddhism.

Vietnamese, especially at weekends and on holidays. Many traders proffer their incense sticks, flower garlands and other devotional objects, whilst birdsong and drums blend in with Buddhist chants.

At the entrance to the pagoda, an impressive tower of seven storeys reaches skywards. On the right-hand side of the site, religious believers with incense sticks bow before a white Quan Am statue. The building with a double roof is typical of real socialist design. Its interior is dominated by a roughly 5m/16ft-high **golden Sakyamuni Buddha**, meditating on a lotus pedestal. On the walls of the great hall, 14 paintings depict important stages in the life of the Enlightened One (a board to the right of the entrance explains the numbered paintings in English, to the left in French). Behind the statue of Buddha to the left is a shrine dedicated to Thich Quang Duc and the other monks who set themselves alight. He is portrayed in the figure to the left, holding pearls.

Along Le Duan Boulevard

At the end of Le Duan Boulevard is the gateway to Saigon Zoo and Botanical Gardens. Swiftly leaving behind the clatter of mopeds and the accompanying exhaust fumes on the busy streets, visitors can immerse themselves in a world of peace and quiet, where the air is filled with the aroma of freshly cut grass and frangipani blossom. Created by the Frenchmen Germain and Pierre in the year 1864, the gardens still hold great charm for young couples and anyone who enjoys a stroll. There is a particularly fine **orchid collection**. Big cats and elephants as well as many birds can be seen in the enclosures and cages, some of which are rather cramped. Of particular note are the **Komodo dragons**, a present from the Indonesian government. Fairground stalls and children's roundabouts are also to be found on the same grounds.

★ **Zoo/Botanical Gardens**
Opening hours: daily 7am–8pm

Within the walls of the Botanical Gardens stands the city's History Museum, founded in 1929. It is well worth investigating this beauti-

★★ **History Museum**

Opening hours:
Mon–Sun
8am–11am,
1.30pm–4pm

ful building as it boasts a wealth of interesting exhibits, including a Dong Son drum from the Bronze Age.

In rooms 11 to 14 are a number of well-preserved artefacts excavated from the Mekong delta and the environs of Saigon. In Room 7, an almost 4m/13ft-high replica of the famous »Lady Buddha with A Thousand Arms« (Quan Am, ►p.1) from But Thap Pagoda is especially noteworthy. Also on display in the museum are Buddha statues from various eras and parts of Asia, along with clothes and furniture from the Nguyen dynasty. Costumes and everyday articles of minority peoples from southern Vietnam can be admired in Room 15.

Room 11 leads to the little **water puppet theatre**, where performances are held during the day as soon as five spectators have taken their seats. The plays star legendary creatures such as dragons, lions, turtles and phoenixes. Three or four puppeteers stand behind the stage up to their waists in water and move the figures on long bamboo sticks. There is a good chance that those sitting in the front row will get wet (►Baedeker Special p.358).

✔ DON'T MISS

- Room 7 with ceramics from the Le dynasty (15th–17th century)
- Room 8 with model ships, items of clothing and instruments from the Tay Son dynasty (18th to early 19th century)
- Room 10 with ceramic vases from various Asian countries

The streets of Cholon are crowded during New Year's celebrations

Cholon Map

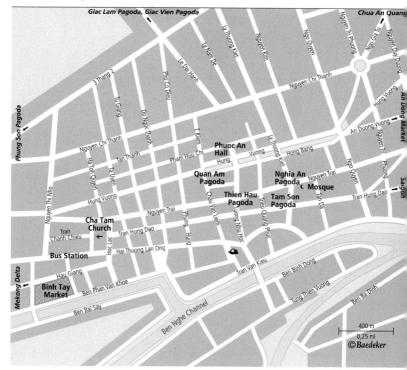

Cholon (Chinese Quarter)

The oldest surviving part of Saigon is Cholon in the southwest of the city, home to the descendants of the Chinese who fled here from Southern China some 300 years ago. The pavements, markets and narrow alleyways are busy with traders, but today the air is no longer laced with the sweet smell of opium. As in days of old, red strips of paper with Chinese characters still hang in the doorways of the houses – talismans from a recent visit to the temple. On the main streets, meanwhile, there are few reminders that this is the exotic Chinese district. The best way to get to know the area is by straying into the side streets. Exotic aromas emanate from the markets, which seem to vibrate with human activity and noise. Most of Saigon's more than **180 pagodas and temples** can be found in Cholon, many of them on Nguyen Trai Street. A visit to one is an absolute must: join the religious followers and enter a world of idiosyncratic deities, colourful adornments and coils of smouldering incense.

✴ Thien Hau Pagoda (Chua Ba)

The »Temple of the Heavenly Lady« was constructed some time between the end of the 18th and middle of the 19th century, a more exact date has not been determined. It was built by the Chinese and is dedicated to the Goddess of the Sea. Restoration work has been carried out on several occasions on this popular Taoist place of worship at 710 Nguyen Trai Street. The picturesque temple is above all worth visiting for its **elaborate façades and ornate roof** with coloured ceramic figures. The structure is typical of South Chinese temple architecture.

The most beautiful pagoda in Cholon

⊙ Opening hours: daily 6am–5.30pm

In the 17th century, many Chinese sought to escape the warring factions of the Ming and Qing dynasties, fleeing to Vietnam by boat and placing their trust in the goddess to protect them from sea monsters, storms and pirates. Having arrived safely, they built this richly decorated temple in her honour.

Thien Hau can be seen on a mural above the main entrance. Colourful mandarins in headdresses stand guard on both sides. In the first courtyard, numerous marble tablets and red strips of paper with Chinese characters hang along the walls – these are the names of donors, sometimes with the amount donated (►see also p.71). The fruits of the many good deeds hangs above the pieces of paper: pictures of buildings financed by the donations, including a clinic and a school. From this atrium it is possible to study the many colourful figures along the **roof crest** more closely: the scholars, guards, kings and princesses, dragons and witches relate stories from Chinese legend. It looks something like a puppet theatre – yet so realistic, that they might jump to life at any moment.

> **? DID YOU KNOW …?**
>
> ■ According to legend, the girl Thien Hau lived around 1000 years ago in the Chinese province of Fujian. One day, she asked the rich owners and captains of the large fishing vessels if she might accompany them out to sea. As they refused her request, she had to make do with a small boat. A sudden storm spared the girl, whilst all other boats which had set out perished. Since then, Thien Hau has been revered as the patron saint of seafarers and fishermen.

✴ **First courtyard**

In the second courtyard, horned devils can be seen on the edge of the roof. Huge coils of incense, made from sandalwood and leaves of the Kapok tree, permeate the air with their smoke: they burn for between two weeks and six months – the longer the better, for the smoke is said to carry the wishes on the red slips of paper to the heavenly goddess Thien Hau. In the small ovens in the courtyard, relatives send symbolic paper gifts to their dead in the afterlife: mon-

✴ **Second courtyard**

← *As long as the incense spirals in Thien Hau Pagoda burn, the smoke carries messages to the gods and departed ancestors*

Scenes from legend and courtly life adorn the roofs

ey or clothing such as shoes or hats, cars and houses made of paper are burned. Incense sticks are also lit in their memory in bronze basins.

Sanctuary

The main shrine features three gold-painted statues of Thien Hau in embroidered garb; the central figure is carried through the streets during a procession in the third lunar month. The shrine to the left is worthy of attention, with the **Goddess of Fertility, Kim Hua**. Married couples often pay homage to her, praying for a child. A small bed stands on the altar complete with a curtain, to help them in their wish – purely in symbolic fashion, of course. A wooden model ship in the corner serves as a reminder of Thien Hau's adventure at sea.

Further rooms

On the left hand side is a bronze bell, 200 years old, which is struck every time a donation is made. Temple employees sit behind a counter and paint the wishes of believers onto coloured strips of paper – these are then hung in the doorways of people's homes. In the rooms to the rear and to the sides, more gods and heroes can be seen, including General Quan Cong and the god of prosperity and happiness Than Tai. Particularly on holidays, large numbers of believers stream into the temple. On the 23rd day of the third lunar month, the annual procession is accompanied by Cantonese singing and dancing.

What to See around Nguyen Trai Street

Nghia An Hoi Quan Temple (Chua Ong)

🕐

Opening hours: daily 6am–6pm

The Nghia An Hoi Quan Temple was constructed in 1840 in honour of the legendary General Quan Cong, who was worshipped like a god. The courageous **hero of the »Three Kingdoms«** is revered for his bravery, sense of justice and his wisdom. The structure of the sanctuary recalls that of the temple described above; with two green courtyards before the main altar.

A magnificently carved wooden boat catches the eye above the entrance. This is said to be the vessel with which the General of China made the journey to Vietnam. A 3m/10ft-high statue of the general stands on the main altar in a glass case. He is flanked by his fellow warriors, generals Chau Xuong and Quan Binh. In the shrine to the right is a statue of the Goddess of the Sea, Thien Hau, and to the left squats the God of Prosperity, Than Tai. Every year, **several festivals** take place in honour of Quan Cong, for example on 24 June and the 15th day of the first lunar month.

In front of Quan Am Pagoda (12 Lao Tu Street) hordes of hawkers await customers who purchase incense sticks or set birds free from their cages to boost their karma. It is worth taking a moment to observe the exterior of the sanctuary more carefully. The roofs are adorned with scenes depicting small figures, houses and temples. Two fierce-looking guards and two stone lions watch over the entrance to the pagoda to ward off evil spirits. Gilded panels depict scenes of courtly life with dancers, musicians and chess players. When the community of Fujian built the place of worship some 100 years ago, it was dedicated to Quan Am, yet it is the Goddess of Heaven (A Pho) whose statue stands in front of the main altar. The open courtyard behind it contains many deities and idols, including Quan Am, clad in white, who attracts many believers. In a small room to the right, the calligraphers can be seen at work, inscribing the red prayer slips and **contribution receipts**.

✱
Quan Am
Pagoda

✱ Binh Tay Market (Cho Binh Tay)

All kinds of market stalls stand alongside each other on the two levels of Binh Tay Market, its courtyard and the surrounding alleyways. Ceramic pots and plastic bowls on one corner, colourful sweets and dried fish piled up on the next. Virtually everything the heart desires can be found here. The traders are used to tourists, who can browse undisturbed. It is nevertheless advisable to keep a firm grip on one's personal possessions! The market is located on Thap Muoi Street in the west of Cholon.

> **? DID YOU KNOW …?**
>
> ■ …that superstition still plays an important role in the healing power of substances and animal extracts in Vietnam? Boiled monkey brain for a healthy life, tiger penis for potency, rhinoceros horn against nosebleeds, with delicacies such as snake meat, frogs and tiger wine regular components of the Asian diet.

In Hai Thuong Lan Ong Street, south of Cha Tam Church, there are shops specializing in traditional **Vietnamese medicine**. The manifold aromas wafting through the air betray their location. Roots and leaves are laid out to dry on the street, whilst, in the shadowy shops, old men and women weigh powder and mix ingredients in mortars.

Sanctuaries in the North and West of the City

✳
Pagoda and temple tours

Adding together all the pagodas, temples, monasteries, mosques, Hindu shrines and other religious centres, there are in the region of **one thousand places of worship** in Saigon. Some of the most noteworthy examples can be found to the north and west of the centre, albeit fairly far apart. The taxi drivers, motorbike taxis and cyclos are, however, used to dealing with foreign tourists in Saigon and have maps of the town with sightseeing highlights clearly marked, enabling visitors to plan their own itinerary.

✳ ✳ Jade Emperor Pagoda and Its Surroundings

Buddhist-Taoist pagoda

The magnificent Phuoc Hai Tu Temple is also known as Chua Ngoc Hoang (Jade Emperor Pagoda), the Vietnamese name for the Jade Emperor. He is one of the most revered figures of Taoist philosophy, ranking higher than all the mythological saints and kings. Ngoc Hoang is worshipped as **ruler of the heavens**. He and his ministers are said to be able to decide the fates of life and death, victory or defeat.

The Taoist shrine is reached via an attractive courtyard

Saigon Jade Emperor Pagoda

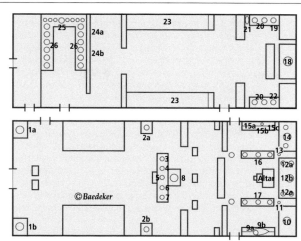

©Baedeker

1a	Tho Than (Tho Dia, God of Earth)	9a	Dai Minh Vuong Quang (riding a phoenix)
1b	Mon Quan (God of the Gate)	9b	Die Tien Nhan (god persons)
2a	General who defeated the White Tiger	10	Phat Mau Chuan De (mother of the five Buddhas of the cardinal directions)
2b	General who defeated the Green Dragon	11	Sun God
3	Phat Mau Chuan De (mother of the five Buddhas of the cardinal directions)	12a	Tu Dai Kim Cuong (the »Four Big Diamonds«)
		12b	Ngoc Hoang (Jade Emperor)
4	Diang Vang Vuong Bo Tat (God of Hell)	13	Goddess of the Moon
5	Sakyamuni (Buddha of the Past)	14	Ong Bac De (reincarnation of the Jade Emperor)
6	Quan Am (Goddess of Mercy)	15a	Thien Loi's guardians (above)
7	Thich Ca Buddha (bas-relief)	15b	Thien Loi (God of Lightning)
8	Duoc Su Buddha (glass case)	15c	Military commander of Ong Bac De (below)

16	Bac Dau (God of the Northern Polar Star and Longevity)
17	Nam Tao (God of the Southern Polar Star and Happiness)
18	Thang Hoang (Chief of Hell)
19	Am Quan (God of Yin)
20	Thuong Thien Phat Ac
21	Thanh Hoang's Red Horse
22	Duong Quan (God of Yang)
23	Depictions of Hell
24a	Dia Tang Vuong Bo Tat (King of Hell)
24b	Thi Kinh (Protector of Mother and Child)
25	Kim Hoa Thanh Mau (Chief of All Women)
26	Figures of 12 women

The well-frequented temple (73 Mai Thi Luu Street) comprises two buildings standing next to each other. It was built by Chinese from the province of Guangdong in the late 19th century and consecrated in a celebration in the year 1906. Unremarkable from the outside, it is, in fact, a masterpiece of Chinese temple architecture, featuring impressive wood carvings, sculptures and colours. The pagoda has been renovated several times, the most recent being in 1985. Inside, innumerable Taoist deities and Buddhist figures stand in unified splendour. Visitors to this temple are allowed to leave their shoes on, but should step over, not on, the high doorsill.

Opening hours: daily 6am–6pm, the monks pray between 4pm and 5pm. The pagoda festival takes place on the 9th and 10th day of the new year following the Tet Festival.

Entrance area ► In the centre and on the right of the parvis, **turtles** swim in small ponds, donated by believers. The Vietnamese and Chinese worship the turtle as a symbol of a long life. Offering the gift of a turtle to a temple promises a long and happy existence. A small guardhouse, with an impressive bronze cauldron for incense sticks, stands immediately in front of the temple entrance. In the building itself, visitors first pass the guardhouses and shrines of the two gods of the earth (left) and the gate (right), followed by devotional stands. At the entrance to the actual temple, two colossal generals of the Jade Emperor stand guard: on the left, a white tiger lies beneath one general (Bach Ho), on the right another heavenly general strikes a victory pose on a green dragon (Thang Long). The next small altar is decorated with various Buddhist figurines and chains of lights. Inside a display case in the centre sits a Sakyamuni Buddha made from sandalwood. To the left stands the Goddess of Mercy **Quan Am with 18 arms**, also worshipped as a Bodhisattva. In her hands she holds a shell, the book of Buddhist teaching, a chalice and a willow branch, various weapons such as a sword and hatchet, a chain and the Wheel of Dharma.

Main altar ► Beyond this space is the main altar with the Jade Emperor resplendent in his glittering robes. Smoke wafts through the room and a bell or drum is sounded for each oblation. In front of the altar, donations are piled up, e.g. fruit and incense sticks or a sack of rice for the monks who live here. The centrepiece of the shrine is the **figure of the Jade Emperor**, made from papier maché and painted gold. He is joined on both sides by his four guards and students. Six life-size figures stand in line in front of him, with the heavenly gods Nam Tao (God of the Southern Polar Star, to the right) and Bac Dau (God of the Northern Polar Star, to the left) closest to him – these two determine the fate of the living and dead. In the altar case to the right of the Jade Emperor is the 18-armed Phat Mau Chuan De with three faces. To the left is another of the Jade Emperor's aides: Ong Bac De, standing on a turtle with a snake in his hands. Further heavenly figures and heroes are lined up on the walls. A dark wooden frame with magnificent animals and mythological scenes surrounds the altar.

Further rooms In a small room on the left, usually thick with smoke, visitors can catch **a glimpse of hell** and the fate of the departed – the gods who reside here reward good deeds and punish evil acts. Behind the altar, which believers or the bereaved sometimes circle in a clockwise direction, the Chief of Hell, Thang Hoang, with his red wooden horse, the Gods of Yin (female) and Yang (male) and mandarins are gathered. To the far left in white robes and headdress sits the God of Wealth, Than Tai, with another collection box – business people commonly turn to him in the hope of his blessing and a good income.

Ten wooden panels along the walls depict the innumerable torments of hell for those whose karma was bad. The graphic **torture scenes**

The Jade Emperor flanked by his guards and students

hauntingly bring home to believers the fate which then awaits them. Ten Judges of Hell watch over the gruesome representations. On the rear wall opposite the altar, the faithful can clutch at hope once again, for it is here that Thi Kinh (one manifestation of Quan Am) offers her blessing and the chance of reincarnation. The figure on the wooden panel is shown holding a baby, as she is also seen as the patron of mothers and children.

On the other side is a tiny room, often filled with acrid smoke, containing twelve ceramic figurines, each carrying a baby. They represent the heavenly women and twelve zodiac signs of the Chinese lunar calendar. Most of those who come to pray here are parents or childless couples. Furthermore, each figure clad in silk exemplifies a positive or negative characteristic of mankind.

Returning to the main altar chamber, a narrow corridor on the other side points the way to another room containing photographs of the two founders of the temple and another statue of Quan Am. Steps lead up from here to the **balcony**, which provides a view of the colourfully designed roof. Like most Taoist temples and older Vietnamese buildings, it is decorated with green ceramic tiles and the four mythological beasts: dragon, unicorn, phoenix and turtle.

✳ Le Van Duyet Temple

A pleasant, tranquil temple, well worth a visit, lies off the beaten tourist track in the erstwhile rural region of Gia Dinh. The northern district is known today as Binh Thanh. This beautiful old wooden structure was built as a memorial tomb for General Le Van Duyet

Magnificent hero's tomb

⊙ Opening hours: daily 6am–6pm

(126 Dinh Tien Hoang/on the corner of Bach Dang). Le Van Duyet (1763–1832), perceived as a **benevolent regent**, ruled in Gia Dinh province under the Nguyen dynasty. During this period, he allowed foreign ships access to the harbour, granted Catholics religious freedom and consented to the Chinese conducting free trade with Cambodia. As supreme commander, the general also played a decisive role in subduing the Tay Son uprising.

The temple consists of several lofty halls and is exemplary of so-called Khai Dinh architecture. Colourful mosaics and ceramics in the form of small savants, dragons and tigers greet visitors on the outer wall and on the roof. Decorative details and antiques can be discovered in the temple, whilst the rituals of the Vietnamese visitors can discreetly be observed. These include the shaking of numbered wooden sticks from a wooden beaker (for prophetic purposes) and the throwing of wooden blocks, also said to bring luck depending on how they fall. Dragons, phoenixes and unicorns wind their way around carved wooden columns in red and gold and marble pillars which surround the **splendid altars**. Two portraits of the honoured general hang in the middle and rear rooms. Temple servants sound the gong when donations are made, although on some days they can barely be seen through the swathes of incense. Particularly on the anniversary of the general's death, the 1st day of the 8th lunar month, and on the day of the Tet Festival, the temple is overrun with visitors come to honour the dead.

✷ Vinh Nghiem Pagoda

Centre of the Buddhist Community

⊙ Opening hours: daily 6.30am–11.30am and 1.30pm–6.30pm

Built during the Vietnam War (1964–71) Chua Vinh Nghiem is the most important pagoda for the Buddhist community of Saigon. The gables of its wide, sweeping double roof take the form of heads of dragons and phoenixes. With the help of the Japanese, the structure was erected in the style of North Vietnamese pagodas. A 40m/130ft bell tower, seven storeys high, rises up directly at the side of the road leading to the airport (399 Nguyen Van Troi Street), each storey housing a statue of Quan Am. The pagoda tower is only opened to the public on special Buddhist holidays.

Main hall

In the vast main hall, **ceremonies** such as burial services are often held, the participants clad in white and wearing white headbands. The altar is graced with three large statues of Buddha: in the centre, a 6m/20ft-tall Sakyamuni Buddha is flanked by his students Van Thu (the Wise) and Pho Hien (the Talisman). Nine paintings on each of the two side walls relate the story of the La Han, the 18 Bodhisattvas and religious figures. On the shrines to the rear of the hall, countless ancestral tablets are on display, featuring photographs and the dates of birth and death of deceased relatives. To begin with, a picture of the departed is placed on the altar and then replaced by the wooden tablets after 100 days – thus enabling the soul to find peace in the holy rooms. For the recently deceased or on the anniversary of a person's death, complete (meatless) meals are sacrificed before the Quan Am statue, commonly small bowls of rice, vegetables and soup, with tea or water.

★ Giac Lam Pagoda and Its Surroundings

Giac Lam Pagoda (Chua Giac Lam) is not only the oldest sanctuary in Saigon, it is also one of the most beautiful – in spite of the flat building with yellow and red tiles looking fairly ordinary from the outside. To the left of the entrance, on Lac Long Quan Street (north of Cholon), comes the first sighting of the seven-storey **pagoda tower**, which can be climbed via a spiral staircase. It contains symbolic relics of famous monks along with Buddha statues on every level. From the top, visitors can enjoy a wide panoramic view of the vibrant Tan Binh district and Saigon. When the pagoda was built in 1744 by the Chinese-born Ly Thuy

The staged roof of Vinh Nghiem Pagoda

Long, students and poets often wandered amongst the many trees and blossoms on this hill, writing or reciting poetry. In the **garden** within the complex, the tall Bodhi tree to the left was a present from Sri Lanka, brought to Vietnam in 1953. In front of the tree is a white Quan Am statue, standing on a lotus blossom. The Goddess of Mercy holds a bottle of holy water in her hand. Eight abbots were buried in stupas further back.

Oldest sanctuary in Saigon
⊙ Opening hours: daily 6am–noon and 2pm–9pm

When entering the pagoda through the small side entrance, shoes should first be removed. Turn left immediately to reach the **main altar**. Mighty columns fashioned from the wood of jackfruit trees catch the eye straight away. Their intricate carvings on dark palisander wood depict, amongst other things, bats, water lilies and the four mythological creatures – dragon, unicorn, turtle and phoenix. The altar pedestal is encased in a gilded, richly decorated wooden frame and boasts an impressive collection of various wooden Buddhas, Bodhisattvas and guards. On a dais at the centre of the back row is a **Buddha of the Past**, between his favourite students Ananda

Monk at the main altar of the Giac Lam Pagoda

and Kasyapa. Standing in front of them, in the middle row, are the bronze Sakyamuni Buddha and the fat, laughing Di Lac Buddha. Alongside Di Lac, the Jade Emperor is enthroned in bronze. Four Bodhisattvas occupy the front row, flanking another Sakyamuni Buddha. Some of the statues are very old and were brought from Hue to Saigon. On the walls, the 18 wooden La Han and the ten Judges of Hell stand guard. In the left-hand corner of the room, a bronze bell is struck when believers place their wish slip here after making a donation. Often the wishes written on the paper ask for the old or sick to make a healthy recovery, with name, address and age noted for good measure. The right hand corner also contains an interesting feature of traditional Vietnamese belief: the Den Duoc Su – a kind of wooden medicine tree. Believers feed its 49 small oil lamps with kerosene and hang their paper wishes to the tree.

Further statues   Returning to the entrance, coloured portraits of nine monks who lived here come into view. Opposite is a shrine for the 18-armed Quan Am and two more bronze figures. A smaller altar at the back of the room is easily missed, but harbours the oldest Buddha: a wooden Sakyamuni, over 300 years old. Altogether, there are more than 120 Buddha statues in the pagoda.

On the 1st and 15th of the lunar month, the monks living in the temple hold a ceremony in memory of their deceased abbots, whilst on other days they congregate several times a day for prayers. Funeral services are held here frequently – hence the proliferation of benches and tables with tea services.

This pagoda is very similar to Giac Lam Pagoda and is located in the same street – roughly 500m/550yd away, yet somewhat hidden at the edge of a leisure park close to Dam Sen Lake. A dusty path through a residential area leads to this dreamy wooden construction in rural surroundings. Containing some 140 statues, it was built by the monk Hay Tinh in around 1850 on an island at the heart of an area of marshland.

The **main altar** is at the rear of the building: again, Buddha and his various manifestations are to be found here, along with the Buddhist students Ananda and Kasyapa. The ten Princes of Hell look down from the walls, as do the 18 Bodhisattvas and a number of guards. Intricate, artistic carvings in teak adorn the altar, its frame and the columns. In a shrine to the right sits the Goddess of Mercy. Another medicine tree with 49 lamps and wishes written on paper can be found in the corner. A door leads onto an **idyllic garden veranda**, where many bonsai trees stand tall. Splendid stupas mark the final resting places of monks who have died.

★
Giac Vien Pagoda (Chua Ho Dat)

🕐
Opening hours: daily 7am–6pm

A wooden bridge at the eastern extremity of the complex connects the temple to the neighbouring leisure park, which can also be accessed via Hoa Binh Street. The Dam Sen Water Park is one of the largest and most modern leisure parks in Saigon for all ages, with rowing boats, giant water slides, »Space Spiral« and miniature railway. The predominantly Vietnamese visitors can eat or drink at one of the innumerable refreshment stalls, soup kitchens and cafés or at a floating restaurant. The sports centre comprises a tennis court, billiard tables, bowling and fitness centre, whilst the health & beauty club offers a range of relaxing treatments and services including acupuncture and a Jacuzzi (3 Hoa Binh, District 11, Saigon, www.damsenpark.com.vn).

Dam Sen Water Park

🕐
Opening hours: Mon–Fri 9am–6pm, Sat, Sun and holidays 7am–7pm

Around Saigon

Having explored the turbulent streets of Saigon, it is well worth venturing into the beautiful region outside the city. As public transport is relatively slow and unreliable, it is advisable to book a tour or hire a car plus driver. Most head northwest to the infamous tunnels of ►Cu Chi and the exotic temple of the Cao Dai in ►Tay Ninh. ►My Tho is less than a day away, offering a first impression of the ►Mekong delta. Those who might prefer to investigate this unusual landscape by boat should, however, allow several days for the expedition. The bathing resort of ►Vung Tau is also worth a visit, or indeed a stay of one or two nights. Nature lovers should make a point of visiting the Cat Tien National Park on the way to ►Da Lat.

Recommended excursions

The region is famous for its **mangrove forest**, the first Vietnamese biosphere reserve to be recognized by UNESCO. Formed by alluvial sand in the Saigon River, the »island« of Can Gio (approx. 80,000ha/

Can Gio

198,000ac, 55km/34mi southeast of Saigon) is described as the »green lung« of Saigon. The mangrove forest, where the trees stand in the murky water as if on splayed stilts, provides shelter for many varieties of **wildlife**, including 137 types of fish and 31 species of reptile, such as monitor lizards. A colony of some 800 macaques (long-tailed monkeys) lives here, happy to be fed by visitors. Tourists can negotiate the dense mangrove canals by motorboat and find overnight accommodation in a simple »eco« guesthouse or middle-class hotel on the beach (www.cangioresort.com). On the southern side is an approximately 10km/6mi-long, fairly wild and windy beach, the closest to Saigon – refreshment stalls proffer fish and seafood (information: Can Gio Ecotourism, tel. 08/8 74 33 33).

★ ★ Tay Ninh · Cao Dai Temple

D 7

Province: Tay Ninh   **Region:** South

Tay Ninh lies at the foot of Nui Ba Den and is famous for its colourful Cao Dai Temple. This unique religious community has its headquarters in the provincial capital – it is possible to participate in the prayers and rituals of the Caodaists during the four services held from the early morning until late into the night.

In the 1940s the Cao Dai enjoyed great financial and political influence, as well as a private army of some 20,000 men, which engaged in shifting alliances. Due to their **oppositional stance**, the Cao Dai sect were earlier attacked and oppressed by the Catholic President Diem. Nor were the Caodaists able to maintain harmonious relations with the Vietcong or the North Vietnamese – they periodically fought at the side of the South Vietnamese Army against the Communists. When the latter were in power (from 1975), the Caodaists were hindered in practising their faith and their estates were confiscated. Only since the mid-1980s have relations eased with the political incumbents of power.

Cao Dai Holy See   Cao Dai means »High« or »Great Palace« and is synonymous with God. A certain Ngo Van Chieu founded the Cao Dai faith in the year 1926, when God is said to have made his third and final appearance on earth. Thus was created a **potpourri** of the moral teachings of Buddhism, Confucianism, Taoism, Christianity and Islam. Its followers still adhere to occult practices to receive heavenly messages from the universe: mediums are put into a trance and suddenly messages appear in sealed envelopes.

The exterior of the temple with dazzling colours and designs →

The bizarre sect enjoyed its heyday in the 1950s, with, by all accounts, around 4 million Vietnamese members. Today, the total number of followers worldwide is estimated at between one and two million.

✶ ✶ Cao Dai Great Temple

Temple design   The beige structure of the main temple is reminiscent of a Baroque church, featuring two square bell and drum towers at the front. Between the towers, a Di Lac figure (Buddha of the Future) sits upon a throne on the curved roof. The resplendent first lady cardinal crowns the left tower, the first pope of Cao Dai the right. The symbols below stand for evil (left) and the divine (right). A ubiquitous feature, for example above the main entrance and on the altar, is a **huge eye**, emanating bright rays and seeing everything – it symbolizes the Divine Eye. On the side walls of the temple, the eye is surrounded by a triangle; some observers see the symbol which appears on the one dollar bill, whilst Caodaists interpret it as a sign of justice. The numerous illustrations are joined by the talismanic mythological figures: dragon (wisdom), turtle (longevity), unicorn (peace) and phoenix (prosperity). In addition, the Hindu trinity of Brahma, Shiva and Vishnu must not be forgotten.

The **interior** of the sanctuary features a cabinet containing figures and statues from religion and mythology, international literature and politics. A mural by the entrance includes representations of

! *Baedeker* TIP

Ceremony without the crowds
The noon service is often overcrowded with tourists, as day-trippers from Saigon can only reasonably attend this one in the time they have. Therefore it makes sense to plan one or two days for Tay Ninh and attend one of the other services. A visit can be combined with a trip to the tunnels of Cu Chi.

Services at 6am, noon, 6pm and midnight ▶   the French poet Victor Hugo and the Chinese revolutionary Sun Yat Sen as saints, signing a tablet with the Caodaist motto »God and humanity, love and justice«.

The main altar is adorned with Laotse (at the rear, to the left), the Sakyamuni Buddha (centre) and Confucius (to the right), in the middle row the Bodhisattva in the form of the benevolent goddess Guan Yin (left), in the centre the holy Pope Ly Tai Pe and the legendary General Quan Cong (right), Jesus Christ at the front and another figure by the name of Khuong Thai Cong. Since 1934, the papal chair has remained unoccupied, as no worthy successor has materialized in real life. The huge globe with the Divine Eye at the centre of the altar is impossible to miss. Relics and genealogical trees of deceased dignitaries are also kept here.

The **mosaic floor** rises to the altar in nine flat steps. The number nine symbolizes the nine steps of the beatitudes and perfection as

The first impression of the temple is of a real potpourri →

well as the nine different hierarchies in Caodaism, from the pope via the bishops and cardinals down to the simple followers. The hall is vaulted by a blue, whitewashed heavenly ceiling, dotted with sparkling mirror stars and crescents and supported by mighty columns: dragons and tendrils wind their way around the richly decorated, motley pillars in two rows of twelve.

Conduct in the temple

Visitors enter the temple through a small entrance on the right of the building. Shoes should be left here. **Suitable clothing** is also an important consideration. A good place to observe the service is from the balustrade inside, as unobtrusively and quietly as possible, of course. **Photography and film recordings** are permitted during the ceremony, although some believers do not like to be filmed or photographed individually – it is better to ask them for permission. When looking around the temple after the ceremony, do not walk through the centre of the hall, but stay between the rows of pillars. The believers enter the temple through separate entrances, divided by gender, although this no longer seems to be expected of tourists.

Religious service

There are four services in total every day: at 6am, noon, 6pm and at midnight. Each ceremony lasts for roughly one hour and is a most impressive spectacle, following a strict **hierarchical composition**, such as strict rules of conduct and predetermined prayer positions. In the lower area, the priests congregate four times a day in their blue, red and yellow robes, along with the laymen, the Tin Do, dressed in white. The Confucianists wear red, the Buddhists yellow and the Taoists blue. Women are theoretically also allowed to be dignitaries, but always wear white. A traditional orchestra and choir accompany the prayers.

In and around Tay Ninh

Nui Ba Den (Black Lady Mountain)

One destination, some 11km/6.5mi northeast of Tay Ninh, is the mountain of Ba Den, usually shrouded in cloud. Standing at a height of 986m/3234ft, »Black Lady Mountain« is tied to a **romantic legend**: the young, pretty seamstress Ly Thi Thien Huong often came here to pray. One day the damsel was threatened by a robber, but a young man by the name of Le Si Triet came to her rescue. They fell in love and wanted to get married, but Le Si Triet had to go to war and Thien Huong again found herself alone as she prayed on the mountain. This time, nobody could come to her aid as she was attacked by the robber. As she fled, she fell down a cliff. Another version claims that a third person was involved – a mandarin, to whom she had long been promised. Today, centuries later, the Black Lady still occasionally appears to the pilgrims who have travelled great distances to make her offerings as if she were a goddess, hoping for a miracle.

► VISITING TAY NINH

INFORMATION
Tay Ninh Tourist
210B Duong 30 Thang 4, Tay Ninh
(in the Hoa Binh Hotel, see below)
Tel. 0 66/82 23 76

EVENTS
Cao Dai Festivals
The Cao Dai sect holds its main festivals on the 14th and final day of each month at midnight. Further annual festivals take place on 15 January, 15 July and 15 October. Days before, thousands of Caodaists and pilgrims in colourful dress gather in the main sanctuary of Tay Ninh to pray together.

Festival of Spring at Nui Ba Den
Thousands of Vietnamese follow the Tet holidays (February/March) by making a pilgrimage up the mountain and into the temples, offering heaps of fruit and whole pigs as a sacrifice.

CUISINE
Scorpions add spice to the menu in the Tay Ninh region – fried with date sauce or deep-fried with chilli. The poisonous creatures have become serious competitors for the traditional delicacies of crickets, termites, grasshoppers and locusts. A crispy, tasty scorpion is said to cost more than the average daily wage.

WHERE TO EAT
► Inexpensive
Thanh Thuy
next to the Hoa Binh Hotel
Tel. 0 66/82 76 06
Classic Vietnamese fare revolving around noodle soup, chicken and pork.

WHERE TO STAY
► Budget
Hoa Binh Hotel
210–30 Thang 4
Tel. 0 66/82 13 15
Fax 82 23 45
Simple hotel with socialist charm and 57 unostentatious rooms, the best the town has to offer.

In the Vietnam War, the almost impassable mountain was used as a hideout by the Vietcong, although, for a period, it was also used as a helicopter landing site by the Americans. Today, paragliders can be seen in action up on high. The sometimes arduous climb across cliffs and streams, past souvenir stalls and refreshment booths, temples and grottoes, takes around two to three hours. Foreigners are officially only allowed as far as the simple Black Lady Pagoda (Chua Ba) at approximately 300m/985ft (approx. 45 minutes up stone steps or with the chair lift). A great temple festival is held on the mountain during the Tet holidays, attracting thousands of Vietnamese. The simple guesthouses at the foot of the mountain are completely booked up at this time. If the weather is fine, **Mieu Son Than Temple** at the summit offers a panoramic view of Dau Tieng Lake and the idyllic Vam Co Dong River, lined with palm trees.

Trang Bang

On the way to ► Cu Chi is a small town whose name resounded around the world during the Vietnam War. The Vietnamese photographer Nick Ut arrived here shortly after a **napalm bomb attack** on 8 June 1972, as villagers and peasants fled from the flames. A naked, nine-year-old girl ran screaming towards him – the photographer pressed the shutter. All around the world, the public was shocked by the picture, which remains today the most striking image of the Vietnam War. The young Phan Thi Kim Phuc (► Famous People) had suffered serious burns, which still incapacitate her years later. In 1996, at a personal meeting in the USA, she forgave the commanding officer for the attack, as so many Vietnamese have done. The former officer, who had claimed he believed the village to be free of civilians, has been working for decades as a reverend for peace in America. Nick Ut was awarded the Pulitzer Prize for his historic photograph (photo ►p.59).

✶ Vung Tau

D 7

Province: Ba Ria–Vung Tau (capital)   **Region:** South
Population: Approx. 200,000

A hilly peninsula on the south coast attracts hordes of Vietnamese, lending the harbour town of Vung Tau a certain Rimini flair, particularly at weekends and on holidays. Does it have something to do with the heartrending legends concerning the region? It cannot be due to the beaches, as there are more beautiful ones elsewhere – oil is extracted right off the turbulent coast.

Special economic zone

In 1979 Vung Tau was declared a special economic zone with international participation, for rich oil and gas deposits lie in the offshore shelf. Since the 1980s, the small town has grown into the **largest oil extraction centre in Vietnam**, initially with predominantly Soviet support. The Soviet influence can still be felt today, with some Vung Tau menus offering Russian dishes such as borscht – in Cyrillic lettering. Western companies have now also set up here and exploit the oil reserves side by side with the Vietnamese. As a consequence the province, with its important deep-sea harbour, has become a magnet for foreign investment in South Vietnam. The first mirror-glass office blocks already overshadow the palms on the beach promenade.

Legends

Vung Tau is awash with legends. A love story is entwined with the mountain of Nui Lon, the highest in the north. It was here that a courageous man rescued the girl from the claws of one of the tigers that roamed the dense forests of the mountain. He cut off the tiger's head with his sword. To show his thanks for the heroic deed, the

Fishing boats at the beach of Vung Tau

girl's grandfather offered her to the hero as his wife and henceforth named the mountain Tuong Ky (the happy meeting).

The legend of the smaller Nui Nho in the south concerns a princess of the sea who was transformed into a goldfish and was only able to meet her fisherman husband in human form every five years on the small mountain.

What to See in Vung Tau

The White Palace, or Bach Dinh Villa, stands proud above the Tran Phu coastal road, accessible via a steep track. The restored colonial building was erected in the late 19th century and initially served as a summer residence for the French gouverneur Paul Doumer. In the years 1909–10, the anti-colonialist Nguyen emperor Thanh Thai was held captive here by the French before his exile to Réunion Island.

★
Bach Dinh Villa

Later on, Emperor Bao Dai and the South Vietnamese presidents Ngo Dinh Diem and Nguyen Van Thieu used the house for recreation. Frangipani and bougainvillea cast their sweet smell throughout the garden. A fantastic view of the town and Bai Truoc Beach can be enjoyed from here.

The interior of the villa exudes the captivating **charm of days long since past**. The original furniture and items rescued from a shipwreck can be admired on the two floors, the latter including rusty muzzles, Cambodian bronze statues, porcelain relics of the Qing and Ming dynasties and a large bronze drum (opening times: daily 7am–5pm).

🕐

Bai Truoc	Bai Truoc Beach is a sweeping bay between the two hills of Nui Lon and Nui Nho, running parallel to Quang Trung Road. This stretch of coast is not really suitable for swimming, but Bai Truoc is an excellent place to watch the fishermen at work.
Nui Nho lighthouse	A small path leads from the broad coastal road close to the Hai Au Hotel onto the summit of Nui Nho (approx. 3km/2mi). At a height of 170m/557ft stands a lighthouse, built in 1910, casting its light a distance of 35 miles from the shore. Looking into the hinterland, the landscape is characterized by fruit trees and coffee plantations, rubber trees, paddy fields and sand dunes.
✶ **Tinh Xa Pagoda**	The Buddhist Tinh Xa Pagoda was constructed from 1969 to 1974 on the western face of Nui Nho. The sanctuary is well worth a visit to see the lying Buddha, although weekends should ideally be avoided. A 21m/68ft-high flagpole can be seen from a distance, marking the location of the pagoda. Its 42 rings represent the 42 pages of Buddha's prayer book. A small street, lined by stalls purveying souvenirs and devotional objects, climbs to the unremarkable entrance portal, which is flanked by the gods of goodness (Than Thien) and evil (Than Ac), the guards standing at the entrance to nirvana. The main shrine features an impressive 11m/36ft-long **lying Buddha**, encased in marble. The wonderfully carved wooden frame is decorated with peacocks, apes, flowers and twiners, designed to evoke the place where Buddha entered nirvana. Leave the main hall on the left

A lying Buddha is the main attraction of Tinh Xa Pagoda

to enter a higher room containing three meditating Buddha statues. A narrow staircase on the left-hand side leads to the roof terrace, where a Thuyen Bat Nha dragon boat stands, 11m/36ft long, with plants and colourful ceramic mosaics. It symbolizes the Buddhist vessel with which man crosses the sea of suffering and finally reaches the other side – like Buddha himself. Also worthy of note is the 3½-ton tower bell cast in bronze, onto which believers stick slips of paper bearing their wishes. One of the nuns rings the bell with a massive bolt so that the wishes may come true. This spot provides a splendid view of the numerous religious statues watching over the coast of Vung Tau.

Bai Dua

Bai Dua Beach can barely be seen beneath the coloured parasols but turns out to be a narrow sandy beach between the quay wall and gently rolling waves, bordered by black cliffs.

★

Statue of Jesus

This figure lends Vung Tau a certain Brazilian flair: as in Rio de Janeiro, Jesus stretches his arms out protectively over the peninsula. Any Western guests taking a cyclo tour are sure to be driven behind Bai Dua Beach to make a stop at the »Catholic Buddha«. Steps lead up to the 33m/108ft-high Jesus monument, built by the Americans in 1971. Inside the white concrete figure, 130 further steps can be ascended. From its 18m/59ft-wide outstretched arms, which are accessible, a broad view from a final height of 136m/446ft over town and sea can be savoured (opening times: daily 7.30am–11.30am and 1.30pm–5pm).

Hon Ba Temple

Back on the main street, the small island of Hon Ba comes into view, where a man named Ho Quang Minh built a temple in 1881. In the year 1939, it came under fire from the French and was partially destroyed, only being completely repaired in 1971. Beneath the structure, there is said to be a **cellar** where Vietnamese patriots held clandestine meetings against the colonial rulers. The 200m/218yd separating the island from the mainland can be negotiated at ebb tide without getting wet feet by crossing the rocks. It can get rather crowded here on the 15th of the month, when pilgrims swarm onto the tiny island, bearing incense sticks and other offerings.

Bai Sau

Bai Sau, the 8km/5mi-long rear beach, is largely hidden behind a row of street-side restaurants and booths along the extended Ha Long Street, called Thuy Van at this point. Sunshades, deck chairs and casuarina trees are dotted along the beach, whilst jet skis roar across the water.
There are changing rooms and restaurants, and anyone who has forgotten a bathing costume has the opportunity of purchasing a new one in the boutiques of the Ocean Park Center. Although the central portion of the beach does get busy at weekends, the extremities of this stretch of coast are far less frequented.

▶ VISITING VUNG TAU

INFORMATION
Ba Ria – Vung Tau Tourist
207 Vo Thi Sau, Ward 2, Vung Tau
Tel. 0 64/85 64-45/-46

TRANSPORT
Airport: no flights to Vung Tau, but three flights a week from Saigon to Con Dao (Co Ong Airport on Con Son, 1 hour; or twice a week from Vung Tau by helicopter, 1 hour) or by hydrofoil from Vung Tau (11 hours).
Boats: hydrofoils commute between Saigon and Vung Tau (45 minutes)

EVENTS
Nghinh Ong Festival
On the 16th day of the 8th lunar month (September) the fishermen of Vung Tau celebrate the anniversary of the stranded whales: offerings are made at Lang Ca Ong Temple accompanied by the sound of gongs and festive processions.

WHERE TO EAT
▶ Moderate
Whispers
15 Nguyen Trai
Tel. 0 64/85 60 28
Generally well-frequented bar and restaurant with steaks, grilled fresh fish and other European dishes (hamburgers, pizza, salads etc.) – all served in huge portions.

▶ Inexpensive
Hue Anh Restaurant
446 Truong Cong Dinh
Tel. 0 64/85 66 63
daily 9.30am–10pm
Large garden restaurant with air-conditioned rooms (seats 300), vast array of Vietnamese dishes.

WHERE TO STAY
▶ Luxury
Anoasis Beach Resort & Residence
Domain Ky Van, Long Hai
(approx. 20km/12mi northeast of Vung Tau)
Tel. 0 64/86 82-27/-28, fax 86 82 29
www.vietnamstay.com/anoasisresort
Prize-winning, rambling complex situated on a lovely beach: from studio apartments to luxurious penthouse villas in a tropical garden (30 bungalows in total), some with a private Jacuzzi. Olympic standard pool, two restaurants, bars, business centre, kids' club.

▶ Mid-range
Petro House
63 Tran Hung Dao
Tel. 0 64/85 20 14, fax 85 20 15
www.vietnamhotels.biz/
petrohousehotel

A French legacy: tasty baguettes on Vung Tau Beach

Elegant colonial building in the town, with rooms and apartments, small pool, exclusive Vietnamese (and French) restaurant »Sao Mai«, booking advised.

Sammy Hotel
157 Thuy Van
Tel. 0 64/85 47 55, fax 85 47 62
sammyhotel@hcm.vnn.vn
Modern three-star hotel with 120 rooms at the end of Bai Sau Beach, restaurant, business centre.

Saigon Con Dao Resort
18–24 Ton Duc Thang
Con Dao-Island
Tel. 0 64/83 01 45, fax 83 05 67
www.saigoncondao.com
sgtcd@hcm.vnn.vn
The small resort nestles beneath verdant mountains on the main island, as yet unspoiled by tourists. Bungalows and rows of rooms in five buildings (40 rooms with satellite TV,

telephone, minibar), veranda with panorama of the sea or view of the garden. Pool, two restaurants, fitness apparatus, sauna and tennis court.

Baedeker recommendation

Binh An Village
1 Tran Phu
(1km/0.6mi outside the centre)
Tel. 0 64/51 00 16, fax 81 02 64
www.binhanvillage.com
vungtau@binhanvillage.com
A chic, architecturally outstanding beach refuge (at a price): just ten beach villas with terrace, each of a different design and beautifully appointed with antique Asian decor and furniture, some with murals, lots of terra-cotta, original open-air bathroom. Two lovely pools (saltwater and freshwater) overlooking the sea, an open-air bar built into the rock, restaurant with jazz concerts on some weekends.

The three sections of the building complex in Hoang Hoa Tham Street house the bones of a number of whales who were stranded and perished on the Vung Tau coast. Almost all fishermen in the south believe reverentially in the miraculous powers of the impressive mammals, honouring whales until this day. In the year 1911, the fishermen of Vung Tau had finally collected enough money to build a suitable tomb for what are now three whales buried at Bai Truoc. In the temple, the bones are preserved behind the three altars decorated with wood carvings.

Lang Ca Ong (whale tomb)

Bau Dau Beach in the northwest of the peninsula is surrounded by the wooded slopes of Nui Lon, on which a temple or giant statues (like the Virgin Mary or the Goddess of Mercy) may break the tree cover. This small, tranquil beach sits beneath a less than picturesque quay wall. The water in the bay is shallow and calm, the sand riddled with stones. Above the beach, small restaurants and simple cafés are especially inviting at sunset.

Bau Dau

Tran Phu Street leads to Thich Ca Phat Dai Pagoda, situated on the north side of Vung Tau at the foot of Nui Lon. Large statues in the

★
Thich Ca Phat Dai Pagoda

Opening hours: daily 7am–5pm

sprawling park (created in 1961–63) depict the various stations in the life of Buddha. As the 5ha/12ac park is so popular, large numbers of children stick to the visitors like glue. Immediately to the left beyond the entrance is a small **exhibition** on the past and contemporary history of the former prison island of Con Dao (see below).

Steps lead up to the main attractions: to the right, a 10m/32ft-high Sakyamuni statue sits atop a lotus blossom, to the rear, an octagonal, 19m/62ft-high Bao Thap tower, said to contain the ashes of the Enlightened One. At the four corners of the tower base stand urns containing holy earth from the four important places in Buddha's life: from Lumbini, his birthplace in what is now Nepal, from Uruvilva, where he achieved enlightenment, from Isipatana where he preached, and from Kushinara, where he attained final nirvana. Another figure to the left portrays the Enlightened One as he receives fruit from an ape and an elephant.

Around Vung Tau

Long Hai

If Vung Tau gets to be too hectic and noisy, it is worth venturing 25km/15mi further north to the more peaceful Long Hai, away from the tourist crowds. Long Hai and Phuoc Hai beaches lie side by side with palm trees offering some shade along the **miles of white sand**. A small villa at the northernmost point of the little fishing village serves as a hotel. Nevertheless, prepare for large numbers of Saigonese to materialize here on weekends.

All kinds of dried fish

North of Vung Tau, more than 70 hot springs bubble in the mangrove woods near the coast. The largest pool measures approximately 100 sq m/120 sq yd and is 1m/3ft deep. The area close to provincial highway 23 is a popular weekend destination for many Vietnamese. Around the springs, a large **leisure and relaxation centre** has been developed. The Saigon Binh Chau Eco Resort welcomes visitors to its range of different bungalows with a total of 200 rooms (tel. 0 64/87 11 31, fax 87 11 30, saigonbinhchauecoresort@hcm.vnn.vn). A large restaurant is on site, as are tennis courts and a golf course. Services include hot baths (also in smaller, separate family pools) massages, mud baths and sauna.

Binh Chau (Xuyen Moc)

Approximately 200km/124mi off the Vung Tau coast lie the 14 islands of the Con Dao archipelago in the South China Sea. The hilly main island was used from 1862 by the French and later by the South Vietnamese and Americans to detain **political prisoners** and opponents of the regime. 10,000–12,000 Vietnamese were held captive and tortured in cells known as »tiger cages«. Amongst the most famous inmates was Ton Duc Thang, Ho Chi Minh's deputy and later president of Vietnam.

Con Dao Islands

The island kingdom was declared a nature conservation area in 1982 and boasts a wealth of **flora and fauna**, with 360 species of tree alone. Whales, dolphins, seabirds, turtles, sea cows and monitor lizards are some of the wildlife to be found here. As well as possessing marvellous sandy beaches, the islands also boast wonderful coral reefs. At present, Con Dao is inhabited by fishermen and several thousand soldiers. There are, however, plans afoot to increase tourism and a mid-range hotel complex and smaller guesthouses have already opened for business. A casino is also on the drawing board, along with the ambition of granting the islands duty-free status. So far, there are three flights per week from Saigon and Vung Tau, as well as ferries.

GLOSSARY OF GEOGRAPHICAL, RELIGIOUS AND CULTURAL TERMS

A Di Da Vietnamese form of ►Amitabha

Agent Orange defoliant (carcinogenic and causes genetic damage) used copiously by the Americans during the Vietnam War

Amitabha Buddha of the Past and Infinite Light

Animism belief that spirits exist in natural elements such as trees and stones

Annam protectorate of French Indochina, covering the coast and highlands of Central Vietnam

Ao dai traditional costume of Vietnamese women

Apsar celestial dancer, commonly portrayed in reliefs

Arhat monk who has realized the goal of nirvana

Avalokitesvara one of the most revered Bodhisattvas, meaning »Lord who looks down with compassion at the world«; see also Quan Am

Bodhi tree tree under which Buddha found enlightenment

Bodhisattva in the Buddhist context an enlightened being, marked by virtue and compassion who refrains from entering nirvana in order to show others the way

Bonze Vietnamese Buddhist monk

Brahma one of the three highest Hindu gods, revered as God of Creation

Buddha the Enlightened One, honorary title for Siddharta Gautama

Cao Dai Vietnamese religious community, influenced by all of the great religions of the world and the European humanist tradition

Cay Son tree from which resin is extracted to make lacquer

Champa Hindu kingdom, dominant in many parts of Vietnam between the 4th and 14th centuries

Chu Nho traditional Chinese character system

Chu Nom Vietnamese characters, closely linked to Chinese system; still to be seen in old scriptures and temples

Chua originally a Buddhist temple or monastery; meanwhile also used to describe temples of other denominations

Cochinchina protectorate of French Indochina, southern third of Vietnam

Confucius Chinese philosopher (approx. 551–479 BC) who developed a form of moral code which established the duties of the individual to the family, state and society

Cyclo pedal rickshaw

Den memorial temple for historical and mythical figures

Di Lac Vietnamese name for the fat, laughing Buddha of the Future; depicted as a 10th-century monk

Dien small Taoist temple

Dinh community house in a Vietnamese village, usually housing a guardian spirit

Doi moi Vietnamese form of perestroika; set of reforms initiated in 1986 aimed at liberalizing the economy

Dong national currency

Endemic term used in biology for species found only in a specific, clearly defined environment (e.g. islands, mountain ranges, tablelands, valleys, river systems, lakes or bays)

Ganesha son of Shiva with elephant's head

Garuda Vishnu's vehicle, a mythical, bird-like creature with claws and human body

Geomancy earth-based method of divination, striving to take into account the flow of earth energy in the planning and construction of buildings

Gia pha wooden panel bearing the names of the deceased and placed on the home altar or ancestral altar

Hinayana Buddhism early, strict form of Buddhism which does not promise release through Bodhisattvas, only from within, through the personal efforts of each individual (doctrine of the lesser vehicle)

Ho Chi Minh Trail route by which the North Vietnamese Army and the Vietcong supported the partisans in the south; large stretches led through Laos and Cambodia (p.58 and p.220)

Indochina generic term for Vietnam, Laos and Cambodia; relates back to Chinese and Indian influences in the region

Jade Emperor highest god of populist Taoism

Jataka tales from early Buddhist literature interspersed with verses in which scenes from a previous life of Buddha (as man, demon or animal) are portrayed as exemplary

Judges of Hell ►Thang Hoang

Kalan Cham temple tower containing a divine statue, god-king relief or lingam

Karma in Buddhism the conduct which determines the form of man's reincarnation, or the present fate delivered on the basis of previous conduct

Khmer ethnic Cambodian

La Ham ►Arhat

Lingam phallic symbol for Shiva, usually made of stone, rising above the yoni

Lotus important symbol of Buddhism, representing purity

Mahayana Buddhism later, popular form of Buddhism (in contrast to Hinayana Buddhism) promising all people deliverance and permitting help from outside, particularly through Bodhisattvas; most prevalent in Tibet, China, Vietnam, Korea and Japan

Maitreya Buddha of the Future, said to have appeared on Earth 4000 to 5000 years after Sakyamuni to herald Buddhism once again; usually portrayed as a trinity with Sakyamuni and Amitabha

Mandapa open or closed columned hall of a Hindu temple

Mandarin state official (civil servant or military personnel) chosen through examination process (pp.263, 264)

Meru universal mountain, seat of the gods

Moi »savage«, derogatory term usually reserved for members of hill tribes (also called Montagnards)

Naga mythical creature, half serpent, half man

Nandi symbolic representation of Shiva as a bull

Nghe temple for guardian spirits

Ngoc Hoang Vietnamese name for the Jade Emperor

Nirvana concept in Buddhist teachings (meaning extinguishing, cease blowing); describes the condition attained when the wheel of reincarnation stops turning

NLF National Liberation Front, official name for the Vietcong

Nuoc mam fish sauce found in almost every Vietnamese dish (p.345)

Oc Eo Indianized kingdom (also known as Funan), ruled South Vietnam from 1st to 6th century

Po Nagar mother goddess of the Cham

Quan Am Vietnamese name for the goddess of mercy; highest female Bodhisattva; depicted as Quan Am Bo Tat (standing and holding the bottle of miracle water), Quan Am Thi Kinh (with child) or Quan Am Thien Tu (as a symbol for benevolence, with a thousand arms)

Quan Cong heroic general from the 3rd century

Quoc Ngu Latin transcription of Vietnamese alphabet, developed in 17th century

Roi Nuoc water-puppet theatre (▶Baedeker Special p.358)

Sakyamuni historic Buddha, born as Prince Siddharta Gautama (approx. 563–483 BC), who founded Buddhism

Sampan small, flat boat

Shiva one of the three highest Hindu gods, venerated as god of destruction and fertility

Stele vertical stone slab or pillar, e.g. to document the history of a temple or the acts of a king; often placed on top of a turtle, the Chinese symbol for a long life

Stupa Buddhist sacral structure, tower to house reliquaries, usually monks' tombs in Vietnam

Sutras statements to be learned by rote about sacrificial offerings and rituals

Tam Quan-style name given to the design of temple structures developed in the 17th century, based on a three-part entrance which leads into the complex; the sanctuary within consists of three rooms behind one another

Taoism philosophy which originated in China (3–4 BC) and declares the harmony of natural forces as its chief principle

Tet Vietnamese New Year or spring festival

Tet Offensive major offensive of the National Liberation Front in all provinces of South Vietnam at New Year 1968, compelling the USA to retreat from Vietnam

Thang Hoang name for the Taoist kings and judges who stand before the ten regions of hell

Thap Vietnamese name for a tower

Theravada school of Hinayana Buddhism

Thich Ca Vietnamese name for the historic Buddha (Sakyamuni) in the form of Thich Ca Cuu Long (as a child, surrounded by nine dragons) or Thich Ca Mau Ni (meditating)

Thien Hau celestial queen and patron saint of seafarers

Thung chai large, round wicker baskets sealed with pitch and used as rowing boats

Tonkin protectorate of French Indochina, northern part of Vietnam; also the name of a stretch of water in the north (Gulf of Tonkin)

Van Mieu Temple of Literature, the first university of Vietnam, where mandarin examinations were held

Vietcong abbreviated form of »Viet Nam Cong San« (Vietnamese Communists), used for resistance groups organized by the Communist Party

Viet Minh abbreviation for »Viet Doc Lap Dong Minh« (League for the Independence of Vietnam), founded in 1941 as a united front of nationalists and Communists against the Japanese and French occupying forces

Vishnu one of the three highest Hindu gods, god of mercy and goodness, sustaining the order of the universe

Yoni symbol of female genitals, counterpart to lingam

REGISTER

LIST OF MAPS AND ILLUSTRATIONS

PHOTO CREDITS

PUBLISHER'S INFORMATION

Illustrations etc: 253 illustrations, 41 maps and diagrams, one large map
Text: Beate Szerelmy and Martina Miethig, with contributions by Dr. Heinrich Motzer, Andrea Lotter, Sabine Stahl and Helmut Linde
Editing: Baedeker editorial team (Robert Taylor)
Translation: Margit Sander, Gareth Davies, Alex Paulick
Cartography: Christoph Gallus, Hohberg; MAIRDUMONT/Falk Verlag, Ostfildern (map)
3D illustrations: jangled nerves, Stuttgart
Design: independent Medien-Design, Munich; Kathrin Schemel

Editor-in-chief: Rainer Eisenschmid, Baedeker Ostfildern

1st edition 2009

Based on Baedeker Allianz Reiseführer »Vietnam« 6. Auflage 2008

Copyright: Karl Baedeker Verlag, Ostfildern
Publication rights: MAIRDUMONT GmbH & Co; Ostfildern

Printed in China

BAEDEKER GUIDE BOOKS AT A GLANCE
Guiding the World since 1827

- Andalusia
- Austria
- Bali
- Barcelona
- Berlin
- Brazil
- Budapest
- Cape Town • Garden Route
- China
- Cologne
- Dresden
- Dubai
- Egypt

- Florence
- Florida
- France
- Gran Canaria
- Greece
- Iceland
- India
- Ireland
- Italy
- Japan
- London
- Mexico
- Morocco
- New York

- Norway
- Paris
- Portugal
- Prague
- Rome
- South Africa
- Spain
- Thailand
- Tuscany
- Venice
- Vienna
- Vietnam

DEAR READER,

We would like to thank you for choosing this Baedeker travel guide. It will be a reliable companion on your travels and will not disappoint you.
This book describes the major sights, of course, but it also recommends the best beaches, cosy pubs and bars, cafés, as well as hotels in the luxury and budget categories, and includes tips about where to eat or go shopping and much more, helping to make your trip an enjoyable experience. Our authors ensure the quality of this information by making regular journeys to Vietnam and putting all their know-how into this book.

Nevertheless, experience shows us that it is impossible to rule out errors and changes made after the book goes to press, for which Baedeker accepts no liability. Please send us your criticisms, corrections and suggestions for improvement: we appreciate your contribution. Contact us by post or e-mail, or phone us:

▶ **Verlag Karl Baedeker GmbH**
  Editorial department
  Postfach 3162
  73751 Ostfildern
  Germany
  Tel. 49-711-4502-262, fax -343
  www.baedeker.com
  www.baedeker.co.uk
  E-Mail: baedeker@mairdumont.com